The Children's World Encyclopedia

Created by: Q2A India
Editor: Rebecca Gerlings
Cover design: Paul Oakley and Beatriz Waller

This edition printed in 2006 by
Arcturus Publishing Limited
26/27 Bickels Yard, 151–153 Bermondsey Street
London SE1 3HA

ISBN-13: 978-1-84193-535-5
ISBN-10: 1-84193-535-2

Printed in China

The Children's World Encyclopedia

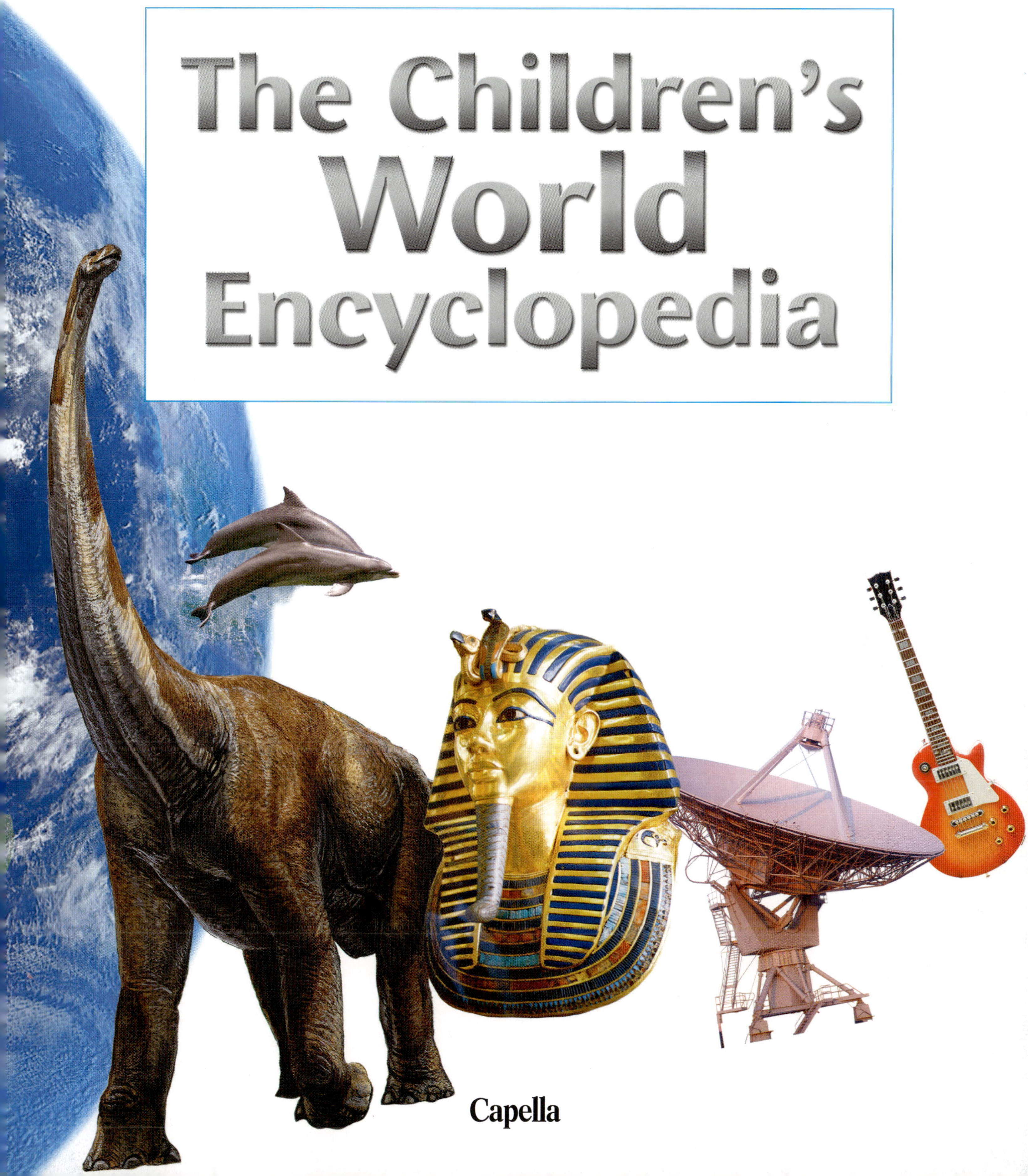

Capella

Contents

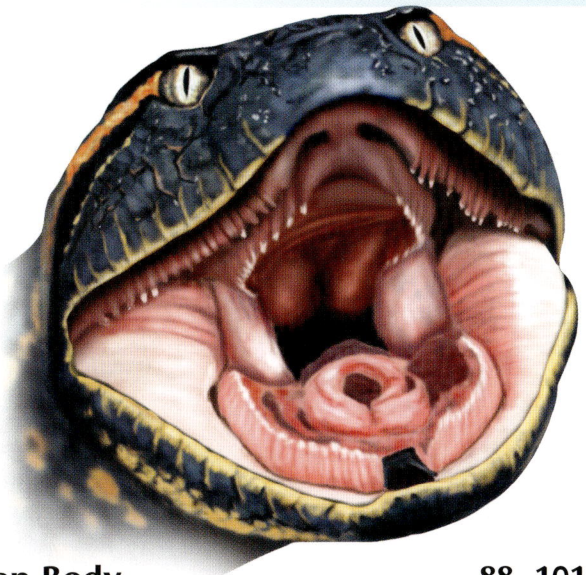

Galaxies and Stars

The Universe is a vast empty region consisting of billions of galaxies and an even larger number of stars. The Sun, the Moon, the Earth and all the other planets are just a very tiny part of the Universe. Some scientists believe that about 15 million years ago the Universe was a small fireball, which slowly grew larger and larger over the next few million years.

▲ **Spiral galaxies** have long, spiralling arms.

▲ **Elliptical galaxies** are shaped like a ball.

▲ **Irregular galaxies** have no shape.

No one knows how big the Universe really is. Until recently, scientists thought it consisted of only one galaxy: the Milky Way. We now know that there are at least 100 billion galaxies in the Universe. Scientists have observed that these are moving away from each other, signalling that the Universe is expanding. Some scientists believe that the Universe will never stop expanding, others think that one day it will begin to shrink, until it becomes a small fireball like it was before.

Galaxies

A galaxy is made up of stars, dust and gas. Billions of galaxies are scattered throughout the Universe. A galaxy can either be on its own, or in a group or cluster. Poor clusters have very few galaxies in them, while clusters consisting of several galaxies are called rich clusters. Galaxies come in different sizes and shapes. According to their shapes, scientists have divided them into spiral, elliptical and irregular galaxies. Our Milky Way is a spiral galaxy. It has more than 200 billion stars in it. The solar system is located on one of its arms, known as the Orion Arm.

Galactic neighbours

Most galaxies are so far away from us that we cannot see them, even with a telescope. However, there are three galaxies (the Andromeda and the Large and Small Magellanic Clouds), which are close enough to be seen without a telescope. The Andromeda, the closest, is more than twice the size of the Milky Way. It is also known as the Messier Object 31 or M31. All of these galaxies, including the Milky Way, are part of a cluster called the Local Group.

Starry nights

Every galaxy in the Universe contains several million, or several trillion, stars. These stars are actually huge balls of gases. A star can live for millions, or billions, of years. There are different kinds of stars. Scientists classify them as giant or dwarf stars based on their size. Supergiants are the biggest in the Universe.

▲ **Star clusters**
Stars are usually found in groups. Some are found in pairs and are called binary stars, while others form clusters, which can be open or globular. Binary stars are often the same size as each other and revolve around a common centre of gravity. An open cluster is a group of stars that are loosely packed together, while a globular cluster is a group of between 10,000 and 1,000,000 stars packed tightly together in a ball.

Patterns in the sky

Sometimes, drawing imaginary lines between stars reveals patterns of familiar animals or objects. We call these interesting star patterns constellations. There are 88 constellations in all. The famous ones include Ursa Major or the Great Bear, Ursa Minor or the Little Bear and Orion or the Hunter. The constellations also include characters from Greek mythology and the twelve zodiac signs.

▲ **Collision course**
The astronomers believe that the Andromeda will collide with our galaxy in about four billion years.

Try these too:

The Rocky Planets (p 10–11), The Gas Giants (p 12–13), Comets and Asteroids (p 16–17), Man in Space (p 18–19)

◂ Stellar explosion
When a massive star nears its death, its core collapses, releasing a huge amount of energy. This causes a big explosion that destroys most of the star. This explosion is called a supernova, and it sends a large amount of light and matter into space. During a supernova, the star would appear a billion times brighter than the Sun. Eventually the remains of the star collapses into itself forming a black hole.

A star's life

Stars are formed when large clouds of dust and gases, mainly hydrogen, form a dense clump. This clump spins faster and faster, causing the atoms to bump into each other. This collision of atoms releases a huge amount of heat that makes the gas glow. This cloud of gas, called a protostar, continues to contract until it becomes a star. The star glows for millions of years until slowly the outer layer of gas begins to cool down, and the star starts to lose its brightness, before it finally fades away. But sometimes stars die in a massive explosion called a supernova.

Key facts:

- The centre of the black hole is called a 'singularity'. The gravitational pull at this point is strong enough to suck in light, making black holes impossible to see.
- The Milky Way is so big that it takes the Sun more than 200 million years to go around it once.
- The Pistol Star is the brightest star in the Universe. Scientists say it is 10 million times brighter than the Sun.
- There are about 70 sextillion known stars in the Universe. That is 7 followed by 22 zeroes. Of these, only 8,000 are visible to the naked eye. The star nearest to the Earth is Proxima Centauri.
- The Universe is about 12 billion years old. Some stars are older than even the Universe.

The Sun and the Solar System

The solar system consists of the Sun, the nine planets and their moons, asteroids, comets and meteors. The solar system was born about 5 billion years ago. Before that it was a gigantic mass of rocks, gas and ice particles that drifted through the Milky Way. This huge mass formed a swirling hot disc called the solar nebula, which kept spinning faster and faster.

▲ **Celestial birth**
The dust, rocks and ice particles around the solar nebula clumped together to form the planets.

Key facts:

- A huge amount of magnetic energy is produced in the Sun. This causes the release of jets of gas into space. Such phenomena are called solar flares. This invariably causes a sudden increase in the brightness of the Sun.
- Solar flares are followed by the release of streams of electrically charged particles, such as protons and electrons. These streams are called solar winds. They can travel at speeds of about 500 kilometres/second (300 metres/second).
- The surface temperature of the Sun is about 5,760 °C (10,400 °F). If you think that is hot, then what about the temperature at the centre of the Sun? It is thought to be an incredible 15 million °C (28 million °F) or even hotter.
- Astronomers have recently discovered what they believe to be the tenth planet in the solar system. The planet is named Sedna, after the Inuit goddess of the sea, and was first observed from the Palomar Observatory located in California, USA.

As the nebula spun faster, the clouds of gas, rocks and ice began to squeeze together until the centre exploded, creating the Sun. The remaining dust, rocks and ice pieces clumped together to form the planets.

The yellow star

The Sun is actually a medium-sized star that is located at the centre of the solar system. All the other objects in the solar system, including the planets, travel around the Sun in an ellipse. It is the Sun's gravity that keeps all of them in their orbits. The Sun is younger and smaller than most known stars in the Universe, but it is very bright and extremely hot. The centre of the Sun is a hotbed of nuclear reactions that turn hydrogen into helium. These reactions produce a large amount of energy that makes the Sun glow. It is this energy that reaches the Earth as heat and light.

The birth of the planets

The heat from the Sun melted the icy particles near it, but the dust particles formed small pieces of rock. Over time, these rocks collided to form the four inner, or rocky, planets – Mercury, Venus, Earth and Mars. The ice particles that were too far away from the Sun to be melted combined with gases to form the four outer planets, or gas giants. Jupiter, Saturn, Uranus and Neptune are bigger and colder than the inner planets.

▼ **Galactic family**
The Sun and the nine planets revolving around it. The planets follow an egg-shaped orbit around the Sun.

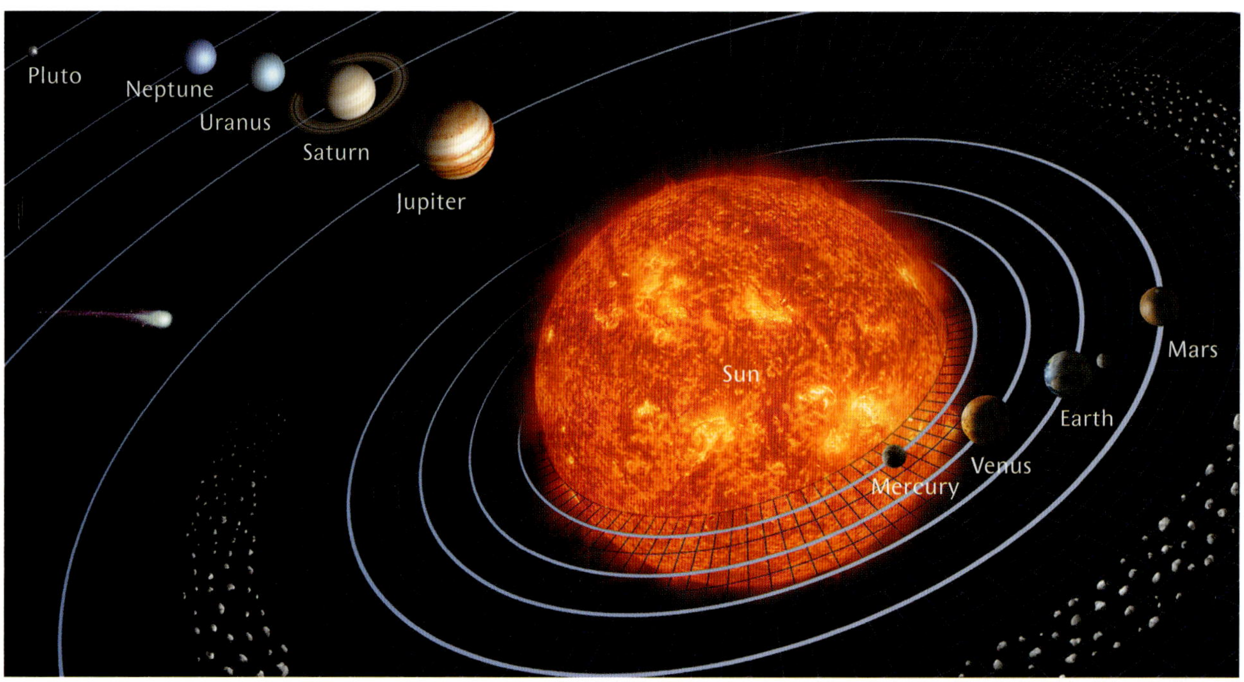

Spots on the Sun?

Have you ever looked up at the Sun and seen spots on it? Most probably not, but that is because the Sun is too far away to be seen clearly. It is also so bright that you must not stare directly at it. Satellite pictures show large, dark spots on its surface. These spots are actually storms that occur on the Sun and are called sunspots.

The oddball

Pluto is the ninth planet. Unlike the outer planets, Pluto is not big. It is the smallest planet in the solar system. It is not composed of gases, but of rocks as well as ice that are largely frozen gases and liquids like methane and ammonia. In fact, Pluto is so different from the other planets that scientists have often wondered whether it is a planet at all.

▲ **Not so big!**
Pluto is smaller than even the Earth's Moon!

▶ **Flaring up**
Sometimes, bright jets of hot gas are released from the regions near sunspots. These jets of hot gas appear as huge explosions known as solar flares. An increase in sunspots causes an increase in solar flare activity. Solar flares can affect Earth by causing changes in the ionosphere. It can also disrupt radio signals and disturb a satellite's orbit.

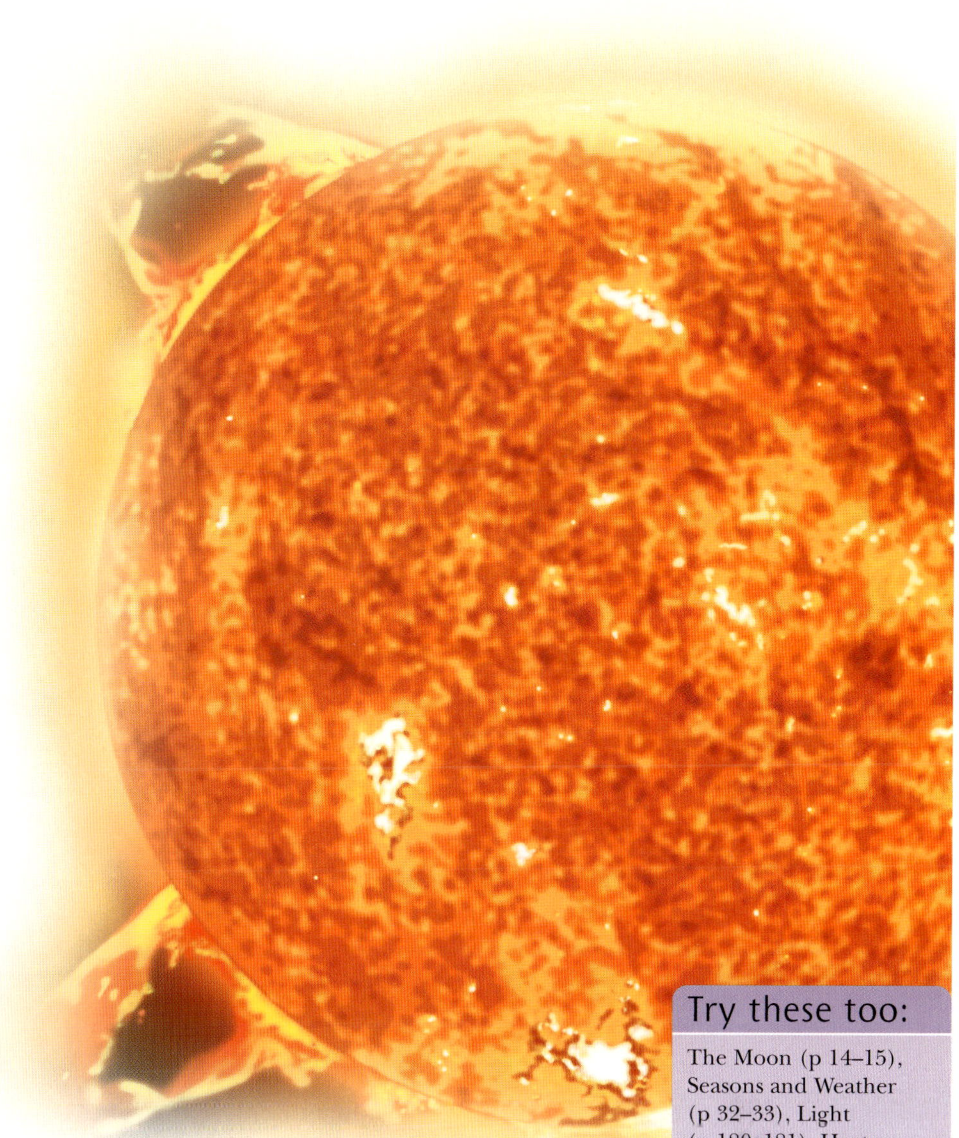

Try these too:

The Moon (p 14–15), Seasons and Weather (p 32–33), Light (p 180–181), Heat (p 184–185), Forces and Motion (p 188–189)

Hide and seek

Ever wonder what would happen if the Sun suddenly disappeared in the middle of the day? Nothing catastrophic really, as this is a phenomenon that is not unheard of. The event in which the Sun disappears during the day for a small period of time is called a solar eclipse. It occurs when the Moon comes in between the Sun and the Earth, blocking the Sun from our view. A solar eclipse can be total, partial or annular. A total eclipse happens when the Moon is so near the Earth that it appears bigger than the Sun and is therefore able to cover it completely. In a partial eclipse only a part of the Sun is covered. An annular eclipse is one of the most amazing sights of all – a thin ring of the Sun is visible around the Moon. The Moon is so far from the Earth that it is unable to cover the Sun completely. The Sun is actually much bigger than the Moon.

The Rocky Planets

The four rocky planets are Mercury, Venus, Earth and Mars. They are made up of rocks and metals like iron and nickel. They are small, with diameters less than 13,000 kilometres (8,078 miles). However, these planets are very heavy and therefore rotate much more slowly than the gas giants. They do not have rings around them.

▲ **Observing Mercury**
Most of what we know about Mercury came from photographs and information sent by *Mariner 10*, the first spacecraft that orbited the planet. After this mission, which was completed in 1975, no other spacecraft was sent to Mercury until 2004, when *Messenger*, the new spacecraft, was launched.

▲ **Water, water, everywhere**
The most unique feature of the Earth is that almost 70 per cent of its surface is covered with water, making it look like a giant blue marble when seen from space.

Of all the planets, Mercury is the closest to the Sun. It is also very small. Only Pluto is smaller. The planet has been named after Mercury, the ancient Roman messenger god. According to legend, this god wore winged sandals that helped him to travel fast. Mercury, the planet, also travels fast around the Sun. It is so close to the Sun that temperatures can be as high as 467 ºC (873 ºF). Unlike the Earth, which has a thick blanket of air around it, Mercury has very little atmosphere to trap the Sun's heat. Therefore nights on Mercury can be a freezing -183 ºC (-297 ºF). Since Mercury's atmosphere is almost non-existent, meteors do not burn up in the air. Instead, they fall on the planet's surface creating huge craters. The largest of these, the Caloris Basin, is about 1,300 kilometres (808 miles) in diameter. The planet goes around the Sun in an elliptical orbit and takes only 88 days to complete one orbit. However, one day on Mercury is as long as 176 days on Earth – that is how slowly Mercury rotates on its own axis.

A planet or a star?

If you look up at the night sky, the second brightest object you would see is not a star, but a planet named Venus. Only the Moon is brighter than Venus. Much-observed by humans for centuries, this planet is similar to Earth in so many ways that it is often considered to be Earth's twin sister. Both planets are almost the same size. They are also similar in their composition and distance from the Sun. But up close Venus is as different from Earth as possible. It is covered with a thick blanket of carbon dioxide containing droplets of poisonous sulphuric acid. This atmosphere traps the Sun's heat and does not let it escape, making Venus hotter than even Mercury. Another strange feature is that Venus rotates in the direction opposite to its orbit – so that on Venus the Sun rises in the west and sets in the east – the opposite of what happens on Earth.

The blue planet

The Earth is the only planet in the solar system known to support life. The thick, protective blanket of air and the presence of water make it possible for living things to exist. The atmosphere protects the Earth from the Sun's harmful rays and prevents meteors from falling on to its surface.

Water on Mars?

Scientists believe that about 3.5 billion years ago, huge floods, the largest in the solar system, swept through Mars. They think that this water collected in lakes or oceans. No one knows where the floods came from or what happened to all of that water. In 2002, the spacecraft named *Mars Odyssey* discovered large quantities of frozen water in the soil near the south pole of the planet. Polar ice caps have also been discovered. All this proves that at one time water existed on Mars.

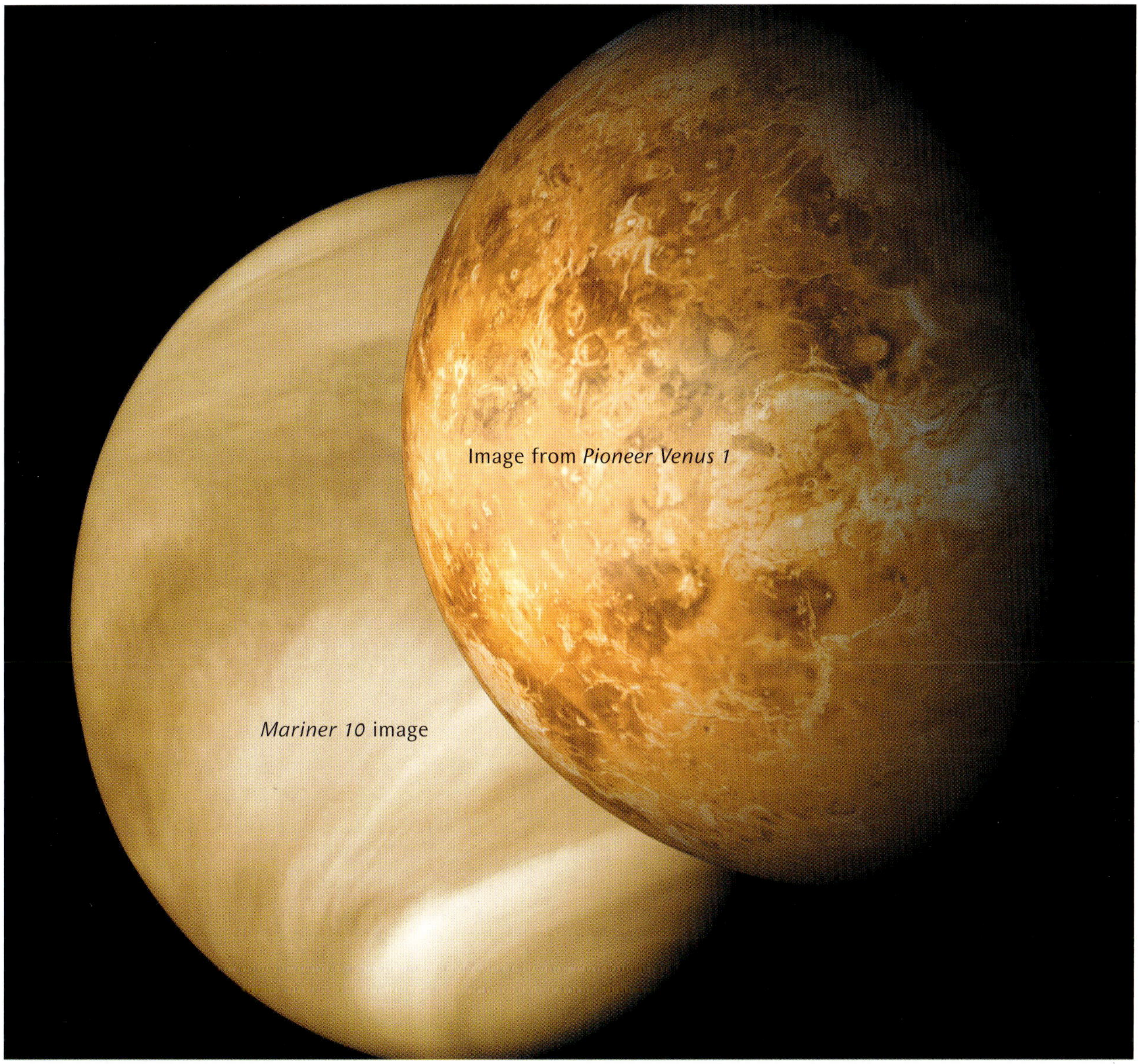

Try these too:

The Sun and the Solar System (p 8–9), The Gas Giants (p 12–13), The Moon (p 14–15), The Story of Our Planet (p 20–21)

◂ Hidden surface!
The first picture of Venus, taken by *Mariner 10*, shows the dense clouds which prevented scientists from learning more about the planet's surface until *Pioneer Venus I* spacecraft obtained a clearer picture in 1978 using radar.

Key facts:

- **Distance from Sun** (in million kilometres/miles)

Mercury – 57.9 (35.9)

Venus – 108.2 (67.2)

Earth – 149.6 (92.9)

Mars – 227.9 (141.6)

- **Diameter of the planets** (in kilometres/miles)

Mercury – 4,878 (3,031)

Venus – 12,104 (7,521)

Earth – 12,756 (7,926)

Mars – 6,787 (4,217)

- **Days taken to go around the Sun**

Mercury – 88

Venus – 225

Earth – 365

Mars – 687

- Like Mercury, the days on Venus are longer than its year. The planet takes about 225 days to circle the Sun, but takes 243 days to rotate on its own axis.
- Phobos and Deimos, the two moons of Mars, are believed to have been asteroids that were captured by the planet's gravity as they drifted too close to it.

The red planet

Mars, the fourth planet from the Sun, has always been the subject of major scientific interest. It has also inspired many theories and science fiction movies about alien life forms. Contrary to the fantastic stories surrounding it, Mars is a cold and lonely planet. The surface of Mars resembles a huge desert with red-coloured sand, which gives the planet its name. The colour of the sand is due to the presence of large amounts of iron oxide, or rust. The planet also has several volcanoes and canyons. One of its volcanoes, Olympus Mons, is the largest in the whole solar system. It is three times the height of our own Mount Everest. The largest canyon on Mars is Valles Marineris.

▾ Probing Mars
Mars is probably the most explored of all planets in the solar system. Several spacecraft and rovers have been sent to the Red Planet to find out more about its surface and whether life really exists there. In 1997, a micro-rover named *Sojourner* became the first of its kind to explore another planet. It analysed the rocks and soil on the planet helping us to learn more about it.

The Gas Giants

The gas giants are Jupiter, Saturn, Uranus and Neptune. These planets are far away from the Sun and are therefore very cold. They are made up of gases and are not heavy, despite their sizes. In fact, Saturn is so light that it would float if placed in a pool of water. These planets also move very fast. All of the gas giants have rings, although Saturn's rings are the most majestic.

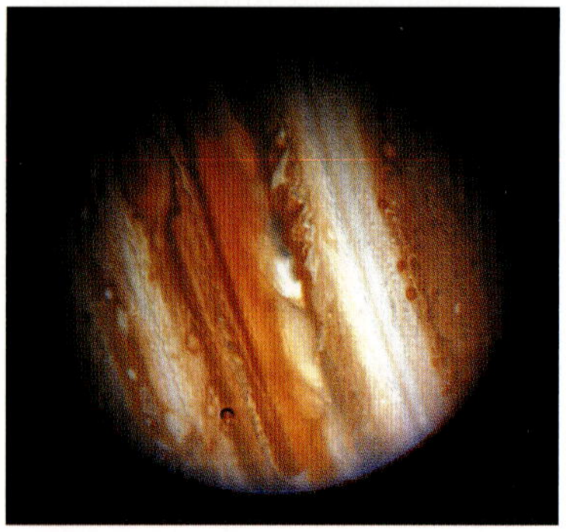

Swirls of poison
The stripes and swirls that can be seen on Jupiter's surface are actually caused by water, along with some extremely cold and windy clouds of ammonia, which is a very poisonous gas.

Stormy surface
The most amazing feature of Jupiter is the Great Red Spot. This is a region on the planet where a huge thunderstorm has been raging for hundreds of years. The red colour is thought to be caused by the chemical phosphorous.

Mystery of the rings
It is believed that the rings around Saturn are in fact pieces of comets, asteroids and moons that were shattered. However, scientists are still not sure why or how they formed the rings.

The fifth planet from the Sun, Jupiter is the largest of them all, and is well named after the king of Roman gods. Jupiter is so big that over 1,300 Earths could fit inside it. It also rotates faster than any other planet and has the greatest number of moons – more than 60. Scientists believe that most of Jupiter's outer moons are actually asteroids that were captured by the planet's gravity when they drifted close to it. The atmospheric pressure is so high that even spacecraft that land on Jupiter get crushed within no time. *Galileo*, the only probe to land on Jupiter, survived for hardly an hour before getting crushed by the pressure on the planet.

Jewel of the solar system

Saturn is a lot like Jupiter in its size and composition. It is the second largest planet in the solar system and, like Jupiter, it is largely made up of gases. But what sets Saturn apart are its beautiful rings. These rings were first observed by Galileo Galilei, the famous Italian scientist, in 1610. Ever since, Saturn's rings have fascinated humans. Saturn has seven huge rings that are made up of thousands of smaller rings. These rings consist of dust particles and pieces of ice that can be as big as snowballs. The ice pieces reflect light, which causes the rings to shine.

Walking on air!

None of the gas giants have a hard surface. Jupiter and Saturn have a semi-liquid centre that is covered by a layer of liquid gas. This ocean gradually meets the heavy blanket of gas surrounding the planets. If we were ever able to land on one of the gas giants, we would have to walk on air.

Saturn's moons

There are 46 known moons orbiting Saturn. Each of them is unique in its own way. One of the moons, Enceladus, is among the shiniest objects in space. It is covered with frozen water that reflects the sunlight, making the moon glow like snow. Iapetus is another very strange moon. One of its halves is ten times brighter than its other half. However, the most fascinating of Saturn's moons is Titan. It is the second largest moon in the solar system and the only known one with a thick atmosphere, thicker than even Earth's. This atmosphere is said to contain chemicals that were present in the Earth's atmosphere before life began. Scientists believe that studying Titan's atmosphere might help us to find out more about the beginning of life on our own planet.

Galilean moons

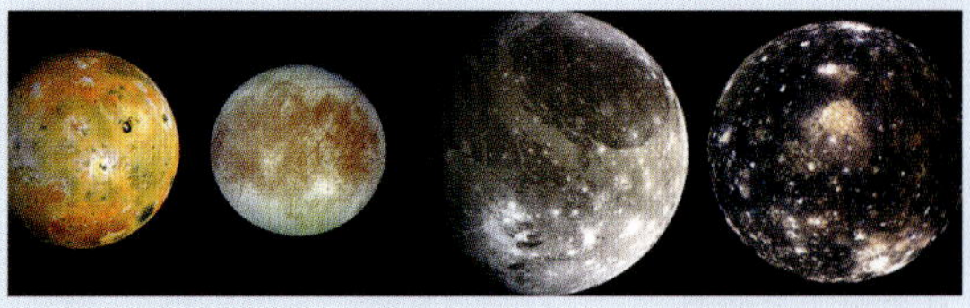

The first four of Jupiter's moons were discovered almost 400 years ago. On 7 January 1610, Galileo observed what he thought were three small stars next to Jupiter. These 'stars' were actually among Jupiter's largest moons – Io, Europa and Callisto. He discovered the fourth moon, Ganymede, a few days later. Together they are known as the Galilean satellites. Ganymede is the largest moon in the solar system. It is larger than two of the planets, Mercury and Pluto.

Try these too:

The Sun and the Solar System (p 8–9), The Rocky Planets (p 10–11), The Moon (p 14–15), Man in Space (p 18–19), Communication and Satellites (p 192–193)

◂ Jets of gas
Triton is the largest of the moons orbiting Neptune, and its most unique feature is its geysers. Unlike those on Earth, which are largely jets of very hot water, Triton's geysers are streams of nitrogen gas formed deep inside its surface.

Key facts:

- **Distance from Sun** (in million kilometres/miles)

Jupiter – 778 (483)

Saturn – 1,427 (887)

Uranus – 2,871 (1,784)

Neptune – 4,497 (2,794)

- **Diameter of the planets** (in kilometres/miles)

Jupiter – 142,796 (88,729)

Saturn – 120,660 (74,974)

Uranus – 51,118 (31,763)

Neptune – 48,600 (30,198)

- **Years taken to go around the Sun**

Jupiter – 12

Saturn – 29

Uranus – 84

Neptune – 165

- Jupiter has three thin rings that cannot be seen from Earth, even with the most powerful telescopes. They are made up of dust particles from Jupiter's moons. It is thought that these dust particles were formed when other space objects, like meteoroids, struck the moons.

Moving sideways

Until recently, Uranus was thought to be very dull. The blue-green planet did not appear to have any unique features, but information sent back by the *Voyager* space mission proved that Uranus is just as exciting as any other planet in the solar system. The calm, blue-green exterior of the planet hides strong winds and 11 known rings. It has also been discovered that the planet has 27 moons and an unusual orbit. Unlike other planets, Uranus orbits on its side, meaning the poles of the planet directly face the Sun. This peculiar feature of the planet is the reason why seasons last longer than 20 years on Uranus.

Hot and windy

Neptune is the windiest planet in the solar system. Winds on this planet can reach speeds of over 2,000 kilometres/hour (1,200 miles/hour). Neptune owes its bright blue colour to the layer of methane gas found above the clouds. Scientists believe that although Neptune looks cold from the outside, it contains an ocean of very hot water. This planet has four rings and 13 known moons. Neptune is the eighth planet from the Sun for most of the time. However, it falls to the ninth position for a period of about twenty years. This is due to the unusual orbit of Pluto, which brings it closer to the Sun once every 248 years.

The Moon

Natural satellites are objects that go around the planets. The word 'moon' is used to describe these natural satellites. Some planets, like Earth, only have one moon while others have more. The gas giants have more moons than the rocky planets. In fact, two of the rocky planets, Mercury and Venus, don't have any, while Jupiter has at least 63.

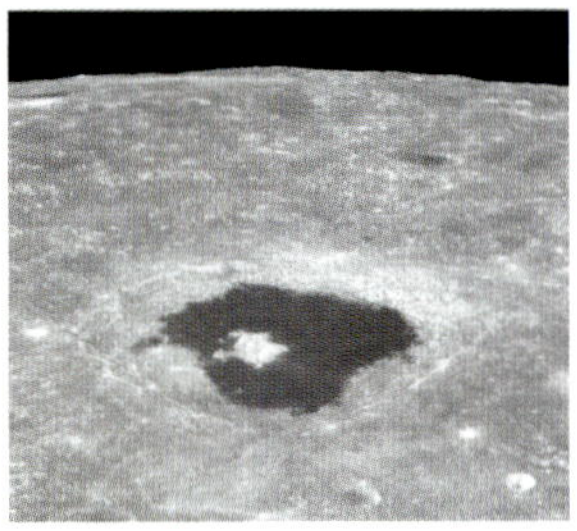

▲ Bumpy surface
The Moon's surface is filled with craters. Tsiolkovsky Crater is one of the largest craters in the far side of the moon, while Tycho Crater is one of the biggest craters on the nearside.

Key dates:

- **14 September 1959** The unmanned Soviet probe *Luna 2* crashes into the Moon. It is the first man-made object to be sent to the Moon.
- **7 October 1959** The Soviet probe *Luna 3* takes the first photographs of the Moon's far side.
- **3 February 1966** *Luna 9* becomes the first probe to make a controlled, successful landing on the Moon.
- **31 March 1966** *Luna 10*, the first artificial satellite to orbit the Moon, is launched.
- **20 July 1969** *Apollo 11* lands on the Moon. Neil Armstrong and Edwin Aldrin become the first humans to walk on the Moon.

When we talk about the moon we are usually referring to the moon we know best – Earth's Moon. Astronomers call it Luna to avoid confusion with other moons. It is closer to Earth than any other celestial object.

In the Sun's glory

The Moon does not give off light. Instead, it simply reflects the sunlight that falls on it. We are able to see moonlight only at night because there is no sunlight falling on the Earth during this time. During the day the bright light of the Sun blocks the soft glow of the Moon.

Not made of cheese

The Moon is a cold and lonely place. It is made up of hard rocks and covered with dust. Ancient people thought the Moon was smooth and spotless. Today, we know that the Moon's surface is bumpy and full of huge craters. Since the Moon does not have an atmosphere, meteors and asteroids crash into it causing these craters. The lack of atmosphere also means that heat from the Sun is not regulated.

The dark side of the Moon

One side of the Moon is permanently turned towards the Earth. This means that we only ever see one side. This is due to the Moon's synchronous rotation – meaning that the Moon takes the same amount of time to rotate on its axis as it takes to go around the Earth. The side we see is called the near side, while the one that is never seen is called the far or dark side. When spacecraft are on the far side, they are completely cut off from communication with the Earth.

▲ Miracle birth?
No one knows how the Moon came into existence. Some scientists believe that years ago a huge object, the size of the planet Mars, struck the Earth's surface. It broke into smaller pieces that later came together to form the Moon.

Lunar eclipse

An eclipse occurs when the Sun, Earth and Moon are in a straight line. If the Moon comes between the Sun and the Earth, a solar eclipse occurs. When the Earth is between the Sun and the Moon, the sunlight makes the Earth's shadow fall on the Moon causing a lunar eclipse. A total lunar eclipse occurs when the Moon passes through the darkest portion of the shadow. If only a part of the Moon comes under the dark shadow during the period, a partial eclipse can be observed.

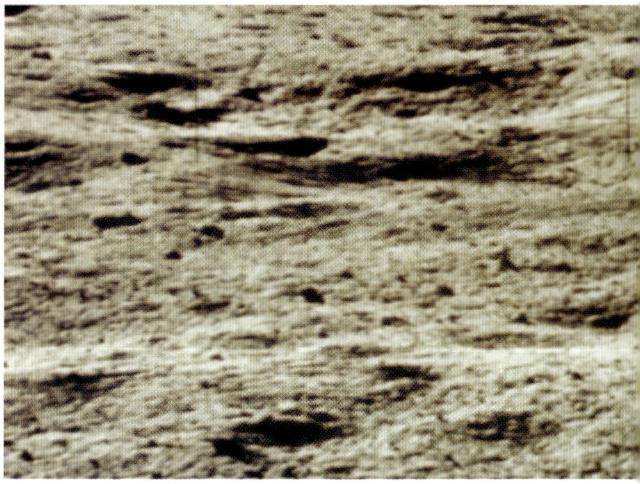

Causing tides

Tides are the regular rise and fall of the level of water in oceans. All objects in the solar system are kept together by the gravitational force they exert on each other. The Sun and the Moon also exert a gravitational force on the Earth. It is this force that causes tides. The Moon is much closer to the Earth than the Sun, so the gravitational force exerted by the Moon is stronger than that of the Sun. The Moon's gravitational pull causes the ocean to bulge out towards it, causing high tides. The ocean on the side facing away from the Moon also bulges out to create high tides. The reason for this is the fact that the Earth itself is attracted towards the Moon. In the area between the two high tides the water level decreases causing low tides. When the Sun, the Moon and the Earth are in a straight line, the gravitational force of the Sun strengthens the gravitational force of the Moon causing tides that are very stronger. These are called spring tides, and occur during the full moon and new moon phases. When the Sun and the Moon are at right angles to the Earth, weak tides called neap tides are formed.

Changing phases

Have you ever noticed that the Moon does not always appear round? Sometimes we only see a thin 'c' shaped Moon. There are also occasions when the Moon is not visible at all. The changing shapes of the Moon, as seen from the Earth, are called phases. The phase when the Moon is invisible is called new moon. During the new moon phase, the side of the Moon that faces the Earth is away from the Sun and so does not receive light. As the Moon travels across the sky, parts of it slowly become visible, until the Moon is on the other side of the Earth and facing the Sun. In this phase, called full moon, we can see the full disc.

◀ **Weightless on the Moon**
It is the gravitational force of the Earth that keeps our feet glued to the ground. If there was no gravity, we would all be floating around like astronauts do in a spaceship. The gravitational force of the Earth is also responsible for the weight of a particular object. On the Moon, this gravitational force is very weak. That is why astronauts wearing heavy spacesuits are able to float around on its surface.

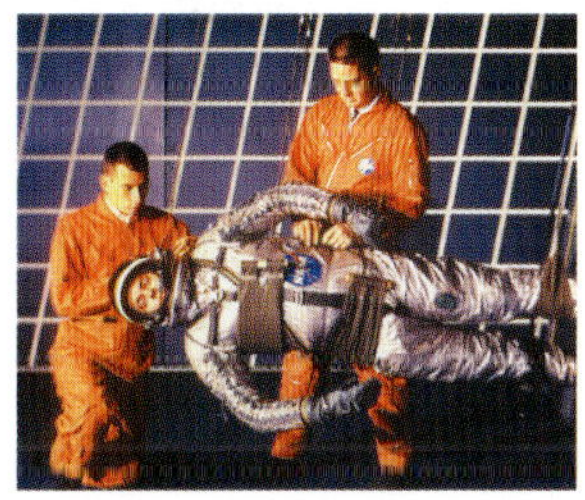

▲ **Moon walking**
The conditions of weightlessness and other irregularities on the Moon are duplicated to train and prepare astronauts for their missions.

Try these too:

The Rocky Planets (p 10–11), Man in Space (p 18–19), Seasons and Weather (p 32–33), Communication and Satellites (p 192–193)

Comets and Asteroids

The solar system contains many small pieces of rocks, metals and ice that orbit the Sun along with the planets. These objects are asteroids, comets and meteors. Asteroids are huge space rocks that are actually fragments that are left over from when the solar system was formed. They are composed of rocks and metals like iron and nickel.

▲ Orbiting an asteroid
In 1993, the spacecraft *Galileo* discovered that the asteroid Ida had a tiny moon orbiting it. This moon was named Dactyl.

Key facts:

- Many astronomers think Pluto is an asteroid. Others think that it is one of the icy objects that came from the Kuiper Belt. Most comets are believed to have been formed from these icy objects.
- About 22,000 meteorites have been found on the Earth's surface. The largest iron meteorite weighs about 54,000 kilograms (120,000 pounds), while the largest rock meteorite weighs 1,000 kilograms (2,200 pounds).
- Halley's Comet takes about 76 years to go around the Sun once. It was last seen in 1986 and will be seen again in 2061. Comet Hale-Bopp, last seen in 1997, will not be seen again for at least 2,300 years!

Asteroids are quite similar to planets and are often called minor planets. Some asteroids even have moons. Most of the asteroids are found in a region between Mars and Jupiter, called the Asteroid Belt. You can find millions of asteroids here, from the very small to the largest. Ceres, the biggest asteroid by far, has a diameter of over 960 kilometres (600 miles). The word 'asteroid', meaning star-like (derived from the Greek *asteroeides*), was coined by the 18th-century astronomer William Herschel.

▼ Belt of asteroids
The Asteroid Belt, also known as the Main Belt, consists of an inner and an outer belt. The inner belt contains asteroids largely made up of metals like iron and nickel. Those found in the outer belt are rocky in nature and appear darker in colour than the ones in the inner belt.

Icy space travellers

Comets are a mixture of ice, gas and dust. Like asteroids, comets are also leftovers from the formation of the solar system that travel around the Sun. They are found in two different regions – the Kuiper Belt and Oort Cloud. The Kuiper Belt is located beyond Neptune. Comets from this region are called short-period comets since it takes them a relatively short amount of time to go around the Sun. Comets from Oort Cloud take as long as 30 million years to complete one orbit and are therefore called long-period comets. There are about a trillion comets in this region.

Sungrazers

Most comets do not go too close to the Sun. Some, however, either crash into the Sun or get so close that they break up into tiny pieces. These comets are called sungrazers.

Shooting stars

Did you know that shooting stars are not actually stars but pieces of burning rocks called meteors? These are formed from meteoroids, which are small pieces of rock and metal that travel around the Sun. Meteoroids are usually leftover fragments of an asteroid that has broken into smaller pieces. When a meteoroid enters the Earth's atmosphere it becomes a meteor. The friction in the atmosphere causes the meteor to heat up. Most meteors burn up in a streak of light. Sometimes fragments called meteorites crash into the Earth's surface. Some meteorites are large enough to make a crater wherever they fall.

▲ **Asteroid menace**
An asteroid can be thrown off its orbit by many things, such as Jupiter's gravity, or encounters with Mars or other asteroids. Stray asteroids often strike the surface of other planets or moons causing widespread destruction and creating huge craters. It is believed that about 65 million years ago an asteroid slammed into Earth near the Yucatan Peninsula in Mexico causing the extinction of the dinosaurs.

▲ **Tails of gas!**
When a comet nears the Sun, the ice on it begins to melt and is converted to gas. As the comet gets warmer, jets of gas and dust particles are released. The solar wind from the Sun blow these materials away from it to form a tail behind the comet's head. This tail can be as long as 10 million kilometres (6.2 million miles), and always points away from the Sun.

Showering meteors

Meteors enter the Earth's surface quite regularly and can be observed evey night. Several meteors can be seen per hour, but sometimes, especially in autumn and winter, there is a dramatic increase in the number of meteors. This is called a meteor shower and is caused by comets. As a comet comes near to the Sun it releases a stream of dust and gas that forms the comet's tail. When the Earth passes through this tail a meteor shower can be seen. These meteors appear to fall from a particular place in the sky, usually a constellation, so meteor showers are named after the constellation from which they appear to fall.

Try these too:

The Sun and the Solar System (p 8–9), The Rocky Planets (p 10–11), The Gas Giants (p 12–13), Man in Space (p 18–19), Earth's Atmosphere (p 30–31), Forces and Motion (p 188–189)

Man in Space

For centuries humans have been looking up at the sky in wonder, trying to unravel the secrets of the Universe. One of the most important inventions that have helped in this endeavour is the space shuttle. This consists of an orbiter, two rocket boosters and an external fuel tank.

Key dates:

- **4 October 1957** The Soviet Union launches the first artificial satellite, *Sputnik 1* into space.
- **3 November 1957** The Soviet spacecraft *Sputnik 2* carries the first living being into space – a dog, named Laika.
- **2 January 1959** The Soviet Union launches *Luna I*, the first ever space probe. The probe flew by our moon at a distance of 5,995 kilometres (3,725 miles) on 4 January.
- **12 April 1981** The space shuttle, *Columbia*, becomes the first of its kind to travel into space. *Columbia* was a major part of NASA's shuttle fleet until it was destroyed on 1 February, 2003, while re-entering the Earth's atmosphere.
- **20 November 1998** The first module of the International Space Station *Zarya* is launched.

The orbiter carries the astronauts. It also contains a cargo bay to hold the supplies. The rockets propel the shuttle into space. Once the shuttle reaches an altitude of about 45 kilometres (28 miles), the rockets fall off and the main engines take over. Just before it goes into orbit, the engines of the orbiter are shut down and the external fuel tank is discarded. The fuel tank re-enters the Earth's atmosphere, burns up and falls into the ocean.

Defying gravity

Every object is glued to the Earth's surface by its gravitational force. This is demonstrated best by a stone that is thrown up. The Earth's gravity pulls the stone back to its surface. That is why objects that are thrown up always fall down after travelling a certain distance. If you want to throw a stone into space, it should travel at a speed of not less than 40,000 kilometres/hour (25,000 miles/hour). This speed is known as the Earth's escape velocity. The term refers to the speed at which an object has to travel if it wants to escape the Earth's gravity. In the case of a space shuttle, a mixture of liquid hydrogen fuel and liquid oxygen is burned under high pressure to help the rockets reach this speed and push the shuttle out of the Earth's atmosphere.

Satellites and probes

Apart from astronauts, we also send man-made satellites and probes into space to learn more about it. A probe is an unmanned spacecraft sent into deep space to collect information about objects other than the Earth. Some satellites are probes.

Watching over space

Developments in science and technology have even enabled us to send a telescope into space. The Hubble Space Telescope was sent into orbit in 1990. The telescope was named after the famous American astronomer, Edwin Hubble, who proved that the Universe is expanding. The Hubble is like any other telescope. It has mirrors that focus light onto the cameras that capture images of space. These instruments let the Hubble see back in time. It took pictures of the Universe when it was barely a billion years old – it's 14 billion years old today. The reason for this amazing feat is that it takes billions of years for light from the far ends of the Universe to reach the telescope. When the light reaches it an image is captured.

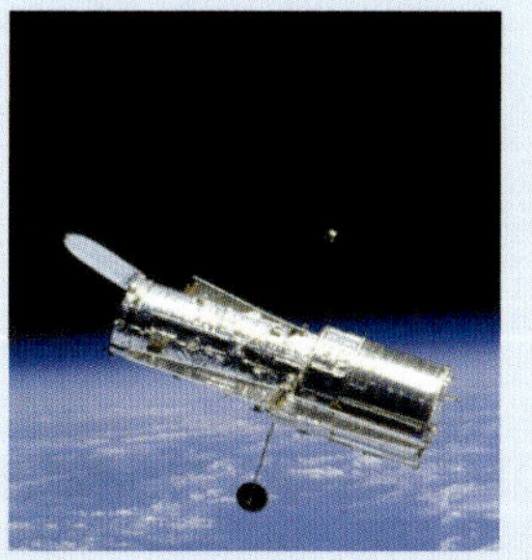

Living in space

Space shuttles, satellites and probes are not the only methods used to study space. Today, it is possible to live in space for a long period of time, in a space station. Like spacecraft, space stations orbit the Earth. Space shuttles transport people and materials to and from space stations. Astronauts live in space stations for weeks, months and even years, to conduct various observations and study the effects of living in space for long periods of time on human beings. Some of the best known space stations include *Salyut*, *Mir* and the International Space Station.

Dressed for space

Astronauts have to be well prepared to go into space. The conditions are harsh, so astronauts need lots of special equipment to protect themselves. The most important part of this equipment is the spacesuit. Astronauts use different suits for different occasions. For example, when breaking through the Earth's atmosphere or re-entering it, astronauts wear a suit called a pumpkin suit because of its orange colour. This suit includes a helmet, gloves and boots. It also has a parachute and a life raft. Aboard the shuttle and the space station, astronauts can wear whatever they like. Outside the shuttle, astronauts wear a suit called an extravehicular mobility unit or EMU. This 14-layer suit is made up of several parts. The undersuit, made of nylon tricot and spandex, has pipes that water flows through. This keeps the astronaut cool. The various layers are made of strong materials, such as those used in bullet-proof and fireproof clothing. Each material has special properties that help to protect the astronaut from temperature changes, harmful radiation and small meteorites. The suit also contains a life support system and communication devices. A special pack filled with nitrogen is attached to the spacesuit. Called the manned manoeuvring unit or MMU, it helps astronauts to fly about in space and take pictures.

▲ **A matter of weight**
Due to the absence of gravity, a spacesuit weighs almost nothing in space.

◀ **First in space**
On 12 April 1961, Russian cosmonaut, Yuri Gagarin became the first human to go to space. He went into orbit aboard the space shuttle, *Vostok 1*.

Try these too:

The Moon (p 14–15),
Heat (p 184–185),
Communication and Satellites (p 192–193)

▶ **Mission renamed**
A space station, named *Freedom* was proposed by NASA in the early 1980s. The project was abandoned at the time, only to be revived as the International Space Station.

The Story of Our Planet

The Earth is over 4.5 billion years old. At its earliest stages, the Earth's surface was continuously hit by space rocks. These collisions produced a huge amount of heat, which caused the rocks on the planet to melt. For the next million years or so, the Earth was covered with an ocean of molten rock.

◂ Fiery Earth
For years, the Earth's surface was rocked by volcanic eruptions such as this one.

Key facts:

- **Earth at a glimpse**
Age: 4.5 billion years

Total area: 510 million square kilometres (196.9 milion square miles)

Area (land): 149 million square kilometres (57.4 million square miles)

Area (water): 361 million square kilometres (139.5 milion square miles)

Average land height is about 840 metres (2,757 feet) above sea level

Average depth of ocean is about 3,795 metres (12,450 feet) below sea level

- The temperature in the inner core can be as high as 7,200 °C (13,000 °F). That is hotter than even the Sun's surface.
- The crust under the ocean is about 7–10 kilometres (4–7 miles) thick, while the continental crust is about 25–70 kilometres (15–44 miles) thick.
- The continents of South America and Africa are moving away from each other at a speed of just over 2 centimetres (1 inch) every year, which is equal to the speed of growth of a fingernail.

During the same time, radioactive elements on Earth also released a lot of heat. This caused heavy metals, such as iron and nickel, to sink into the Earth's core. Lighter elements such as silicon were forced to the surface. As the Earth began to cool the elements solidified, but the molten rocks beneath pushed through cracks in the surface causing volcanic eruptions. These eruptions spewed large amounts of carbon dioxide, water vapour, ammonia and methane. The water vapour condensed and formed clouds that eventually brought rain. The rain fell in torrents until the volcanic activity decreased and the Earth started to cool once again.

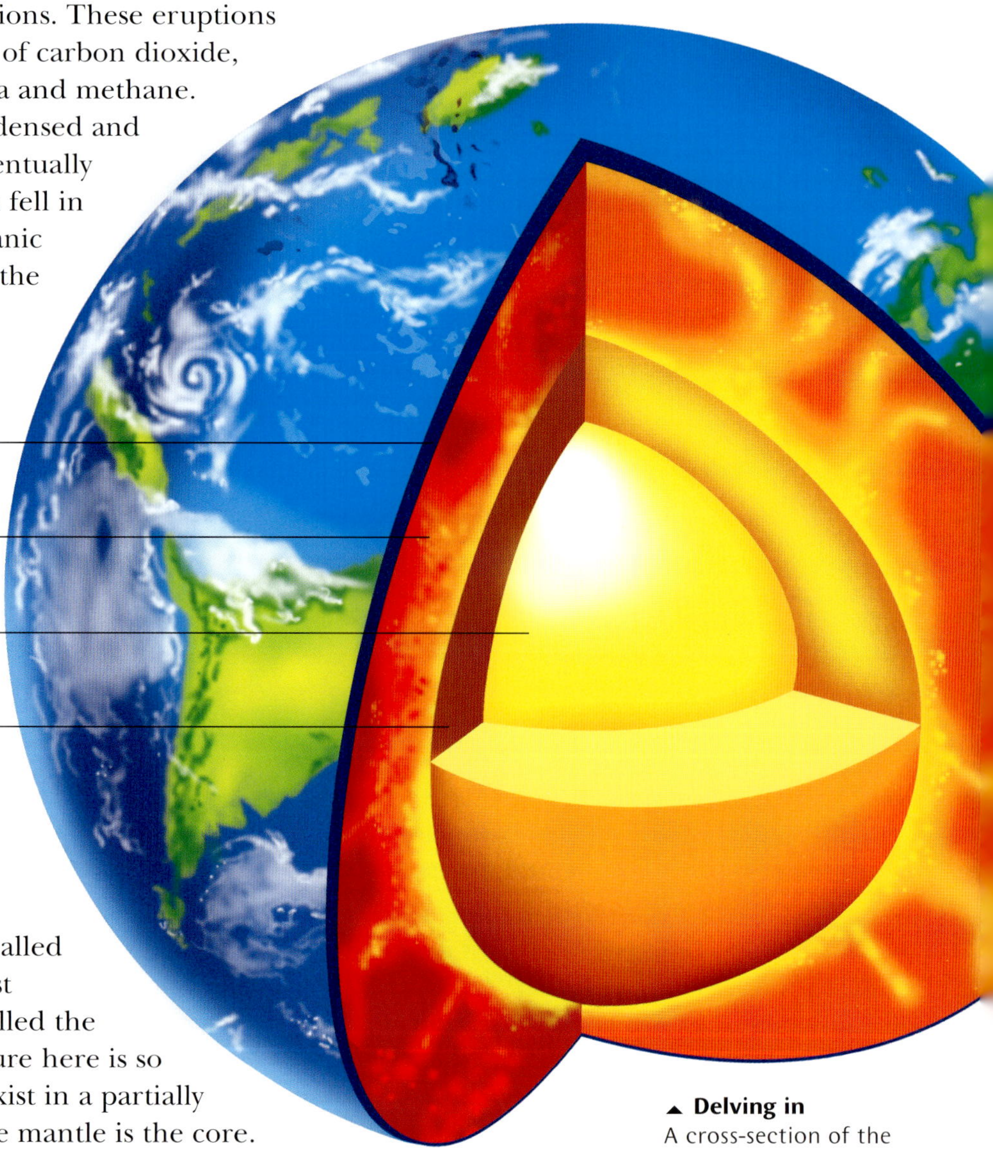

Earth layers

The Earth can be divided into three different layers. The topmost solid layer is called the crust. The layer just beneath the crust is called the mantle. The temperature here is so high that even rocks exist in a partially molten state. Below the mantle is the core. It contains metals like iron and nickel.

▴ Delving in
A cross-section of the various layers of the Earth.

Always changing

Pangaea was not the only supercontinent to have existed on the Earth's surface. Another supercontinent, which scientists now call Rodinia, is thought to have existed about one billion years ago. Scientists believe that Rodinia consisted of all the modern continents. Then, about 750 million years ago, Rodinia broke up into three pieces. The ever-changing surface of our planet made certain that these new land masses came together once again – this time to form another supercontinent called Pannotia.

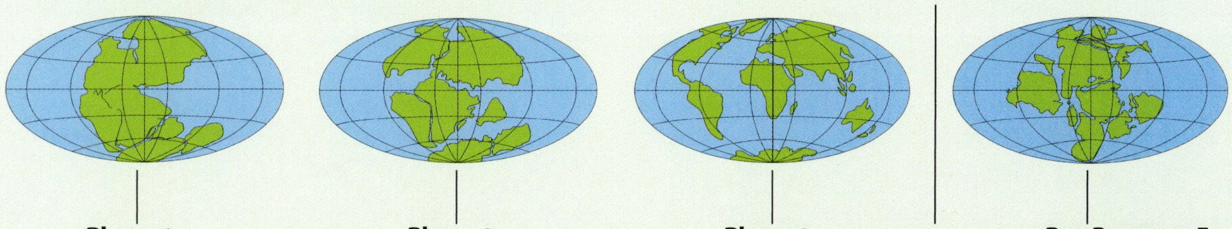

Phase 1
Supercontinent Pangaea

Phase 2
Gondwanaland and Laurasia

Phase 3
Gondwanaland and Laurasia breaking up to form modern continents

Pre-Pangaea Era
Ancient supercontinent of Rodinia

▾ Hard ground
The plates that form the crust can be divided into continental and oceanic plates. Continental plates are thicker than oceanic plates but are lighter in weight. They are made of granite, while the oceanic plates are basalt. Today, the Earth's crust consists of about a dozen major tectonic plates and several minor ones.

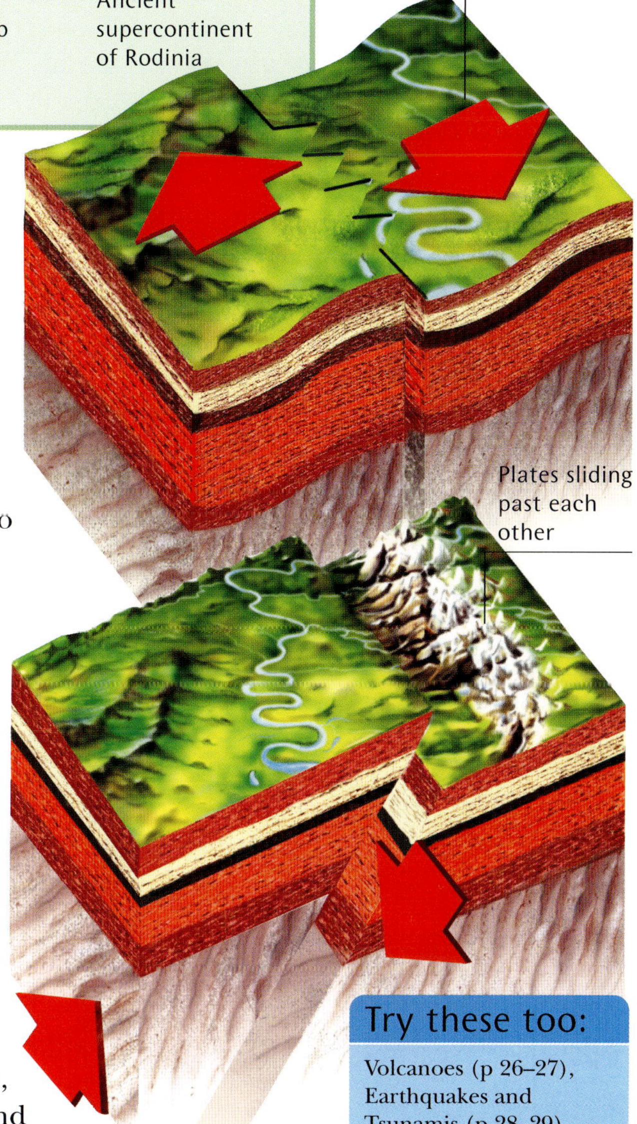

Forever in motion

The Earth's crust along with the solid part of the upper mantle is called the lithosphere. Beneath the lithosphere is the semi-liquid part of the mantle known as the asthenosphere. The molten rocks in the asthenosphere are in constant motion. This is because hot, molten rocks rise up to replace the cooler, heavier material above it, which in turn sinks below to be melted by the heat. This movement of molten rocks is known as convection. The crust is not made up of one single piece, but of several pieces of rock called tectonic plates. These plates float on the asthenosphere. The convection currents in the asthenosphere cause the tectonic plates to move.

Drifting away

If you look at the world map closely, you will see that the shapes of the continents almost seem to fit together like a jigsaw puzzle. Alfred Wegener, a famous German scientist, also noticed this strange coincidence and proposed the first fully detailed continental drift theory to explain this occurrence. According to this theory, the continents were a part of a supercontinent named Pangaea. A vast ocean surrounded this supercontinent. Scientists named this ocean Panthalassa. About 180 million years ago, the supercontinent Pangaea began to break up and soon two separate continents were formed. These contients were called Gondwanaland and Laurasia. Over the next few million years, Gondwanaland divided into the present Antarctica, Africa, South America, Australia, New Zealand, Madagascar, India and Arabia (consisting of Saudi Arabia, Yemen, Oman, Kuwait, UAE, Qatar and Bahrain). Later, Laurasia broke up into North America and Eurasia – now Europe and Asia.

Try these too:

Volcanoes (p 26–27), Earthquakes and Tsunamis (p 28–29), Countries and People (p 102–115), World History (p 116–157)

Features of the Earth

The Earth's surface is not one flat plain. It is filled with several natural features like mountains, rivers, lakes, plateaus, valleys, canyons, caves and beaches. These natural features affect the weather as well as the variety of animals and plants found in each region. None of these land features were formed in a day. It took millions of years for Earth to look like it is today.

Key facts:

- **Highest mountains** (in metres/feet)

Everest, Nepal/Tibet: 8,844 (29,028)

Godwin Austen (K2), Pakistan/India: 8,611 (28,250)

Kanchenjunga, India/Nepal : 8,586 (28,208)

- **Longest rivers** (in kilometres/miles)

Nile, Africa: 6,695 (4,160)

Amazon, South America: 6,387 (4,000)

Yangtze, China: 6,380 (3,964)

- **Largest lakes** (in square kilometres/ square miles)

Caspian Sea (saline), Asia/Europe: 371,000 (143,244)

Superior (freshwater), North America: 82,103 (31,700)

Victoria, Africa: 68,870 (29,828)

- **Largest deserts** (in square kilometres/ square miles)

Sahara, Africa: 9,096,000 (3,500,000)

Gobi, Mongolia/China: 1,295,000 (500,000)

Kalahari, Southern Africa: 500,000 (200,000)

- **Longest beach**
Long Beach, USA, 45 kilometres (28 miles)

A mountain is a feature that stands very high above its surrounding area. Mountains are formed when two continental plates collide. Continental plates are light so neither of the colliding plates can be pushed downwards. Instead, when the plates crash into each other the resulting force pushes them either upwards or sideways, creating a mountain. For example, about 10–15 million years ago, the continental plate of India crashed into that of Asia to form the Himalayan mountain range in which Mount Everest, the tallest peak in the world, is found. Hills are smaller than mountains and do not have such steep sides.

Rivers and lakes

When it rains or when snow on mountains melts, the water flows down the slopes, forming small water bodies called streams. Several such streams join together to form a river. Small rivers drain into larger rivers. The water in rivers keeps flowing until it reaches the sea. Sometimes, rainwater can collect in big hollows in the ground to form lakes. These hollows can be formed by various causes like plate movement and glaciers. Lakes are also formed by landslides that leave huge depressions in the ground. Most lakes and rivers contain freshwater. In some places where the amount of salt in the soil is very high, lake water can be salty.

▲ **Plateaus**
A plateau is a landform that is higher than its surrounding area but has a flat top. Like mountains, plateaus are formed when two continental plates collide, but erosion due to wind and water flattens the top. Some plateaus, such as the Tibetan Plateau, lie between two mountain ranges.

Valleys

A valley is a low-lying area of land surrounded by mountains or hills. They are usually formed by running water eroding the land. A deep valley with cliffs on both sides is called a canyon. Valleys can also be formed by glaciers or flowing ice. When glaciers slowly flow downhill, they collect a large amount of rock pieces on the way. These pieces scrape against the valley floor, digging deeper into it until a U-shaped valley is formed.

▸ **The grandest of all!**
The Grand Canyon in Arizona, USA, was formed by the Colorado River. It is believed that millions of years ago this region was covered by sea. Slowly, a part of the sea floor was pushed up to form a plateau. Over the next few years, rainwater collected on the plateau to form a river. This river ran through the plateau, cutting into the rocks like a knife to form the canyon.

Caves

Caves are huge holes under the ground, in cliffs or under the sea. Caves can be formed in various ways. Most rock caves, especially limestone caves, are formed by rainwater that seeps into the cracks in the rocks. The rainwater slowly causes the rock to dissolve leaving behind a large hole. Sea caves are formed by waves that wear away rocks at the base of a cliff. The continuous pounding of the waves causes these rocks to crumble and form small hollows. These hollows keep expanding as sand, gravel and rocks brought by the waves erode their inner walls. Some sea caves are submerged in water during high tide and can only be seen when the water recedes.

Coastlines and beaches

A coast is a long stretch of land that borders a sea or ocean. A beach is a small part of a coast. It is made up of sand, mud and gravel. Coastal features of a particular area depend on the wind, rocks and currents in that place. Strong winds whip up powerful waves that are responsible for the formation of cliffs, sea arches and sea stacks. A cliff is formed by the pounding of waves on the face of a huge rock. At first, a tiny gap is created in a weak spot, which enlarges with time until the roof collapses.

Wave power

Sometimes waves pound a headland from two sides to form caves on each side. When two back-to-back caves meet, a sea arch is formed. The top portion of the arch links the headland to the mainland. After years of erosion, the sea arch breaks up to form a column of rock known as a sea stack.

The softer rocks at the base of a cliff erode first and collapse on to the shore. They break into even smaller fragments until an expanse of sand and gravel lie between the cliff and the sea. This saves the cliff from further erosion and slows down the waves. Soon the waves begin to deposit more sand on the coast, forming wide beaches.

Try these too:

Mammals (p 34–53), Birds (p 54–59), Fish (p 60–63), Reptiles and Amphibians (p 64–69), Insects (p 70–73), Plants (p 84–87)

◂ Land of arches
The Delicate Arch in the Arches National Park in Utah, USA, was formed by continous erosion of a slab of sandstone by wind, water and frost. The National Park is filled with such arches.

Oceans of the World

Oceans occupy about 70 per cent of the Earth's surface. The water in the oceans cannot be used for drinking since it is very salty. However, the ocean is home to a huge variety of fish and other creatures. There are five oceans in the world. They are the Atlantic, Pacific, Indian, Arctic and Antarctic oceans.

Key facts:

- **Size of the Oceans** (in million square kilometres/miles)

  Pacific: 70 (43.5)

  Atlantic: 41 (25.5)

  Indian: 28.4 17.6)

  Arctic: 5.54

- The temperature of the water from a hydrothermal vent can be as high as 400 °C (752 °F). This water is rich in minerals and hydrogen sulphide.
- Most ocean currents flow in gyres, or large loops, which spin clockwise in the Northern Hemisphere and anti-clockwise in the Southern Hemisphere. This is called the Coriolis Effect and is caused by the Earth's rotation.
- The Arctic Ocean is the smallest and the shallowest of all oceans. Its deepest point is only 5,450 metres (17,880 feet). This is not even half the depth of the Challenger Deep, which is the deepest point in the Pacific Ocean and the world.
- The Pacific Ocean gets its name from the Spanish word *pacifico*, meaning peaceful. It was named by Ferdinand Magellan, the Portuguese explorer, who thought that it looked calm.

The surface under the oceans is called the ocean floor. This consists of continental shelves, continental slopes and abyssal plains. The edges of islands and continents gently slope into the surrounding water to form the continental shelves. These usually extend to a distance of 75 kilometres (47 miles), and much of the marine life can be found here. The point where a shelf starts to plunge steeply towards the ocean floor is called a continental slope. It is here that one can find the deep canyons of the ocean. The sediments in continental slopes often pile up to form gentle slopes called continental rises. A continental shelf, slope and rise are together known as a continental margin. In many places, the ocean floor forms vast, flat expanses called abyssal plains.

▲ **One ocean, many names**
There is only one ocean in the world. It is made up of four major ocean basins – Pacific, Atlantic, Indian and Arctic. The Southern Ocean is also part of these oceans.

Ridges

Like the continents, the ocean floor also contains tectonic plates. The movement of these plates creates features like ridges, trenches, seamounts and valleys. The ridges are connected to form a single chain called the mid-ocean ridge that is over 80,000 kilometres (50,000 miles) long and the longest mountain chain on Earth.

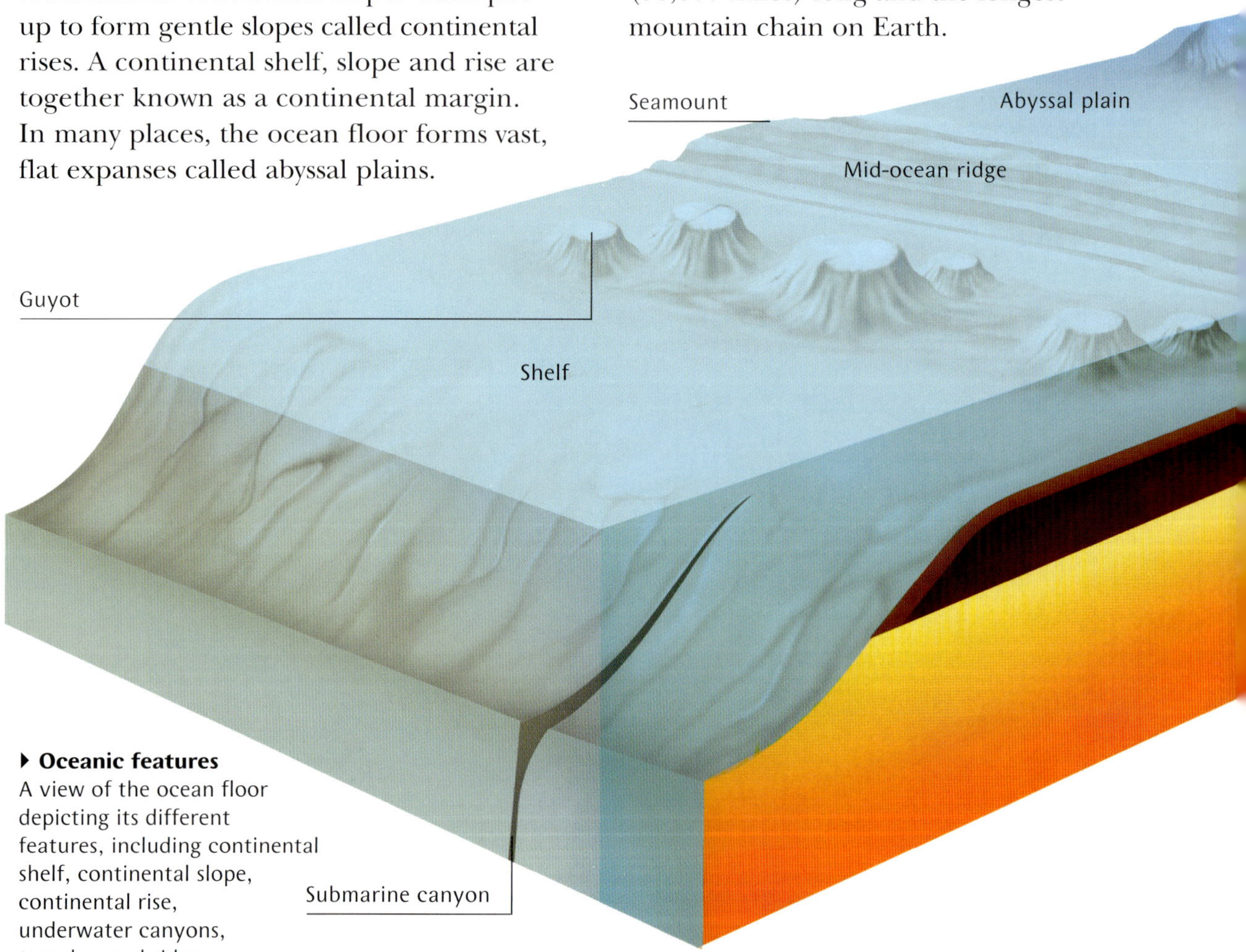

▶ **Oceanic features**
A view of the ocean floor depicting its different features, including continental shelf, continental slope, continental rise, underwater canyons, trenches and ridges.

Trenches

Trenches are formed when the heavier plate plunges beneath the lighter one. Mariana Trench in the Pacific Ocean is the deepest of its kind. The Challenger Deep is the deepest point of this trench, and also on Earth.

Volcanoes under water

Almost 90 per cent of the world's volcanic activity takes place under the ocean. These underwater volcanoes are called seamounts. A seamount with a flat crest is known as a guyot, while those with peaks are called seapeaks. Most undersea volcanoes are found along the mid-ocean ridge. Undersea volcanoes also form volcanic islands.

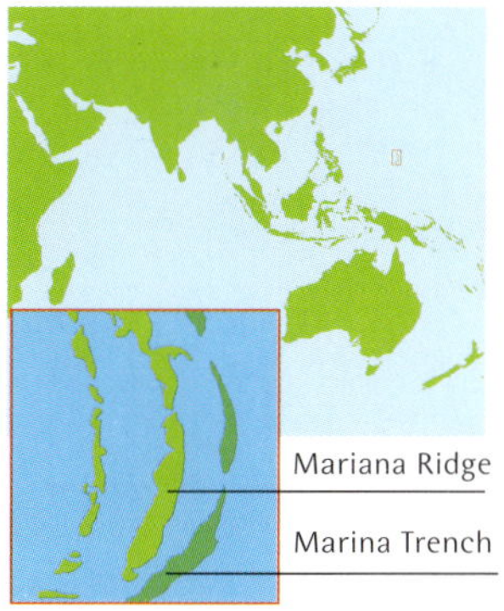

▲ **Plunging deep**
The Challenger Deep – the deepest point of Marina Trench – is about 11,033 metres (36,200 feet), deep.

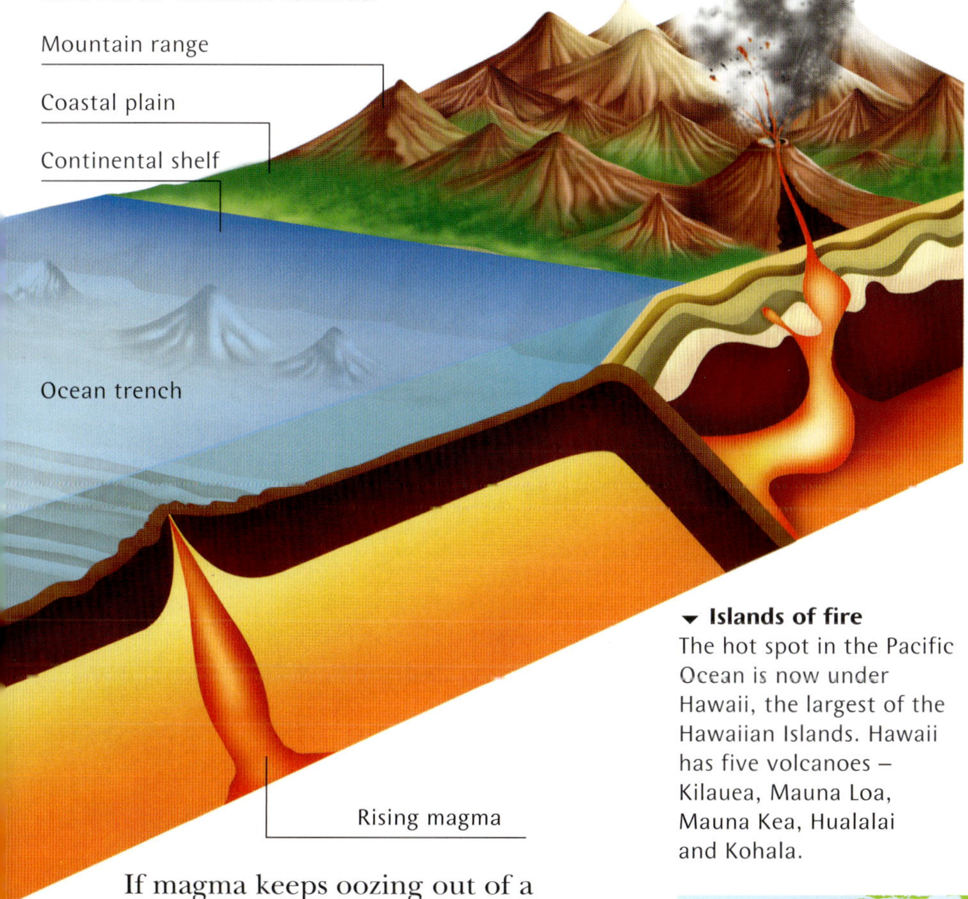

▼ **Islands of fire**
The hot spot in the Pacific Ocean is now under Hawaii, the largest of the Hawaiian Islands. Hawaii has five volcanoes – Kilauea, Mauna Loa, Mauna Kea, Hualalai and Kohala.

If magma keeps oozing out of a seamount for millions of years, the mount can slowly rise above the ocean surface as an island. Sometimes, volcanic activity takes place over a hot spot. The constant movement of tectonic plates eventually shifts the volcano away from the hot spot. Soon, another volcano is created in the area near the hot spot. This often leads to the formation of a chain of islands, such as the Hawaiian Islands.

Hot water

The ocean contains hot springs, also known as hydrothermal vents. When water seeps into the crust through cracks, it is often heated by the magma found beneath. As the pressure builds up within the crust, the hot water shoots up through cracks in the ocean floor forming hydrothermal vents. When the scalding water comes in contact with the cold water above, chimney-like jets of warm water are created. These jets are often black because of the mineral content in the water, so they are also called black smokers.

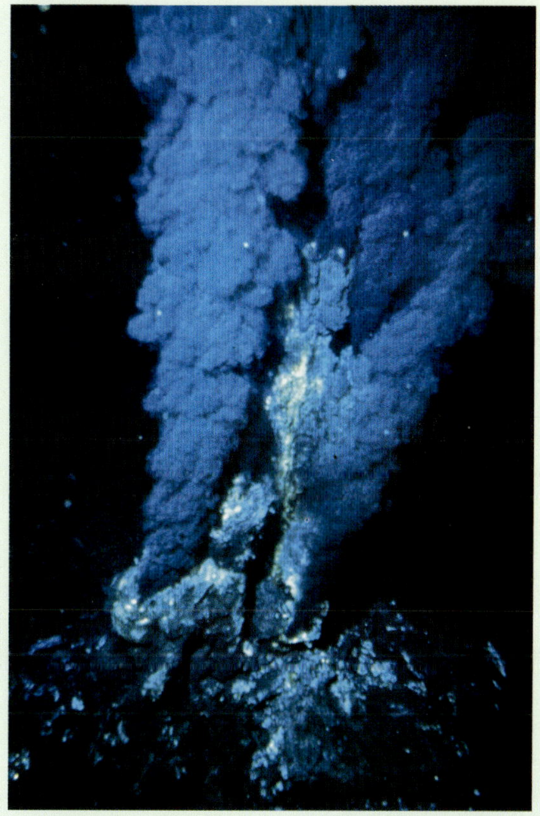

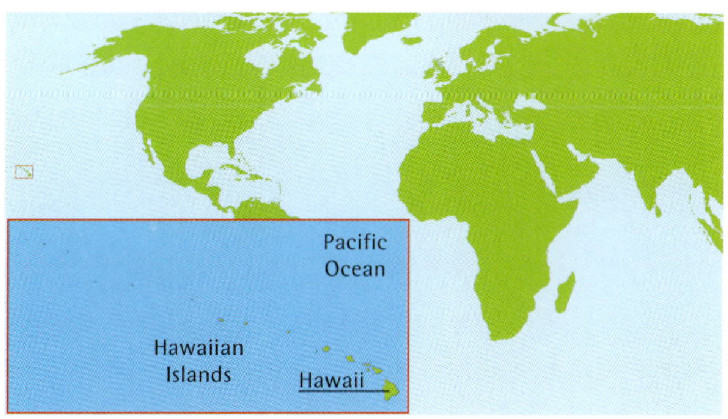

Try these too:

Volcanoes (p 26–27),
Earthquakes and Tsunamis (p 28–29),
Marine Mammals (p 50–51),
Fish (p 60–63),
Life Begins (p 74–75),
Water Transport (p 196–197)

Volcanoes

Volcanoes are mountains formed by the accumulation of molten rocks and ash around an opening on the Earth's surface. They are usually formed when an oceanic plate slips beneath a continental plate. The sudden movement generates a lot of heat, which melts part of the oceanic plate. The magma, or molten rock, which is formed collects below the Earth's surface.

Key facts:

- **Top five deadliest volcanic erutpions**

Tambora, Indonesia in 1815 – 92,000 killed

Krakatau, Indonesia in 1883 – 36,000 drowned

Pelee, Martinique in 1902 – 30,000 dead

Nevado del Ruiz, Colombia in 1985 – about 25,000 killed

Unzen, Japan in 1792 – over 15,000 killed

- There are over 500 active volcanoes in the world. Eighty per cent of these volcanoes are found in the ocean.
- The jets of hot water and steam that are ejected from geysers are known to reach heights of about 500 metres (1,640 feet).
- Mauna Loa, which makes up a large part of the Hawaiian Islands, is the largest active volcano in the world. It is more than 4,100 metres (13,450 feet) tall and has erupted 33 times since the first time in 1843.

◂ Jets of hot water
When surface water trickles into the mantle it is heated. Soon, the pressure builds up and the hot water erupts through cracks in the crust. These jets of hot water are called geysers.

When a large amount of magma is collected beneath the surface, the pressure inside ejects the magma, causing an eruption. Volcanoes are usually found on the boundaries of plates. However, they can also be formed over regions known as hot spots. A hot spot is an area in the mantle where a large amount of magma is produced. This magma comes out through tiny cracks in the crust to form volcanoes. The hot spot stays in one place as the plates above keep moving to form a string of volcanoes.

◂ Volatile region
The Ring of Fire stretches from New Zealand, along the eastern coastline of Asia, across the Aleutian Islands and along the western coast of North and South America. This region is known for frequent earthquakes and volcanic eruptions.

Volcanic zone

Most of the world's biggest volcanoes are found around the Pacific Ocean, in the Ring of Fire. This area is composed of the Pacific Oceanic plate and three smaller plates. The edges of the oceanic plates lie near several continental plates, making this region highly vulnerable to volcanic activity.

Volcanic material

During an eruption, a volcano ejects various substances like lava, rock fragments, ash and gases. The magma that comes out at the surface is called lava. It is extremely hot and is reddish orange in colour. Lava can be thrown high up into the air if the eruption is explosive. Sometimes, it just spills over the sides of the vent and flows down the slopes of the volcano. It can come out of a single vent on top or ooze out of vents on the sides. Thicker lava travels slowly and covers shorter distances before cooling, while fluid lava can flow several kilometres (miles) away from the volcano before it solidifies. All materials that are thrown into the air during a violent eruption are called pyroclasts. These include ash, cinders and balls of molten lava called volcanic bombs.

▸ Fiery lava
Inside the magma chamber, the temperature of the magma can be as high as 1,200 ºC (2,200 ºF). When the magma reaches the surface and flows out as lava the temperature decreases, but even lava is as hot as 900 ºC–1,170 ºC (1,600 ºF–2,140 ºF).

Types of volcanoes

There are different types of volcanoes – active, intermittent, dormant or extinct, depending on the frequency of eruption. Active volcanoes erupt constantly, while intermittent volcanoes are those that erupt at regular intervals. The most dangerous volcanoes are those that are dormant or extinct. Dormant volcanoes are merely 'sleeping' and can erupt without any warning. Extinct volcanoes are those that have not erupted for several thousands of years. It is difficult to distinguish clearly between the two, since some volcanoes remain quiet for a very long time before suddenly becoming active once again. Volcanoes are also classified according to their shapes and the type of materials they are composed of.

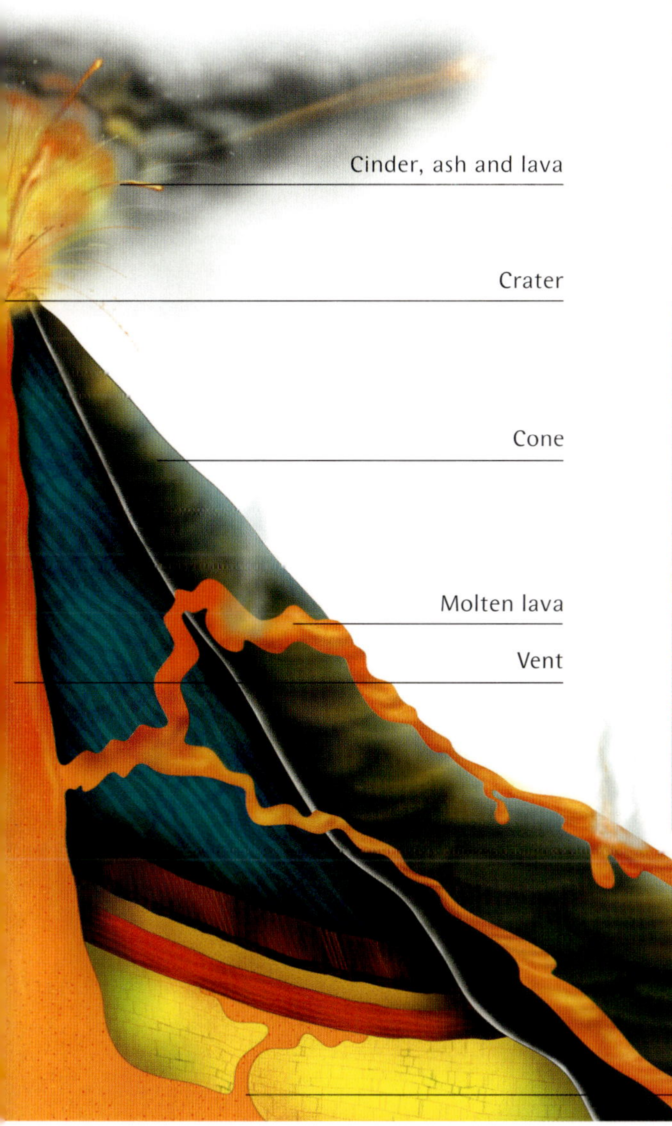

What's that noise?

Eruptions can be explosive or non-explosive depending on the thickness of the lava and the amount of gas formed inside the magma chamber and the vent. If the lava is thick, it will block the opening making the eruption explosive. During explosive eruptions thick lava and fragments of volcanic and non-volcanic rock are thrown out of the vent. In non-explosive eruptions the lava flows out of vents located on the sides of the volcano.

Cinder cones are volcanoes that are formed by tephra, or the solid material, ejected from the vent. These solid pieces fall back on to the ground to form a cone-shaped mountain. A shield volcano is formed when a large amount of liquid lava flows out of a vent. This lava spreads around to form a broad, dome-shaped mountain. Composite volcanoes, also known as stratovolcanoes, are huge and steep. They are composed of alternating layers of lava, volcanic ash, cinders and rocks. Most of them have a crater on top with a single central vent or a group of vents. Some of the biggest mountains in the world, including Mount Fuji, Mount St Helens and Mount Vesuvius are composite volcanoes.

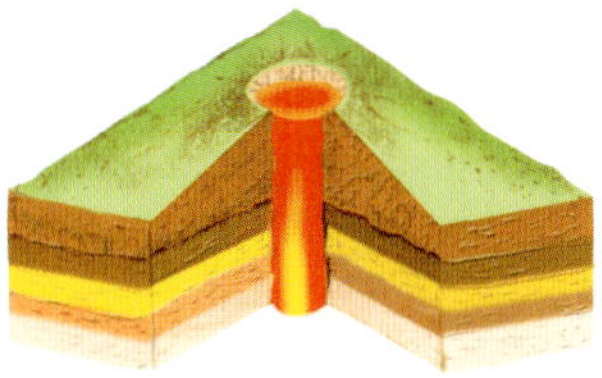

Shield volcano

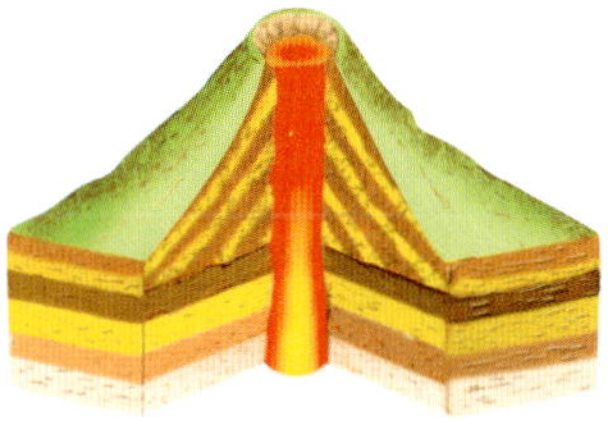

Cinder cone

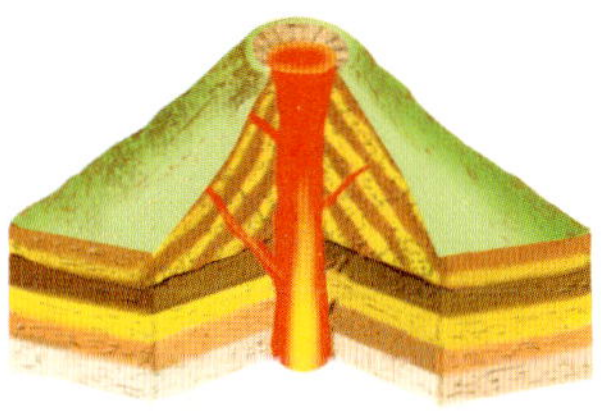

Composite volcano

▲ **Lava domes**
Sometimes the lava is so thick that it does not flow far, but piles up around the vent to form lava domes, which are usually found near composite volcanoes. Some domes take years to grow. The Santiaguito Dome in Guatemala began to erupt in 1922 and is still growing.

▲ **An active life**
Kilauea in the Hawaiin Islands is the most active volcano in the world, with eruptions occurring almost continuously.

Try these too:

The Rocky Planets (p 10–11), Oceans of the World (p 24–25), Earthquakes and Tsunamis (p 28–29), Earth's Atmosphere (p 30–31)

Earthquakes and Tsunamis

Like volcanoes, earthquakes are caused by the movement of tectonic plates. When the plates separate or slide past each other suddenly, it makes the Earth tremble. This is called an earthquake. Most earthquakes are too small to be felt. But massive earthquakes cause the ground to shake so hard that even houses and other buildings can collapse.

Key dates:

- **18 April 1906**
  An earthquake hits San Francisco. It only lasts for about 60 seconds, but kills more than 700 people.
- **1 September 1923**
  The Japanese cities of Tokyo and Yokohama are hit by the Great Kanto earthquake. The quake kills more than 100,000 people.
- **26 December 2004**
  An earthquake measuring 9.0 on the Richter scale originates in the Indian Ocean. It triggers a tsunami that kills more than 200,000 people across 15 countries, making it the worst tsunami in history.
- **8 October 2005**
  An earthquake measuring 7.6 on the Richter scale hits Pakistan and parts of Kashmir, India, killing over 100,000 people.

It is possible to measure the strength of an earthquake. However, it is impossible to predict where and when an earthquake would occur. People who live in earthquake-prone cities have to be well prepared and trained to protect themselves during emergencies. Nowadays, buildings are constructed so that they can withstand the strongest earthquakes.

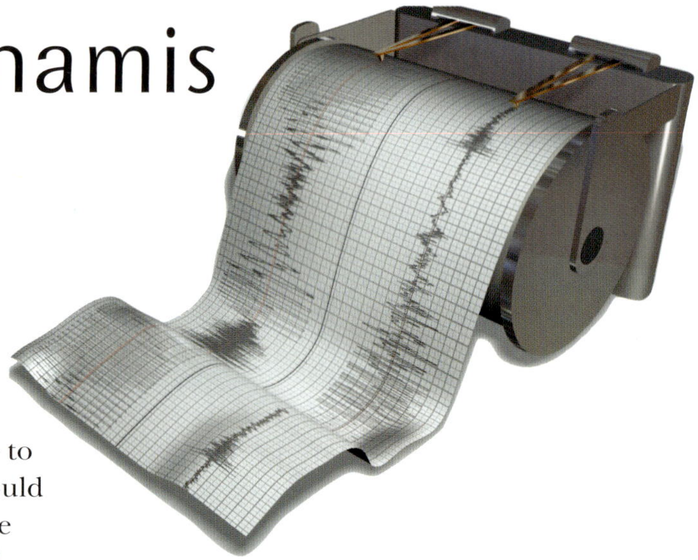

▲ **Recording a quake**
The changes in the intensity of an earthquake cause vibrations. These vibrations are recorded by a seismograph in the form of zigzag lines.

Line of fault

Most earthquakes occur along a fault. A fault is a region where pieces of broken rocks found under the Earth's surface slide past each other. These faults are marked by cracks on the Earth's surface, caused by plate movement. Most faults are located near the plate boundaries. However, small faults can be found far away from the boundaries. The presence of faults allows the rock fragments that form the crust to shift. Over a period of time, plate movement builds up pressure causing large blocks of rocks along a fault to bend or break with a jolt. This sudden movement releases energy that moves through the surface in the form of waves. This is what is commonly known as an earthquake.

Measuring tremors

Earthquakes are measured using the Richter scale. This scale was developed in 1935 by the famous American seismologist Charles F. Richter, along with his fellow scientist Beno Gutenberg of Germany. The Richter scale uses numbers from 1 to 10 to measure the intensity of an earthquake. Each increase of one point on the scale indicates a ten-fold increase in the magnitude of an earthquake and about 33 times the amount of energy released. So, a level 5.0 earthquake is ten times stronger than a level 4.0 earthquake. The instrument used to measure the intensity and location of an earthquake is called a seismograph. This instrument contains sensors, known as seismometers that can detect even the slightest movement in the ground.

▸ **Focus of disaster**
The point within the Earth where the rocks first begin to break is called the focus or hypocentre of the earthquake. The point on the Earth's surface that lies directly above the focus is the epicentre. The earthquake is strongest near its epicentre.

Side effects of quakes

Earthquakes can be very destructive. A strong quake can topple even the largest of buildings and bridges, trapping people underneath them. It can also cause gas pipes and electrical wires to break starting fires that can rage for several days. The violent shaking of the ground can cause liquefaction, where loose, moist soil or sand turns into a quicksand-like slurry that can suck in entire buildings. Earthquakes can also cause landslides and avalanches. Strong tremors sometimes loosen chunks of snow or mud that slide down the slopes of mountains and hills. Houses and people can get buried under tons of snow or mud.

▲ **Terrible tremors**
The San Fernando earthquake of 1971 was one of the worst earthquakes in the history of California. The quake was responsible for enormous property damage. It also caused many landslides in the regions near the San Gabriel Mountains.

Waves that kill

Massive earthquakes under the ocean can create giant, destructive waves called tsunamis. These waves move at great speeds (about 800 kilometres/hour or 500 miles/hour) and can travel thousands of kilometres (miles) across the ocean. In deep water, these waves are not very high. They gain strength and height as they approach the shore. Tsunamis can be as tall as 30 metres (98 feet). These huge waves break on to the shore with such force that they can bring down trees and large buildings. The term tsunami in Japanese means 'harbour wave'. Tsunamis are often mistakenly called tidal waves. A tidal wave is generated by high winds, but a tsunami is caused by underwater earthquakes, landslides and, occasionally, volcanic eruptions. Moreover, a tidal wave is not destructive.

◂ **Total devastation**
The two pictures on the left are of Aceh in Indonesia. The first picture showing a calm coastline was taken before the tsunami struck on 26 December 2004. The second picture shows the extent of the devastation caused by the tsunami.

Try these too:
The Story of Our Planet (p 20–21),
Features of the Earth (p 22–23),
Oceans of the World (p 24–25),
Communication and Satellites (p 192–193)

Earth's Atmosphere

The Earth is surrounded by a protective blanket of air called the atmosphere. When the Earth was newly formed, the atmosphere mainly consisted of hydrogen and helium, just like the atmosphere of all the other planets. This atmosphere was destroyed due to extreme heat. Then about 3.5 million years ago, the Earth's present atmosphere was created.

Key facts:

- Water vapour is responsible for over 60 per cent of the greenhouse effect. Carbon dioxide is the second most important greenhouse gas. Chlorofluorocarbons, or CFCs, are capable of trapping more heat than any other greenhouse gas. An increase in the atmospheric CFCs is largely responsible for global warming.
- The increasing levels of CFCs are also responsible for the destruction of the ozone layer. The chemicals in CFCs destroy the ozone, creating a hole in the ozone layer. This will in turn allow harmful ultraviolet rays to enter the atmosphere. These rays can cause severe health problems, including skin cancer.
- Global warming can cause significant changes in the climatic conditions across the world. An increase in the temperatures of the atmosphere will lead to increased evaporation, melting of glaciers and polar ice caps and an alarming rise in sea levels. It will change the Earth as we know it. In fact, global warming is thought to have ended the Ice Age.

Like the Earth's surface, the atmosphere can also be divided into several layers – troposphere, stratosphere, mesosphere, thermosphere and exosphere. The layers are based on temperature and density.

Troposphere

The troposphere is the layer closest to the Earth's surface. It stretches about 8 to 14.5 kilometres (5 to 9 miles) above sea level. The process of weather takes place in this layer. As you climb higher, the temperature drops from about 17 to -52 °C (62 to -62 °F).

Stratosphere

The layer above the troposphere is called the stratosphere. It extends upwards to about 50 kilometres (31 miles). The stratosphere contains a gas known as ozone, which absorbs the harmful ultraviolet rays of the Sun. The temperature in this region increases gradually to -3 °C (26 °F) due to the absorption of ultraviolet rays.

The final layers

The final layers of the atmosphere are the mesosphere, thermosphere and exosphere. The mesosphere extends above the stratosphere to about 85 kilometres (53 miles). The thermosphere extends to 600 kilometres (372 miles). Part of the thermosphere, known as the ionosphere, contains high-energy particles called ions that reflect radio waves, making long-distance radio communication possible. The exosphere, the final layer of the Earth's atmosphere, it merges with outer space. The air in the exosphere is very thin and mainly contains hydrogen and helium gases.

A natural greenhouse

The atmosphere sends most of the Sun's heat back into space. Gases like water vapour, carbon dioxide, methane, nitrous oxide, ozone and chlorofluorocarbons, or CFCs, trap a part of this reflected heat, keeping the Earth warm even at night. This process is called the natural greenhouse effect because it is similar to what happens in a greenhouse filled with plants. Greenhouse gases in normal quantities are essential, but an increase in the level of greenhouse gases in the atmosphere causes more heat to be trapped, leading to global warming.

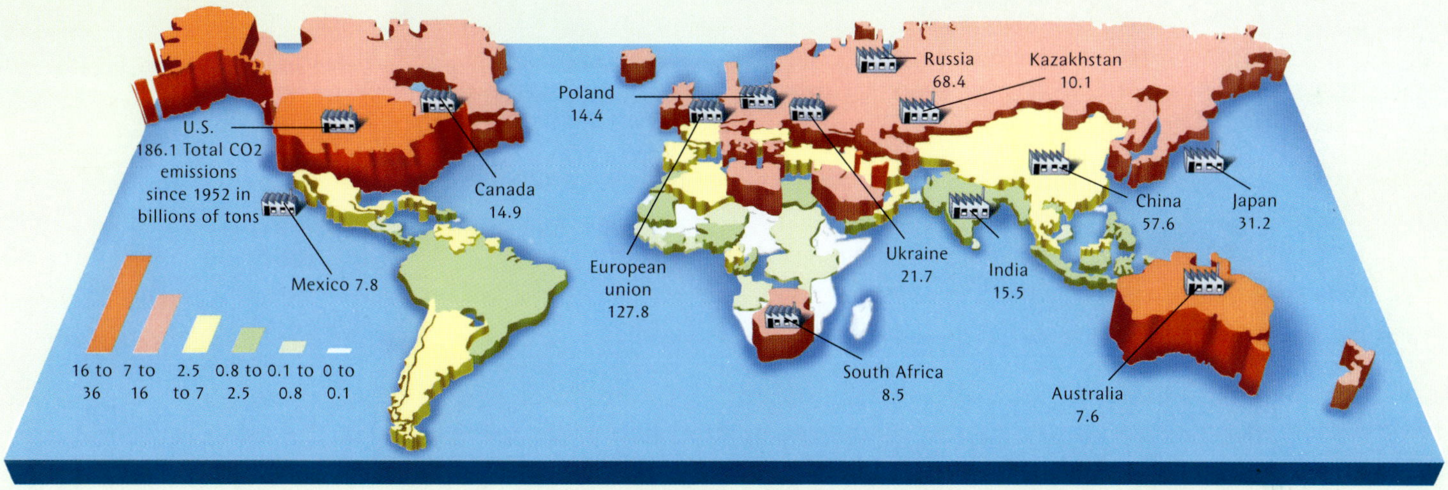

◂ A complex atmosphere
Nitrogen makes up 78 per cent of the atmosphere, while 21 per cent is composed of oxygen. The remainder is a combination of carbon dioxide, water vapour, argon, and trace gases like neon, helium, krypton and xenon. Trace gases are only present in extremely small amounts.

Air pressure

The Earth's gravity pulls the atmosphere towards its surface. The air in the upper atmospheric layers exerts weight on the layers below. This weight is known as pressure. The force exerted on the lower layers is stronger than on the upper layers, leading to less pressure at the top. Atmospheric pressure depends on the amount of gas molecules present and their speed. As we go up the atmospheric layers the number of molecules decreases. This in turn causes the atmospheric pressure to decrease. Since atmospheric pressure decreases with height, it changes according to location. For example, the atmospheric pressure on a mountain is lower than that at sea level. Atmospheric pressure also changes according to temperature. The atmospheric pressure usually decreases as the temperature increases.

▲ Measuring pressure
Atmospheric pressure is measured using an aneroid barometer. As the pressure increases the barometer is squeezed; as the pressure decreases the barometer is released. The barometer is connected to a pen and paper on a slowly rotating cylinder. The increases and decreases in pressure cause the pen to move up and down the paper and thereby record the changes.

Try these too:

The Rocky Planets (p 10–11), The Gas Giants (p 12–13), The Moon (p 14–15), Comets and Asteroids (p 16–17), The Story of Our Planet (p 20–21), Communication and Satellites (p 192–193)

Seasons and Weather

As the Earth goes around the Sun, it also rotates on its own axis. The Earth's axis is tilted, meaning that the poles of the Earth receive sunlight at different times. The Earth's movement is largely responsible for seasons, climate and weather patterns. It is also responsible for day and night.

Key facts:

- The highest shade temperature of 57.7 °C (136 ºF) was recorded at Al'Azizyah, Saudi Arabia in 1922.
- The coldest temperature ever of -89 °C (129 ºF) was recorded in 1983 at Vostock, Antarctica.
- At an average of 11,700 millimetres (463 inches) Tutunendo, in Columbia, receives the highest amount of rainfall every year. Arica in Chile receives the least rainfall. It gets only 0.76 millimetres (0.03 inches) of rain each year.
- In the Northern Hemisphere the longest day falls during the summer, on 21 June, when the northern half of the Earth is tipped towards the Sun. This is knows as the summer solstice. During the winter solstice (22 December), the northern part is tipped away from the Sun, resulting in the longest night of the year.
- On 23 September and 21 March the Earth is positioned in such a manner that the length of day and night is equal (12 hours each). These days are known as autumnal and spring equinoxes.

The Earth's axis is an imaginary line passing through the North Pole and the South Pole. This line is slightly tilted to one side. That is why both poles receive sunlight. At any given point of time, half of the Earth faces the Sun, and therefore it is daytime in that part and night in the half that faces away from the Sun. Since the Earth spins in an eastwards direction, the Sun appears to rise from the east and set in the west.

▲ **Tilted axis**
If the Earth's axis had been vertical neither pole would receive light and there would be no life in these regions.

Earth's revolution

As well as spinning on its own axis, the Earth also revolves around the Sun. The Earth takes about 365 days to complete one revolution. Throughout its orbit, the Earth's tilted axis remains pointed towards the same direction. Therefore, different parts of the Earth receive varying amounts of sunlight all through the year. For example, the North Pole faces the Sun for a part of the year. During this time, the Sun's light falls on the northern part of the world more directly. At the same time, the southern part receives less sunlight. It is this difference that causes the four seasons – spring, summer, autumn and winter.

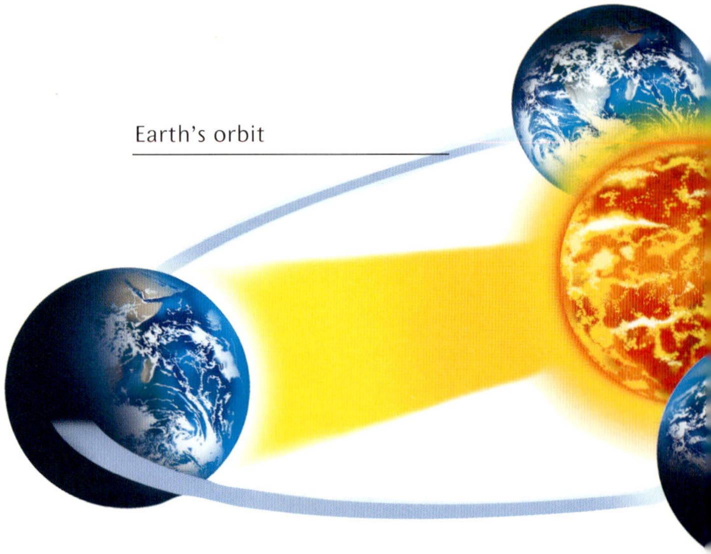

Weather and climate

The tilted axis is also responsible for weather and climatic patterns. Since sunlight falls at varying angles onto the Earth's surface, it heats up different parts of the planet differently. This causes temperature differences that result in the generation of wind and eventually leads to various weather conditions. A particular weather condition in a place for an extended period of time is known as climate.

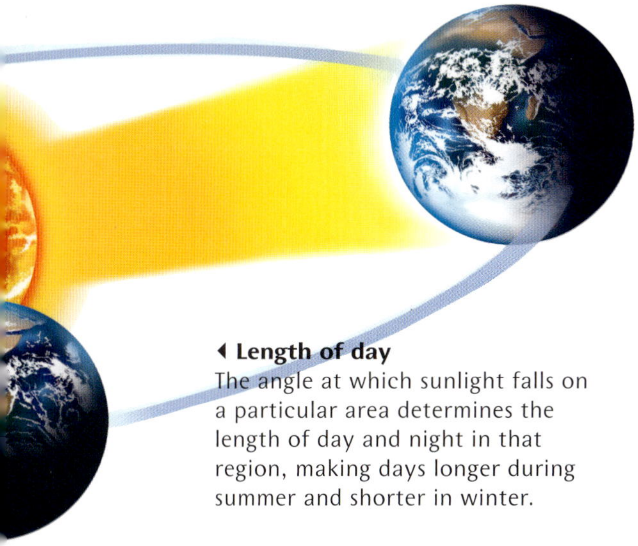

◀ **Length of day**
The angle at which sunlight falls on a particular area determines the length of day and night in that region, making days longer during summer and shorter in winter.

Extreme weather

Weather is not always pleasant. Sometimes, nature unleashes her fury in the form of hurricanes and tornadoes. There are many reasons for such extreme weather conditions. Hurricanes are tropical storms with strong winds that travel at speeds of about 117 kilometres/hour (73 miles/hour). They are formed in places close to the equator. Hurricanes are born when the heated air above the sea rises up to create a low-pressure area at the surface. The cooler trade winds (winds over the equator) move into this region. The Earth's rotation causes the rising air to twist and form a cylinder. The warm air slowly cools down to produce huge clouds. Tornadoes are produced by huge thunderstorms that are formed when cold, dry polar winds mix with warm, moist tropical air.

▶ **Climates of the world**
The five main types of climates include tropical, dry, warm temperate, cold temperate and cold climates.

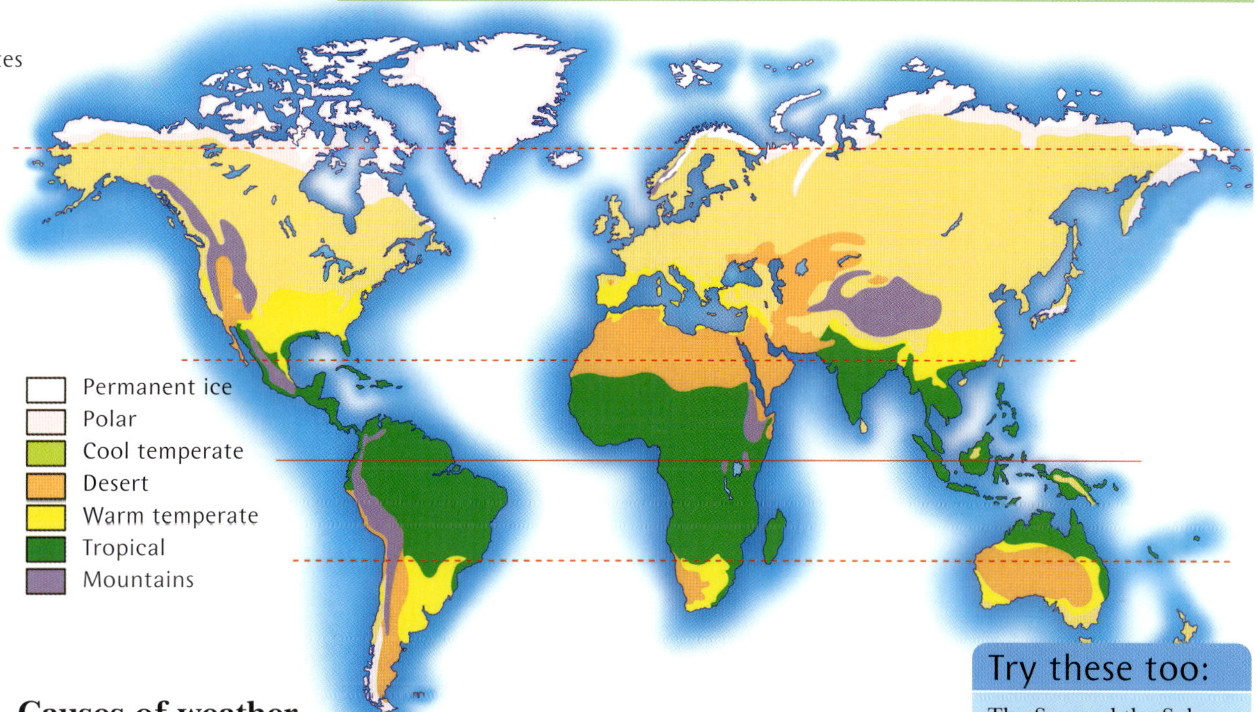

▼ **Seasonal change**
Changes in weather conditions, such as a drop or rise in temperatures, are indicative of a change in the season.

Causes of weather

Weather patterns are influenced by temperature, atmospheric pressure, wind, cloud and precipitation, all of which are affected by sunlight. Water in the oceans, rivers and lakes evaporates due to the Sun's heat. This process forms water vapour that is absorbed by the air near the Earth's surface. When the air containing water vapour is heated, it rises up and begins to cool down. As a result, the water vapour in the air condenses to form clouds containing tiny droplets of water. These droplets grow larger in size and finally fall down as rain. Sometimes, these droplets freeze into ice crystals – snow – on their way to Earth.

▼ **Clouds of change**
Different types of clouds are responsible for different kinds of weather conditions.

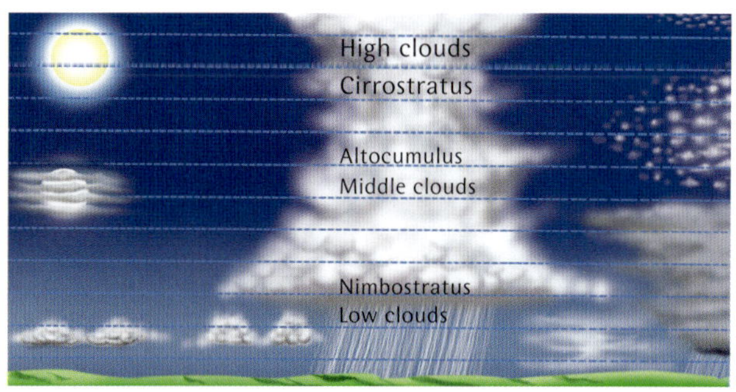

Try these too:

The Sun and the Solar System (p 8–9), Man in Space (p 18–19), Forces and Motion (p 188–189), Communication and Satellites (p 192–193)

Mammals

Mammals are vertebrates (animals with a backbone) that suckle their young. They are warm-blooded animals with highly developed organs and four limbs. Most mammals are covered with hair or fur and almost all have teeth that can cut and chew food. Mammals can be found in all kinds of habitats, including the hottest and the coldest regions of the planet. Some common animals, including elephants, lions, whales, dolphins, cats, dogs and even humans, are mammals.

▲ **Mum's the word**
Most mammals give birth to live young and look after their babies until they can take care of themselves.

▸ **Footsie**
The feet of each mammal are adapted to that mammal's habitat and position in the food chain.

Key facts:

- The blue whale is not only the largest mammal, but it is also the largest living animal in the world. It can grow to a length of more than 30 metres (98 feet). The smallest of all mammals in the world is the Kitti's hog-nosed bat.This tiny bat is as small as a bumblebee.
- Most mammals have a long life span. Horses and dogs can live up to 20 years, while chimpanzees have been known to live longer than 50 years. However, humans live the longest with an average life span of 80 years. Some people live to the ripe old age of 110 or sometimes even longer.
- Each year grey whales migrate between the Arctic waters and the Mexican coast, covering a total distance of 20,000 kilometres (12,427 miles). This is the largest distance covered by any migrating animal on the planet. Only the Arctic tern, a bird, covers a distance longer than that. The Arctic tern flies over 35,405 kilometres (22,000 miles) to reach its new home.

There are over 5,000 species of mammals in the world. They have been divided into various families, including primates, big cats, hoofed animals, rodents and canines. The rodent family consists of about 2,000 species, including rats, squirrels, beavers, moles and mice. All meat-eating mammals belong to the group, carnivore, while plant-eating mammals make up the group, herbivore. Carnivores include big cats like lions and tigers, bears, wolves, foxes and marine mammals such as seals and walruses. Herbivores include deer, horses, rhinoceros, antelope, camels, giraffes, hippopotamuses and zebras. All mammals with hooves are called ungulates and are further divided into even-toed and odd-toed ungulates. We belong to a family called primates. This family includes monkeys, apes and lemurs. Some mammals spend their whole life or part of their life in water. Such mammals, including whales, seals, dolphins, sea lions, walruses and manatees, form the family of marine mammals.

Smart mammals

Mammals are the most intelligent of all animals. They are able to think, learn fast and imitate actions. The brain of a mammal, like that of other vertebrates, is divided into three parts – hindbrain, midbrain and forebrain. The hindbrain controls bodily functions like breathing. The midbrain deals with nerve impulses and the forebrain helps a mammal to think and respond to its surroundings. The forebrain is highly developed with millions of nerve cells. Among mammals, humans are considered to be the most intelligent.

Defence tactics

Most mammals depend on their excellent senses and reflexes to escape from dangerous situations. Smaller mammals usually flee. Mammals like skunks release foul-smelling chemicals to deter the enemy, while porcupines have spines that are erected in times of danger. Larger mammals use their limbs and teeth to cause serious injury to their attacker.

Mammalian diet

Mammals eat food not only to grow, but also to keep themselves warm. That is why they eat more often than cold-blooded animals like reptiles, fish and amphibians. The smaller the mammal, the bigger its appetite. This is because small mammals lose heat faster than larger mammals. The teeth of mammals are highly specialized and adapted to their individual diet, but all mammals have teeth that fit together when the mouth is closed. This allows them to carry out a variety of processes like gnawing, biting and chewing. Smaller mammals feed on insects and worms, while bigger meat-eating mammals hunt down other mammals and birds. The senses of smell, sight and hearing are highly developed in all mammals, but in mammals that hunt these senses are heightened. Herbivorous mammals have a stomach that helps them to digest the plants they eat. Almost all herbivores spend a long time chewing their food since certain plant parts are difficult to digest.

Try these too:

Birds (p 54–59),
Fish (p 60–63),
Reptiles and Amphibians (p 64–69),
Countries and People (p 102–115)

▼ **Tooth matters**
Carnivores have specialized teeth that help them to crush bones and tear through flesh.

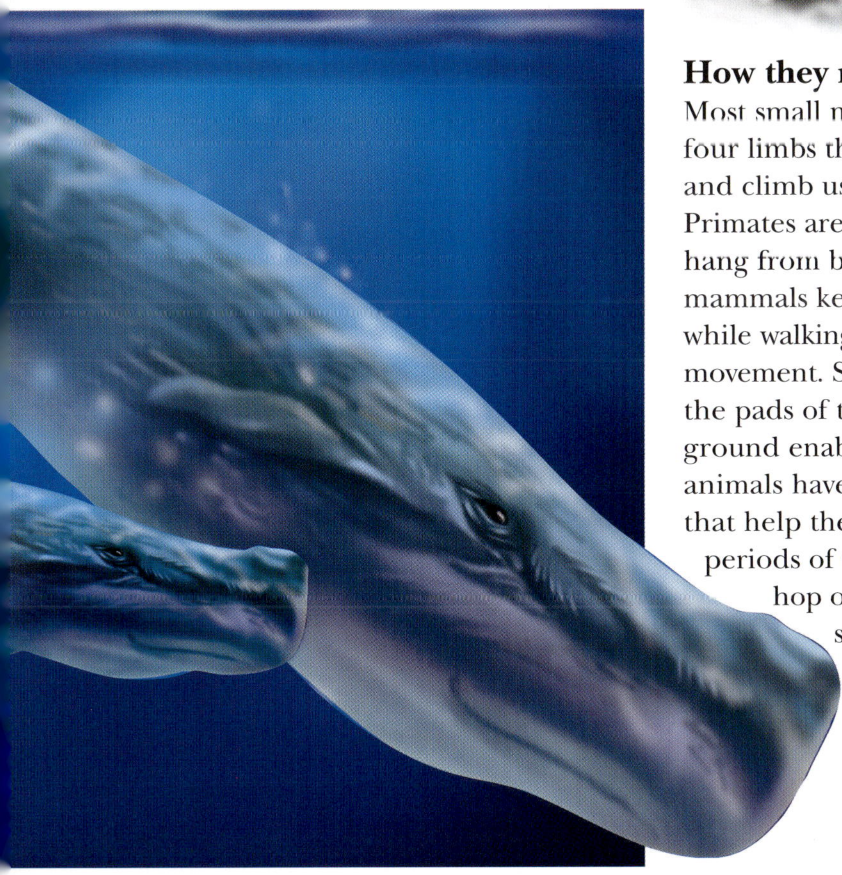

How they move

Most small mammals, such as rodents, have four limbs that are almost equal. They run and climb using all four of their limbs. Primates are good climbers. Some can also hang from branches of trees. Most heavy mammals keep their feet flat on the ground while walking. This does not allow for fast movement. So, hunting mammals walk on the pads of their toes with their heels off the ground enabling them to run fast. Hoofed animals have hard hooves and long strides that help them to run quickly, and for long periods of time. Mammals like kangaroos hop on their hind legs. Some mammals, such as flying squirrels, have flaps of skin that act like wings to help them to glide from tree to tree.

◀ **Flipper power**
Marine mammals have flippers instead of legs to help them swim better.

▲ **To greener pastures!**
Many large mammals are known to migrate. Animal migration is influenced by climate and food supply. Whales migrate to warmer waters during the breeding season. Animals, such as zebras, migrate in search of water. Herbivores that live in the Arctic regions migrate to warmer climates during the winter.

Primates

Monkeys, apes (gorillas, chimpanzees, gibbons and orang-utans) and humans make up the order called Primate. All primates have five flexible fingers and toes, opposable thumbs, arms and legs that move more freely than other mammals, forward-facing eyes enabling them to judge distances accurately, and large brains.

Key facts:

- The gorilla is the largest primate in the world. The adult male can be as tall as a full-grown man and can weigh a maximum of 170 kilograms (375 pounds).
- The world's smallest primate is the pygmy mouse lemur found in Madagascar. This animal is only 20 centimetres (8 inches) tall and weighs about 30 grams (1 ounce).
- African vervet monkeys use different alarm calls for each of their main predators – eagles, leopards and snakes. The monkeys react differently to each call. When they hear the eagle alarm call, the monkeys hide among dense vegetation. At the sound of the leopard call they climb as high as possible. They simply go 'on alert' at the snake call.

Primates are commonly found in tropical jungles, dry forests, grasslands, and cold, mountainous regions. There are more than 350 species of primates in the world. They are broadly divided into prosimians and anthropoids. The prosimians, or 'primitive primates', consist of only 60 species, including lemurs and lorises. The rest fall under the anthropoid category. The term 'anthropoid' means 'humanlike'. This group consists of about 175 species. Most anthropoids have flat faces and a poor sense of smell. They depend on their eyesight to find food. Opposable thumbs and big toes help primates to grip branches as well as pick up objects. Most monkeys and prosimians have tails, which help them to maintain balance while moving from tree to tree. Many species have prehensile tails that can be wrapped around branches and act like an extra foot or hand.

▸ Aping about
Apes are found only in Asia and Africa. They have arms that are longer than their legs and do not have tails.

▸ Strong shoulders
Primates have a collarbone that helps to stabilize the shoulder. This is vital for a primate since the shoulders support its body weight while hanging down from branches with its arms.

Monkeys from Asia and Africa are known as Old World monkeys. Like humans and apes, these monkeys have narrow noses and downward-facing nostrils. These monkeys are also called catarrhines, meaning downward-nosed. Monkeys from Central and South America have broad noses and nostrils that open sideways. These monkeys are called platyrrhines, meaning broad-nosed. Platyrrhines are more commonly known as New World monkeys.

Primate diet

Most primates are omnivorous, meaning they eat both meat and plants. However, there are a few species that live entirely on either meat or plants. Most monkeys are opportunistic feeders, meaning they will eat whatever they come across, including bird eggs, fruit and plant sap. Several species of monkeys even attack and eat other monkeys. Some monkeys love to eat leaves. Howler monkeys of South America and colobus monkeys of Africa eat the leaves of any tree. The digestive system of leaf-eating monkeys is similar to that of other herbivores like deer and cows.

Fussy monkey

The proboscis monkey, which is found on the island of Borneo, is very selective about its food. It usually prefers to eat the leaves of mangrove and pedada trees, although it feeds on seeds and green fruit when its favourite is unavailable.

Primate language

Primates use several methods of communication. Solitary species use scent as a means of communication. Urine, faeces or special scent glands are used to mark territory or to announce a particular individual's desire to mate. Primates that live in groups use both visual and vocal signals. The majority of monkeys and apes communicate visually using a variety of facial expressions, some of which are very similar to those we humans use. Sound is yet another important mode of communication. Primates use a wide array of sounds, from soft clicks and grunts to elaborate songs and roars. Courtship calls are loud and vary with each species. Chimpanzees have been known to use as many as 34 different vocal signals. One of these calls is used to communicate the location of food.

◂ **Tarsier terror**
Tarsiers have long back legs that are used to leap onto their prey. They then hold the prey down with their hands and kill it with sharp, pointed teeth.

Behaviour

Primates, especially anthropoid primates, are the most intelligent of all animals. They are extremely curious and are quick to learn. They usually learn by imitating. Primates are completely dependant on their power of sight to move about and to locate food. Species that live in groups are highly interactive. They clean and groom each other's fur. Their high level of intelligence has enabled primates to learn several new skills, including making tools. This skill is most pronounced in humans, followed by chimpanzees.

▾ **Healthy relationships**
Removing parasites from the fur of other members of the group helps many primates to forge new relationships and maintain old ones.

Try these too:

Birds (p 54–59),
Fish (p 60–63),
Reptiles and Amphibians (p 64–69),
Countries and People (p 102–115)

▾ **Howl to be heard**
The barking sound made by howler monkeys can be heard 3 kilometres (1.9 miles) away. It is this sound that gives the monkey its name.

Big Cats

From the graceful domestic cat to the more ferocious species, cats are truly amazing animals. All cats are carnivorous and hunt smaller animals. They usually hunt at night, but tigers prefer to hunt at dawn or dusk. Cats have large eyes, sharp teeth, a good sense of hearing and powerful limbs with sharp claws. Most of them have long tails and coats that have patterns. Lions, tigers, leopards and jaguars all belong to the group called big cats.

▲ **Multi-purpose tongue**
A cat's tongue has hook-like projections called papillae. Cats use their tongue to clean the flesh from the bones of their prey and to groom themselves.

Key facts:

- The jaguar uses its powerful jaws and sharp teeth to pierce the skull of its prey between the ears. The jaguar's strong teeth can even break open turtle shells.
- White tigers are not a result of albinism. A true albino would not have stripes, but white tigers have very prominent stripes. The colour variation is due to mutation. White tigers rarely occur naturally. They are usually bred in captivity and so can only be seen in zoos.
- Lionesses do most of the hunting, while lions mainly defend the pride. The large golden mane of the lion gives it away while hunting.

All cats have small faces and short, broad skulls. They have strong jaws with three pairs of incisor teeth, one pair of canines, two or three pairs of premolars, and one pair of molars. Cat paws have soft pads. The forelimbs have five toes and the hind limbs have four. All cats walk on their toes with the heel raised off the ground. They also have long, sharp claws that can be drawn into their paw. The cheetah is the only cat that cannot retract its claws. All cats are sticklers for cleanliness and spend a lot of time licking their bodies, and cleaning and rubbing their face with their paws.

Feline senses

Big cats are specialist hunters that rely on their senses of sight and hearing to locate their prey. The eyes of the cat face forwards, which helps them to judge distances and the size of their prey accurately. Their large pupils allow more light to enter their eyes at night.

▸ **Show of strength**
Leopards are extremely strong animals. They have been known to carry full-grown antelopes, which are about three times their size, up to treetops to eat in peace.

During the day the pupils can be shrunk into slits allowing less light to enter the eyes. Cat ears can be round or pointed. They are held erect and can be turned in any direction to pick up the slightest sounds. Cats also have long whiskers that help them to feel their way around. The whiskers are very sensitive to movement and touch. Sometimes, cats use their whiskers to locate hidden prey.

◂ **Burning bright!**
Some big cats' pupils appear circular when dilated and, as in domestic cats, mirror-like tissue in their retinas reflects the light back, making their eyes glow in the dark.

Coat of many patterns

Big cats have fur coats that protect them from extreme heat and cold. The tiger has a striped coat that allows the cat to conceal itself in vegetation while hunting. Lions have sand-coloured coats that help them to blend into the landscape of the open savannahs. Leopards and jaguars have spots that serve as good camouflage. The spots of jaguars are more like paw prints and are different from those of leopards. Like the fingerprints of humans, leopard and jaguar spots are unique – no two individuals have the same spots.

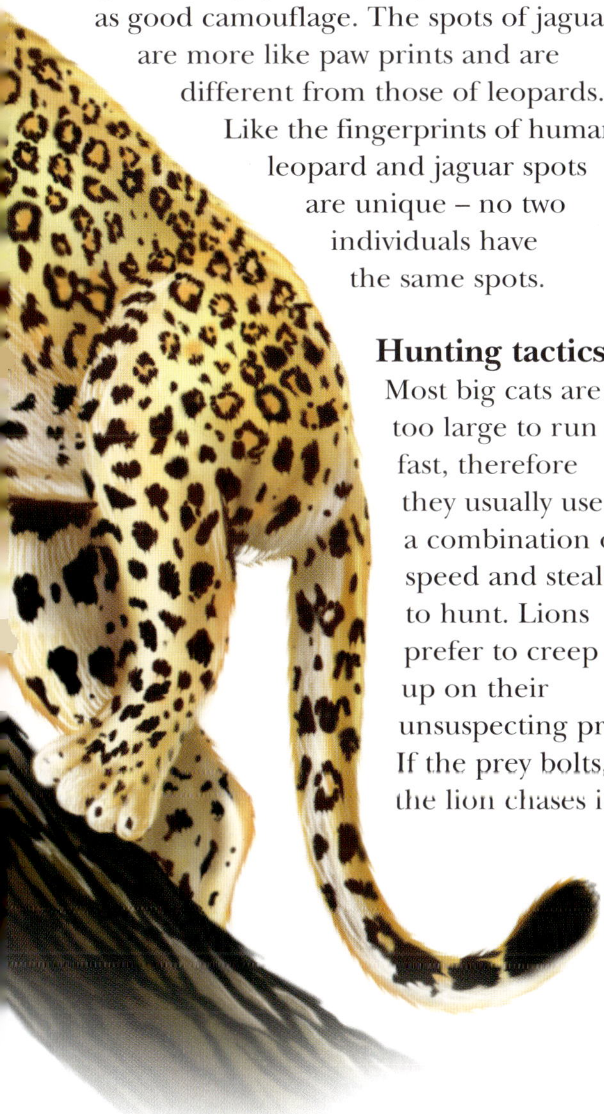

Hunting tactics

Most big cats are too large to run fast, therefore they usually use a combination of speed and stealth to hunt. Lions prefer to creep up on their unsuspecting prey. If the prey bolts, the lion chases it. If the prey is too fast the lion gives up the chase. Tigers like to stalk their prey. They hide in the tall grass, waiting for the prey to pass by. Then they pounce on it. Tigers can leap up to 9 metres (30 feet), making it one of the most successful hunters. The leopard also uses stealth tactics to capture prey, which it then carries off to the top of a tree so that no other animals can steal its food.

Behaviour

Lions are social animals. They live in groups called 'prides'. A typical pride consists of 3 to 30 individuals, but on average have 4 to 6. One to five adult lions and several lionesses and cubs make up a pride. Tigers, jaguars and leopards, on the other hand, are solitary creatures. They come together only during the mating season. All big cats are territorial. Tigers leave claw marks on the bark of trees and a urine trail to let other tigers know that the territory is occupied. Jaguars and leopards also mark their territories in a similar fashion. Both tigers and jaguars are good swimmers and can often be seen lazing in ponds and lakes.

Colour variations

Melanism – the over-production of a skin pigment, melanin – is common among jaguars and leopards. Affected animals are black in colour and are commonly referred to as black panthers, but are not a separate species as, on closer examination, the typical spots of a jaguar or a leopard can be seen. Albinism – the absence of pigment – is rare among cats, but has been reported in some jaguars and leopards. These individuals are called white panthers. White tigers, however, are not albinos, nor are they a separate subspecies, but are the result of a recessive gene.

◂ Judge by the cover
The coat of each big cat contains a unique pattern that serves as a camouflage and helps in the identification of the particular species.

▴ On guard
Adult lions and lionesses are fierce when it comes to protecting their pride.

Try these too:

Birds (p 54–59),
Fish (p 60–63),
Reptiles and Amphibians (p 64–69)

Bears

All bears have a stocky body, powerful limbs, thick fur and a short tail. Bears can be found in a wide range of habitats, including mountains and Arctic regions. There are eight species of bear – spectacled bear, sun bear, giant panda, Asiatic black bear, American black bear, brown bear, sloth bear and polar bear. All species are similar in appearance, although there are slight differences in size, habitat and diet.

Key facts:

- Sun bears are the smallest of all bear species. They grow up to 1.5 metres (5 feet) in length and weigh 66 kilograms (146 pounds).
- Bears can run at speeds of about 50 kilometres/hour (30 miles/hour) when required.
- Polar bears do not drink water. They get all the water they need by breaking down body fat and from the animals that they eat.
- In traditional Asian medicine, a bear's body parts are thought to cure even the most fatal diseases. In Taiwan, sun bears are killed for their paws, which are used to make soup.

Bears have an elongated head, rounded ears and a long snout. They have a keen sense of hearing and smell. All bears, except the polar bear, are omnivorous. Their varied diet includes roots, nuts, fruit, berries, honey and insects. Their teeth are small, and mainly used for defence or as tools. The molar teeth are broad and flat, helping the bear to shred and grind fruit, nuts and berries. Bears have four limbs with paws. Each paw has five long, sharp claws, which are used to climb trees, open termite nests and beehives, dig for roots, and catch prey. All bears have long, shaggy fur. The colour of fur varies from species to species. Most bears are solitary creatures, but usually come together during the mating season.

Polar bear

The polar bear is a native of the Arctic regions. It has creamy white fur that blends in with the Arctic ice. Polar bears are one of the largest bear species. They can grow to a length of 2 metres (7 feet) and can weigh up to 800 kilograms (1,760 pounds).

▼ Born to swim
Polar bears are excellent swimmers and are fast on both land and in water.

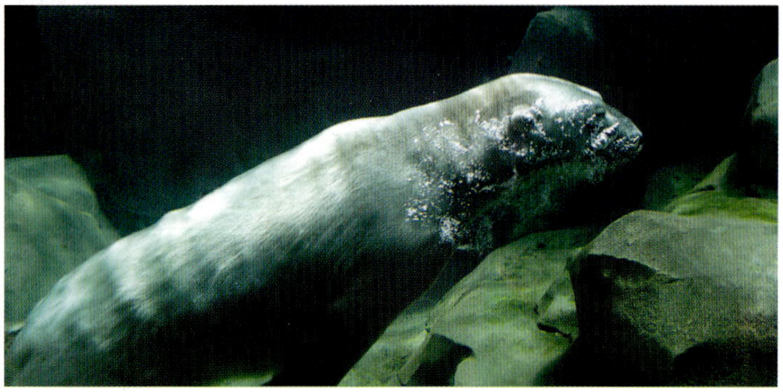

Brown bear

The brown bear can be found in a variety of habitats, including tundra, dense forests and deserts. The brown bear's coat can vary from creamy white and various shades of brown to almost black. The hair on the back of some brown bears is white at the tips, giving the coat a greyish appearance. An adult male brown bear can weigh about 500 kilograms (1,100 pounds).

▼ Telling marks
The brown bear is distinguished from other bears by the hump on its shoulder and its upturned snout.

▲ **Giant appetite**
The giant panda eats about 18 kilograms (40 pounds) of bamboo leaves and stems or about 40 kilograms (85 pounds) of bamboo shoots each day. It spends up to 14 hours a day just eating.

Giant panda

Like most bears the giant panda has a big, bulky body. It is covered with black and white shaggy fur. The giant panda is the most endangered of all bear species. There are only about 1,000 individuals surviving in south-central China. The main danger facing this cuddly-looking animal is the loss of their bamboo forests. The giant panda lives almost entirely on a diet of bamboo shoots and, in recent years, bamboo forests have been destroyed to make way for human progress.

Winter sleep

Some bears, like brown bears, black bears and polar bears, live in places that have very cold winters. These bears spend the coldest period sleeping in warm, cosy dens. Pregnant female bears usually give birth during the winter in these dens. Before they go into their winter sleep, bears fatten themselves up during the summer and autumn when food is readily available. Since food is scarce in winter, bears sleep through that part of the year to conserve energy. Winter sleep is not the same as hibernation as the bear can easily wake up anytime. Also, a bear's body temperature does not drop as drastically during the winter as that of other hibernating animals.

Black bear

There are two kinds of black bear – Asiatic and American. As the names suggest, the Asiatic black bear inhabits the temperate forests of Asia, while the American black bear is native to North America. The Asiatic black bear is also known as the moon bear because of the white, crescent-shaped mark on its chest. Its coat is mostly black in colour, although brown coats are not uncommon. Asiatic black bears feed mainly on fruit and nuts. Many of these bears migrate to higher regions in warmer months and return to lower areas during winters.

The American black bear is the smallest of all North American bear species. This bear grows up to 1.8 metres (6 feet) in length and weighs about 40–300 kilograms (90–660 pounds). The American black bear is primarily a vegetarian. It eats grass, berries, walnuts and acorns. They are, however, occasionally known to eat deer fawns and moose calves.

Other bears

The spectacled bear gets its name from the white rings around its eyes. It is the only bear found in South America. It builds a nest on a tree for sleeping during the day. These nests are usually built near a food supply so that the bear can simply pluck fruit or other fare from nearby branches anytime it needs to. The sun bear has a sleek, black coat marked with a golden-coloured crescent on the chest. Also known as the Malayan sun bear, this bear is found in the rainforests of Southeast Asia. It has a very long tongue that helps it to capture insects and dig out honey from tree holes. The sloth bear, or the honey bear, has a long coat that can be black, red or reddish-brown in colour with a white v-shaped mark on the chest. It mainly feeds on ants and termites, although it can also eat honey, bird eggs, fruit and meat. Its white snout is flexible and is used to dig out food. The sloth bear uses its long claws to rip open the nests of ants and termites. It then uses its snout and hairless lips to form a kind of suction tube that sucks in its prey.

▲ **Exceptions to the rule**
Most American black bears have a glossy black or honey-coloured coat. However, the Kermode bear, a type of American black bear found in the rainforests of British Columbia, Canada, is the only black bear to have a white coat.

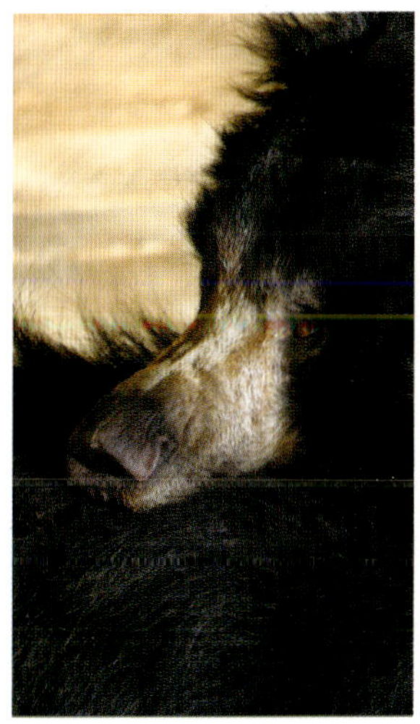

▲ **Namesake**
The sloth bear looks like the sloth of Central and South America, which is how it got its name.

Try these too:

Birds (p 54–59), Fish (p 60–63), Reptiles and Amphibians (p 64–69), Countries and People (p 102–115)

Canines

Domestic dogs and their relatives are commonly known as canines. This family includes wolves, foxes, coyotes, dingoes and jackals. The canine family can be broadly divided into true dogs and foxes. True dogs include the wolf, coyote, jackal, African hunting dog, dhole, raccoon dog, bush dog, domestic dog and some species of foxes.

▲ **All in the family**
Grey wolves are close relatives of domestic dogs and look a lot like them.

Key facts:

• Greyhounds are among the fastest canines in the world. They have been known to run at speeds of up to 70 kilometres/hour (44 miles/hour). African hunting dogs are also very fast and can maintain speeds of 50–60 kilometres/hour (31–37 miles/hour) for very long distances.

• Fennecs are the smallest of all canines. These small foxes are only 65 centimetres (2 feet) long from the top of their ears to the tips of their tails, and do not weigh more than 1.5 kilograms (3.3 pounds). These desert animals have oversized ears that help them to dispel excess heat from their body.

• With swift foxes, the female is dominant over the male. It is the female that guards the territory and defends the pups. The male has no role in these activities. Male swift foxes leave the den if the resident female dies or is removed.

Canines can be found on every continent except Antarctica. They are extremely adaptable and can live in a variety of habitats. For example, bush dogs inhabit the humid tropical forests of South and Central America, while Arctic foxes live on the ice floes of the Arctic regions. Some species like the grey wolf and the red fox are found across the world in a variety of environmental conditions.

Hunters by nature

Most canines have medium-sized bodies covered with fur. They also have long, bushy tails, and a pointed snout and mouth. Their ears are usually erect and pointed. Some species, like the bat-eared fox, have extraordinarily large ears. All canines are excellent hunters. They have a keen sense of sound and smell. Contrary to popular belief, canines do not have very good eyesight. All canines have several sharp teeth used for killing, feeding and defence.

Built for speed

Canines are very good at chasing prey for long distances. They can run extremely fast and have a large amount of stamina. This ability is due to their long legs, wrists and anklebones. These animals are also digitigrade, meaning that they stand on their toes. Furthermore, canines have a highly flexible backbone that can be arched as they run. Their feet are small, and in most cases have only four toes that touch the ground. The fifth toe, called the dewclaw, can be found high up on both forelegs. All toes have strong but blunt claws. Their small, light feet and limbs help them to run more efficiently than other animals with larger legs.

▶ **Canine teeth**
Canines use their chisel-like incisors, in the front of the mouth, for cutting food and grooming. Next to them are a pair of dagger-shaped teeth used for fighting and hunting.

▼ **Varied appetite**
Jackals eat just about anything from antelope and reptiles to insects and even berries.

▲ **United effort**
African hunting dogs prefer to hunt in packs. This allows these small canines to hunt animals that are much larger than themselves.

Life in a group

Most canines live and hunt in closely-knit groups. Members of a group use a series of sounds like barks, whimpers, growls and howls to communicate with each other. Canines also use various head movements, tail movements and scents to mark hunting territories, display strength or to show that they are prepared to mate. Most groups have a main breeding pair who set the rules for the rest of the pack. For example, wolf packs have a breeding male, called the alpha, which rules over the others in the pack using growls, barks, scent marking and at times, even fighting. The size and composition of the group is largely influenced by its habitat and the availability of food. On average, a canine group usually consists of 10 to 30 individuals. The dominant female is the only female in the pack that breeds, while the rest of the female members help to raise the young. Lower ranking females might mate and even produce pups, but they are not given the freedom or the necessary help to look after their babies.

One at a time

Canine packs are known to hunt larger animals using a technique called relay hunting. In this method, one member of the pack chases the prey for a while, then another takes over. Each member of the pack takes a turn in chasing until the prey becomes exhausted. The canines then immediately move in for the kill. Canines are able to hunt animals as large as a bison in this way.

Try these too:

Birds (p 54–59), Fish (p 60–63), Reptiles and Amphibians (p 64–69), Countries and People (p 102–115)

▼ **Defending territories**
Some species of fox, like the red fox, live in very small groups and usually hunt alone. A red fox pair defends the territory in which they hunt and raise their young.

Elephants

Elephants are the largest of all existing land animals in the world. Modern elephants are divided into three different species – savannah, forest and Asian elephants. Savannah and forest elephants are together known as African elephants. The African and Asian elephant are quite different from each other. The African species are larger in size than their Asian counterparts.

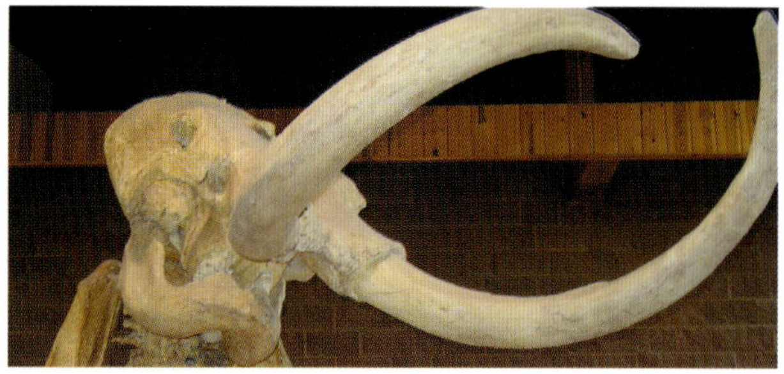

▲ **White gold!**
Elephants have been poached for their tusks, which are used to make jewellery, furniture and other such items.

Key facts:

- A newborn calf can drink a maximum of 11 litres (2.5 gallons) of milk every day.
- The elephant has the longest gestation period of all mammals. A female remains pregnant for almost two years, before giving birth to a single calf.
- The elephant's digestive system is very weak. It can digest only 40 per cent of the total food it eats. The elephant has to make up for this weakness by eating a lot. An adult consumes about 140–270 kilograms (300–600 pounds) of food a day, 60 per cent of which is excreted without being digested.
- All elephants have four molar teeth with jagged ridges that help to grind leaves and stems. The teeth are very large, each weighing more than 5 kilograms (11 pounds). One pair is located near the front of the mouth. When these molars drop out, those at the back shift forwards. Two new teeth grow at the back of the mouth to replace the ones that moved forwards.

African elephants also have bigger, fan-shaped ears and less hair on their body. Both male and female African elephants have tusks.

In contrast, only the male members among Asian elephants have tusks. The tusk of an African elephant is between 1.8–2.4 metres (6–8 feet) in length, whereas that of an Asian male is about 1.5 metres (5 feet) long. The savannah elephant is light grey in colour, while forest and Asian elephants have dark grey skin. An elephant's trunk is actually a combination of its nose and upper lip. It is long, muscular and flexible. The elephant uses its trunk to grasp objects, pluck leaves, break off branches and carry heavy objects like logs. The trunk is also used to suck in water for drinking or to bathe. When lying in water, the elephant sticks its trunk out to breathe. Elephants use the nostrils at the tip of their trunk to capture the scent in the air. The trunk is then placed in their mouth, where special organs identify the scent. Small, finger-like projections at the end of the trunk help elephants to pick up small objects.

▲ **Angry loner**
Solitary male elephants can be dangerous and have been known to attack without provocation.

A tale of tusks

The tusks of an elephant are actually elongated incisor teeth. Elephants use their tusks for digging for water, stripping tree bark for food, fighting each other during the mating season, and protecting baby elephants from predators. A calf is born with a pair of incisors that are replaced within 6 to 12 months. The second set grows into tusks. The tusks grow at a rate of about 17 centimetres (7 inches) per year throughout its life. However, years of wear and tear scale down their length.

Living in a herd

Elephants live in huge groups called herds. The members of a herd are headed by the oldest female elephant. There can be as many as 30 members in a herd, mostly females. The herd usually stays together for life, but if the family grows too big, some of the female members can leave to start a new herd. The members of a herd feed, bathe and migrate together. They usually stay very close to their leader and protect each other from predators. The young, sick and old are well taken care of. When faced with danger, the head leads the rest in a stampede. When the leader dies, the next oldest female takes over.

Power struggle

Males in a bachelor herd fight among themselves to prove their worth. Only the powerful ones are allowed to lead the herd and breed with adult females. Most of the fights involve aggressive displays of strength. The weaker animals usually back off before any damage is done. However, during the mating season, fights can become fatal.

Try these too:

Birds (p 54–59), Fish (p 60–63), Reptiles and Amphibians (p 64–69), The First Mammals and Birds (p 82–83), Countries and People (p 102–115)

Friendly bout ▲
Fights between males appear fierce, but those involved are careful not to injure each other seriously.

▼ **Shown the door!**
At around six years old, male elephants who are ready to mate wander off alone or are driven away by older females. Such males often form bachelor herds.

Beasts of burden

For years man has tamed elephants for all kinds of reasons. Female elephants were used extensively by various Asian militaries to uproot trees and carry heavy objects. Elephants were also used as a means of transport, in circuses and as mounts for hunting. They continue to be used as mounts in religious ceremonies and in temples across India and many other Asian countries. The military of ancient India used male elephants in wars. These elephants were made to charge and trample the enemy. Male elephants were preferred as they are faster and more aggressive than females. Moreover, female elephants often ran away from other male elephants.

Even-toed Ungulates

Some mammals have hard nails, called hooves, that are large enough to walk on. These animals are called hoofed animals, or ungulates. The two main groups of ungulates are artiodactyls and perissodactyls. Artiodactyls are hoofed animals with two or four toes. They are further divided into suidae and ruminants. Suidae include pigs and hippopotamuses, while ruminants include deer, antelope, cattle, camels, llamas, giraffes and okapi.

Key facts:

- Impalas can jump over fences that are 3 metres (10 feet) high, and can cover distances of 10 metres (33 feet) in a single leap.
- The royal antelope, which is about 25 centimetres (10 inches) high at the shoulder, is the smallest of all antelope, while the common eland, which can be as heavy as 900 kilograms (2,000 pounds) is the largest of the species.
- Giraffes can run at speeds of about 56 kilometres/hour (35 miles/hour), but they do not appear to go very fast because of their extremely long legs.
- The pygmy hippopotamus is the world's smallest hippopotamus. It is only 75 centimetres (30 inches) tall and weighs just about 160–270 kilograms (350–600 pounds).

Suidae have four toes, short legs, simple molars and tusks. Ruminants have longer legs with two toes, grinding teeth and a highly developed digestive system. The animals that fall into these two groups chew their cud.

Hippopotamuses

Hippopotamuses are found only in central, western and southern Africa. They live partly in water and partly on land. There are two species of hippopotamuses – the common and the pygmy hippopotamus. The common hippopotamus can weigh up to 3,200 kilograms (7,055 pounds), and is one of the largest land animals. Most hippos spend a large part of their day in shallow water and usually come out only at night. But pygmy hippopotamuses prefer to stay near the water rather than in it and go underwater only when they are in danger. The skin of all hippos is almost hairless. Most common hippos have grey-brown skin, while pygmy hippos are blackish-brown in colour.

▸ Watery life
Hippos usually remain underwater for less than five minutes, but can do so for up to half an hour. They can walk or run along the riverbed and even sleep underwater.

▲ A large family
Artiodactyls, also called even-toed ungulates, include pigs, hippopotamuses, camels, giraffes, goats and cattle.

The pores of the common hippo secrete a reddish-pink fluid, which is often mistaken for blood. This fluid gives the skin a shiny appearance and prevents it from cracking in the heat. Pygmy hippos secrete a colourless fluid for the same purpose. The eyes of common hippos are on the top of their head and are set in sockets that bulge upwards. This helps them to keep their eyes above the water when floating. Their nostrils also face upwards and can be sealed when they dive.

Camels and llamas

Camels and llamas are ruminants. Their upper lip is split into two parts, both of which can move separately. There are two species of camels and four species of llamas. The camel species are the Bactrian and the dromedary, or Arabian camel. The Bactrian camel has two humps on its back, while the dromedary only has one. Contrary to popular belief, humps do not store water. Instead, the hump contains a large amount of fat that provides the animal with nutrition when food is not available. Both camel species can be found in the deserts of Asia and northern Africa.

Built for the desert

The Arabian camel is well adapted for the desert life. It has thick, broad sole pads and callosities – corn-like projections on its leg joints and chest that prevent its skin from cracking while kneeling on the hot desert sand. The nostrils of the Arabian camel can be closed at will to prevent dust from entering the nose. The camel also has very long eyelashes that protect its eyes from the desert heat and dust.

Antelope and deer

Antelope are ruminants with a pair of pointed, hollow horns. Most antelope inhabit open grasslands, but some of the smaller species live near vegetation, so that they can take cover in the thick undergrowth to escape predators. Those that live in open habitats rely on speed to escape from enemies. Unlike antelope, deer have branched antlers that they shed every year. Deer antlers are solid and bony. Only male deer grow antlers, while both male and female antelope have horns.

◂ **Distant cousins**
Llamas are found in South America. Although they are distant relatives of camels and fall under the same category, llamas do not have humps. They are usually white, with black and brown patches. Some llamas are completely white or black in colour. Alpacas are similar to llamas but are much smaller in size.

Giraffes

The giraffe is the tallest living mammal. An adult male giraffe can grow to a height of about 6 metres (20 feet). Giraffes inhabit the savannah and open woodland. The giraffe's body is shorter than that of most other hoofed animals. Its front legs are slightly longer than the hind legs. Adult giraffes have very large hooves. Their necks can be over 1.5 metres (5 feet) in length, but only have seven vertebrae. These vertebrae are long and separated by highly flexible joints. Its long neck and extraordinary height help the giraffe to pluck leaves that are beyond the reach of other animals. It also has a tongue that can be extended as far as 45 centimetres (18 inches). The tongue and lips of the giraffe are covered with hard growths called papillae that allow it to pluck leaves even from trees with thorns. Both male and female giraffes have a pair of bony horns covered with skin. A tuft of black hair grows out of the ends of these horns.

▸ **Moving about**
While walking, giraffes move their feet on one side of their body together, followed by the two feet on the other side. However, when running, they move their front feet together, followed by their back feet. They also swing their hind feet up, putting them in front of their front feet. The neck of a running giraffe moves backwards and forwards to maintain balance.

Try these too:

Birds (p 54–59),
Fish (p 60–63),
Reptiles and Amphibians (p 64–69),
Countries and People (p 102–115)

▾ **Armed with horns**
Although there have been instances when an antelope has impaled and even killed powerful predators like lions, these shy animals are more likely to run away when faced with danger.

Odd-toed Ungulates

Animals such as horses, zebras, rhinoceros and tapirs all belong to the group of mammals known as perissodactyl. All the animals in this group have an odd number of toes and are therefore also known as odd-toed ungulates. Other modern hoofed mammals include elephants and aardvarks. Marine mammals like whales, manatees and dugongs are also believed to have evolved from hoofed land mammals of the prehistoric times.

Key facts:

- The modern Sumatran rhinoceros is a descendant of the woolly rhino that became extinct about 10,000 years ago. The woolly rhino was a native of northern Europe and eastern Asia. This Ice Age rhinoceros had two horns and a body covered with thick, long hair.
- Both the mountain zebra and the Grevy's zebra have suffered from habitat loss and extreme hunting. The pelt of Grevy's zebra with its narrow stripes was considered very fashionable. It was therefore used extensively for making handbags, rugs, slippers and clothes.
- The Grevy's zebra was named after the French president, François Paul Jules Grévy, who received one of these species in the 1880s as a gift from the Abyssinian (modern-day Ethiopia) government.
- The Quagga is a type of plains zebra that is now extinct. It had stripes only in the front part of its body. These stripes faded towards the middle, and the hindquarters were plain brown.

Zebras belong to the same family as horses. There are three main kinds of zebras all of which are found in Africa. All zebras have black and white vertical stripes on their body that act as a camouflage and also defend the animals from the blood-sucking tsetse fly, by confusing it. The three species of zebra are the plains, mountain and Grevy's zebra. The plains zebra is the most common of the three species. It is found in the south and east African grasslands. Mountain zebras are native to the mountainous regions of southwest Africa. They have a white belly and their stripes are narrower than those of the plains zebras. The Grevy's zebra is the largest of the zebra species. It has an erect mane, large ears and narrow, closely set stripes that extend to the hooves. Both the Grevy's zebra and the mountain zebra are endangered.

Rhinoceros

There are five species of rhinoceros in the world. They are the Sumatran, Javan, Indian, white and black rhinoceroses. The white and black rhinoceroses are found in Africa, while the others inhabit Asian forests. All rhinos have thick skin with folds. They have short, thick legs and a tiny tail. They are solitary animals that come together only during the mating season. The mother and calf stay together until the calf can take care of itself. The white rhino, also known as the square-lipped rhino, has a wide mouth used to cut grass. It has two horns on its snout and a hump on the back of its neck, while the black rhino does not have a hump on its neck and has a pointed, prehensile upper lip that is used to grab leaves and twigs.

▼ **All sorts**
There are several types of African plains zebras such as these, all featuring variations in their stripes.

Of the Asian species, the Indian rhino, also known as the great one-horned rhino, is the most common. Unlike the African species, the Indian rhino has only one horn. The Sumatran rhino is the only one with thick fur, while the Javan species is grey in colour and has no hair on its body. Both Sumatran and Javan rhinos are endangered.

Strange relative

The tapir is a pig-like animal with a short, prehensile trunk that is closely related to zebras and rhinos. It is about 2 metres (6.5 feet) long and about 1 metre (3.2 feet) tall. This animal has splayed hoofs, with four toes on its front limbs and three on its hind legs. Its hooves help the tapir to get a firm grip on soft, muddy ground. There are five species of tapirs in the world, three of which are found in the rainforests of South America, while the other two inhabit parts of Southeast Asia and Iran. All tapirs prefer water to land and spend a great deal of time in lakes and streams. They feed on fruit, leaves and aquatic plants. Brazilian tapirs often sink to the bottom of streams and rivers in search of food.

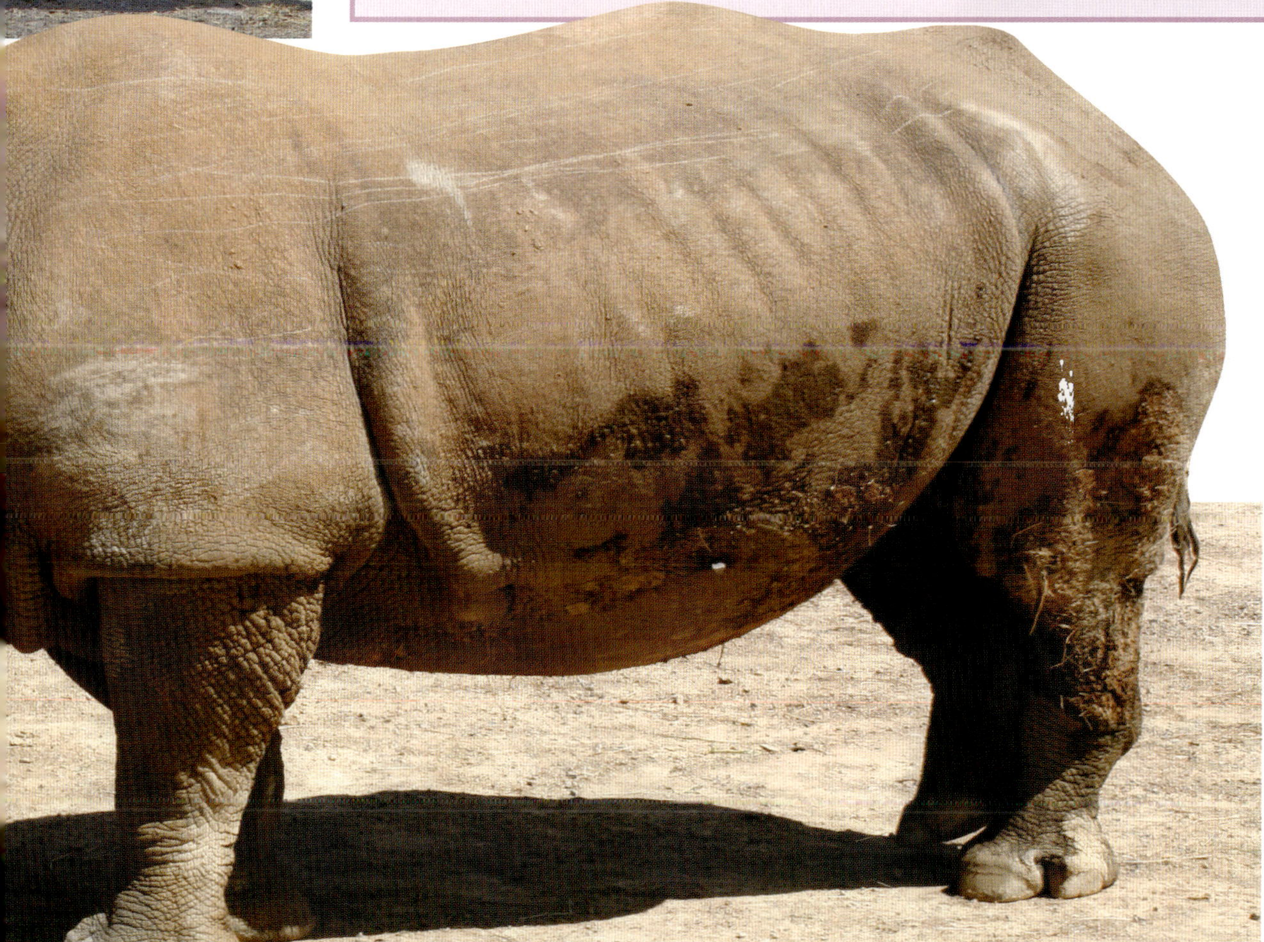

▲ **Not white!**
Contrary to its name, the white rhinoceros of north-eastern and southern Africa is greyish-brown in colour. It is believed that the term 'white' is a misnomer for the Afrikaans word *weit*, meaning 'wide', which is believed to have been used to refer to the white rhino's wide mouth.

▲ **Trading in horns**
In some countries, like Yemen, daggers with handles made from rhino horns were a status symbol. The worldwide oil shortage in the 1970s made these countries, which had lots of oil, rich. Soon people were able to afford more rhino horns, leading to an increase in the poaching of rhinos.

Try these too:

Birds (p 54–59), Fish (p 60–63), Reptiles and Amphibians (p 64–69), Countries and People (p 102–115)

Marine Mammals

Some mammals spend most of their life, or at least part of it, in oceans. These marine mammals have special features that help them to adapt to their surroundings. These animals share many characteristics with other mammals, but are different in some ways. Unlike most other mammals, marine mammals do not have hair.

Key facts:

- Whales use a series of moans and clicks to communicate between themselves. Most of these sounds are either too low or too high for humans to be able to hear. Blue whales and fin whales produce the loudest noises of all animals.
- Weddell seals are the best divers of all seals. They can dive to depths of 700 metres (2,300 feet) and stay there for over an hour.
- Toothed whales give out sound waves that bounce off an object, helping them to identify the size, shape and location of that object. Most toothed whales use this method, called echolocation, to locate prey, enemies or other members of their pod.

Instead, they have a layer of thick fat called blubber to keep them warm in icy cold water. Their limbs have been modified into paddle – like extensions called flippers that help them to swim. However, like other mammals, all marine mammals breathe using their lungs. They also give birth to live young and look after their babies. Some well-known marine mammals are whales, seals, sea lions and walruses. Whales are one of the largest animals in the world. They spend their entire life in the water. They look like fish, but are very different from them in every other way.

▲ **Whales with teeth**
Toothed whales include dolphins, killer whales, sperm whales, beluga whales and porpoises.

Whales do not have gills like fish. Instead, they breathe through nostrils, called blowholes, located on top of their head. The blowholes are kept closed underwater. Whales come up to the surface at regular intervals and open their blowholes to breathe. After taking in a few gulps of air, they dive into the water again. Like fish, whales have tail fins, but they are horizontal and are called flukes. Whales move their flukes up and down to propel themselves through the water.

Classification of whales

Whales are divided into toothed and baleen whales. Toothed whales have small, sharp teeth in their jaws. Baleen whales are toothless. Instead, they have sieve-like structures, called baleen, that hang from their upper jaws. These whales swim with their mouths open, taking in water rich in krill, plankton and other tiny marine creatures. The prey gets trapped in the comb-like edges of the baleen plates and the whale licks the food off them. Baleen whales, also known as great whales, include grey whales, humpback whales, right whales and blue whales.

◀ **Pause for breath**
Sometimes when a whale comes up to the surface of the ocean to breathe you can see a fountain shoot up from the blowhole at the top of its head. This fountain is called the blow, or spout. Contrary to popular belief, the blow is not actually a fountain of water. It is in fact stale air, which condenses and vaporizes the moment it is released into the atmosphere. The blow of some whales can shoot up to heights of 10 metres (33 feet).

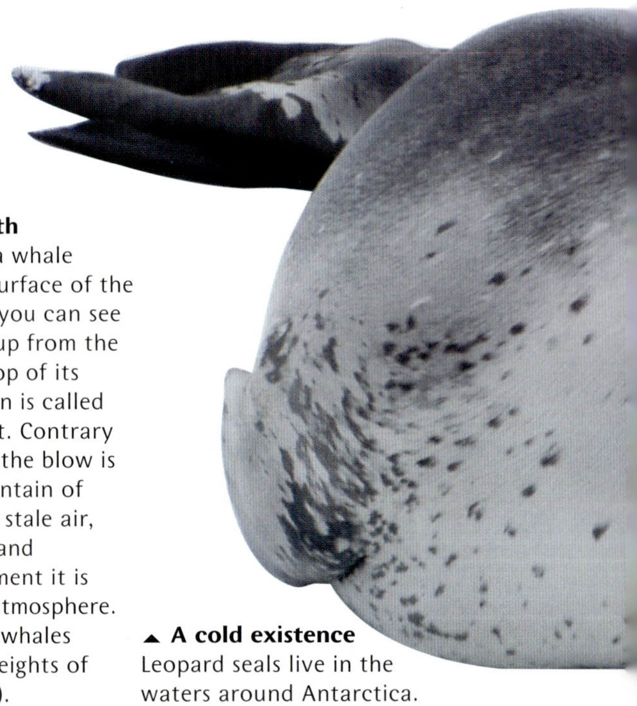

▲ **A cold existence**
Leopard seals live in the waters around Antarctica.

Seals and walruses

Seals and walruses fall into one group called pinnipeds, meaning fin-footed. All species in this group have limbs that look like fins. Seals are classified into true seals and eared seals. True seals do not have external ear flaps, while eared seals do. There are 19 species of true seals, making this group the largest among pinnipeds. Eared seals include sea lions and fur seals. Seals have powerful flippers and a strong torpedo-shaped body that make them great swimmers. However, true seals are very clumsy on land, sliding on the ice with great difficulty. The rear flippers of eared seals are longer and more mobile than those of true seals and better adapted for moving on land. Their front flippers are also larger and more powerful. Eared seals use their front flippers to row through the water. Seals range in size from 1 metre (3 feet) to over 4 metres (13 feet). Galapagos fur seals and ringed seals are the smallest, while the male southern elephant seal is the largest in the world.

Seals spend most of their lives in water, but they come ashore to breed and look after their young. They mainly eat fish, squid, crab and shellfish. However, some species, like leopard seals, also hunt other seals and penguins.

Having a whale of a time!

Whales do more than just swim and dive. They are known to leap out of the water and indulge in playful behaviour. Sometimes they pop their head above the surface and float motionless. This behaviour is known as 'logging'. Some whales, like humpback whales and orcas, leap right out of the water, which is known as 'breaching'. Whales also stick their tails out and splash them around. This is called 'lob-tailing'. Some species like dolphins and orcas can be seen popping their heads out of the water. This behaviour, known as 'spyhopping', is believed to give the whale a good view above the surface.

◂ **Handy tusks**
The most unique feature of the walrus is its tusks, which are actually a pair of elongated upper canine teeth. Walruses use these tusks not only to defend themselves, but also as hooks to climb out of the water onto the ice. Male walruses have bigger tusks, which they use during courtship fights.

Walruses are much bigger than seals. They inhabit the Arctic regions, at the edge of the polar ice sheet. Like all marine mammals, walruses have a layer of blubber that protects them from the cold.

Sea cows

Manatees and dugongs are together called sea cows. They are large, thick-bodied mammals, which live completely in the water. They get their name from the fact that they graze on seagrass and other aquatic plants found on the seabed. Manatees have a long, rounded body that tapers towards the tail. They have a short, square snout, and are grey in colour. Dugongs are very much like manatees, except smaller. Other differences between the two include the forelimbs, which in manatees are set close to the head. Dugongs have forked and pointed tails, while those of manatees are rounded at the end and paddle-like.

▴ **Slow swimmers**
Both the manatee (pictured) and the dugong are slow swimmers and use their forelimbs and tails to move in the water. Neither of these animals have hind limbs.

Try these too:

Birds (p 54–59), Fish (p 60–63), Reptiles and Amphibians (p 64–69), Countries and People (p 102–115)

Odd Mammals

Most mammals share certain common characteristics despite their differences. By definition a mammal is one that gives birth to live young and looks after them. However, there are exceptions, such as the platypus and the echidna. Mammals also have four limbs to walk on land. But some mammals can swim, while others like bats can even fly.

Hanging Around
Bats' thumbs are not attached to the wing, and have claws that are used to cling to tree bark or to the walls and ceilings of caves.

Key facts:

- There are about 1,000 species of bats that are divided into two major groups – Megachiroptera, or megabats, and Microchiroptera, or microbats. Megabats are found in Africa, India and Australasia, while microbats are found almost everywhere. Megabats mainly eat fruit, so are known as Old World fruit bats. Microbats are not too fussy about food and eat just about anything from small mammals to fish.
- After mating, the female platypus constructs a nest of weeds, leaves and grass at the end of the burrow in which she lays her eggs. The male platypus is not allowed to come anywhere near the nest. The female lays about two to four eggs in a clutch.
- There are two types of echidnas – the short-nosed and the long-nosed, or New Guinean echidna. The short-nosed echidna grows to about 35–53 centimetres (1–1.7 feet) long. The New Guinean echidna has a long, curved snout. This species can be as long as 75 centimetres (2.5 feet).

The duck-billed platypus and the echidna, or spiny anteater, are the only mammals that lay eggs. Together they are known as monotremes. They were also one of the first mammals to appear on the planet. Like other mammals, monotremes are warm-blooded, have hair and produce milk to feed their young. However, adult monotremes lack teeth and have snouts that look like beaks. The platypus is a semi-aquatic animal. It has a snout that looks like a duck's bill, giving the animal its name. The snout is covered with soft skin and is used for finding prey. The platypus has small eyes and no external ears, but its senses of sight and hearing are very good. Adult males have a horn-like spur on the inner side of their hind leg, which secretes poison. At first glance echidnas look like porcupines, since their bodies are covered with spines. However, they are completey different from porcupines. They have short, powerful limbs with large claws that help them to dig up their prey. They also have a long, thin snout, with a tiny mouth and a toothless jaw.

Flying mammals

Some mammals, like bats, flying squirrels and colugo, have modified flaps of skin that act like wings. However, bats are the only mammals that truly fly. The others can only glide from one tree to another. The flying squirrel has a membrane of furry skin between its limbs and a long flattened tail that helps it to glide. In the colugo, or flying lemur, the furry membrane extends along the limbs to the tips of its toes and tail. When the legs are stretched out, the membrane expands like a parachute, helping the animal to glide. Bats have modified front legs that act as proper wings. Each leg has four long fingers that support the wing. The wings consist of a double layer of skin called the patagium, which is stretched between the finger bones and attached to the side of the body and hind legs. Three pairs of flight muscles attached to the upper arms and chest give bats the power to fly.

Sticky business
Echidnas use their long, sticky tongues to feed on termites, ants and other tiny insects.

Non-stop reproduction!

Kangaroos often mate again soon after a baby comes out of the mother's uterus and climbs into the pouch. After mating, the fertilized egg begins to develop and stops at the blastocyst stage. During this stage, the baby is just a hollow ball of cells. It remains inside the mother until the newborn leaves the pouch. The blastocyst then begins to develop again and the new baby emerges from the uterus to move into the vacated pouch. This ability of the kangaroo helps it to continuously produce babies.

◂ Amazing mothers!
Some marsupials, such as kangaroos, have one baby at a time but others, such as possums, give birth to as many as twelve babies in one litter. The mother carries all of them in her pouch for at least two months. Of the twelve only eight or nine actually survive.

Pouched mammals

The female of some mammals, like kangaroos, wallabies and koalas, have a pouch on their bellies used to carry their babies. This pouch is called a marsupium and the animals that fall under this group are called marsupials. There are about 280 species of marsupials, most of which are found in Australia and New Zealand. Unlike other mammals, pregnant marsupials do not have a true placenta. The placenta is an organ that provides nutrients and removes waste products from the developing baby. Instead of a fully developed placenta, the pregnant marsupial has a yolk sac in her uterus from which the baby absorbs nutrients. About four to five weeks later, the baby comes out, but in an undeveloped state. The tiny newborn that weighs about 1 gram (0.03 ounces) climbs into the mother's pouch where it remains for several weeks until it is strong enough to move about on its own. The baby may remain in the pouch for more than a year, climbing in and out for milk or protection when needed.

Try these too:

Birds (p 54–59), Fish (p 60–63), Reptiles and Amphibians (p 64–69), The First Mammals and Birds (p 82–83), Countries and People (p 102–115)

▾ Leading a quiet existence
The platypus is a very shy animal. It is active only at dawn and dusk. The platypus is an excellent swimmer and diver. It leads a very quiet existence in burrows. These burrows are usually dug by females and can be found on the banks of rivers or streams. The burrows are blocked with earth in several places. The platypus is believed to do this purposely so as to prevent flooding and the entry of enemies.

Birds

Birds, like mammals, are warm-blooded vertebrates (animals with backbones). Unlike most mammals, birds have only two legs. Their front limbs have been modified into wings that help them fly. Birds do not give birth to young ones like mammals. Instead, they lay eggs. They have strong beaks and bodies that are covered with feathers.

Key facts:

- Some birds have what is known as powder down. These are special feathers that produce a kind of powder that acts as a waterproofing agent and conditioner.
- Cuckoos are lazy birds. They do not make nests. Instead, most cuckoos lay eggs in the nests of other birds. The female cuckoo usually searches for a host bird, whose eggs are similar to her's in appearance. Once the eggs hatch, the young cuckoo sometimes destroys the other eggs in the nest to avoid being detected.
- The arctic tern travels the longest distance during migration. It covers about 30,000 kilometres (18,640 miles), travelling between the Arctic and Antarctic regions every year.
- Some birds, like the hummingbird, have to flap their wings rapidly to help them hover. They extend their wings and flap them up and down several times as they hover near a flower, drinking the nectar. Some hummingbird species can beat their wings as many as 52 times in one second.

Feathers are one of the most distinguishing features of birds. They form a protective cover over the bird's body. Feathers keep birds warm and keep water off their bodies. They are often brightly coloured and so add to the beauty of birds. There are two types of feathers – vaned and down feathers. Vaned feathers are the ones that we see. They cover the exterior of the body. Down feathers provide the birds with insulation and are found under the vaned feathers. A vaned feather consists of a main shaft, called a rachis. A series of branches, or barbs, are attached to the rachis. The barbs further branch out into barbules, which have tiny hooks called barbicels that hold the feathers together. Down feathers are soft and fluffy because they do not have barbicels. The rachis forms a hollow tubular calamus, or quill, at the base, which is attached to a follicle in the skin. The flight feathers of the wings and tail are in fact modified vaned feathers.

Built to fly

Wings are the most important feature for flight. The size and shape of the wings determine how fast and high a bird can fly. Wings can be different shapes. Elliptical wings are short and rounded and do not help birds fly very high or for very long. They help the bird to move about in confined spaces.

▸ Migration
Most birds migrate to breed or to search for food. The change of seasons often leads to a decrease in food supply. This causes birds of one particular region to move to a place where food is abundant. Even during the breeding season, migration is related to food supply since plenty of food is required to feed the growing chicks.

▾ Tearing beaks
Birds like eagles have curved beaks with hooks at the end that help to tear the flesh of their prey.

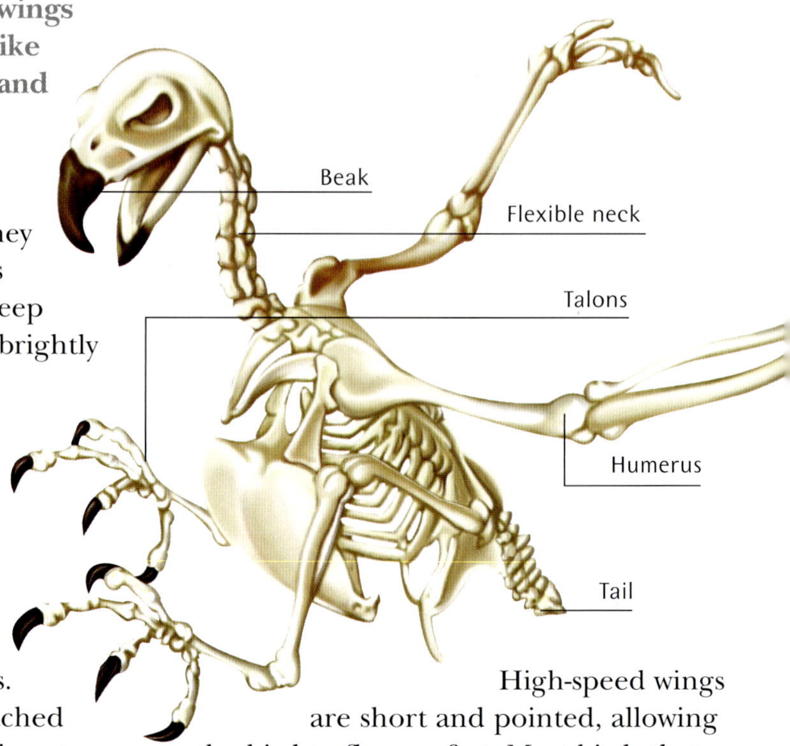

High-speed wings are short and pointed, allowing the bird to fly very fast. Most birds that soar, glide and hover have long wings, and do not have to run a bit before taking off. However, some soaring birds, like eagles, vultures and pelicans, with shorter wings have slots at the end that help them to take-off without taxiing. As well as wings, birds have other adaptations that improve flying. The bird's skeleton is hollow and light. They have strong lungs and a very efficient respiratory system that provides them with enough energy while flying.

◂ **Young and vulnerable**
The newly-hatched chicks of some species are covered with feathers and are capable of feeding on their own. However, the young ones of most birds are born blind and without feathers. These chicks are weak and need to be kept warm as well as fed by their parents. Some species swallow the food and regurgitate it at the nest to feed the young. This way the parent can carry more food and since it is half-digested, the young birds find it easier to swallow than whole pieces.

Beaks

All birds have beaks, also known as bills. The beak is a bony structure composed of an upper jaw called a maxilla, and a lower jaw called a mandible. A bird's beak varies according to the kind of food it eats. Meat-eating birds have cutting beaks that help them to tear the flesh of their prey. Hummingbirds have long, narrow beaks that help them to suck nectar from flowers. Apart from eating, birds use their beaks for many other purposes. Some, like the woodpecker, use their beaks to drum on trees to attract a mate or make hollows in trees for use as nests. Birds carry twigs for their nests and food for their young in their beaks. They also use their beaks to defend themselves.

Home sweet home

Almost all birds build nests. Some of them build nests with twigs and leaves, while others make simple holes in the ground to hide in. Certain other species use the old nests of other birds to lay their eggs in. Nests come in various shapes and sizes. They can range from simple, cup-shaped nests to elaborate dome-topped hanging nests like those of the tailorbird. A particular species of cave swiftlet makes a nest from its own saliva. This nest is the main ingredient of bird's nest soup, a delicacy in China.

Hard-working stomach!

Birds do not have teeth, so they have to swallow their food whole. How do birds break up their food? Birds have a very strong, muscular stomach called a gizzard, the muscles of which rotate the food around inside and crush it. Sometimes the bird swallows small stones or gravel to make the gizzard's work easier. These stones are called gizzard stones and break up hard food like seeds as they are rotated inside the gizzard.

Loving father!

Most birds mate with one partner at a time, with some mating for life. After mating the female lays her eggs in a nest usually built by her. In most species the mother incubates the eggs, but for some birds the work is divided equally between both partners. In some species the male carries out the incubating all by himself. When not brooding, male birds stay by their nests to protect the female and the eggs, and bring back food for the mother. Once the eggs have hatched, both partners take turns feeding and protecting the chicks. Birds make great fathers and take an interest in raising their young ones more than the males of most other animal groups.

▾ **Watch me!**
During the breeding season, most birds observe specific mating rituals. Some birds spread their wings and dance, while others, like the eagle, perform complicated aerobatics while flying. Sometimes, birds undergo a change in their physical appearance during mating. For example, the male frigate bird has a red-coloured inflatable pouch on its neck. The bird inflates this pouch during mating and shakes it to catch the female's attention.

Try these too:

Mammals (p 34–53), Fish (p 60–63), Reptiles and Amphibians (p 64–69), Countries and People (p 102–115)

Birds of a Feather

Birds have been divided into various families depending on common characteristics and behaviour. They are also classified according to their diet and habitat. The most common groups include seabirds, waders, songbirds, birds of prey (raptors), waterfowls and flightless birds. Seabirds spend a large part of their life at sea. They usually come ashore only during the breeding season. Seabirds live longer, have fewer chicks than other birds and undertake long migrations.

Seabirds have special adaptations to help them cope with their lifestyle. Those that spend a lot of time flying over open seas have long, strong wings that help them to fly and glide, while divers have shorter wings. Almost all seabirds have webbed feet that help them move over the surface of water and dive deep into it. The most unique feature of seabirds is the salt glands that help them to expel the salt consumed while feeding or drinking. All seabirds, except cormorants, have waterproof feathers. Seabirds are not as brightly coloured as some land birds. They are mostly black, grey or white in colour. This is believed to provide camouflage for them.

◂ **Turning heads**
Raptors have long, flexible necks that can be turned almost towards their back.

▾ **Bare necessities**
All birds of prey have sharp talons, strong beaks, good hearing and keen eyesight.

▴ **Head on**
Birds come in many different sizes and colours. They also differ in their behaviour, the environment in which they live and their feeding habits. Some birds feed on nectar and seeds, while some, like eagles, prefer meat.

Birds of prey

A bird of prey is also known as a raptor. These birds use their beak and talons to hunt for food. Eagles, vultures, hawks, kites, falcons and owls are among the most common birds of prey. Of these, only owls hunt at night. Eagles are large birds with long, broad wings and powerful legs. Kites and vultures also have long wings but they feed mainly on dead animals, hunting only occasionally. Falcons are not big, but they are extremely fast and are great hunters. Raptors have curved talons made of keratin, the same substance that our nails are made from. The length and the curved nature of the talons make walking very difficult. Strong leg muscles and talons help these birds to carry their prey even while flying. Birds of prey have large eyeballs that enable them to spot prey a kilometre (mile) away.

▸ Flapping away
Waterfowl have powerful wings, which they must flap continuously to fly.

Waders

Birds that feed on the shores of water bodies are known as waders. They feed on worms that live in the mud. They often wade through shallow waters, dipping their beaks into the mud in search of food. Some waders, like cranes and storks, have long legs that allow them to venture into deeper water in order to catch fish. Most waders have long beaks that help them to dig deeper into the mud for worms.

Waterfowl

This group includes about 150 species of swans, ducks and geese. One of the most unique features of waterfowl is their webbed feet that help them swim. Another interesting fact is the way in which their feathers moult. The flight feathers in most birds are replaced gradually. But the waterfowl shed theirs all at the same time, rendering them flightless until the feathers grow back. Most species in this group have broad, flat bills that help them to sieve water or mud to extract food.

Songbirds

There are about 4,000 species of songbird all of which are known for their musical sound. All songbirds have well-developed vocal organs that enable them to produce sound notes. The 'songs' are mainly used as a means of communication. Songbirds also 'sing' to attract mates during the mating season. Interestingly, not all species that belong to this group have a musical tone. Some, like the crow, make sounds that are harsh and unpleasant.

◂ Keeping dry
The powder down of waterfowl produces fine powder, which is distributed throughout the body as the bird preens. This powder keeps the bird's feathers waterproof.

Key facts:

- The peregrine falcon is the fastest flying bird. It can fly at heights of about 600 metres (2,000 feet) and can achieve speeds of about 290 kilometres/hour (180 miles/hour) while diving downwards to capture its prey. The peregrine has a series of small, cone-shaped projections called baffles in the openings of its nostrils. These baffles slow the wind speed during a dive, protecting the bird's lungs and helping it to breathe even during high speed dives.
- The pelican is the largest diving bird. It has a long neck and short legs, but the most unique feature of this bird is its long beak and throat pouch. The pelican uses its throat pouch as a net to catch fish. Once it grabs its prey, it draws the pouch close to its chest to squeeze the water out and to swallow the fish. The pouch is also used to carry food to the chicks.
- Songbirds are also known as perching birds. They have four toes, with three facing forwards and one facing backwards. These unique feet help the perching birds to hold on tightly to branches as they sing their hearts out.

Try these too:

Mammals (p 34–53), Fish (p 60–63), Reptiles and Amphibians (p 64–69), Countries and People (p 102–115)

Flightless Birds

Did you know that some birds like ostriches and penguins cannot fly? This does not mean that these birds are wingless, but that their wings are too short and weak to help them fly. According to scientists, flightless birds might have been able to fly in the past. They just lost their need and power to fly since they had no predators. Some of the world's biggest birds are flightless. They include ostriches, greater rheas, emus and emperor penguins.

Key facts:

- The Inaccessible Island rail is the smallest of all flightless birds in the world. This bird grows to a length of about 17 centimetres (2 inches) and weighs only 30 grams (1 ounce). It inhabits the Inaccessible Island, from which it gets its name, in the Tristan Archipelago in the South Atlantic Ocean.
- The ostrich is the largest of all birds. It can grow up to 2.5 metres (8 feet) in length and weigh about 150 kilograms (330 pounds).
- Aepyornis, also known as the elephant bird, was a species of flightless bird that is now extinct. This bird, was found in Madagascar, an island off the eastern coast of Africa. It was the largest bird that ever existed. It was believed to have been more than 3 metres (10 feet) tall and it weighed up to 500 kilograms (1,100 pounds).
- The ostrich makes up for its inability to fly by running at speeds of about 65 kilometres/hour (40 miles/hour). This makes the ostrich one of the fastest animals on land.

The main advantage a flying bird has over a flightless bird is a pair of long, powerful wings. The wings of flightless birds are short, and they have a small keel or no keel at all. In flying birds the keel on the breastbone anchors the strong muscles that aid wing movement. The absence of this keel in flightless birds makes their wings weak. So, even if these birds had long wings they still would not be able to fly without a keel. Flightless birds have more feathers than flying birds and are heavier.

Tough life

Flightless birds have developed unusual adaptations to overcome their handicap. Some species of flightless birds can run very fast, saving them from any potential danger. Others, like penguins, are great swimmers. Penguins also have a protective colouring that helps them to blend into their surroundings, making it difficult for predators to spot them. The ostrich is known to lie flat on the ground with its neck stretched out. This keeps the enemy from spotting the bird on the open plains. If cornered ostriches use their strong claws to cause serious harm to their attacker. Their legs can also deliver a painful kick.

▼ Living on the edge
Many species of birds have become extinct because they could not fly. A large number of surviving flightless birds – like the emu – are endangered for the same reason.

Penguins

There are about 17 species of penguin in the world and many of them can be found in the Antarctic region. These flightless birds have a black head and wings, and a white underside. They have sharp bills, a short tail and a streamlined body. Their flipper-like wings help them to swim at speeds of up to 24 kilometres/hour (15 miles/hour) in search of food. Penguins are also good divers. These birds, however, are very clumsy on land. They have paddle-shaped feet that are not good for walking, so penguins waddle about slowly. They are often seen sliding across ice and snow on their bellies. Penguins have several other unique adaptations that help them to live in extremely cold conditions. They have a thick layer of fat similar to that of seals and whales, which protects them from the freezing temperatures. They also have stiff feathers that are tightly packed and coated with oil produced in a gland near the tail. This oil makes the bodies of penguins waterproof, keeping them dry and warm.

▼ The more the merrier
Penguins are considered to be one of the most social birds. They live, swim and feed in large groups.

▲ Wings of change
The male ostrich spreads its wings during mating displays. Ostriches also use their wings to provide shade to the chicks.

Ostriches

The long necks and legs of the ostrich have almost no feathers. Their wings might not be suitable for flight, but ostriches have many other uses for them. The soft, curling feathers of the wings protect the bird from extreme heat and cold. During the summer, the bird uses its wings to fan itself, while in the winter it covers its thighs with them. The ostrich has only two toes. The inner toe is larger and hoof-like. This helps it to run. The toes have claws that help the ostrich defend itself.

Try these too:

Mammals (p 34–53), Fish (p 60–63), Reptiles and Amphibians (p 64–69), Countries and People (p 102–115)

The land of flightless birds

New Zealand has the most types of flightless birds, including kiwis, penguins, and extinct birds like the moa. The reason for this is that until about 1,000 years ago there were no land mammals in New Zealand. The only predators of these birds were larger birds, which they had no trouble keeping at bay. When human settlers arrived, they introduced land mammals that fed on the meat and eggs of these birds. Humans also hunted them for their meat, driving many species into extinction and endangering the others.

Fish

Fish are cold-blooded vertebrates (organisms with a backbone) that live in water. They breathe with their gills. Most of them have fins for swimming, scales and streamlined bodies. They come in a variety of sizes, shapes and colours. Fish can be divided into jawless and jawed fish. The jawless are one of the earliest types of fish and have been around for millions of years.

Key facts:

- Like birds, fish also migrate to breed and to search for food. The salmon, which actually lives in the sea, migrates to freshwater during the breeding season. Interestingly, it is capable of travelling hundreds of kilometres (miles) to return to the same stream where it was born.
- The whale shark is the largest fish in the world. It grows to about 14 metres (46 feet) in length. The smallest known fish is the stout infant fish, which grows to a length of only 7 millimetres (0.3 inches).
- Fish do not usually make very good parents, but male seahorses are an exception. These creatures make great fathers. The female seahorse lays eggs in a pouch on the male's body. The males carry these eggs until they hatch.
- Some species of fish, such as minnows, can recognize the smell of chemicals that may be present on the skin of other members of the same species. When attacked, minnows release this chemical into the water to warn other minnows.

Some of the better known species of jawless fish that survive today are hagfish and lampreys. Jawed fish is further divided into bony and cartilaginous fish. Bony fish have skeletons made of rigid bone, while the skeletons of cartilaginous fish are made of a flexible material called cartilage. Cartilaginous fish include all sharks, rays and chimaeras. There are two groups of bony fish – lobe-finned and ray-finned. Lobe-finned fish include lungfish and the prehistoric coelacanth. Other fish, like herring, tuna and salmon, are ray-finned.

Life under water

Fish have special adaptations that are important for their life under water. Most fish have a streamlined body that is pointed at the front and tapers towards the end. They also have strong, moveable tail fins that propel them through the water. Dorsal, anal, pelvic and pectoral fins provide the balance and thrust required to swim. Fins are in fact thin membranes that are stretched over a series of fanlike spines or rays. All bony fish have an air-filled organ called the swim bladder. This organ helps the fish to stay afloat without moving. This way, a fish can save energy since it does not have to swim to stay in place.

Since they spend all their lives in water, fish also have special 'lungs' that help them to breathe. The respiratory organs of a fish are called gills. When water enters the mouth of a fish, it passes over the gills. The oxygen dissolved in the water is extracted and passed through the gills into the blood, while carbon dioxide exhaled by the fish is dissolved in the water. Some fish, like lungfish, however do not have gills. They breathe using lungs.

◂ Home under water
Fish can be found in both freshwater and saltwater environments. Freshwater rivers and lakes contain about 40 per cent of the world's fish species, while the rest live in oceans. Most marine fish are found either living on the seafloor or in and around reefs. Very few inhabit the deepest waters.

▾ Scales to the rescue
The body of a fish is covered with scales that protect it from predators and injuries. Some fish have spines that keep their enemies away.

Try these too:

Mammals (p 34–53), Birds (p 54–59), Reptiles and Amphibians (p 64–69), Countries and People (p 102–115)

Reproduction

All fish lay eggs. However, the number of eggs, the type of birth, and the method of egg fertilization vary from species to species. Male sharks insert a sexual organ into the female to pass their sperm into her. The eggs are fertilized inside the female's body. Some sharks lay the fertilized eggs among rocks and seaweed on the ocean floor. These eggs hatch within a few days or weeks. In certain shark species the eggs hatch inside the mother's body and she gives birth to live young. Most fish release their eggs and sperm into the water. The sperm fertilize the eggs in the water. This type of reproduction is called spawning.

◂ Spawning young
Adult salmon swim hundreds of kilometres (miles) back to the stream they were born in, fighting against strong currents, only to breed and then die.

A matter of sense

Like all the other animals, fish can see, smell, hear, taste and feel. In addition to this, most fish have a sixth sense organ. This sixth sense is called a lateral line, which is a sensitive canal that runs through the length of the body of the fish from its gills to its tail fin. Tiny hair-like structures, or cilia, found on the lateral line (see right) can detect even the slightest movement in water. These then send a message to the brain, helping the fish to avoid collisions with other creatures or objects under water and to detect prey.

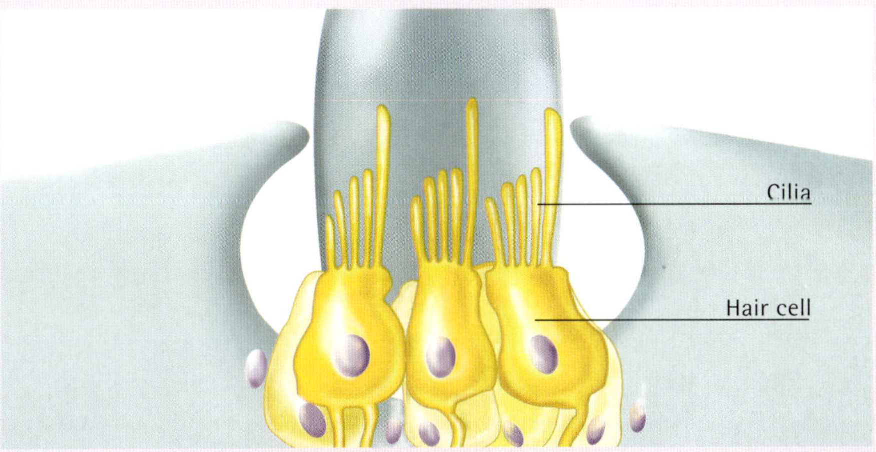

Aquatic Adaptations

Each fish species has developed special adaptations depending on its lifestyle and habitat. Fish are different from each other in many ways – from their feeding style to the ways in which they defend themselves. The ocean is home to many species and each of them has found unique ways to survive, despite the dangers lurking in the water.

Key facts:

- The deep-sea anglerfish has a long spine protruding from above its eyes. A fleshy growth is attached to the tip of this spine. The spine glows in the dark and the fish uses it like a fishing rod to lure prey.
- A great white shark can smell a drop of blood in 100 litres (26 gallons) of water even from a distance of 400 metres (1,310 feet).
- Flounders are flat and almost round in shape. Both their eyes are located on the same side of their bodies. Flounders that have both eyes on the left side lie on their right side and those with eyes on their right side lie on their left side. When they sense a predator, flounders bury themselves in the sand, with only their eyes visible. They stay still, only moving their eyes to see if the enemy has passed by
- Eels look like snakes, but are in fact fish with elongated bodies. Unlike other fish, eels do not have tail fins. Instead, they use their dorsal and anal fins to swim. Most eels do not have scales. Their bodies are covered with a slimy layer of mucus.

Most fish live near the surface or on shallow seabeds. However, some fish like the anglerfish and the viperfish live in the deep, dark region of the ocean known as the twilight zone. This region does not receive any sunlight and the water here is extremely cold. Since it is pitch dark in the twilight zone, many fish that live here are bioluminescent – that is, certain chemicals in their body produce a glowing light that helps them to find their way through the dark water.

Feeling about
Deep sea fish have large mouths, and feelers which help to locate prey and attract mates.

Built to kill

Sharks are the largest predators in the ocean. and very different from other fish. Special features make sharks fierce hunters. Despite their terrifying image, only three or four of the 370 known shark species pose a major threat to humans. Most sharks have sharp, pointed teeth that help them to tear chunks of flesh off their prey. Some of the largest species, like megamouth, basking and whale sharks, feed by filtering tiny marine creatures like shrimps and krill from the water. Most sharks have long, tapering bodies that help them to move swiftly. They also have a very keen sense of smell and are sensitive to even the slightest movements in water. All sharks have denticles on their bodies instead of scales. Denticles are small, tooth-like structures that make the shark's skin hard and rough.

Spiny puffers
Some species of puffer fish have spines that stand up when their bodies are inflated.

Fighting to survive

Every fish species has unique and sometimes strange ways to protect itself. Predators, like sharks, are not in much danger except from their own species and humans. Smaller sharks often fall prey to larger species. Most sharks, especially those that live on the seabed, have protective colouring that helps them to blend into their surroundings. Many reef fish also use camouflage as a defensive option. Some species of fish release certain chemicals that are either distasteful or poisonous to their predators. The puffer fish and other related species swallow water to puff up their bodies to twice, sometimes even three times, their normal size to scare predators away. Some fish bury themselves in the sand to avoid being seen. Certain species of parrotfish make a protective cocoon of mucus around their bodies at night to fool their enemies. This sac of mucus hides the scent of the fish, protecting it from nocturnal predators that use their sense of smell to locate prey.

Living in harmony

Certain marine animals form a unique relationship known as symbiosis. In a symbiotic relationship, two different species depend on each other for food, protection, cleaning or transportation. There are different types of symbiosis – mutualism, commensalism and parasitism. In mutualism both species benefit from their relationship. Wrasses and shrimps are good examples of mutualism. These fish are found at the 'cleaning stations' in coral reefs, where they remove parasites, dead skin and tissue from bigger fish including sharks. The big fish in turn do not harm these 'cleaners'. In commensalism, one species benefits and the other is unaffected. The relationship between remoras and sharks fall under this category. Remoras attach themselves to sharks to hitch a free ride and feed on the scraps of their hosts. In parasitism, one species benefits at the expense of the other. The one that benefits is called a parasite. Lampreys are well known examples of parasites.

Unique senses

Sharks live in all kinds of habitats. Some live near coral reefs, while others are found on the seabed. Some, like the great white and the blue shark, swim in the open seas, although they venture into shallower waters from time to time. All of them have unique sensory organs suited to their environment. Sharks, such as blind and nurse sharks, have whisker-like projections called nasal barbells under their snouts. Nasal barbells help the sharks feel for tiny creatures hiding in the sand. Sharks also have tiny pores on their snouts. These pores lead to jelly-filled sacs called ampullae of Lorenzini. Sharks use this organ to detect weak electric impulses produced by other creatures. Sharks also have powerful eyes that help them to see in dim light. The eyes of sharks that hunt actively are protected by the nictitating membrane. This is a fold of skin that is drawn across the eyeball when hunting. It protects the shark's eyes from getting hurt by its prey.

Try these too:

Oceans of the World (p 24–25), Mammals (p 34–53), Birds (p 54–59), Reptiles and Amphibians (p 64–69), Countries and People (p 102–115)

◂ **Give and take**
The relationship that exists between the clownfish and the sea anemone is an example of mutualism. The clownfish cleans the anemone by removing parasites and is in turn protected from its enemies by the anemone's poisonous tentacles.

▸ **Sink or swim**
Unlike bony fish, sharks do not have a swim bladder and so have to keep swimming to stay afloat. However, sharks get some help from their livers, which are filled with oil. Since oil is lighter than water, it keeps the shark from sinking.

Reptiles

Reptiles are vertebrates that share many characteristics with other animal groups. Like birds, reptiles lay eggs that have a protective outer shell, but they are cold-blooded like fish, meaning that they cannot produce their own body heat. Like mammals, reptiles breathe with their lungs and most of them have teeth. However, the similarities end there.

Getting tanned?
All reptiles bask in the sun during the day. They often lie on a rock or log.

Key facts:

- Leatherback turtles are the largest turtles in the world. They can grow up to 3 metres (10 feet) in length and weigh over 900 kilograms (2,000 pounds). The 11 centimetre- (4 inch) long American bog turtle is one of the smallest turtles.
- The Gila monster and the Mexican bearded lizard are the only species of lizard that are poisonous, but neither are harmful to humans since the poison is introduced slowly by chewing.
- When attacked, the Australian frilled lizard flares up the frill around its neck to display bright orange and red scales. It also opens its mouth wide to show a bright pink or yellow lining inside to scare the enemy away.

Turtle alert!
There are seven species of sea turtles in the world, all of which are listed as endangered. Over the years, sea turtles have been hunted for their eggs, meat and shell. The green sea turtle was extensively hunted for the cartilage, called calipee, found in its bottom shell. Calipee was used to make turtle soup.

Most reptiles do not look after their eggs or take care of their young. They also have a rough skin that is not covered with scales or feathers. Reptiles can be found almost everywhere, except the polar regions since they cannot survive there due to their cold-blooded nature. There are more than 7,000 species of reptiles, belonging to four main groups – turtles and tortoises, snakes and lizards, crocodiles and alligators, and tuataras.

Reptilian life

All reptiles have a well-developed brain and most have two lungs. All reptiles, except crocodilians, have a three-chambered heart. Crocodiles and their relatives have four-chambered hearts like mammals. The tough skin of reptiles keeps their internal organs from becoming dry, and also protects the reptile from injuries.

All reptiles shed their skin periodically as they grow. Most reptiles are meat eaters and feed on a variety of prey including insects, birds, rodents, fish, amphibians and even other reptiles. Most reptiles wait for their prey to come close, and then ambush it. Some kill their prey by suffocating it, while others bite or inject poison into their victims.

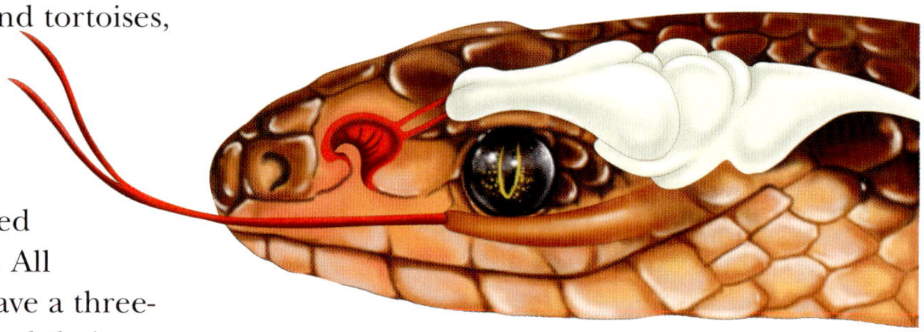

The scent of life!
The forked tongue of a snake picks up chemical traces, which are then carried into the Jacobson's organ to be identified. This is why snakes keep flicking their tongues in and out.

Reptilian senses

All reptiles taste and smell with the help of the Jacobson's organ found in the roof of the mouth. It is a small cavity lined with sense detectors that can recognise chemical changes in the mouth. This organ not only aids in locating prey and finding a mate, but also helps the reptile get a general bearing of its surroundings. Some reptiles rely on their eyesight to find prey. The eyes of reptiles that actively hunt are located at the front of their head to provide them with a sense of depth.

Tuatara

There are only two species of tuatara in the world today. They are the only survivors of a group of reptiles that first emerged about 225 million years ago – even before the dinosaurs came into being, which is why they are sometimes called living fossils. Tuataras are found only on a few islands off the New Zealand coast. These reptiles grow very slowly and are thought to live for as long as a hundred years.

Turtles and tortoises

There are more than 250 species of turtles and tortoises. The term 'turtle' is mainly used to describe the species that live in water, while tortoises live entirely on land. Tortoises and sea turtles can grow to be quite large, while freshwater turtles are often small. All of them have a protective shell made of flat bones. This shell is joined with parts of the spinal column and ribs. The upper shell is called the carapace and the lower one is called the plastron. The two pieces are connected by a 'bridge'. The shell of a turtle is flatter and lighter than that of a tortoise. Tortoises usually have strong and heavy shells. Sea turtles have large flipper-like forelimbs that help them to swim under water. Turtles are known to live very long. Some species can live longer than 150 years. Although turtles spend a lot of time under water, they have to come up to the surface frequently to breathe. They also lay their eggs on dry land. When the eggs hatch, the young ones immediately begin their long journey from land to water.

▸ Catch me if you can

When in danger, the first instinct of a reptile is to hide or escape. If cornered, reptiles resort to a variety of defence tactics. Some appear larger than they really are to frighten their attacker, while others make loud noises and release foul-smelling chemicals. Most snakes, lizards and turtles deliver a painful, sometimes poisonous, bite. Lizards, like chameleons, change their colours to escape their enemies.

Lizards and snakes

The order Squamata consists of lizards, snakes and worm lizards. There are more than 4,300 species of lizard, making them the most diverse family among the reptiles. Most lizards have long, slender bodies and narrow, pointed tails. Almost all of them have four legs with clawed toes. However, some species have reduced limbs or no limbs at all. Most lizards feed on insects. Larger species feed on smaller reptiles and mammals, while some lizards eat plants. The other families related to lizards are snakes and worm lizards. Most species belonging to these families lack legs, but the similarity between the two ends there. Worm lizards spend most of their lives underground. They have short tails and blunt snouts that help them to dig. Some worm lizards have large front legs. Snakes are believed to have evolved from burrowing lizards. But unlike most lizards, snakes do not have external ears and moveable eyelids. Instead, their eyes are protected by transparent scales.

Crocodilians

Crocodiles, alligators, caimans and gavials are together called crocodilians. These giant lizard-like reptiles spend most of their time in water. All families in this group have powerful, flat tails that help to propel them through the water. Their eyes and nostrils are located on top of their head. This allows these reptiles to lie submerged but still be able to breathe and keep an eye on their surroundings. It also helps them to sneak up on unsuspecting prey.

Try these too:

Mammals (p 34–35), Birds (p 54–55), Birds of a Feather (p 56–57), Flightless Birds (p 58–59), Fish (p 60–63), Life Begins (p 74–75), The Rise of Reptiles (p 76–77), The Age of the Dinosaurs (p 78–79), Monster Lizards (p 80–81), Countries and People (p 102–115)

Snakes

Snakes vary in size from 10 centimetres (4 inches) to 9 metres (30 feet). They usually move around alone, in cold and temperate climates, but are known to hibernate in large numbers in burrows. They mainly feed on insects, other reptiles and smaller mammals.

▸ **Arboreal life**
Many species of boas and pythons live in trees in forests, but some live in burrows in deserts.

Snake families

Snakes can be broadly divided into three groups. The first family includes all blind snakes. These primitive, non-venomous snakes look a lot like earthworms. They have large shovel-like heads to burrow into the ground. The eyes of most blind snakes are reduced to tiny eye spots under the scales. They eat small insects, and their eggs and larvae. When faced with danger, blind snakes play dead or rub themselves in smelly secretions and faeces. The second group includes large non-venomous snakes like boas and pythons as well as several types of pipe snakes, shield-tailed snakes and short-tailed snakes. Boas and pythons kill their prey by squeezing it to death. Pipe snakes, shield-tailed snakes and short-tailed snakes live in burrows and have strong, hard skull bones, as they use their heads for burrowing. All of these snakes give birth to live young instead of laying eggs.

Unlike other carnivores that have strong teeth, snakes use their teeth mostly for biting and catching, not so much for chewing. They usually swallow their prey whole. The food is then broken down and digested in their body.

Killer teeth

There are an astounding 2,500–3,000 species of snakes in the world. Only one-fifth of these is venomous. Venomous snakes have two types of teeth – small, solid backward curving teeth as well as a pair of hollow fangs. The small teeth prevent the prey from slipping out. The fangs are longer and connected to special poison glands in the head. The poison from the glands flows into the prey through a groove in the fang. There are three types of fangs – fixed front, rear and folding front fangs. Some, like the spitting cobra, spit venom into the eyes of their attackers.

Fangless

Rear Fang

Front Fang

▴ **Fang mania**
Fixed front fangs are thick and short with grooves, rear fangs are large and grooved, and folding front fangs are very long and hollow and fold back when the mouth is closed.

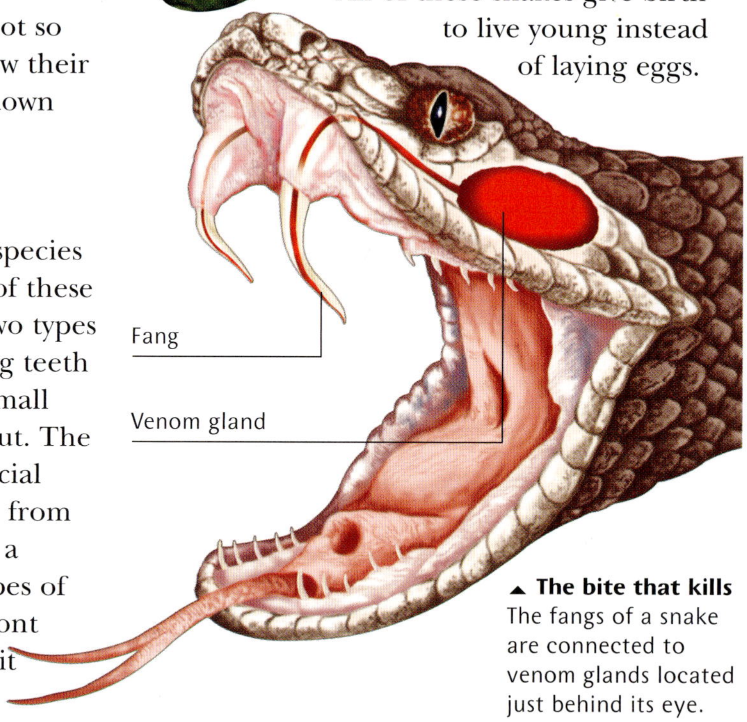

▴ **The bite that kills**
The fangs of a snake are connected to venom glands located just behind its eye.

Divine snakes

Snakes have been feared and worshipped throughout the ages. Prehistoric Toltecs and Aztecs revered a 'feathered serpent' as the great teacher of mankind. In ancient Egypt and Greece, snakes were associated with their respective sun gods, Ra and Apollo. The Mesopotamians and Sumerians believed that snakes were immortal and divine, as they could keep shedding their skin and emerging freshly covered. In China, since time immemorial, snake-like dragons have been considered ferocious but divine guardians.

Venomous snakes

The third group includes colubrids, vipers and elapids. Colubrids form the largest of all snake families. Most of the species in this family are small and harmless. However, a few colubrids are venomous. Some colubrids lay eggs, while others give birth to their young. Non-venomous colubrids include colourful racers and bronzebacks, rat snakes, reed snakes and wolf snakes. Some mildly venomous colubrids are vine snakes, flying snakes and cat snakes and the venomous ones include African boomslangs and rear-fanged water snakes.

Elapids include front-fanged snakes that live only on land. The most dangerous elapids include African mambas, cobras, kraits and coral snakes. Vipers are the most well developed creatures in the entire snake family. They live in forests, deserts or mountains and can adapt to all kinds of weather, even the icy cold climate near the Arctic. Vipers have front fangs that are longer than those of the other snakes. When these fangs are not being used they are folded up inside the mouth. Vipers give birth to live young. Russell's vipers, Gaboon vipers and mangrove vipers are some of the deadliest members of this group. Pit vipers form a sub group of the viper family.

Key facts:

- The jaws of snakes are specially designed to be flexible. As both jaws can move independently, they can open their mouths very wide to swallow their prey. Their skin is also extremely elastic and expands to accommodate huge bellies stuffed with large prey.
- Snakes produce two types of venom: hemotoxic and neurotoxic. Hemotoxic venom affects the blood and organs, causing difficulty in breathing, and neurotoxic venom affects the nervous system, causing seizures and quick death. Most snakes produce a combination of both types of venom.
- Snakes move in a variety of ways aided by the contraction and expansion of their muscles. They can wriggle, move by side winding, move in a straight line using a concertina-like movement or move themselves like caterpillars by using their belly muscles.

◂ Record holder!
The Asiatic reticulated python is the longest of all snake species in the world. Females of this species have been known to grow up to 9 metres (30 feet), in length.

Try these too:

Mammals (p 34–53),
Birds (p 54–59),
Fish(p 60–63),
The Rise of Reptiles (p 76–77),
Countries and People (p 102–115)

Amphibians

Amphibians are cold-blooded vertebrates that combine the features of both fish and reptiles. There are about 6,000 species of amphibians in the world. Frogs, toads, salamanders, newts and a small group of limbless, tropical creatures called caecilians, are all amphibians.

Key facts:

- Females of most amphibian species lay eggs directly in water, while some frogs, salamanders and almost all caecilians prefer to lay eggs on land in moist places like burrows or logs. The eggs are usually suspended in a jelly-like substance and are not protected by a hard shell-like cover.
- Salamanders can regenerate injured or lost body parts like a leg or a tail.
- Some adult species of newt are able to survive in water even though they lose their gills and grow lungs.
- Adult frogs can breathe through their lungs, but they prefer to absorb oxygen through the thin lining of their mouths. In fact, in moist conditions, frogs can absorb oxygen directly through their skin.

The name amphibian means 'double life', describing the ability of these creatures to survive both on land and in water. Amphibians are born in water, as they lay their eggs in water or in a moist place close to water. The larvae that hatch from the eggs are limbless. They have gills through which they breathe and they use their fish-like tails to swim. As they grow, they develop limbs and lungs that help them to survive on land. Amphibians do not have dry scaly skin like reptiles. They have smooth, moist skin that needs to be in regular contact with water. The bodies of amphibians vary greatly, depending on the type of species and its environment. Frogs and toads have short squat bodies, with long hind legs and no tail. Salamanders and newts have longer bodies, long tails and short legs.

Adult frog

Frogs and toads

Frogs have muscular, well developed hind limbs and webbed feet that are helpful for jumping. Most of them have smooth green or brown skins, while some rare species are brilliantly coloured. Toads are distinguished from frogs by their thick skin and heavy bodies. Some varieties also have warts all over and enlarged salivary glands behind their eyes. Frogs and toads have huge, bulging eyes that are covered by transparent membranes that keep them constantly moist. Both species have voice boxes and are capable of making a variety of sounds. Frogs and toads have eardrums on each side of their heads, rather than ears. They have long forked tongues which they whip out to catch small insects. Some of the larger varieties are known to even eat small snakes and mammals. Some rare varieties of frogs and toads can secrete poison from their skin and salivary glands.

Truly aquatic Some species of salamander spend their entire life in water.

▾ Aquatic metamorphosis
The eggs of a frog hatch into oval shaped larvae called tadpoles, which live in the water as they slowly change into an adult.

Try these too:

Mammals (p 34–53),
Birds (p 54–59),
Fish (p 60–63),
Life Begins (p 74–75),
The Rise of Reptiles (p 76–77),
Countries and People (p 102–115)

Salamanders and newts

Salamanders are smooth skinned, lizard-like creatures that are mostly nocturnal. Most grow to only about 15 centimetres (6 inches) in length, but some, like the giant Japanese salamander, can grow up to 1.5 metres (5 feet). Newts are a type of salamander and also begin life in water, adapting to live on land as they grow up. Salamanders and newts mainly stay close to water, though some varieties live in trees, in burrows or in caves. They feed on small insects, worms and snails. Like frogs and toads, some species of salamander secrete poisonous or irritating substances.

▾ False salamanders
Sirens form a sub-group of salamanders, native to southern USA and northern Mexico. They have lizard-like bodies and moist skins but, unlike salamanders, sirens only have two short forelegs and no hind legs.

Caecilians

Caecilians are a small group of amphibians that resemble eels or earthworms. Most caecilians normally grow to a length of around 38 centimetres (15 inches), but rare species can grow up to 1.37 metres (4.5 feet). These worm-like creatures have no limbs and no tail. Caecilians normally live in burrows throughout their lives, which could be the reason why their eyes are shielded with a skin covering, and in some species covered with bone, making them blind. Like all other amphibians, caecilians are carnivores, but unlike the others, some species of caecilians can bear live young.

The World of Insects

Insects are the most common life forms on the planet. There are 800,000 known insect species and millions more not fully known to science. This is more than all the mammals, birds, reptiles, amphibians and fish put together. Insects can be found everywhere – in forests, on ponds and in our own backyards. The only places you will not find these creepy crawlies are in the ocean and the polar regions.

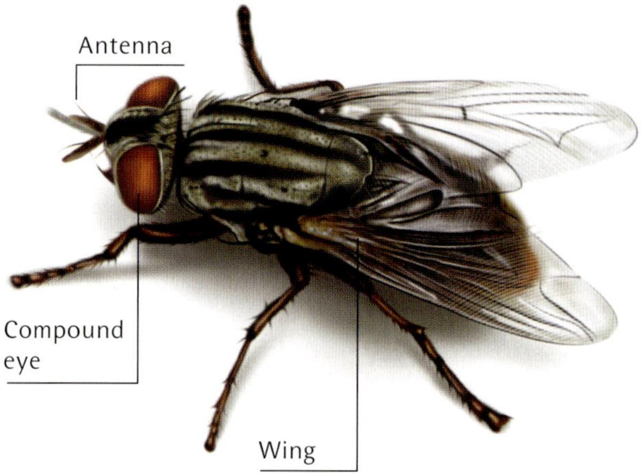

▲ The truth about wings
Wings are important in identifying the different species of insects. Some, like flies and mosquitoes, have one pair of membranous wings. Butterflies and moths have wings covered with powdery scales, while the hard outer wings of beetles provide protection to their back wings.

Key facts:

- The hard, but light, exoskeleton of an insect is largely made of a substance called chitin. It is made up of several layers and protects the insect from enemy attacks and changes in the environment.
- Insects feed on other insects, small animals, plants and dead vegetable or animal matter. Some insects, like lice or fleas, are parasites, living off other animals.
- Fossils show that insects haven't changed very much since their first ancestors lived on Earth 350 million years ago, in the early Bashkirian Age. Their small sizes, ability to reproduce in large numbers, and ability to hide easily or fly away from danger are probably the reasons why they have been able to survive for so long.
- Some insects protect themselves using the method of camouflage, as in the case of the praying mantis or the stick insect. Others, such as wasps, bees and hornets, have venomous stings that they use to defend themselves.

All insects have six legs, a pair of antennae, and a pair of compound eyes. Some insects also have wings. The body of an insect is divided into three parts – the head, the thorax and the abdomen. The soft body of an insect is covered by a thick, protective outer layer called the exoskeleton.

Special characteristics

Insects are the only invertebrates (animals without a backbone) that can fly. Insects such as flies, mosquitoes, bees, cockroaches and grasshoppers have wings attached to the thorax. When flying, these wings are well supported by muscles inside the thorax. The thorax also supports the legs. Insects have legs that are suited for swimming, jumping, digging or holding, depending on the species. Their mouthparts are also varied so that they can pierce and suck (mosquitoes), bite and chew (caterpillars and beetles), or sponge (flies). The eyes of an insect are situated on top of, or on each side, of their heads. Insect eyes are made up of several hundred tiny lenses. Unlike humans or other animals, insects cannot move their eyes and they are in fact quite short-sighted. This means that they cannot see very well or very far. It is the feelers, or antennae, placed above the eyes, that help insects to search for food and to warn them of danger.

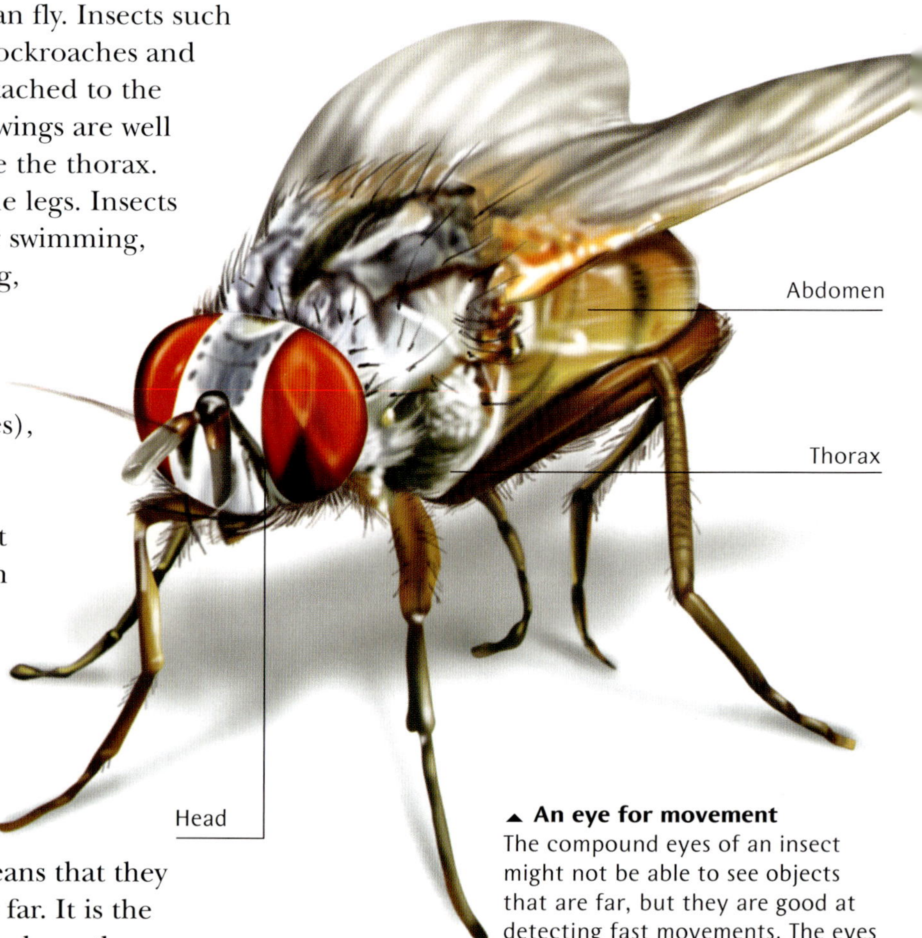

▲ An eye for movement
The compound eyes of an insect might not be able to see objects that are far, but they are good at detecting fast movements. The eyes also help the insect to fly at high speeds without bumping into any object and chase fast moving prey.

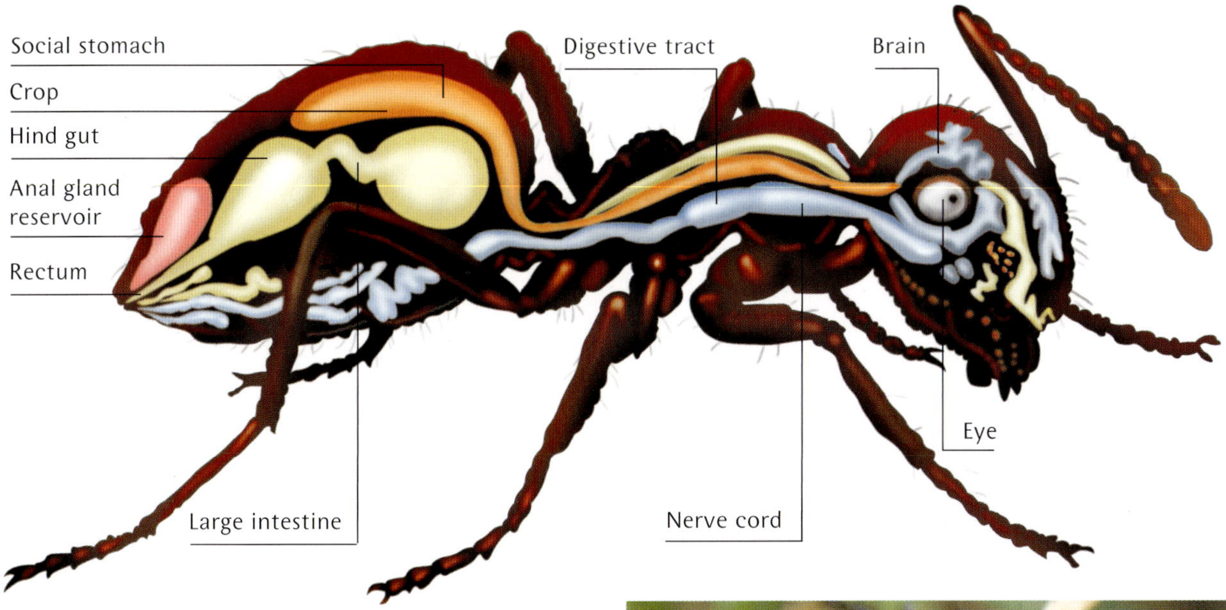

Try these too:

Mammals (p 34–53),
Birds (p 54–59),
Fish (p 60–63),
Reptiles and Amphibians (p 64–69),
Life Begins (p 74–75),
Plants (p 84–87)

◂ Insight into insects
The digestive system of an insect consists of a tube running from the mouth to the anus. This tube is specially designed to control the amount of water in the insect's body.

The inside story

Insects have several tiny openings, called spiracles, along the sides of their bodies. Oxygen enters the insect's body through these spiracles and is circulated by thin air tubes called tracheae. The larvae of some species breathe through gills. Insects have an 'open' circulatory system. Like in humans and other animals, the insect's heart pumps blood. However, the blood is not carried through the body by blood vessels. Instead, it flows freely around the internal organs and back to the heart. Insects also have a well developed nervous system, with a brain and sense organs. Insects reproduce through eggs, which are sometimes hatched in the mother's body. In some species, females reproduce without the help of males, whereas in others, unfertilised eggs produce males and fertilised eggs produce females.

▴ An armour of dung
Beetles are the largest group of insects. There are 350,000 types of beetle on Earth. The dung beetle shown here makes a ball of animal dung and drags it away to a safe place where it can lay its eggs and hide them in the ball. The dung ball protects the eggs and provides the larvae with food until they are strong enough to step out on their own.

Scourge or saviours?

Most of us see insects as fearful or irritating creatures, which are responsible for spreading diseases or attacking our food supplies. Mosquitoes spread diseases like malaria and filaria, termites destroy wood, locusts destroy entire fields of food crops and weevils eat into our grain supplies. However, did you know that without insects the world would probably be filled with dead animals and plants? For example, the dung beetle is responsible for the breakdown of animal waste matter and plays an important role in cleaning up our environment. Bees and butterflies play an important role in the pollination of plants. Flowering plants bloom and food crops thrive when they are busy. Insects are also the source of useful products like honey, lac, silk and wax.

Insect Life

Some insects, such as mosquitoes and flies, live only for a few days or even a few hours. Others, like cicadas, can live as long as 13 years or more. The life cycle of an insect is limited to the time that it needs to hatch from an egg and grow into a mature adult capable of reproducing the next generation of its species. The life cycle of most insects consists of four stages – egg, larva, pupa and adult.

Key facts:

- In warm temperatures, species like the fruit fly can produce as many as 25 generations within one year. However, in most species, only one generation is produced within one year.
- In the early part of their life cycle larvae feed on things that are completely different from their adult forms. For example, caterpillars feed on leaves, while butterflies drink nectar from flowers.
- When two insects run into each other, they rub their antennae and use their sense of smell to find out where each of them came from and what kind of work they were engaged in.
- The smallest insect is the dwarf beetle. It grows no longer than 0.25 millimetre (0.01 inch). The atlas moth's wingspan is about 25 centimetres (10 inches), giving it the largest wingspan of all insects.
- Dragonflies are the fastest flying insects. They can fly at speeds of 95 kilometres/hour (60 miles/hour). Locusts and butterflies can fly non-stop for over 160 kilometres (100 miles).

In some cases the larva grows into a nymph, which looks a lot like the adult insect, but does not have some of the adult features, like wings. The four-stage life cycle is called 'complex metamorphosis' and the three-stage cycle is called 'simple metamorphosis'. In simple, or incomplete metamorphosis, there is no pupal stage. The eggs hatch into nymphs, which moult or shed their exoskeleton as they grow. Most nymphs moult 4–8 times before turning into adults, after which they stop moulting.

A complex lifecycle

In complete metamorphosis, the eggs are laid by adult female insects in safe places like burrows, on the underside of leaves or logs, inside fruit and even inside another insect's body. These eggs hatch into tiny babies. The young of the mosquito are simply called larvae, while baby beetles are called grubs. Young flies are called maggots, and caterpillars are the larvae of butterflies. Insect larvae eat constantly and grow very quickly. As a larva grows, it moults several times. The larval phase is followed by the pupal stage. During this phase, the young insect wraps itself in a cocoon or hard shell made from ceratin secreted by its body and then hibernates until it is ready to emerge as a fully grown adult. As insects are cold-blooded creatures they depend on nature to provide them with the warmth that is essential for their growth.

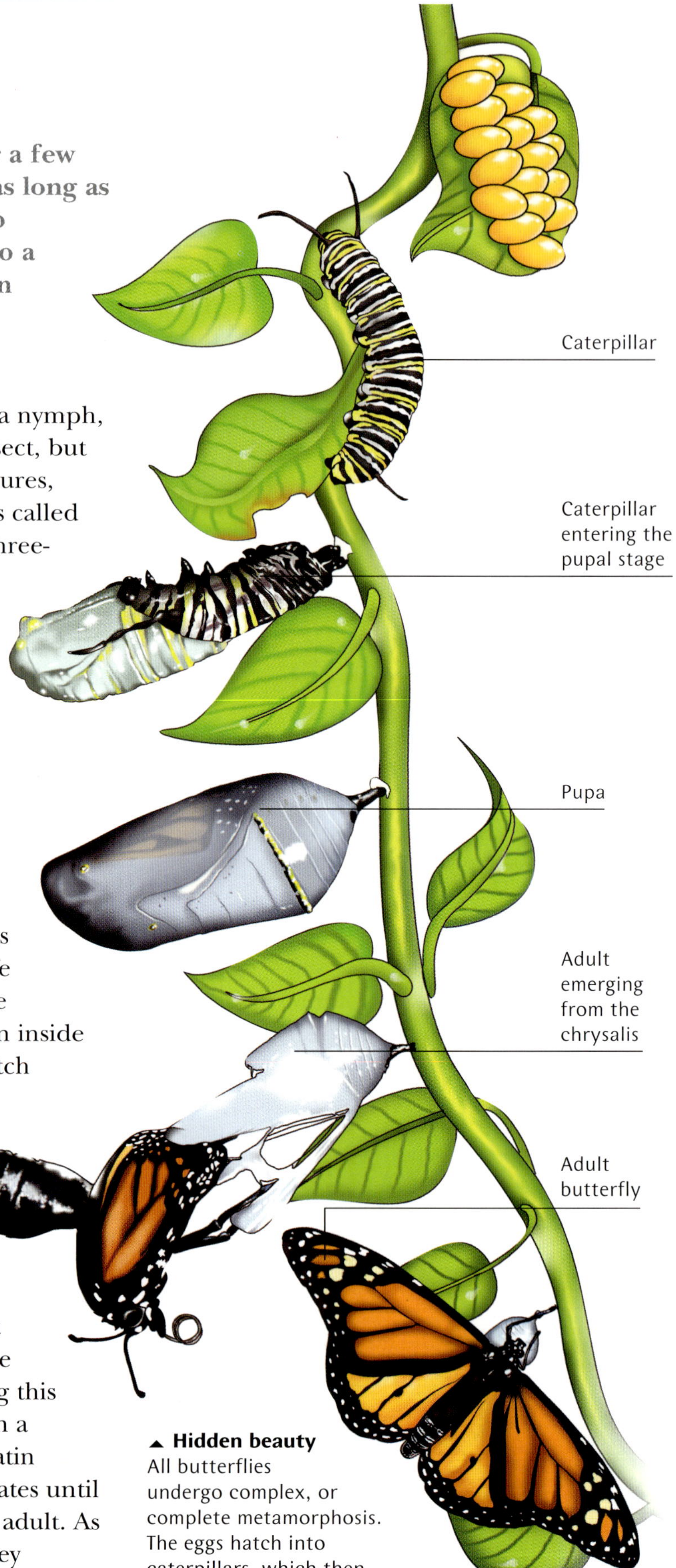

▲ **Hidden beauty**
All butterflies undergo complex, or complete metamorphosis. The eggs hatch into caterpillars, which then enter the pupal stage before finally emerging as an adult.

Pheromones

Pheromones are chemical substances that are produced by animals and insects. They help to attract and control members of their own species. Studies show that in some species of colonized insects, the queen uses her pheromones to prevent her daughters from mating and reproducing. In this way, she maintains her powerful position as the sole reproducer in the colony. Modern science has found a new and revolutionary use for insect pheromones. Farmers use pheromones to protect their crops from insect attacks and to prevent insects from multiplying. This is a much safer alternative to using harmful pesticides.

▲ Winged wonders
Insect wings are merely extensions of the exoskeleton. The first pair of wings protects the fragile second pair. The wings of the dragonfly are delicate, transparent sheets with fine tubes running through and supporting them, while butterfly and moth wings have soft overlapping scales.

Social colonies

Insects, like ants, bees, wasps and termites, are social creatures that normally live and work in large colonies. Such colonies are usually referred to as 'superorganisms'. Insect colonies have many advantages because the responsibilities of gathering food, building the nest and protecting it, and caring for the young are shared by all members. They are usually ruled by a queen, who reproduces with the help of a drone.

The rest of the colony members are called workers, and are usually all children of the queen. The queen is also the biggest insect in the colony, followed by the drone and then the workers. Some insects feed their larvae and queen with special food. For example, the larvae and the queen in a beehive feed on royal jelly, a substance that is specially produced by the workers. In contrast, the drone and the workers feed on a simple mixture of nectar and honey.

Try these too:

Mammals (p 34–53), Birds (p 54–59), Fish (p 60–63), Reptiles and Amphibians (p 64–69), Life Begins (p 74–75)

◀ Brooding young
Worker bees build the beehive from beeswax. The hive has a brood chamber, or nursery, at its centre. The queen lays her eggs in this chamber. The worker bees tend to the eggs and take care of the newborn grub.

Life Begins

When the world began, the air was hot and dusty. There was no oxygen on Earth, so naturally, there could be no life. However, about 3,400 million years ago the first cells came into being. The first living things were microscopic single-celled bacteria and blue-green algae. The algae could produce their own food and oxygen using sunlight (photosynthesis). Slowly, the oxygen in the atmosphere increased, and larger organisms emerged.

Key facts:

- The number of animals with protective shells may have increased during the Cambrian period due to the absence of the ozone layer that could keep out the harmful ultraviolet rays of the Sun.
- The development of the hard and leathery waterproof egg allowed animals to move away from water, as unlike the soft eggs that had to be laid in water, the new eggs could now be laid anywhere.
- By the end of the Palaeozoic era (570–245 million years ago), glaciers covered the southern parts of the Earth, while large areas in the northern parts became desert-like. At the end of this period, the Earth experienced its largest ever mass extinction.

The first animals appeared in the oceans about 650 to 543 million years ago. They were soft-bodied creatures that were the ancestors of sea anemones, jellyfish and worms. In the next 50 to 60 million years there was a sudden growth in animal life – popularly known as the 'Cambrian Explosion'. At this time, the ancestors of almost every known animal group appeared in the oceans, although they did not look anything like their modern descendents. The first vertebrate, the jawless fish, also appeared at this time. Gradually, several varieties of clams, mussels, oysters, snails and corals as well as starfish and sea urchins were born. Thick-armoured water insects, called trilobites, were the most important and commonly found species of this period. Luckily for us, the number of creatures with protective shells increased at this time. This means that we have several good fossil records of this period.

Fishy tales

About 439 million years ago, freshwater fish appeared and life on dry land began. Plants began to grow and soon the early ancestors of spiders and centipedes also appeared. They were the animals with feet. In the next 50 million years, plants and trees grew swiftly, and insects such as cockroaches and dragonflies appeared. Fish multiplied in number and variety, and some of them grew to terrifying sizes.

◂ True survivors
About 600 million years ago during the Cambrian period, the ancestors of crabs, shrimps, spiders and insects appeared in the shallow seas. These creatures, called trilobites, survived for about 350 million years.

◂ Double act
Early cells, such as bacteria and blue-green algae, reproduced themselves simply by dividing in two.

Among these new varieties of fish were an early shark species called Cladoselache. Another was the antiarch family – fish that were partly covered with a hard armour-like shell. However, the most remarkable of all the fish species that appeared during this period were the coelacanths and lungfish. Both had limb-like fins and the lungfish had the ability to breathe even on the surface of water.

Animal imprints

Fossils are impressions of animals and plants that lived millions of years ago. Sometimes, when an animal or plant dies it is gradually buried under several layers of soil. The soil hardens over the years and due to tectonic changes is buried deep below the surface, until it is discovered several million years later. By studying the fossil records of creatures and plants that lived so many years ago palaeontologists have been able to tell us much about the origin and evolution of our world.

On land at last!

The movement of landmasses and the shifting of the seabed kept changing the Earth's climate. Each change led to the extinction of certain species, and the birth of new ones. About 363 to 290 million years ago, the climate became warm and insects like mayflies and dragonflies, and little animals like snails and millipedes began to rule the Earth. Many of the marine animals began to adapt to life on land. Those which could not became extinct. It is believed that some lobe-finned fish used their fins to walk on to land for short periods. This practice may have led to the evolution of the first amphibians. Soon the heads of these amphibians flattened. They grew short strong legs, snouts and reptilian bodies that were suited to life on land. This change led to the appearance of crocodiles, water and land reptiles, lizards and dinosaurs.

▸ **Taking to land**
Westlothiana lizziae is believed to be one of the earliest land animals. It had four legs and laid eggs with hard shells, allowing the reptile to live away from water.

▾ **Living fossil**
The coelacanth is one of the earliest known fish that still exists. This lobe-finned fish can grow to a length of up to 2 metres (6.5 feet). Until a coelacanth was caught at the mouth of the Chalumna River on the east coast of South Africa in 1938, this species was thought to be extinct. The only other lobe-finned fish that survives today is the modern lungfish.

Try these too:

Mammals (p 34–53), Birds (p 54–59), Fish (p 60–63), Reptiles and Amphibians (p 64–69), The World of Insects (p 70–71), Insect Life (p 72–73), The Rise of Reptiles (p 76–77), The Age of Dinosaurs (p 78–79), Monster Lizards (p 80–81), The First Mammals and Birds (p 82–83)

The Rise of Reptiles

The extinction of many marine life forms ended the Palaeozoic era and signaled the beginning of the Mesozoic era (245 to 65 million years ago). This was the Age of the Reptiles, when aquatic animals decreased in number and importance, giving way to large killer land animals that ruled the Earth for many centuries.

Key facts:

- Aquatic reptiles and flying reptiles existed along with dinosaurs until the very end of the Cretaceous period. In the mass extinction that happened around 65 million years ago, almost all these species were wiped out.
- Reptiles shed their teeth and grow new ones several times in their lives. This is probably why most reptile fossils found are of their teeth.
- Some prehistoric reptiles that began life on land returned to water eventually. Many of these creatures could live both on land and in water. These reptiles hunted for food in water and rested on land.
- Ichthyosaurs were excellent swimmers and divers. They could swim at speeds of 40 kilometres/hour (25 miles/hour).

The Lystrosaurus was a mammal-like reptile and the only land vertebrate to survive extinction of the Permian period. This small and heavy herbivore looked like a mammal but was very reptilian in nature. It had a short tail and, instead of teeth, it had two short tusk-like fangs. It moved on all fours. Reptiles like Lystrosaurus became a prominent feature of the Mesozoic era. Some of them were more like mammals than others. By the end of the Triassic period these reptiles evolved into the first mammals. The beginning of the Mesozoic era also witnessed the emergence of a new group of animals, called the archosaurs, or 'ruling' reptiles. Crocodiles, dinosaurs, pterosaurs and birds are all archosaurs. The early crocodile-like reptiles were called thecodonts or 'socket-toothed'. This was because they were among the first animals to have strong jaws with teeth set in sockets. Prehistoric reptiles lived on land and in water, and some of them even flew. The Ichthyostega and Acanthostega were among the first amphibians. They had some features of fish, along with four paddle-like limbs with fingers, a broad tail and lungs to breathe out of the water.

The Acanthostega could not walk very well or breathe properly through its lungs, so it continued to use its gills. The Ichthyostega's limbs were stronger and it could walk on dry land and in swamps, and breathe through its lungs. These early amphibians were mostly herbivores.

▼ Powered for flight
Pterosaur wings were bat-like. They consisted of flaps of skin instead of feathers. These membranous wings were supported by one finger that extended the entire length of the wings.

▶ Early amphibian
Palaeontologists consider the Acanthostega a link between lobe-finned fish and land vertebrates. This amphibian may have lived in swamps. It had webbed feet but was not well-adapted for life on land. Therefore it is thought that the legs were not used for walking on land, but were actually meant for some other purpose.

Dinosaur, reptile or bird?

The pterosaurs or 'flying lizards' were large flying reptiles. They were the first flying vertebrates, the other two being birds and bats. Pterosaurs had small, light bodies and large wings. They stood on two legs and had two hands to which the wings were attached. They had a bird-like face with a long beak and the body was covered with fur. Pterosaurs were meat eaters and may have eaten fish, as well as crabs, clams and dead animals. There were different types of pterosaurs, the biggest of them was the Quetzalcoatlus. This huge reptile had wings that measured more than 13 metres (42 feet) across, making them the largest flying creatures that ever lived.

Tanystropheus

The Tanystropheus was one of the oddest looking prehistoric reptiles. Its neck, at 3 metres (10 feet) in length, was longer than its body and tail put together. However, the neck had only ten vertebrae making it very stiff. This reptile lived in shallow water and ate fish. It is believed that the Tanystropheus also spent a lot of time on land. Like lizards, the Tanystropheus could drop its tail to protect itself while fighting, and grow it back later.

Marine reptiles

The earliest water reptile, the Mesosaurus, looked a lot like an alligator. It was about 1.8 metres (6 feet) in length and fed on crabs and fish. This animal was first a land reptile, that later took to living in water. Ichthyosaurs, sea turtles, and mosasaurs were some of the other big and dangerous Mesozoic water reptiles. These creatures combined features of fish along with those of reptiles. All of them were meat-eating animals.

In fact, the mosasaur seems to have been the T. rex of the oceans. The ichthyosaur looked somewhat like a dolphin and grew to about 2.7 metres (9 feet) in length. It had a crescent-shaped tail and limbs that were like paddles. The ichthyosaur was a swift swimmer and caught prey with its long snout and sharp teeth. Fossil records show that it gave birth to its young instead of laying eggs. There were two types of plesiosaurs – those with long necks and small heads and those with short necks and big heads. Prehistoric sea turtles looked much like the sea turtles of today. Giant turtles, called Archelon, measured 4 metres (13 feet) across.

Try these too:

Mammals (p 34–53), Birds (p 54–59), Fish (p 60–63), Reptiles and Amphibians (p 64–69), Life Begins (p 74–75)

▾ **Resilient reptiles** Plesiosaurs looked like turtles with a pointed tail and four flippers. They were also the only aquatic reptiles apart from turtles to survive until the end of the Cretaceous period.

The Age of the Dinosaurs

Ever since the first fossils of this species were discovered in the early 19th century, the dinosaur has been the most popular of all prehistoric animals. It was about 230 million years ago that dinosaurs evolved from early reptiles.

Key facts:

- Dinosaurs varied in size. For example, Brachiosaurus could grow to be a height of about 16 metres (50 feet). In contrast, the smallest dinosaur Compsognathus was no bigger than a chicken.
- The Giganotosaurus was the largest of all meat eaters. It was about 14 metres (45 feet) long and 4 metres (12 feet) tall.
- The awe-inspiring sizes of dinosaurs made the English scientist, Richard Owen, give these animals their name, which means 'fearfully great lizards' in Greek.
- Some of the larger dinosaurs, like the Brachiosaurus, are thought to have eaten about 200 kilograms (440 pounds) of leaves and plants in one day.

Dinosaurs ruled the Earth for over 150 million years – the longest period that any particular species has ever lived! They first appeared in the Triassic period of the Mesozoic era and lived through the Jurassic and Cretaceous periods. Dinosaurs only lived on land, and none of them could fly, but by the end of the Cretaceous period, about 65 million years ago, birds descended from some types of dinosaurs.

A varied life

Dinosaurs came in many sizes and shapes. The tallest were about 43 metres (140 feet) in height and the smallest were just 60 centimetres (24 inches). Dinosaurs could be found everywhere. They lived in forests, in swamps, near rivers, lakes and oceans. They ate either plants or meat or both.

Unique features

Dinosaurs might have had several reptilian features, but they were also quite different in some ways. Unlike other reptiles, the feet of dinosaurs grew downwards instead of sideways, helping them to walk on four or two legs, instead of crawling like other reptiles. No one knows if dinosaurs were warm-blooded or cold-blooded. Palaeontologists believe that dinosaurs were able to adjust their body temperature according to their surroundings. Some dinosaurs brooded over their eggs to keep them warm and took care of their young. Many dinosaur species lived and moved in large herds, but some lived alone or in very small groups. Dinosaur skin was tough and scaly like most reptiles. Some of them had armour-like covers, spikes, crests, or frills around their necks.

▸ Marked difference
Their skeletal structure was the feature that set dinosaurs apart from their thecodont ancestors. The unique structure allowed for a nearly vertical posture with their rear legs positioned directly under the body. However, like all the other reptiles, dinosaurs had four-chambered hearts and teeth set in sockets in their jaws. Like their reptilian ancestors, the dinosaurs also reproduced through eggs.

▼ **Dinosaurs' rule**
The first dinosaurs that appeared during the early Triassic period were small, bipedal predators. By the end of this period large species began to emerge. Over the next few million years, until their mass extinction, strange-looking dinosaurs of all sizes walked the Earth.

Where did they go?

Some scientists believe that the climate changed once again towards the end of the Cretaceous period, and that there were alternating spells of very hot and very cold weather. Dinosaurs could not protect themselves against these drastic changes and they gradually died out. Others believe that a huge asteroid crashed against the Earth and the smoke and dust from this collision blocked out the sun for several months. Plants died, the atmosphere became icy cold, and dinosaurs starved and froze to death.

Types of dinosaurs

There were two major groups of dinosaurs – the saurischians and the ornithischians. The saurischians had 'lizard hips' and the ornithischians had 'bird hips'. The dinosaurs of the Triassic and Jurassic periods were mostly saurischians and those that lived in the Cretaceous period were mostly ornithischians. The saurischians were further divided into dinosaurs with reptile feet (sauropoda) and beast feet (theropoda). The ornithischians were made up of dinosaurs with bird feet (ornithopoda), horns (ceratopsia), armour (ankylosauria), roofed or plated reptiles (stegosauria) and thick-headed reptiles (pachycephalosauria).

Try these too:

Mammals (p 34–53), Birds (p 54–59), Fish (p 60–63), Reptiles and Amphibians (p 64–69), Life Begins (p 74–75)

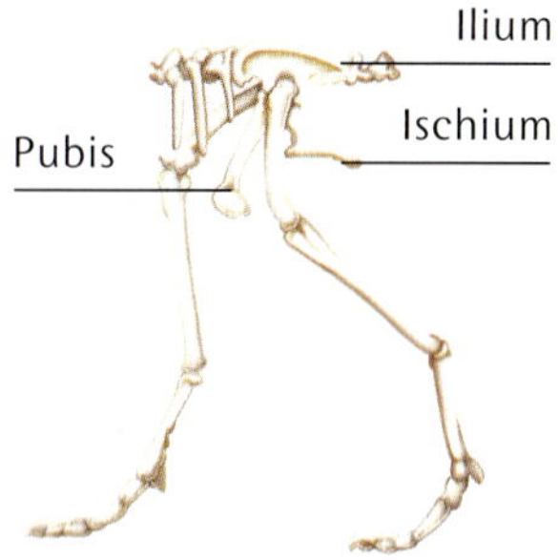

Saurischian Pelvis

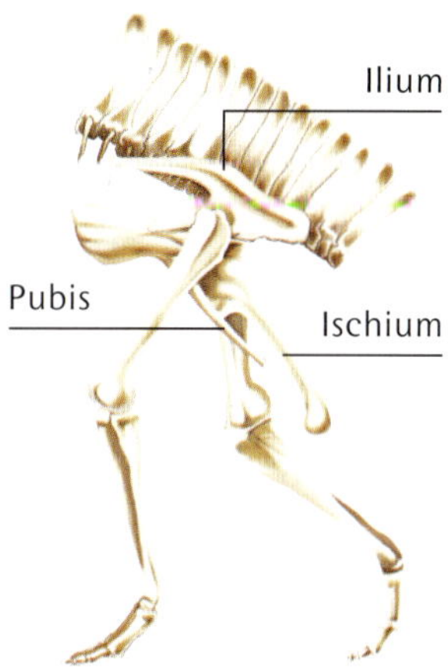

Ornithischian Pelvis

▶ **Hippy matters**
The hip bones of saurischians and ornithischians consisted of ilium, ischium and pubis. In saurischians the hip jutted forward and in the ornithischians the hip bone slanted backwards.

▲ **Terror unleashed**
The herbivores often used their size to scare away predators. Some, like the Triceratops, had horns with which they protected themselves.

Monster Lizards

About 300 different dinosaur species have been found, many just from a single tooth. The major groups of dinosaurs (the ornithischians and saurischians) each consisted of many species.

Key facts:

- One of the few sauropods that survived until the Cretaceous period was the Argentinosaurus. This massive South American dinosaur was probably the largest sauropod – larger than even the Brachiosaurus. Some of them were about 45 metres (150 feet) and weighed as much as 110 tonnes.
- The gigantic Brachiosaurus had several holes in its skull. This was nature's way of reducing the weight supported by its long neck.
- The medullary bone was a special bone in the thigh of the female dinosaur. This bone was rich in calcium, and was used by the female dinosaur to make eggshells for her embryos.

▸ Pricey bones
In 1990, Sue Hendrickson, a fossil hunter discovered the bones of a T-rex in South Dakota, USA. The fossil, named 'Sue' after the discoverer, was found on land owned by a Native American rancher. Since the land was held in trust by the government, a dispute over the ownership of Sue began. The rancher finally won the legal battle and sold Sue at a Sotheby's auction for 8.4 million dollars – the largest amount ever paid for a fossil!

The ornithischians were all plant-eaters and divided into ornithopods, ceratopsia, stegosauria and ankylosaura, while the saurischians were both plant- and meat-eaters and consisted of theropods and sauropods.

Theropods included dinosaurs that walked upright on two legs and had short hands with sharp claws. Their sharp teeth and powerful jaws helped in chewing meat, though some ate plants as well. Some theropods looked very similar to ostriches and some even had feathers all over their body. Theropods usually had three toes on their feet (like birds) and light, hollow bones. Birds are believed to have descended from this group of dinosaurs, instead of ornithischians.

Theropod terrors

The most well-known and fierce dinosaur, the Tyrannosaurus rex, was a theropod. It was larger than others in its group.

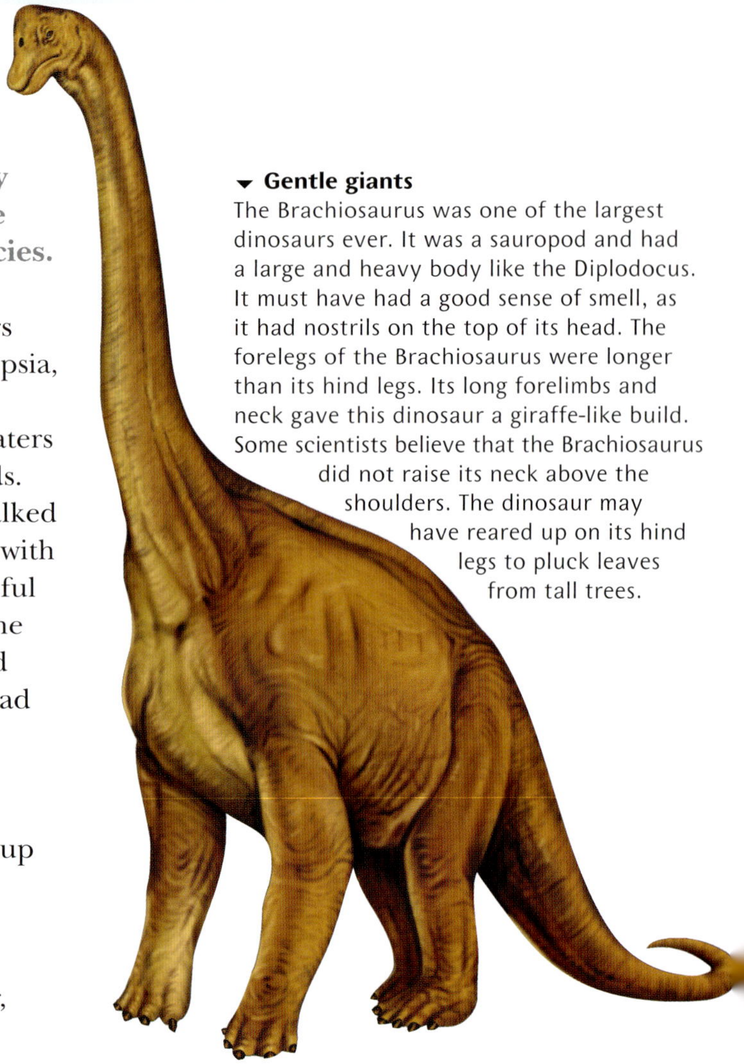

▾ Gentle giants
The Brachiosaurus was one of the largest dinosaurs ever. It was a sauropod and had a large and heavy body like the Diplodocus. It must have had a good sense of smell, as it had nostrils on the top of its head. The forelegs of the Brachiosaurus were longer than its hind legs. Its long forelimbs and neck gave this dinosaur a giraffe-like build. Some scientists believe that the Brachiosaurus did not raise its neck above the shoulders. The dinosaur may have reared up on its hind legs to pluck leaves from tall trees.

It had a big head, powerful jaws and very sharp teeth that could even break bones.The T-rex had a large brain and was considered far more intelligent than most dinosaurs. It could grow up to 13 metres (43 feet), and probably could not run fast due to its massive size.The velociraptor was a light and swift theropod. It had sharp teeth and long curved claws, which gave it a very fierce look. These raptors (running lizards) grew up to about 2.5 metres (8 feet). Their bodies and arms were covered with soft feathers.

Feathered dinosaurs

Sinosauropteryx was a small, about 91 centimetres (3 feet), feathered dinosaur. This bird-like dinosaur had a short body and a long tail. The Caudipteryx was another feathered dinosaur. It had a short tail with peacock-like feathers. Its short wing-like hands also had feathers.

Try these too:

Mammals (p 34–53), Birds (p 54–59), Fish (p 60–63), Reptiles and Amphibians (p 64–69), Life Begins (p 74–75)

◂ Spiked for attack?
Some of the larger plates on the back of a Stegosaurus may have been about 60 centimetres (2 feet) tall and wide. Scientists believe that the plates might have been used to control body temperature as well as for protection and mating displays.

Sauropods

Sauropods were four-legged, plant eating dinosaurs. They had huge bodies, small heads, long necks and tails, and chisel-shaped teeth. This group consisted of some of the largest land animals ever. Even dwarf sauropods were 6 metres (20 feet) long. The Diplodocus was a sauropod that grew to a height of 23 metres (75 feet). Its long thick tail balanced its heavy body when it reached out to bite off leaves from the tree tops.

Ornithopods

These were a group of herbivorous dinosaurs that lived during the Cretaceous period. They had three-toed bird feet, beaks and long stiff tails. Ornithopods were swift runners, and walked on two feet at first. They later began moving on all fours. The Iguanodon and the Hadrosaurus belong to this group. The hadrosaurus had a flat head, shaped like a duck-bill. Unlike sauropods, ornithopods had incisors and molars that helped them to bite and chew well.

Ceratopsia

Ceratopsia were plant-eaters with beaks, one or more horns and muscular frills around their necks. The frills may have supported the neck in earlier species, but later they were more decorative or used to defend the neck while fighting. The Triceratops and the Protoceratops both belonged to this group.

Stegosauria and ankylosauria

These were large herbivorous dinosaurs with armour-covered bodies. The Stegosaurus had thick scaly skin and spikes or plates along its back. This dinosaur must have been about 12 metres (40 feet) long. Nobody knows what the plates were used for, but they must have scared away other smaller and weaker animals. However, in spite of its scary appearance, the brain of a Stegosaurus was only the size of a walnut. The Ankylosaurus had hard armour-like skin and a club-shaped tail which it could swing at its enemies.

▾ Head to head
Pachycephalosauria were herbivorous dinosaurs that had thick, round heads. Some had short spikes on top. They probably used their spiky, hard heads to butt their enemies or to fight each other during mating. Both the Stygimoloch and the Pachycephalosaurus belonged to this group.

Gizzard stones

Dinosaurs' teeth were not well developed and not capable of biting and chewing everything they ate. To break down their food and grind it, they swallowed gastroliths, or gizzard stones. Several fossilized dinosaurs had these smooth pebbles in their stomachs.

The First Mammals and Birds

The first mammals appeared in the Jurassic period. They evolved from reptiles. Their number and variety increased over the years, but they were dominated by the mighty dinosaur. About 65 million years ago, when dinosaurs died out, several other species also became extinct. However, some survived and grew to become as big and powerful as the dinosaurs.

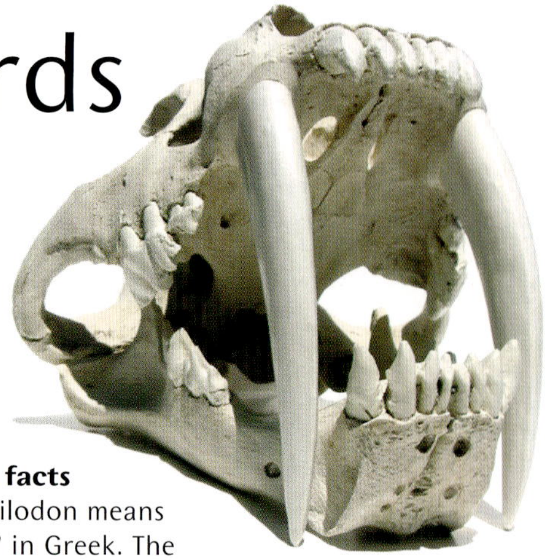

Smilodon facts
The term smilodon means 'knife-tooth' in Greek. The name is appropriate considering the long fangs of the animal. An adult Smilodon weighed about 200 kilograms (450 pounds). The fangs were about 17 centimetres (7 inches) long.

Key facts:

- The Cenozoic era saw the dominance of mammals, most of them massive in size. The giant ground sloth of the ice ages was one of them. Megatherium, the largest of all ground sloth species, was as large as the modern elephant.
- Many prehistoric animals are said to have died in the last ice age, which ended about 10,000 years ago. At the time most of North America and Europe were covered by glaciers and it was extremely cold all over the world.

The prehistoric creatures of the Cenozoic era included: birds, which reproduced through eggs; mammals, which carried their young inside their bodies in placenta; and marsupials, which carried their young partly in placenta and later in a pouch on their belly.

Archaeopteryx

About 150 million years ago, the first bird appeared on Earth. It was the Archaeopteryx. This creature was partly reptile and partly bird. Even today, nobody is sure whether the Archaeopteryx could fly at all or if it merely hopped about. What we do know is that it was no bigger than a crow, and had short, wide wings. The creature also had a long bony tail and sharp teeth. The feathers of the Archaeopteryx were quite similar to those of modern birds.

Too weak to fly
The ability of the Archaeopteryx to fly has been questioned due to the absence of a large breastbone.

Sabre-tooth cats

Sabre-tooth cats included a number of prehistoric cat-like species with large, sharp sabre or knife-like canine teeth. These cat-like animals first appeared during the Cenozoic era and were alive until about 10,000 years ago. One group were marsupials but all the others were placentals. These big cats used their terrifying teeth to injure their prey and bleed them to death. The Smilodon, or sabre-tooth tiger, was as big as a modern-day lion. It had a large head, muscular legs, a short tail and large fangs. Its huge powerful jaws could open very wide. The Smilodon moved with its pack and the young adults took care of the babies and older members. There were five species of Smilodon in the prehistoric world. Another variety of sabre-tooth tiger was the scimitar cat, whose teeth were smaller and flatter than those of the Smilodon. Both these varieties lived in North and South America. The Thylacosmilus was a marsupial sabre-tooth cat that lived in South America. Its sabre teeth kept growing in length throughout its life. In terms of its appearance, the Thylacosmilus was quite similar to the other sabre-toothed mammals.

Mammoths

A class of extinct elephants are called mammoths. These animals had long curved tusks and those that lived in cold northern countries like Siberia had woolly coats. These ancient creatures lived until 2000 BC.

Mastodons

Mastodons first appeared over 30 million years ago and became extinct only about 12,000 years ago. They looked a lot like prehistoric mammoths, but were actually quite different.

The mastodon was smaller than the mammoth, but had huge tusks (almost twice its height). They were herbivores and had blunt conical teeth. Early man hunted these animals for their flesh.

Woolly rhinoceros

The woolly rhino was a powerful animal with short, thick legs. It lived in the northernmost parts of Europe and Asia. It was a plant-eating mammal with a thick woolly coat. The woolly rhino had two horns on its snout, which it used to dig and move snow to graze.

Try these too:

Mammals (p 34–53),
Birds (p 54–59),
Fish (p 60–63),
Life Begins
(p 74–75)

▲ **Unknown roots**
Until recently it was believed that the Neanderthal man was the ancestor of modern humans. However, new DNA studies have questioned this theory.

◀ **Mammoth sized?**
Most mammoths were only as large as modern-day Indian elephants.

Early man

4.2 million years ago: Australopithecus, the first hominid, appeared. They were only 1.2 metres (4 feet) tall. They walked on two legs and looked a lot like chimpanzees. **2.4–1.5 million years ago:** Homo habilis, the first humans, lived. They were only about 1.3 metres (4 feet 3 inches) tall, and they made weapons of stone to hunt for food. **230–30 thousand years ago:** Neanderthal man lived. Neanderthals were about 1.7 metres (5 feet 6 inches) tall, and very muscular. They are not the ancestors of modern man. In fact, the ancestry of modern man still remains unresolved. Homo sapiens, otherwise known as modern man, actually only appeared 200,000 years ago.

Plant Life

Plants are one of the biggest groups of living things on Earth. Almost all plants are green in colour, they cannot move and they do not have sense organs to smell, hear, see, touch or taste like animals or human beings. Plants appeared on Earth for the first time around 400 million years ago. Today there are more than 300,000 types of plants on this planet.

▲ Pretty important
Flowers are the most attractive part of a plant and play an important role in pollination.

Key facts:

- Some plants have underground stems which send out leaves above the ground and roots below. Examples of underground stems are bulbs like onion, rhizomes like ginger and tubers like potato.
- Plants in dry places and deserts have very few or no leaves. They are covered with spines or hairs and are thick and fleshy so that they can store a lot of water.
- Mangrove forests are found in the shallow coastal areas of some tropical countries. The trees in these forests are specially adapted to growing in salty water.

Plants are divided into four major groups, depending on the way they reproduce. They are: bryophytes (mosses and liverworts), pteridophytes (ferns, horsetails and club mosses), gymnosperms (conifers, yews, cycads and ginkgos) and angiosperms (flowering trees and shrubs).

Mosses and liverworts

These are small plants that grow close to the ground in moist places. They absorb water from the atmosphere to transport food around their bodies. These plants have spores in capsules at the end of long stalks. The mother plant provides food to the spores and when the capsule, or sporophyte, dries, the spores burst out and fall onto the ground.

Ferns, club mosses and horsetails

These first appeared in the Palaeozoic era. They have stems, leaves and roots and can transport food, water and minerals around their bodies. This is taken care of by the vascular system, which is made up of a number of water-carrying tissues. Like the bryophytes, these plants reproduce through spores. The spores are produced and stored in sporangia, or seed sacs, on the underside of the leaves.

▸ Bearing spores
The developing sporangia on the underside of fern fronds are at first green in colour. They slowly turn brown, black or yellow as they mature. When ripe enough, the sporangia split open to release the spores into the air.

Conifers, cycads and ginkgos

Conifers, cycads and ginkgos are trees or shrubs with roots, stems and leaves. The leaves of these trees are like needles or scales. The seeds of these plants are called 'naked seeds' because they are not hidden within fruit. Instead, they are stored on cones that grow on these trees.

Flowering trees and shrubs

There are of two types of flowering trees and shrubs – monocotyledons and dicotyledons. In both these types the seeds grow in the ovary of the flower. When the flower dies, a fruit grows around the seeds. Monocotyledon seeds have single seed leaves within them. The leaves of these plants have narrow veins that are parallel to each other and do not branch out. Dicotyledons have seeds with two seed leaves and their foliage leaves have a thick main vein that branches out into several thinner veins over the leaf. Flowering and fruit-bearing plants grow in an amazing variety of sizes and forms. They can be trees (apple, mango, banyan, oak or chestnut), woody plants (rose, hibiscus or frangipani), green herbaceous plants (tomato, chrysanthemum or strawberry), or vines (also called climbers) and creepers (honeysuckle, sweet pea or pumpkin). Flowering plants can be annuals that live only for one year and flower for three to four months (marigold, aster, phlox). They can be biennials that live for two years and flower only in the second year (parsley, foxglove, carrot). Some plants may also be perennials that live for many years and flower every year (water lily, begonia, banana).

◂ **Not trees**
Unlike trees, shrubs have many stems and are short. They also have small branches covered with leaves.

Biomes

Plants can be roughly divided into three major biomes. A biome is a large area with a distinctive climate and plants and animals adapted to living in that climate. The three major biomes on Earth are the tropical forests near the equator, the temperate forests between the tropics and the polar regions, and the boreal or taiga forests just south of the Arctic.

◂ **Weak stems**
Creepers and climbers (vines) have weak stems that cannot support the rest of the plant. So these plants either creep along the ground or climb up rocks, walls or other plants for support.

▴ **Tree basics**
Trees are tall and have branches coming out of a single stem, or trunk.

Try these too:

Mammals (p 34–53), Birds (p 54–59), Fish (p 60–63), Reptiles and Amphibians (p 64–69), Countries and People (p 102–115)

Food for Plants

The parts of a plant consist of the root, stem, leaves, flowers, fruit and seeds. These parts can be grouped as reproductive or vegetative parts. The root, stem and leaves are vegetative parts. They help in manufacturing food and transporting it throughout the various parts of the plant. Flowers, fruit and seeds are the reproductive parts. Vegetative parts can also be used to grow plants asexually – a stem cutting can grow into a new plant.

Key facts:

- Bees and butterflies carry pollen from one flower to another and deposit it on the stigma. The stigma is found on the top of the pistil, which is a long stalk that goes down to the ovary at the centre of the flower. The pollen grows tubes that go downwards and fertilize the seeds in the ovary.
- The banyan is an unusual tree in which the young plants grow aerial (upward growing) roots that attach themselves to another tree. Banyans normally keep spreading and have several such roots attached to them.
- Water plants, like hyacinth and lily, float on water and are not rooted in soil. Their stems, leaves and roots have several air spaces, which make them light and help them to float. Water lily leaves have stomata on top, so that they can breathe easily.
- Flowers are the most beautiful and sweet smelling parts of plants so that they attract insects for pollination. However, the rafflesia, which is the largest flower in the world, smells of rotten meat.

In plants with vascular systems (plants that can transport water and food on their own) the roots grow below the ground. There is a main, or primary, root with several root hairs growing out of it. Roots absorb water and minerals from the soil and send it to the stem and leaves. In some plants, like carrot and radish, the root stores the minerals, while in others like ivy and money plant, they grow above the ground and support the plant.

The support system

The stem is the main part of the plant. It rises above the ground and supports the entire weight of the plant. The leaves, flowers and fruit grow from it. The stem supports the plant. It also transports the water and the minerals sent up by the root to the other parts of the plant. Small shrubs and creepers have green stems while trees have woody brown stems covered by bark.

Food factories

Leaves are the food factories of a plant. They are responsible for producing food required for plant growth. Leaves come in different shapes and sizes. Some of them are simple leaves, which are attached to the stem by stalks. Others are compound leaves with several small leaflets attached to one stalk that grows out of the stem. Leaves are mostly green in colour. They have a thick vein running through the middle with small veins branching out from it.

Building new generations

Buds grow at the tip of the stem or at the joints of the leaves and stem. These grow into flowers. The stalk of a flower is attached to green sepals, which hold the petals together. Inside the sepals and petals is the ovary, which contains the seeds of the plant. When the seeds are fertilized the flower withers away and the fruit begins to grow in its place.

▸ **The root of the matter**
Food in plants is usually stored in leaves or stems, but in some plants the food is stored in the roots. In carrots, the taproot is used to store food, and in sweet potatoes the lateral roots are modified for storage.

◂ **Flower power**
The pistil, the female part of a flower, consists of stigma, style and ovaries. The male part, called the stamen, includes the anther, or the pollen sac, and the filament that supports it.

Parasitic existence

Some plants get all of their water, minerals and food from other plants. Such plants are known as parasites. These parasitic plants attach their roots to the roots and stem of the host plant and grow by sucking nutrients from them. As these parasitic plants do not make their own food, they do not have chlorophyll or green leaves. Some plants are partial parasites. They take water and minerals from the host plant but make their own food through photosynthesis. Mistletoe is an example of a partial parasite. Plants like rafflesia depend completely on their host.

Try these too:

Mammals (p 34–53), Birds (p 54–59), Fish (p 60–63), Reptiles and Amphibians (p 64–69), Countries and People (p 102–115)

▼ **Self-sufficient life**
The carbon, hydrogen and a part of the oxygen present in water and carbon dioxide is converted into glucose. The leftover oxygen is released into the atmosphere, while the surplus glucose is stored in roots, leaves and stems for future use.

Photosynthesis

Plants make their own food by combining water from the soil with sunlight and carbon dioxide from the air. Leaves contain chlorophyll, a green substance that can absorb energy from sunlight. On the underside of leaves are several tiny openings called stomata. Leaves breathe in carbon dioxide through these openings. The carbon dioxide is combined with water and energy from sunlight to make glucose, which helps plants grow. During this process, the carbon dioxide is changed into oxygen and released into the atmosphere by the leaves.

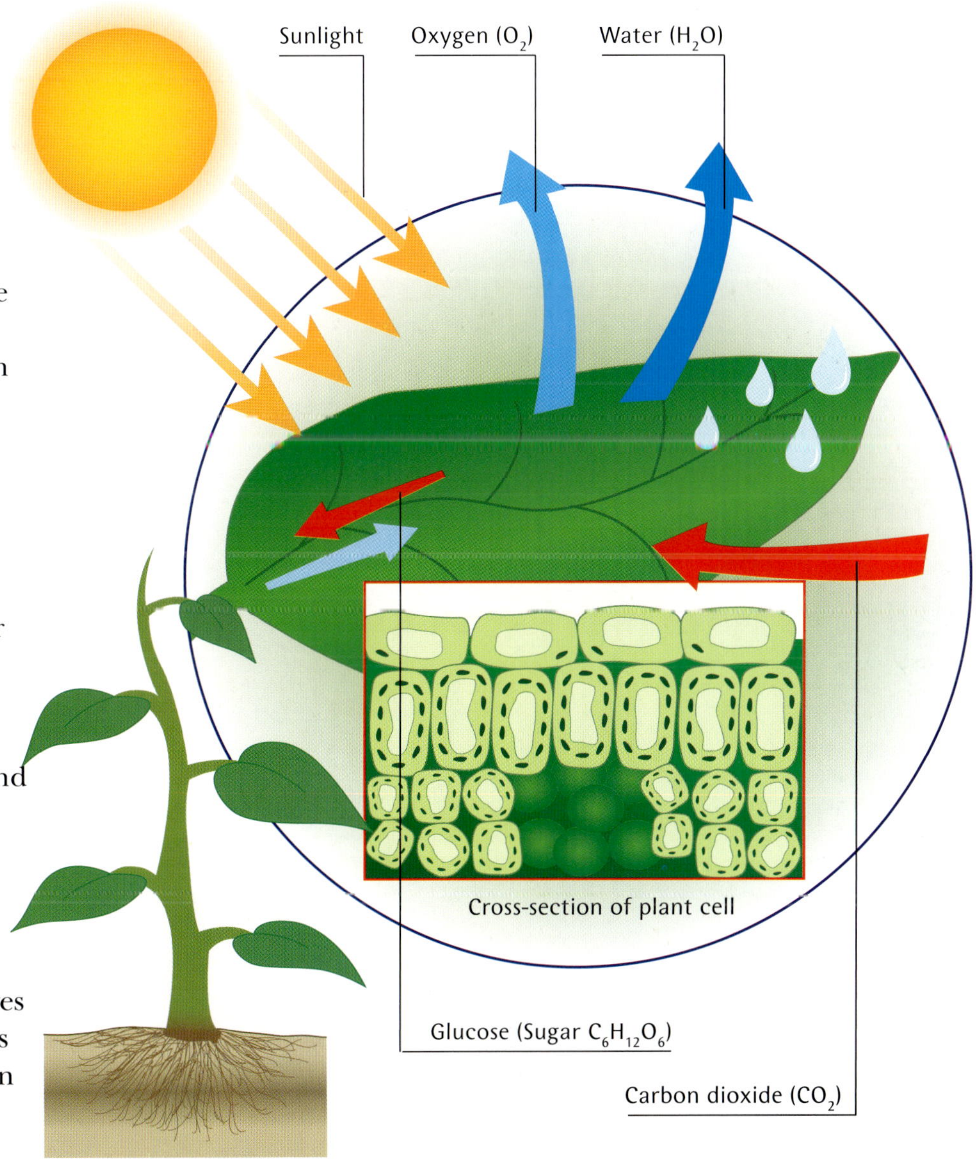

Preying on insects

In some places the soil might lack minerals, especially nitrogen that is necessary for their growth. Plants that live in such places make up for the deficiency by eating insects and even small animals. Such plants are known as insectivorous plants. They are usually found in marshes and on rocks. The Venus flytrap and the pitcher plant are popular examples of insectivorous plants. Both plants have brightly coloured leaves that are modified into insect traps. The pitcher-like leaves of the pitcher plant contains a liquid that dissolves the trapped insect. The top part of the leaves of a flytrap has teeth-like projections. When an insect sits on this part, the leaf snaps shut, trapping the prey inside.

External Body Parts

The population of the world is more than six and a half billion, yet no two people can look completely alike. There are always differences in the colour and elasticity of our skin, the shape of our muscles, the amount of fat within our bodies and the size and shape of our skeletons. However, all human beings have the same body parts. The visible parts of the human body include the skin, hair, nails, hands and feet.

Key facts:

- The body continuously sheds tiny particles of dead skin. It grows completely new skin at least once every month. It is estimated that a human being sheds at least 18 kilograms (40 pounds) of skin in their lifetime.
- The kind of hair a person has is determined by the shape of their hair follicles. Asians have round follicles, Europeans have round to oval and Africans have flat follicles. Straight hair grows out of round follicles and curly or frizzy hair out of flat follicles.
- The palms and fingers of human hands have ridged patterns. This ridged texture helps us to grasp and hold things better. These patterns are unique – no two people can have identical ones.

Skin is the largest organ of the human body. It is a protective covering that prevents too much heat or harmful bacteria from entering the body. It also prevents the body from losing too much water and other nutrients. Skin is made up of three layers – the epidermis, the dermis and fat. The epidermis is the outermost layer, and is made up of a thin layer of dead cells that are replaced continuously. When the dead cells wear away, new cells are formed. A substance called keratin makes the epidermis tough and waterproof.

The epidermis also produces melanin, a substance that protects the skin from harmful rays of the sun. The dermis is a thicker and more elastic layer. It contains follicles from which hair grows. It also contains sebaceous glands, which produce an oily substance called sebum that keeps the skin from becoming dry and cracking. Sweat glands excrete water and salt from the body and are situated in the dermis. This layer also has sensory nerves, which help the skin to feel sensations and changes in temperature. The fat layer is responsible for storing energy and keeping the body warm.

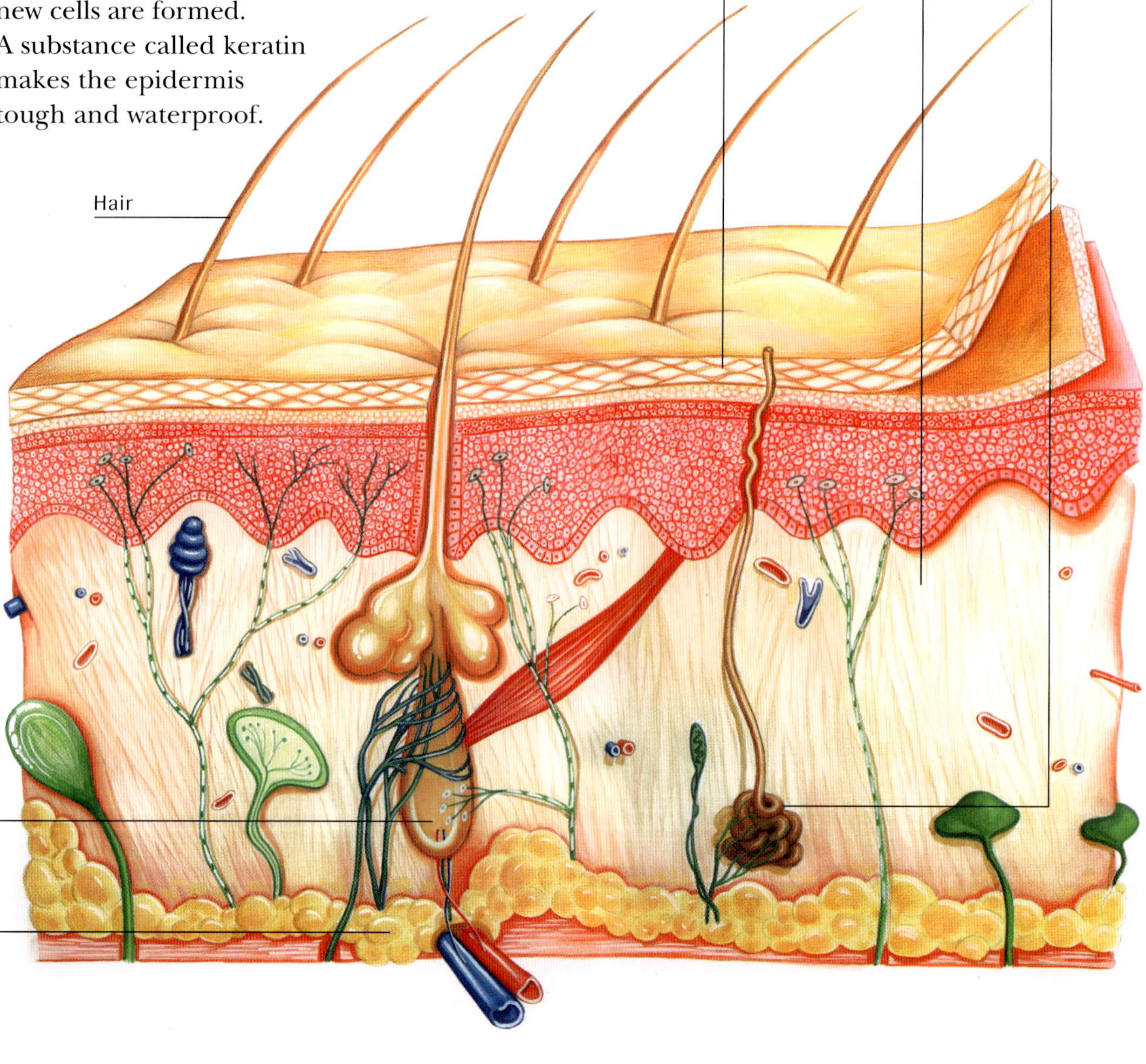

Getting under the skin
A cross-section of the skin showing various layers.

Hair and nails

Hair grows out of the skin all over the body, except on the lips, the soles of the feet and the palms of the hands. Hair is made of keratin, the same substance that is found in the outermost layer of skin. The nails on fingers and toes are attached by their roots, which fit into grooves in the skin. Nails are flexible and horn-like in appearance. The roots of nails produce new cells, which make the nail grow. This means that the oldest part of the nail is at the fingertip.

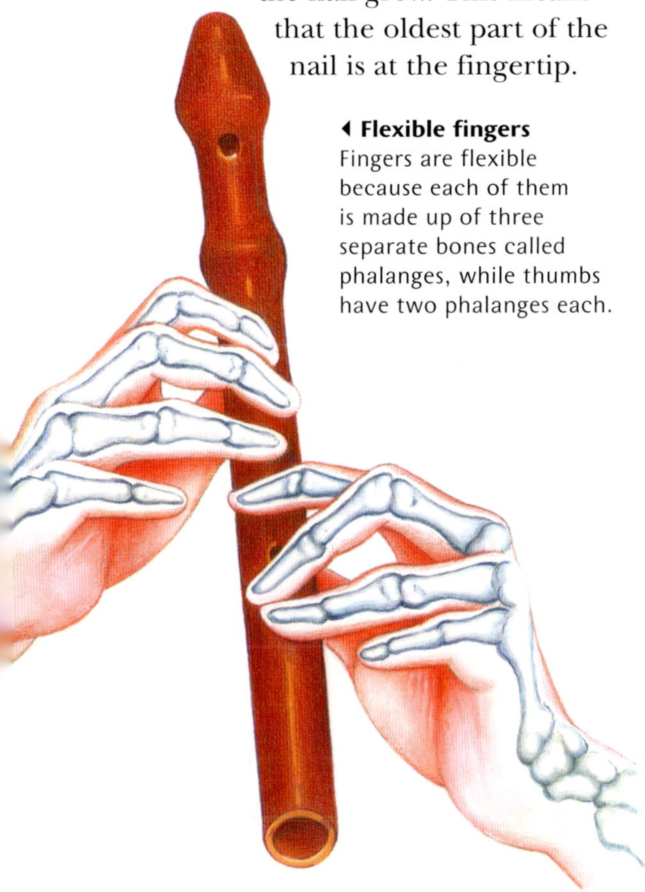

◂ Flexible fingers
Fingers are flexible because each of them is made up of three separate bones called phalanges, while thumbs have two phalanges each.

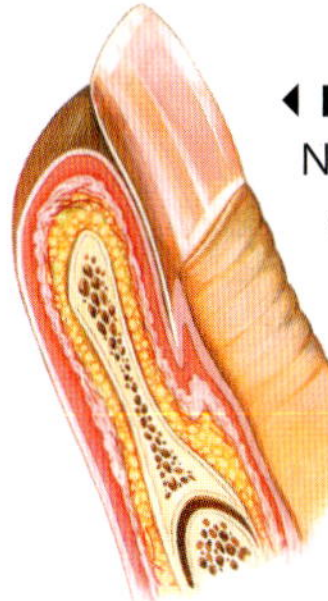

◂ Hardy nails
Nails protect the soft skin of our fingers from injuries and bacteria. We are able to cut our nails without feeling any pain because they do not have nerves. This is also the case with our hair.

Limbs

Human beings use their hands and feet for various activities. They are two of the most useful parts of the human body. A hand consists of a palm, a wrist, and five fingers, or digits, including the thumb. The wrist is a flexible bone that attaches the hand to the forearm. Our two hands are mirror images of each other. Fingertips have sensory nerves, which help us to feel texture, temperature and pain. Feet are essential for movement and balance. The human foot is made up of six parts – ankle, heel, instep, sole, ball and toes. The ankle connects the foot to the leg, while the toes help in gripping and walking. The ball is the soft spongy part located just behind the toes. The heel and the arch (the curve found at the bottom of the foot) support the body and absorb shock while walking or running. The instep is the raised, curved part on top of the foot, between the ankle and the toes.

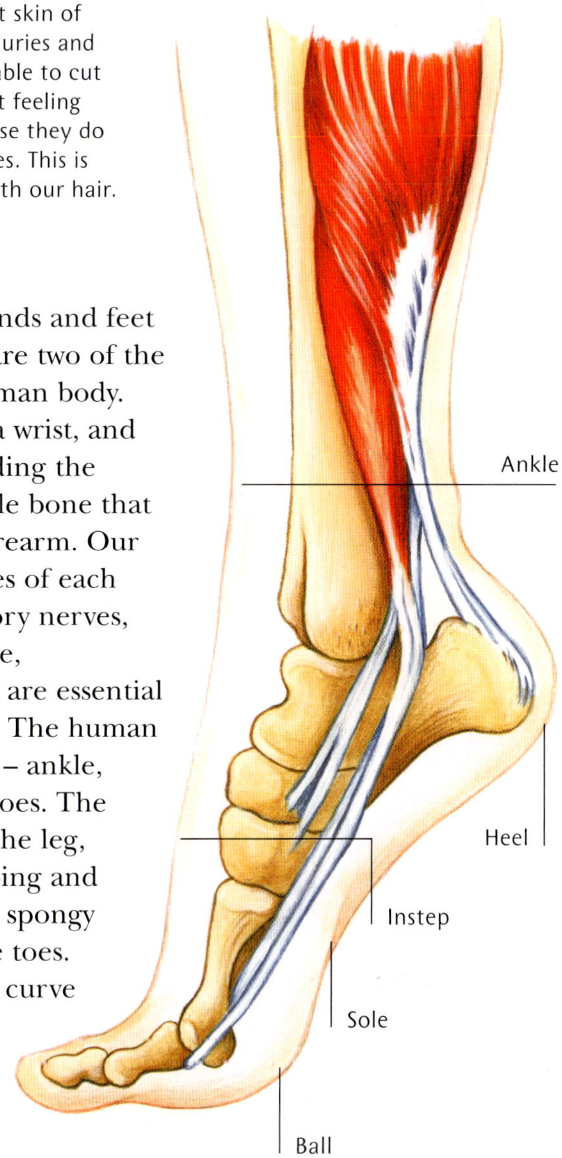

▲ Best foot forward
Humans use their legs and feet for a variety of activities like walking, running and dancing. Most of the body weight is carried by the two largest bones in the feet.

Natural protection

The skin colour of different races is determined by a substance called melanin that is present in the epidermis. There are two types of melanin – pheomelanin, which ranges from red to yellow in colour, and eumelanin, which is dark brown to black. Light skinned people have pheomelanin, and that is why they get sunburnt easily. Dark skinned people, on the other hand, have eumelanin, which protects them against the ultraviolet rays of the sun.

Try these too:

Bones and Muscles (p 90–91), The Heart and Blood Circulation (p 94–95), The Brain and Sensory Organs (p 96–97), Falling Sick (p 100–101)

Bones and Muscles

The skeleton is a framework of bones, which gives shape to the human body. The skeleton of an adult human being consists of 206 bones. These bones not only protect the internal organs of the human body, but also support the muscles connected to it.

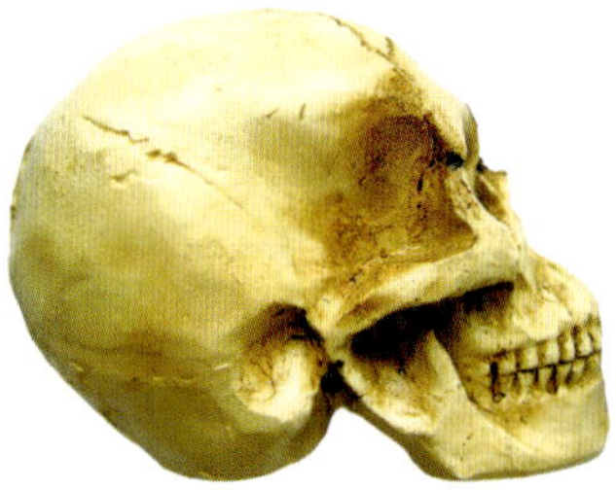

▲ Heady issues
The skull consists of the cranium and facial bones. The cranium is a bony case that protects the brain.

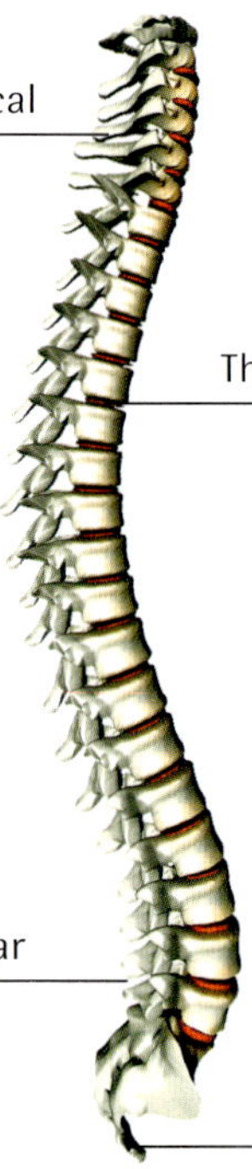

▲ Spinal curves
When seen from the side, the backbone is curved at four different regions. These regions are called cervical (neck), thoracic (upper trunk), lumbar (lower back) and pelvic. The curves allow for an increased flexibility and provide more room for the internal organs.

The bones that make up the skeleton are hard on the outside and spongy on the inside. This reduces their weight. Deep inside the larger bones is bone marrow, which produces blood cells. Bones also store calcium and phosphate, two important body-building minerals. The skeleton consists of the skull, the backbone, the ribcage, the shoulder and hip girdles, and the bones of the arms and legs. Arm bones are attached to the body at the shoulder blade and leg bones are attached to the hipbone, or pelvis.

Facial bones

The skull is a hard shell made up of 28 bones fused together. It gives shape to the face and protects the brain. The only skull bone that is not completely fixed is the jawbone. The jawbone is hinged below the ear, so it can move up and down easily.

The spine

The spine, or backbone, supports the body and protects the delicate spinal cord. It is made up of 33 vertebrae that are joined together. The last bone is longer than the rest of the vertebrae. It is triangular in shape and looks like a tail. The ribcage is connected to the backbone at the back and to the breastbone at the front. It forms a protective cover for the heart and lungs.

Soft bones

Some parts of our body are shaped by cartilage instead of bone. Cartilage is more flexible than bone, but it is also damaged or worn out more easily. The nose, ear, ribs and throat are made of cartilage. Small discs of cartilage are also present between each of the vertebrae in the backbone.

▶ Face up!
The facial muscles in humans are arranged in flexible sheets, which overlap each other.

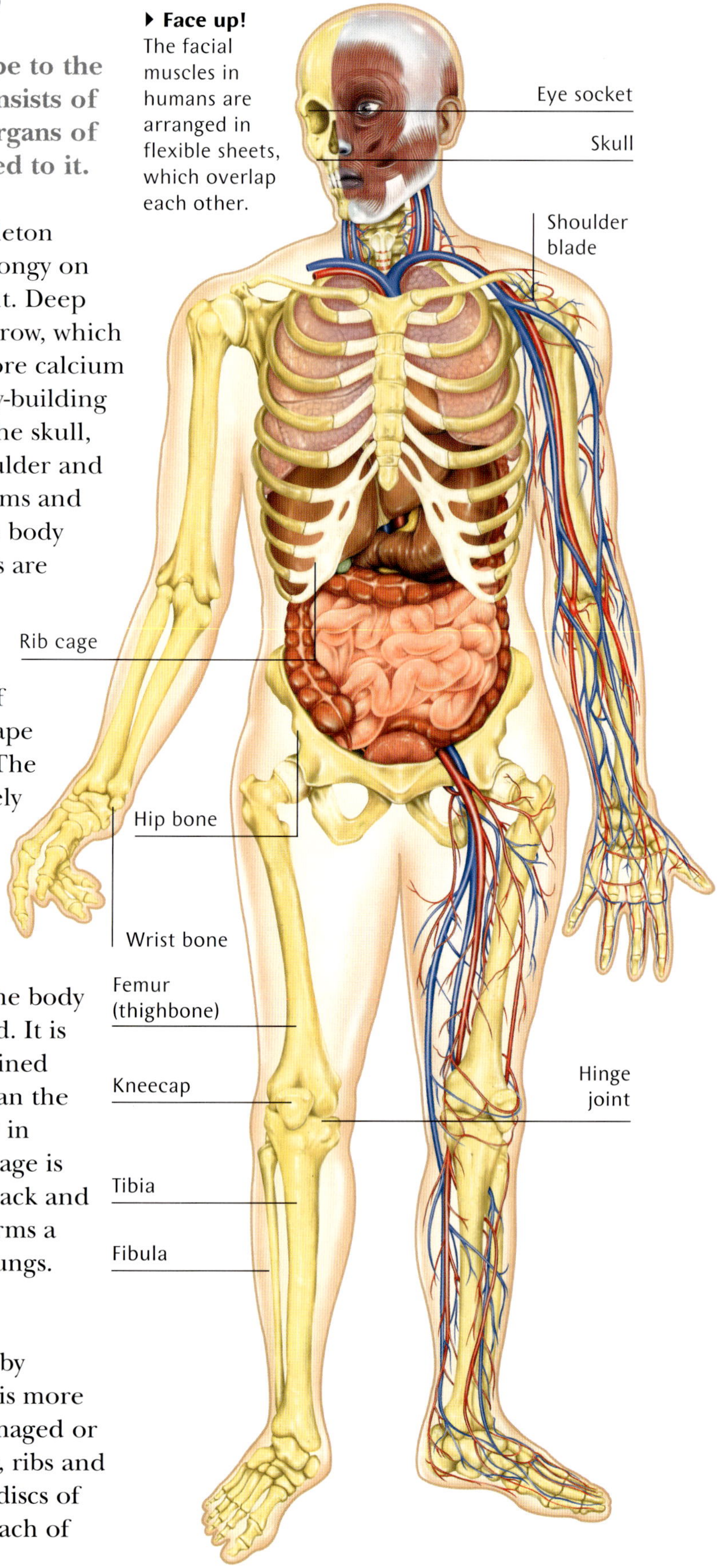

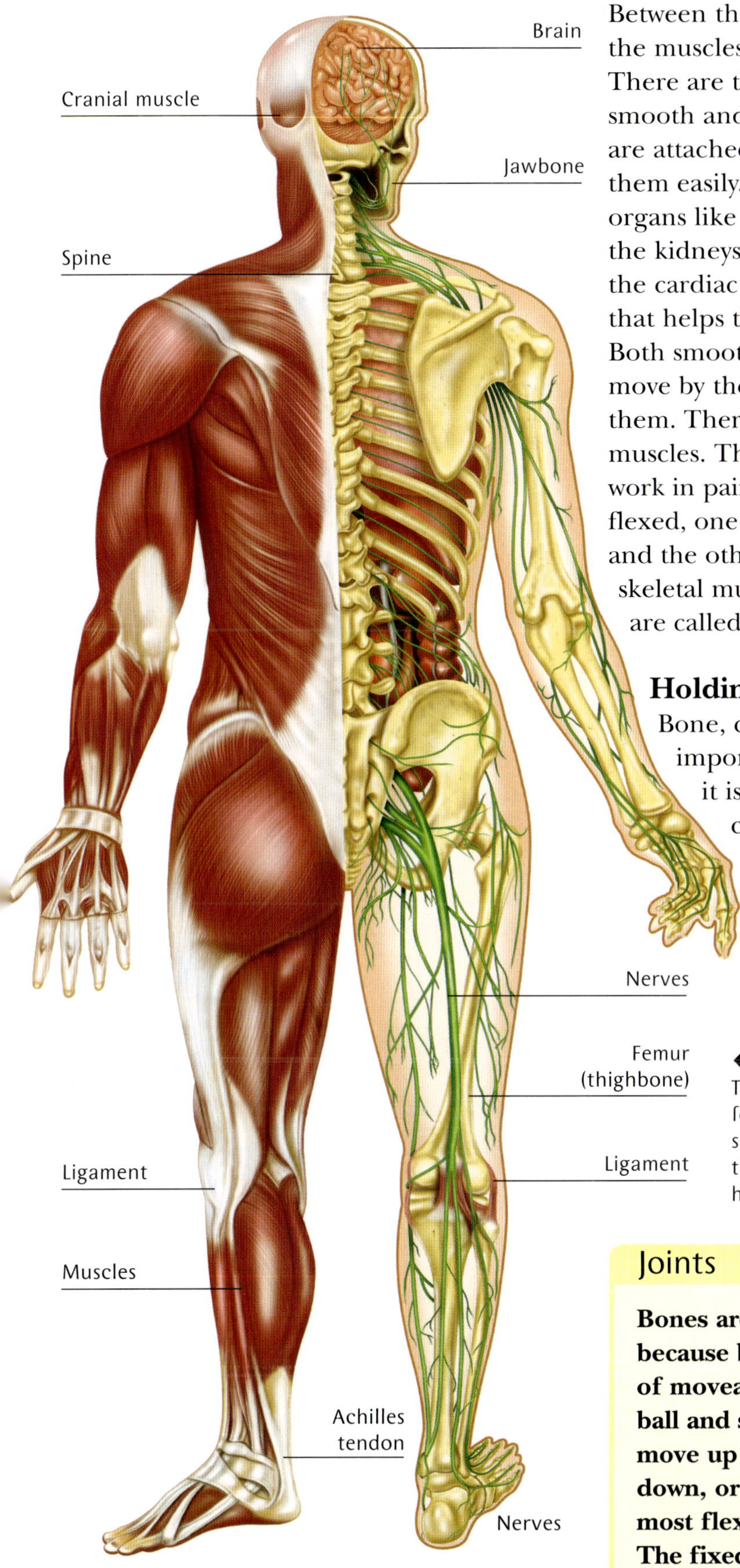

Muscle power

Between the skin and the skeleton are the muscles that help the body to move. There are three types of muscles – skeletal, smooth and heart muscles. Skeletal muscles are attached to the bones and we can control them easily. The smooth muscle is found in organs like the stomach, the intestine and the kidneys. The heart muscle, also known as the cardiac muscle, is a special type of muscle that helps the heart to function continuously. Both smooth muscle and the heart muscle move by themselves and we cannot control them. Therefore we call them involuntary muscles. The muscles attached to the skeleton work in pairs. When a hand or leg is bent or flexed, one muscle contracts, or tightens up, and the other relaxes. Since we can control skeletal muscles and move them at will, they are called voluntary muscles.

Holding together

Bone, cartilage and muscle may be important parts of the human body, but it is the tendons and ligaments that connect these parts and help them to move easily. Tendons connect muscles to bones and ligaments connect bones to each other. Both are strong flexible bands that are located at the joints.

◂ Flex those muscles!
The muscles in the human body account for almost half of the body weight. Of these, skeletal muscles aid all body movements. In the process, these muscles produce heat to help maintain the body temperature.

Key facts:

- Human beings are born with about 300 bones. The bones of new born babies are soft and flexible. As they grow, some of these bones fuse, or join together, and the skeleton becomes strong and tough.
- The hyoid bone is a small U-shaped bone in the neck that supports the tongue. It is the only floating bone in the body. This means that the hyoid is not attached to any other bone in the body. Instead, the hyoid bone is well-supported by the muscles in the neck.
- The human body contains about 650 muscles. All of these muscles are made up of several stretchable fibres that are bunched together. When muscles contract they can become just one-third of their actual size.

Try these too:

External Body Parts (p 88–89), Digestion and Excretion (p 92–93), The Heart and Blood Circulation (p 94–95), The Brain and Sensory Organs (p 96–97)

Joints

Bones are stiff and cannot bend. We can bend our arms and legs because bones meet at joints, which are flexible. The main types of moveable joints in the human body include pivot, hinge, and ball and socket joints. Pivot joints allow the bone to rotate and move up and down. Hinge joints allow the bone to move up and down, or backwards and forwards. Ball and socket joints are the most flexible and allow the bone to move in many different ways. The fixed joints do not move at all – the skull bones, for example.

Digestion and Excretion

The body gets rid of waste matter in different ways. The skin gets rid of excess water and salt, we breathe out carbon dioxide and water vapour, the urinary system sends out urine and the digestive system gets rid of solid waste. The digestive system is responsible for nourishing all parts of the body. It breaks down the food that is eaten, helps the body to absorb the nutrients in it and gets rid of any waste matter that remains.

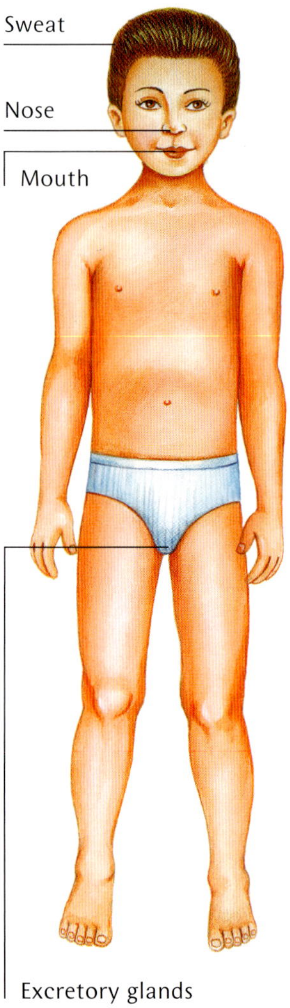

▲ Excretion points
The toxins that enter the body are either absorbed by the fibre you eat or dissolved in water and flushed out of the body through the excretory system. Therefore, it is important that you drink at least eight glasses of water every day and your diet consists of food with lots of fibre.

When we put food into our mouth, we trigger a series of actions in our body. This process is called digestion. An adult usually has 32 teeth in his or her mouth. They are the incisors, the canines, the molars and the premolars. The incisors and canines help bite and tear the food into small pieces, and the premolars and molars grind the food. The mouth produces saliva, which helps us to break the food down and move it around in the mouth. The saliva turns the food into a mush making it easy to swallow it.

Down the tube

The food travels down the oesophagus, or food pipe, to the stomach, which produces chemicals called enzymes. These enzymes further break down the food. The partly digested food goes from the stomach to the small intestine. Here, it is broken down completely and all the nutrients and water pass through the intestines into the bloodstream. The blood takes these nutrients to other parts of the body. The small intestine uses bile, sent from the gall bladder, and enzymes and acids from the pancreas to break down the food. Excess fat is converted into fat molecules (by the liver) and fat cells under the skin, and stored for future use.

At the very end

The excess water and undigested parts of food, which is termed fibre, are sent to the large intestine. Here, all the remaining water is absorbed, while bacteria present in the intestine change the rest of the waste food into faeces. As the excess water is reabsorbed it causes the faeces to harden. The large intestine secretes a slimy substance called mucus that lubricates the faeces so that it passes out easily. The faeces is sent into the rectum where it is pushed out of the body through the anus.

Liquid waste

The urinary system consists of a pair of kidneys, a bladder, two thin tubes called ureters (which connect the kidneys to the bladder) and a tube called the urethra (which passes the urine out of the body). The kidneys remove the waste matter in blood by filtering it. The waste that it collects is called urine. Urine is a watery substance that contains urea. Too much urea can be harmful to the body. The ureters carry the urine into the urinary bladder. As more and more urine is sent to the bladder, it stretches until it can hold no more. At this point the nerves in the bladder alert the brain that the bladder has to be emptied. A muscle called sphincter controls the opening between the bladder and the urethra. When the brain receives the message it in turn tells the sphincter to relax and let urine pass through. The bladder squeezes to force the urine down the urethra.

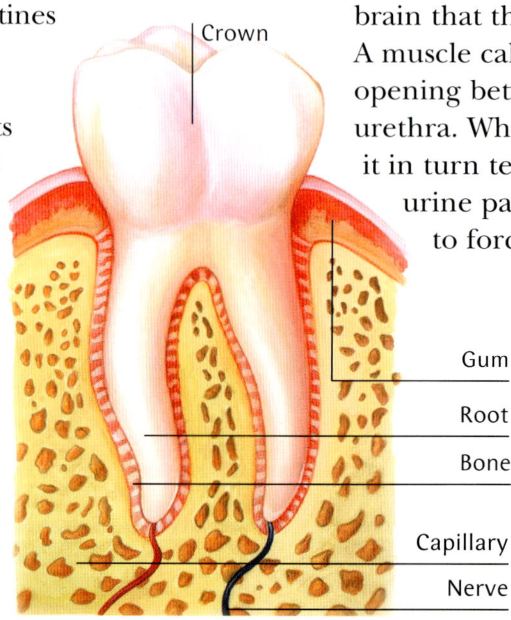

◀ Toothy tales
A human tooth consists of two main parts – crown and root. The crown is the exposed part of the tooth jutting above the gum. It has an outer covering of enamel, which is the hardest substance in the human body. Inside the tooth there is a cavity filled with tissue, blood vessels and nerve fibres. This region is called the pulp and is very sensitive.

▸ Long and winding
The small intestine is the longest section of the digestive tract. The total length of the tract is 12 metres (40 feet). The small intestine alone constitutes about 5 metres (16 feet) of it.

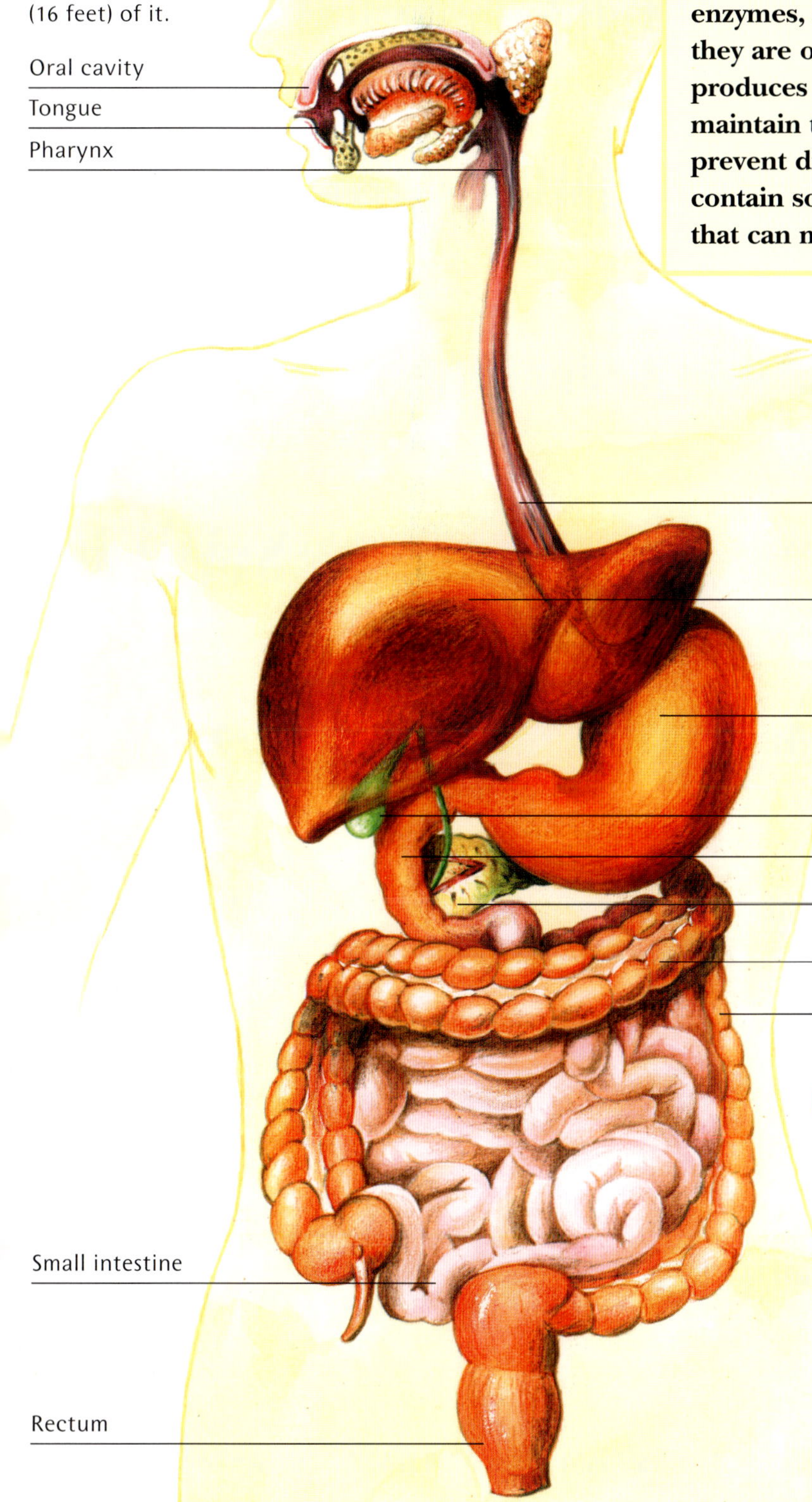

Pancreas

The pancreas is a small but very important organ situated behind the stomach. It releases enzymes that break up proteins, fats and carbohydrates into the small intestine. In fact, if the pancreas does not produce these enzymes, a person can starve even if they are overeating! The pancreas also produces insulin and glucagons, which maintain the glucose level in the body and prevent diabetes. Pancreatic juices also contain sodium bicarbonate, a chemical that can neutralize acid in the stomach.

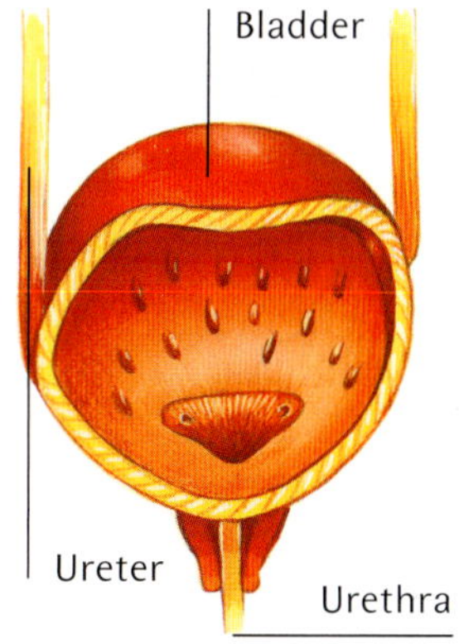

▲ Storing urine
The bladder can store about 1.5 litres (3 pints) of urine, or even more.

Key facts:

- The digestive system is made up of a long tube that starts at the mouth and ends at the anus. This tube, called the alimentary canal, is about 12 metres (30 feet) long – that is five times the height of an average adult.
- Each bean-shaped kidney contains about one million filters, or nephrons. Both kidneys work continually to clean blood. About 190 litres (42 gallons) of blood pass through the kidneys every day.
- On the right side of the lower abdomen, attached to the large intestine, is a short tube called the appendix. The appendix plays no known part in the digestion process, or any of the other functions of the body.

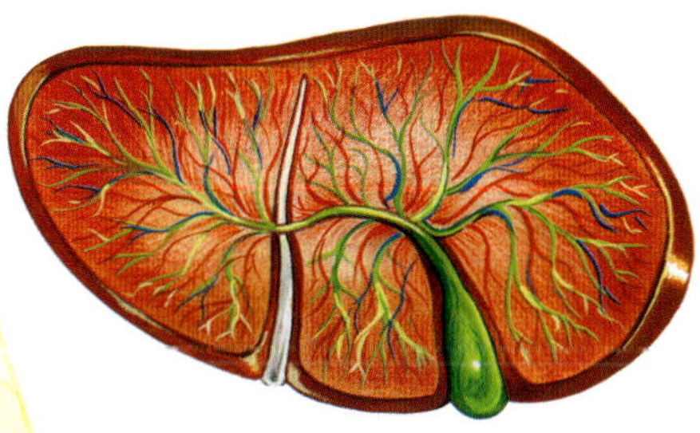

▲ Amazing liver!
The liver is the largest internal organ, and probably one of the busiest. It processes sugar and fats for storage, manufactures bile for digestion and contains a reservoir of blood that is released if the body loses too much.

Try these too:

External Body Parts (p 88–89), Bones and Muscles (p 90–91), The Heart and Blood Circulation (p 94–95), Falling Sick (p 100–101)

The Heart and Blood Circulation

The heart is one of the most important organs in the human body. The heart, along with numerous blood vessels, keeps the body healthy and fit. Any breakdown in the heart and circulatory system will result in almost immediate death.

Key facts:

- The heart is only as big as a fist. It begins functioning from the time the foetus is formed and does not stop until the person dies. During this time it beats more than two and half billion times.
- The lungs and the heart need clean blood and nutrients to work well. The heart gets back the clean, oxygenated blood it needs through the coronary arteries, and the lungs get it through the bronchial arteries.
- Blood cells are produced in bone marrow. Each red blood cell lives for up to 120 days, whereas white blood cells only live for a few days or weeks.
- Blood is mostly made up of red blood cells. These cells contain a substance called haemoglobin, which is rich in iron and gives blood its red colour.

The heart is a muscular organ situated towards the left side of the chest, between the lungs. It is responsible for pumping blood to all parts of the body. The blood that goes out of the heart carries oxygen and nutrients, and the blood that comes back is full of carbon dioxide. The human heart is divided into four chambers. A muscle known as the septum divides the heart lengthwise into two chambers. These chambers are in turn divided horizontally by valves that can open and close. The chambers on top are called atria and those at the bottom are called ventricles. Large blood vessels called arteries carry clean blood from the heart, while veins bring unclean blood back to the heart.

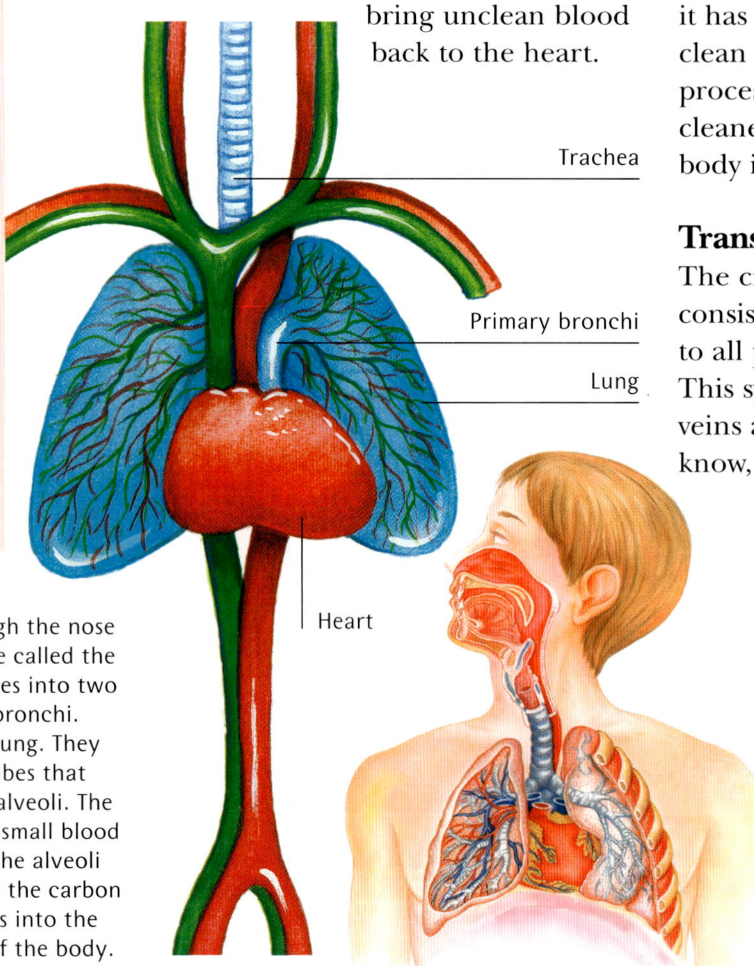

▸ Respiratory tract
Air enters the body through the nose and is carried down a tube called the trachea. The trachea divides into two tubes, known as primary bronchi. One of these enters each lung. They branch out into smaller tubes that lead into tiny air sacs, or alveoli. The alveoli are surrounded by small blood vessels. The oxygen from the alveoli passes into the blood, and the carbon dioxide in the blood passes into the alveoli to be carried out of the body.

The path of circulation

Blood containing carbon dioxide is brought to the heart by the superior and inferior vena cava, or 'heart veins'. This impure blood enters the right atrium. When the atrium is full, the valve opens and the blood flows down into the right ventricle. From here the blood is sent to the lungs through the pulmonary artery. The lungs breathe out the carbon dioxide that comes with the blood and breathe in the oxygen from the air. The oxygenated blood then re-enters the heart, into the left atrium, through the pulmonary veins. When the atrium is full, the valve connecting it to the left ventricle is opened and the clean blood flows down into it. The blood is then sent out into the body through the aorta, which is the largest artery in the human body. The left ventricle is more muscular than the rest of the heart because it has to pump with greater force to send the clean blood to all parts of the body. The process of receiving unclean blood, getting it cleaned and finally pumping it back into the body is called a cardiac cycle.

Transport network

The circulatory system is a complex network consisting of delicate tubes that carry blood to all parts of the body and back to the heart. This system is made up of the heart, arteries, veins and capillaries. Arteries and veins, as we know, carry blood to the heart and back.

▾ The number game
Organs that are more active than others require more capillaries.

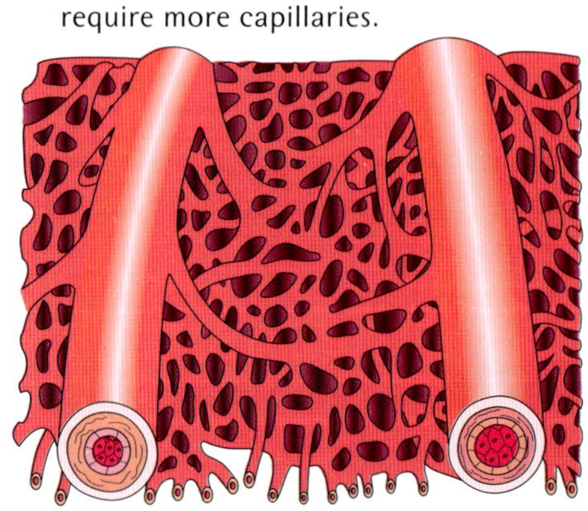

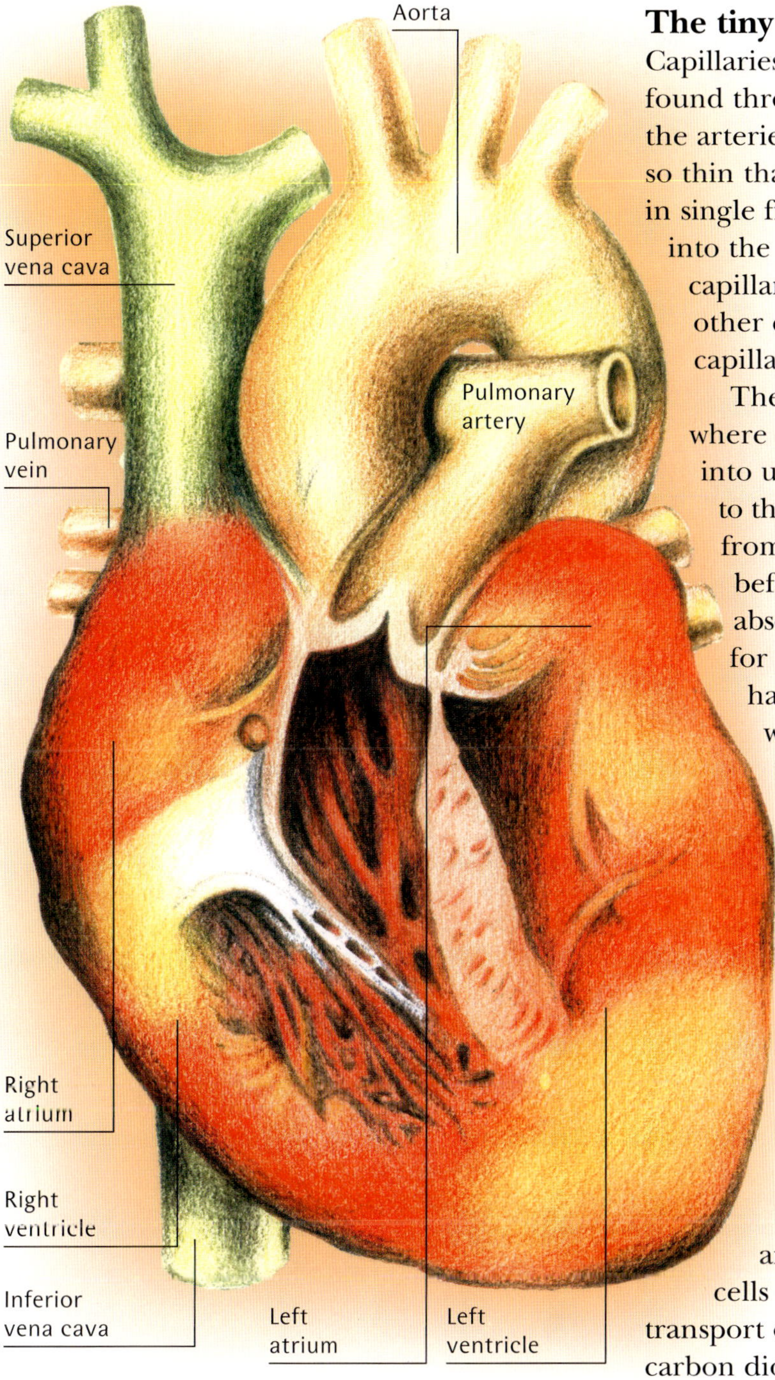

▲ Hearty life
As well as pumping blood, the heart also secretes a hormone called atrial natriuretic factor, or ANF, which regulates blood pressure.

The tiny carriers

Capillaries are fragile blood vessels that are found throughout the body – they connect the arteries and veins. The capillaries are so thin that blood cells travel through them in single file. Oxygen in the blood is passed into the tissues through the thin walls of the capillaries. Similarly, carbon dioxide and other chemical wastes also pass into the capillaries to be taken away.

The blood is taken to the kidneys, where the urea in it is filtered and made into urine. The filtered blood then goes to the small intestine. Here, the nutrients from digested food enter the blood, before it goes to the liver. The liver absorbs the nutrients and converts them for storage. It also reduces the effect of harmful substances, like enzymes, which come from the intestine. The blood is then sent through the inferior vena cava back into the heart.

Blood is the source of life for all human beings and animals. It is the vehicle in which food, water and oxygen are sent to all parts of the body. An average human being has about 5 litres (10 pints) of blood circulating in their body. Blood is a liquid tissue made up of plasma and cells. Suspended in the plasma are the red blood cells, white blood cells and platelets. Red blood cells transport oxygen to the tissues and carry away carbon dioxide, while white blood cells help fight infections and diseases. Platelets form clots to help prevent too much bleeding when a blood vessel is punctured.

▼ When the heart beats
The contraction of the muscles of the left and right atria forces blood into the ventricles. The pressure in the ventricles increase, forcing the valves between the atria and ventricles to close. At the same time, the aortic and pulmonary valves are forced open to carry the blood out. This opening and closing of valves causes the characteristic lub-dub sound made by the heart as it beats.

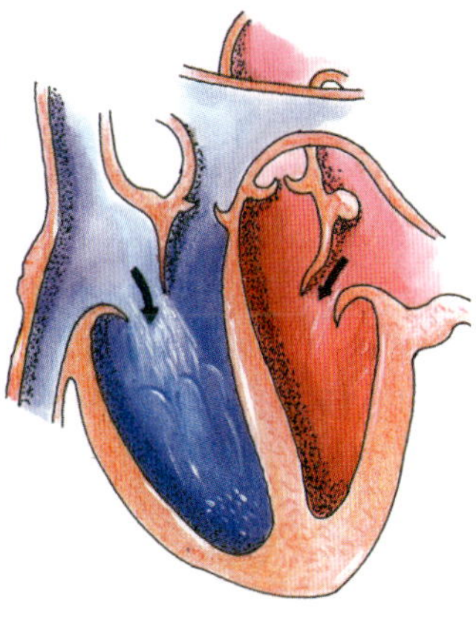

Blood flowing into the ventricles

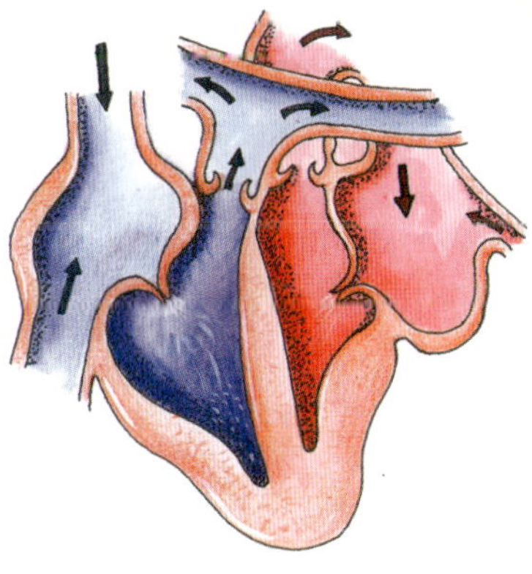

Blood flowing out of the ventricles

Types of blood

Although human beings have the same kind of blood, there are some differences that can only be seen with the help of a microscope. Based on these differences, blood has been divided into four groups – A, B, AB and O. In addition, some people have a certain blood protein present in their blood. This is called the Rhesus, or Rh, factor. Blood types that have this blood protein or the Rh factor have a + sign and those that do not, have a – sign, for example A+ or A-, O+ or O-, and so on.

Try these too:

Bones and Muscles (p 90–91), The Brain and Sensory Organs (p 96–97), Reproduction and Birth (p 98–99), Falling Sick (p 100–101)

The Brain and Sensory Organs

The nervous system is the messaging system of the body. The brain and spinal cord are the most important part of this system and are together called the central nervous system. They are supported by millions of nerves and the sense organs – ears, eyes, nose, tongue and skin.

▾ It's just cerebral
The cerebrum is the largest and most important part of the human brain. The front part of the cerebrum, known as frontal lobe, is responsible for speech, thought and emotion. The parietal lobe, located behind the frontal lobe helps to understand touch and feel pain.

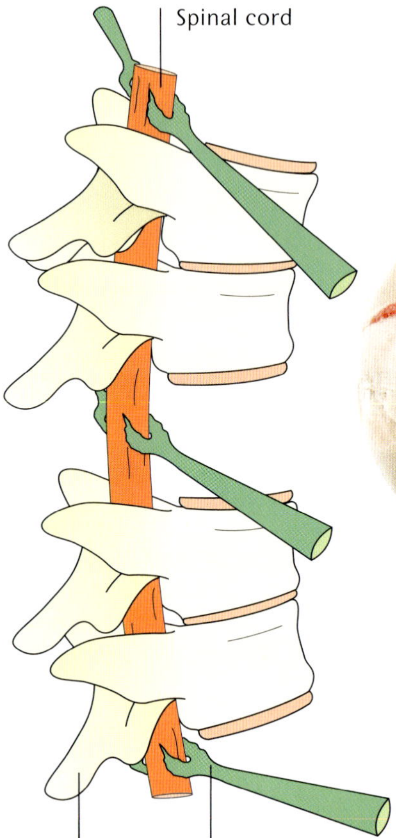

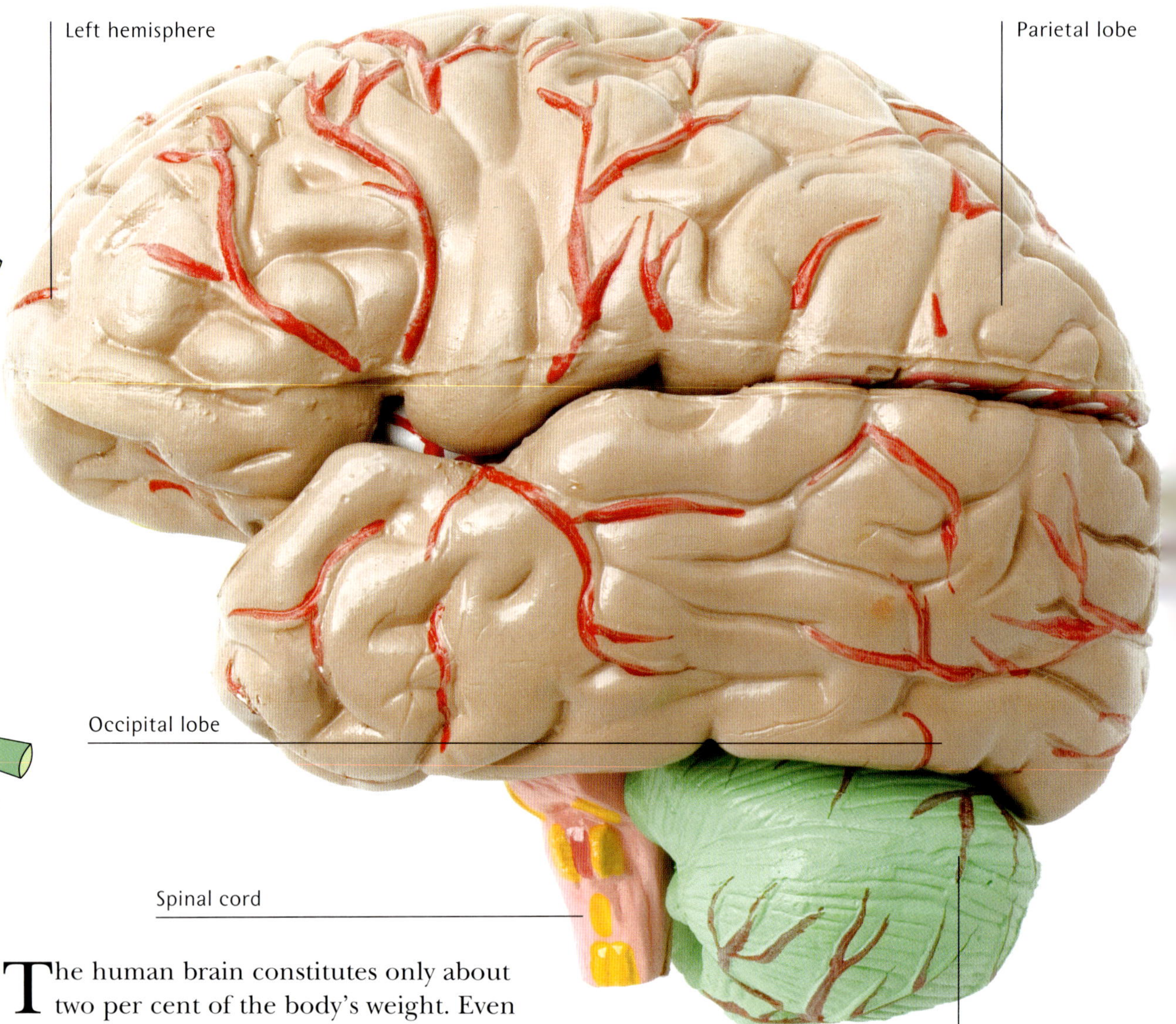

▴ Decoding the message
The spinal cord along with the brain constitute the central nervous system. Thirty-one pairs of spinal nerves also connect the spinal cord to the rest of the body. These nerves help to carry messages to and from the spinal cord to other parts of the body. In most cases, the spinal cord conveys the impulses to the brain for processing. However, in reflex actions, such as pulling one's hand away from fire, the spinal cord processes the impulses.

The human brain constitutes only about two per cent of the body's weight. Even then it is responsible for every activity of a person. It plays a role in every thought that humans think, every memory that they have, and every skill that they develop. The brain also determines a person's personality. In short, a human being cannot function without a brain. This very important organ is also the most vulnerable and delicate part of the body. Even the smallest injury can affect the brain's function.

Therefore, the brain is well protected. Three membranes called meninges surround the brain. The space between the meninges and the brain is filled with cerebrospinal fluid that absorbs shock and protects the brain from infections. The skull forms the outermost layer of protection.

▸ Nerve fibres
A neuron consists of a cell body with a nucleus and one or more fibres. These fibres vary greatly in length. The fibres that carry impulses towards the nucleus are called dendrites, while those which carry impulses away from the nucleus are known as axons.

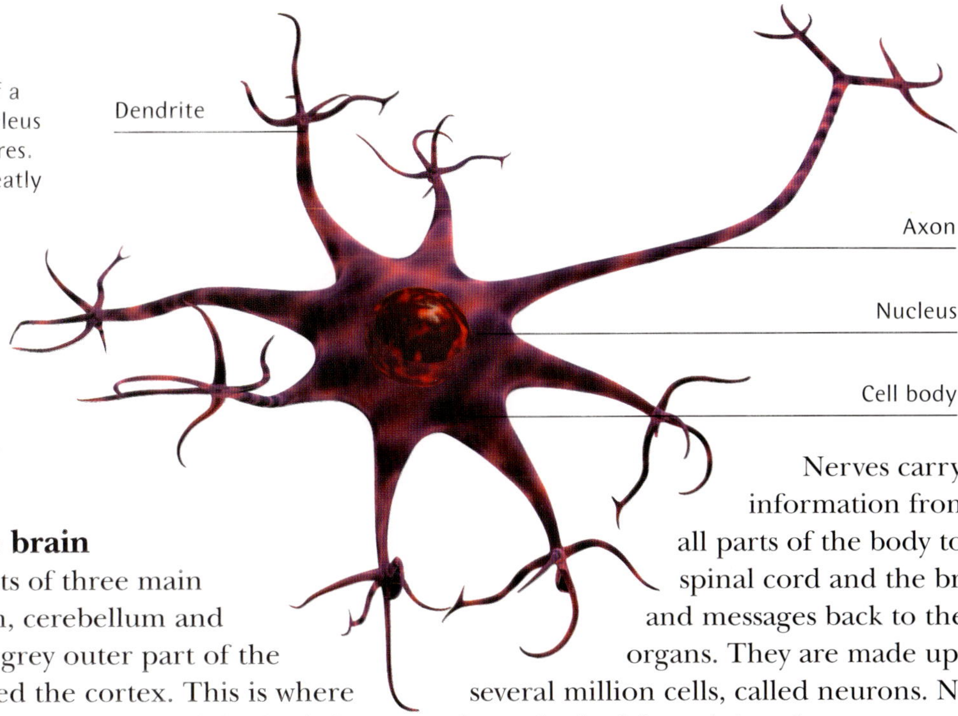

Nerves carry information from all parts of the body to the spinal cord and the brain, and messages back to the organs. They are made up of several million cells, called neurons. Nerves form the body's peripheral nervous system.

Dissecting the brain

The brain consists of three main parts – cerebrum, cerebellum and brain stem. The grey outer part of the cerebrum is called the cortex. This is where information from other parts of the body is received. Within the cortex is a large white matter, which sends messages to the other parts of the body. The cerebrum is further sub-divided into several sections and each section is responsible for a particular function – each communicates with a particular sense organ. Below the cerebrum, towards the back, is the cerebellum. This part of the brain controls our body movements. The brain is connected to the spinal cord through the brain stem. All involuntary activities like breathing, heartbeat and digestion are controlled by the brain stem. It also takes messages from the brain to the spinal cord, which runs from the brain to the lower back, through the backbone. The spinal cord has an outer white layer and an inner grey layer, within which is cerebrospinal fluid. The spinal cord carries information to the brain and messages from the brain to the other organs.

How we see, hear and taste

The brain controls all activities – both of the body and the mind. However, the brain is able to tell us what to do, how to do it, and when to do it, only because it gets all the required information from the five sense organs it is connected to. The eyes, ears, nose, tongue and skin help us to experience a wide range of sensations. The sights that we see, the sounds that we hear, the odours that we smell, the flavours that we taste and the texture, temperature or pain we feel are all converted into electric signals by these sense organs. The electric signals are then sent through nerves to the relevant parts of the brain. The brain processes all the basic information it gets from the sense organs and sends back messages to these organs, helping us to see, hear, smell, taste, feel and respond.

Hormones

The endocrine glands play a very important role in the nervous system. These glands release chemicals called hormones, which travel to the brain and other parts of the body. These hormones affect our bodily functions. There are eight major glands in the human body that produce hormones. Some glands are present only in men and others can be found only in women. The hormones affect the growth of bones and muscles, the balance of minerals and chemicals in the body, and reproduction.

Key facts:

- The right side of the brain is used more by people who are creative, whereas people who are good at mathematics and science tend to use the left side of their brain more often.
- Messages are passed in the form of electrical signals through neurons. However, while moving from one neuron to the next, the electrical signal has to change into a chemical signal. This is because neurons do not touch each other.
- Endocrine glands are ductless glands. This means that they do not have tubes to transport the hormones. Hormones travel through the blood stream by entering the blood stream.

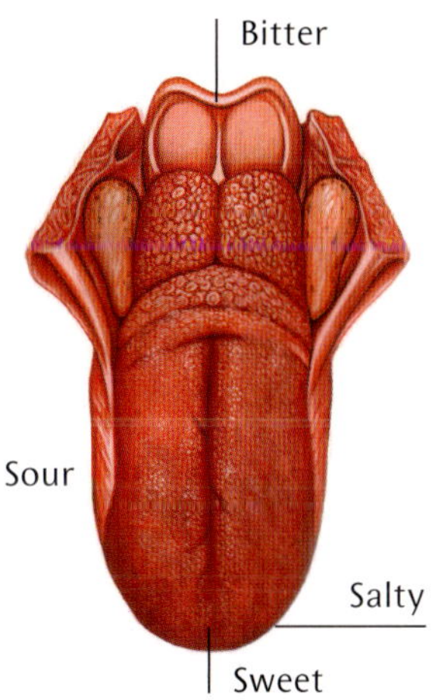

▲ A matter of taste
Different parts of the tongue help to detect different tastes.

Try these too:

External Body Parts (p 88–89), Bones and Muscles (p 90–91), The Heart and Blood Circulation (p 94–95)

Reproduction and Birth

The human body becomes capable of reproduction when the body begins changing and growing during puberty. Puberty in girls begins between the ages of 8 and 11, and in boys it takes place between the ages of 9 and 14.

▾ Born with it!
A woman will have all the eggs that she will ever produce throughout her life from the time she is born. On the other hand, a man begins to produce sperm only when he reaches maturity.

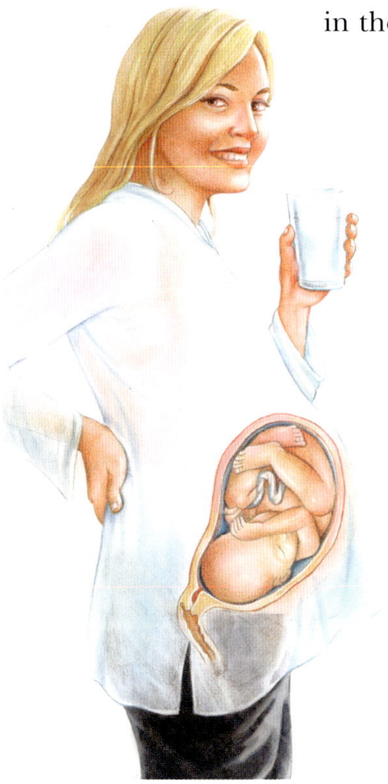

▸ Strong and muscular
The uterus contains some of the strongest muscles in a woman's body. The uterus of a woman who is not pregnant is only 7.5 centimetres (3 inches) long and 5 centimetres (2 inches) wide. However, the strong muscles of the uterus help it to expand to make space for a growing foetus and contract to push the baby out of the body during delivery.

During puberty, endocrine glands release hormones that change the appearance of a person. The body grows and matures, and starts developing adult characteristics. In girls, the body develops breasts and the hips widen. Boys begin to grow body hair and their voice changes. Male and female hormones are produced by special glands in the reproductive system.

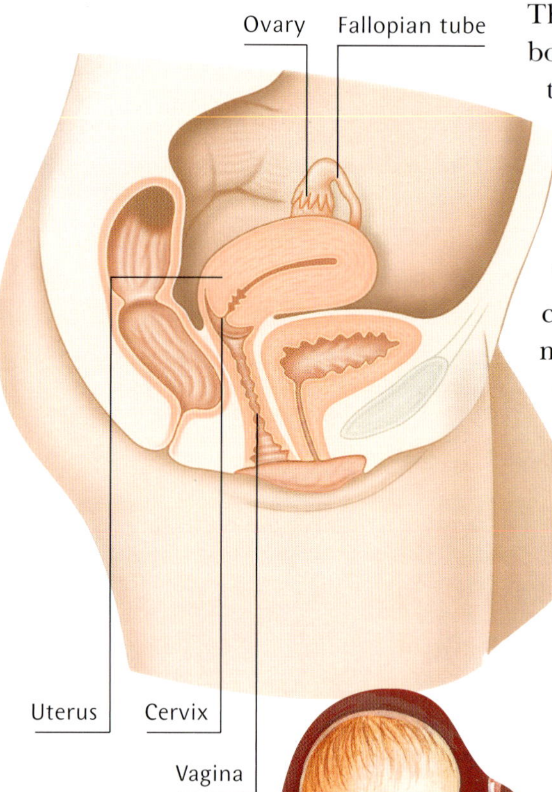

The reproductive organs

The female reproductive system is situated in the pelvic region. It consists of a pair of ovaries, the uterus, two fallopian tubes, the cervix and the vagina. The ovaries are the female endocrine glands – they produce oestrogen, the hormone that changes and prepares the body for adulthood and reproduction. With the onset of puberty, the ovaries begin to produce an egg approximately once a month. This egg is sent into the uterus through the fallopian tubes. The uterus is a sac-like organ that receives the egg. It is connected through an opening called the cervix to the vagina. The vagina provides a passage out of the body. Unfertilized eggs break up and leave the body through the vagina. This is called menstruation. The male reproductive system is situated near the pelvic region, but outside the body. It consists of a pair of testes, their related ducts, and the penis. The testes are protected by a sac-like cover called the scrotum. The testes produce the male hormone called testosterone as well as sperm. The sperm mature within three weeks, after which they are either ejaculated out through the penis or reabsorbed by the man's body.

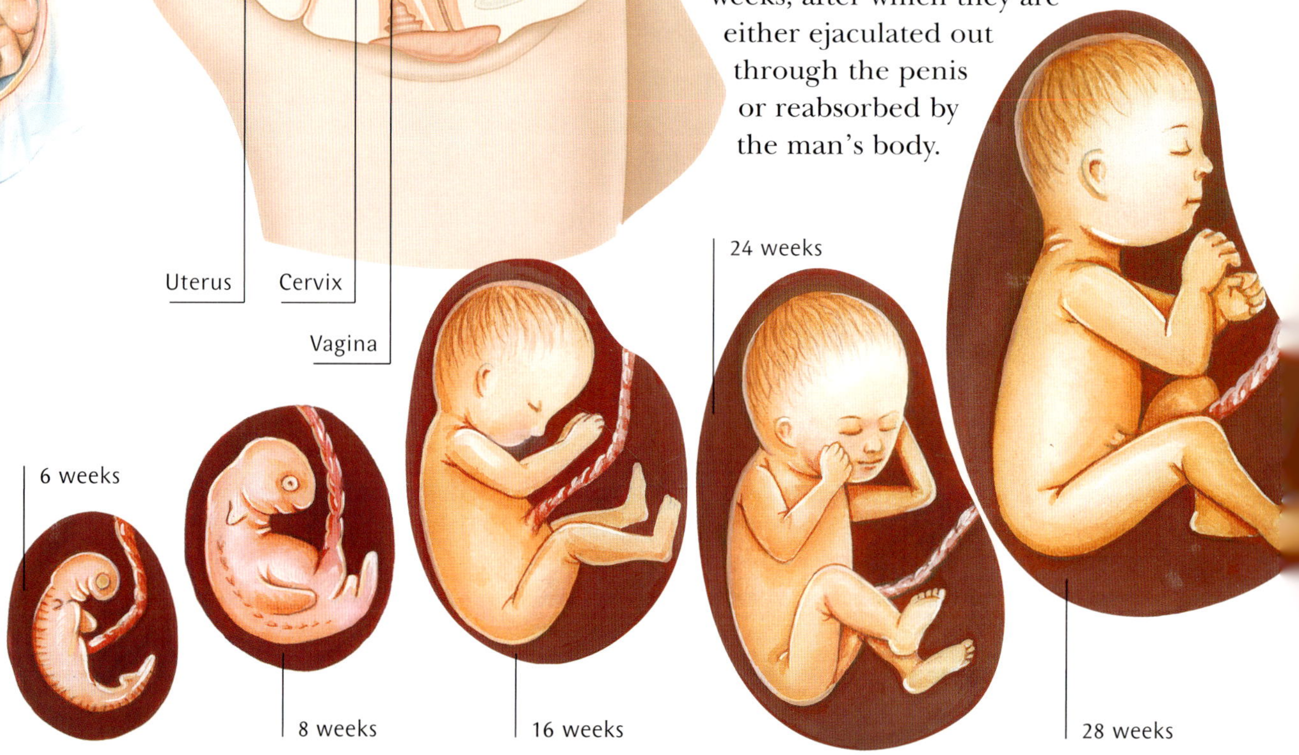

Inside the uterus

When sperm enter the female body, many die, but those that survive travel through the uterus to the egg within the fallopian tubes. If a sperm is able to attach itself to the egg, fertilization takes place. The fertilized egg then attaches itself to the uterus wall and prepares itself for growth.

A baby is born

The period during which the fertilized egg grows until it becomes a baby and is ready to come out is called 'pregnancy'. A woman is pregnant for 38 to 40 weeks. At the beginning of the pregnancy, the fertilized egg grows a cover to protect itself. This protective cover is called the placenta and is attached to the wall of the uterus. The egg gradually grows into an embryo, and after a few weeks it is called a foetus. The foetus gets food, water and clean blood from the mother through the umbilical cord, which is connected to the foetus at its belly button. The umbilical cord absorbs the necessary nutrients through the wall of the uterus. It also passes out unclean blood and waste matter into the blood to be excreted.

When the foetus is fully grown and ready to come out, the uterus begins to push it out. The head of the foetus usually comes out first. Sometimes the uterus and the cervix have to go through several hours of labour before the child can be delivered. After the baby is born, the placenta also is pushed out. The umbilical cord is then cut, as the new born baby is now ready to be fed through its mouth.

▾ Soft and sensitive
Part of the penis is covered by a loose fold of skin called the foreskin. The penis is a spongy organ, which contains several million nerve endings making it the most sensitive organ in a man's body. The penis does not have a bone. It becomes erect when the arteries in the penis dilate, filling the spongy erectile tissue chambers with more blood and causing the penis to lengthen and become stiff.

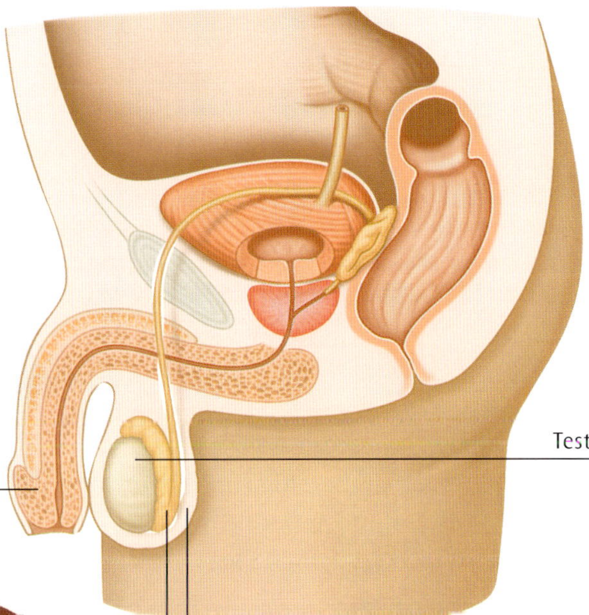

▾ Growing up!
The picture shows the various stages of foetal development throughout the three trimesters.

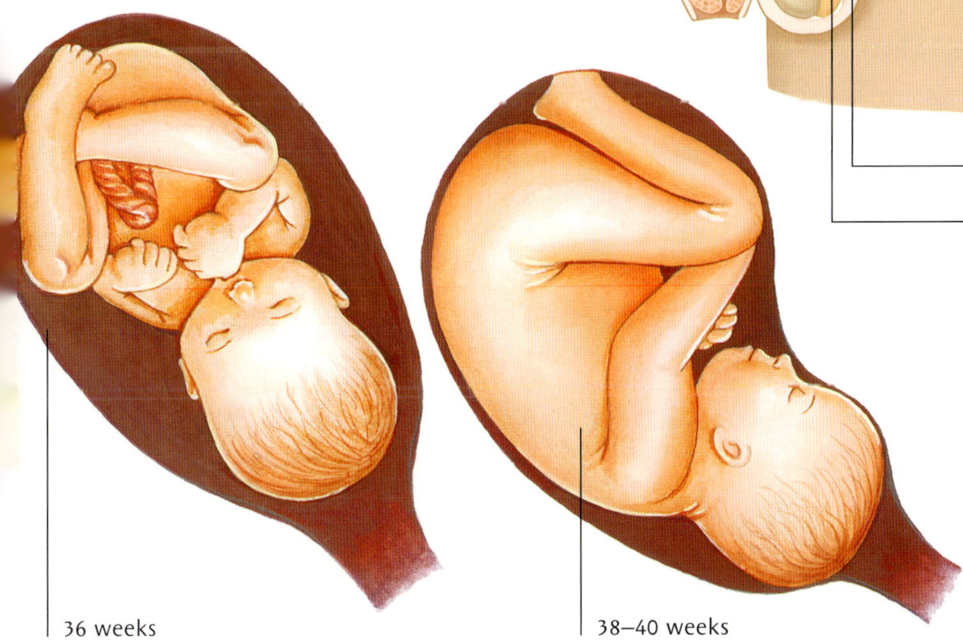

Key facts:

- The 40 weeks of pregnancy are divided into three trimesters of roughly 13 weeks each. It is only in the second trimester that the embryo begins to resemble a human being. A foetus has to complete the first two trimesters for it to have a chance of surviving.
- The female reproductive cycle ends at about the age of 50. The body stops producing oestrogen and eggs, and menstruation stops. However, the male reproductive system can continue to produce sperm until the very end.
- Sperm is suspended in a milky white, sticky fluid called semen. This is a mixture of secretions from three glands in the male reproductive system. Semen provides energy to the sperm. Every millilitre of semen contains between 50–130 million sperm.

Try these too:

Bones and Muscles (p 90–91), Digestion and Excretion (92–93), The Brain and Sensory Organs (p 96–97), Falling Sick (100–101)

Amniotic fluid

Within the placenta, the embryo is cushioned in amniotic fluid. This is a watery liquid that contains proteins, carbohydrates and other energy-giving substances. Low or high levels of amniotic fluid may be dangerous for the embryo and in some cases can mean that it suffers from birth defects.

Falling Sick

When all our organs, systems, bones and muscles are working well, we enjoy good health. However, when any one of these has trouble, it affects other parts of the body as well – and we suffer from discomfort or disease.

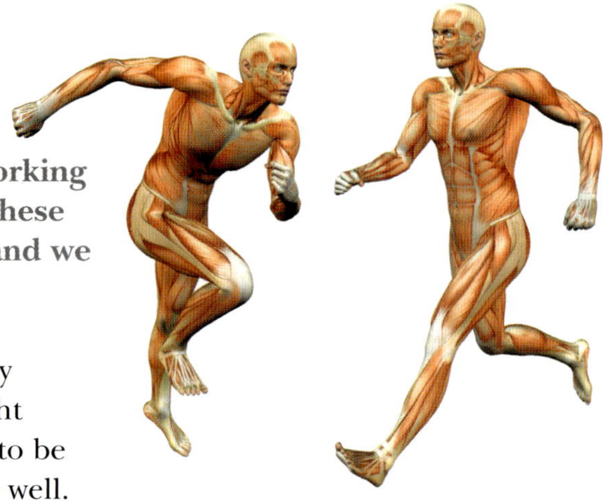

◂ Keeping fit
Exercising helps you to stay fit. Routine exercise strengthens the muscles and improves the functioning of the other organs in the body.

Key facts:

- In 1796, Edward Jenner, an English doctor, invented the vaccine to fight smallpox. He noticed that people who had had cowpox, a mild disease, did not get smallpox. So he inoculated a small boy with the cowpox virus and, after a few days, he inoculated him with smallpox only to prove his theory correct. Vaccines have put an end to smallpox, one of the most infectious diseases known to man. They have also reduced the occurrence of polio, measles, mumps, rubella and chickenpox.
- When we suffer from pain, the hypothalamus and the pituitary glands of the endocrine system produce chemicals called endorphins. Endorphins are natural painkillers that act on the nervous system and lessen pain.
- Doctors sometimes give tablets called placebos to treat illnesses. Placebos do not contain any medication. They are just used to reassure the patient and make them believe that they will recover.

The human body is much like any other machine. It needs the right fuel, at the right time. It also needs to be exercised regularly and looked after well. We can fall ill for many reasons. Bad eating habits, no exercise, and lack of hygiene can cause several of the illnesses that we suffer from. An imbalanced or unhealthy diet slows down the working of our organs and results in diseases like diabetes and hypertension. Similarly, lack of exercise makes our bodies stiff and inflexible, and more prone to diseases like osteoporosis and spondylitis.

Alien attacks

Not all diseases are caused by carelessness alone. Sometimes diseases are caused by harmful viruses or bacteria entering our circulatory system. These may enter our bodies from others who are unwell, from stale and unhygienic food or water, or from our surroundings. The common cold, pneumonia and flu, as well as more life-threatening illnesses like cholera, tuberculosis and AIDS are all infectious diseases.

Body breakdown

Another cause of disease is body malfunction. Sometimes organs speed up their functions, slow down, or stop working. This causes imbalances in the body because of too much or too little of certain chemicals, leading to depression and thyroidism. Cancer is caused when sometimes bad cells in a specific part of the body multiply swiftly and destroy the good cells.

▸ Eating healthy
A balanced diet is very important for a healthy life. This food pyramid explains the kind and amount of nutrients required each day to keep a person healthy.

Diagnosing disease

As the number of diseases keeps increasing, science finds more and more ways to understand and treat the human body. Early doctors treated patients after checking their pulse and the colour of their eyes and tongue. Today, doctors diagnose diseases using complex and more precise equipment like ultrasonographs, CT scanners and endoscopes. The endoscope, a slim instrument with a camera, is inserted into the body so that doctors can have a close look at the organs inside.

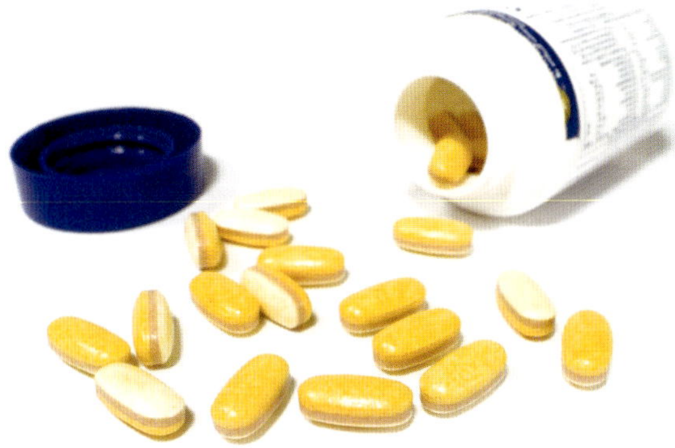

▲ Bitter pill
Swallowing that pill can be very hard. Pills usually leave a bitter taste in the mouth. Some, however, have a smooth gelatinous covering that contains the bitter medicine inside. These capsules are also easy to swallow. Once the pill enters the body, the gelatin case is dissolved by the digestive juices to release the medicine

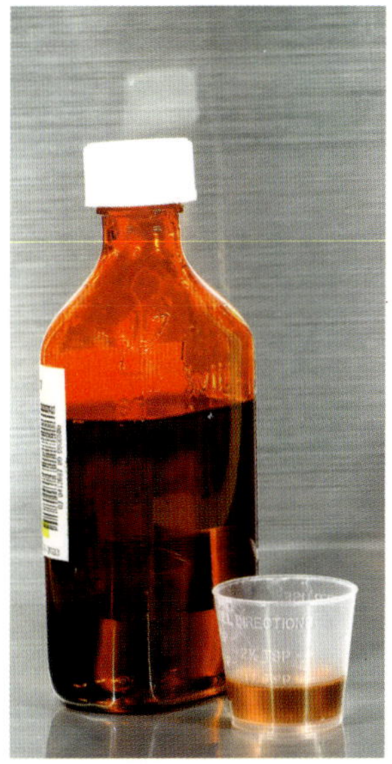

▲ ▼ Sting of health
Apart from introducing disease-fighting agents through oral medications like syrups and pills, doctors can also inject them into the body using syringes. Liquid medicine is administered through a hollow needle into the skin, muscles or directly into the bloodstream through the veins.

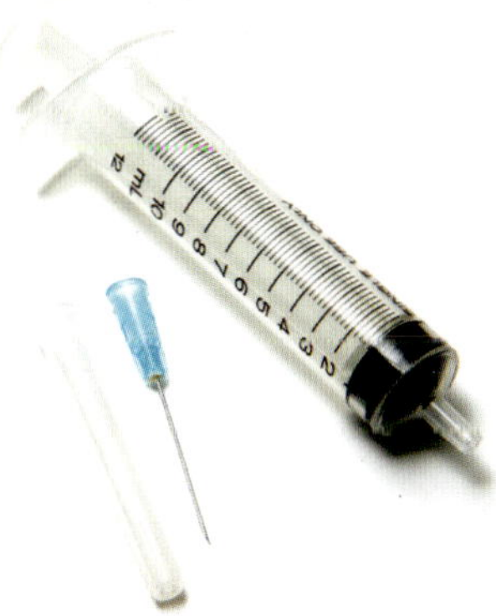

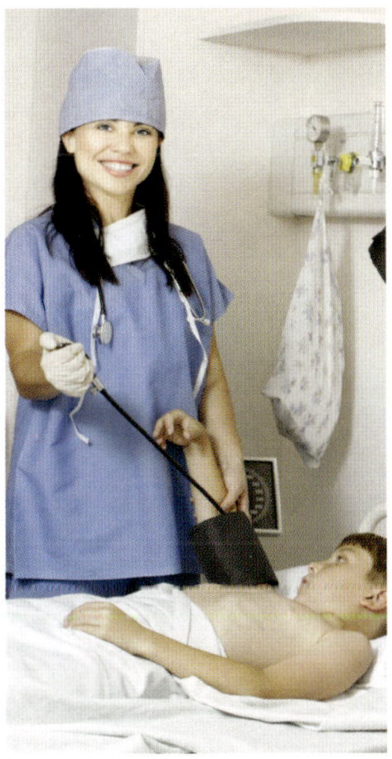

▸ Checking up
People usually visit doctors when they are not keeping well. They can also go for routine check-ups to make sure that their body is functioning properly.

Fighting back

When infections and disease attack the body, its first response is to fight back. In the process, the body raises its own temperature to kill the infectious bodies that have entered the blood stream. The white blood cells immediately start attacking the alien bodies in an attempt to kill the infection. These cells even make special antibodies, or proteins, that can match the strength of the infections and fight against them. However, the immune system is not always able to fight the illness all by itself. Therefore, we have to help it by taking medicines. Medicines can be in the form of pills or syrup. They mostly contain chemicals that help to fight diseases. Some medicines can be bought from supermarkets, while the stronger ones can be bought only at a pharmacy, and with a doctor's prescription.

Being prepared

Some illnesses can be avoided by taking medication beforehand. This can be in the form of a vaccination. Vaccinations are injections containing a strain of weak bacteria that causes a particular disease. The injected bacteria immunizes the body and prevents similar bacteria from attacking it. Diseases like measles, mumps, hepatitis and tetanus can be avoided by vaccination.

Try these too:

External Body Parts (p 88–89), Bones and Muscles (p 90–91), Digestion and Excretion (p 92–93) The Heart and Blood Circulation (p 94–95), The Brain and Sensory Organs (p 96–97), The Scientific Revolution (p 142–143)

North America

North America forms the upper part of the continent of America. The continent is separated from South America by a narrow strip of land called the Isthmus of Panama. This strip of land is usually considered a part of North America alone. North America is the third largest continent after Asia and Africa, and the fourth most populated continent in the world. It is situated in the Northern Hemisphere (above the equator).

Key facts:

- Lakes Superior, Huron, Erie and Ontario, on the border of Canada and the United States, and Lake Michigan, in the United States, are together known as the Great Lakes. They form the largest freshwater surface on Earth. They are interconnected by channels and flow into the Atlantic through the St Lawrence Seaway, the world's longest navigable waterway.
- The Grand Canyon is a 446 kilometre- (277 mile-) long gorge in Arizona, in the United States. It was formed by the Colorado River, which has, over time, eroded the soil to make a steep-sided passage that is about 1.6 kilometres (1 mile) deep in some places.
- The western part of North America is one of the most earthquake-prone regions in the world. At least 4,600 earthquakes have occured in parts of Canada, the United States and Mexico in the past 100 years. This is because the Pacific Plate under the ocean keeps colliding with and rubbing against the North American Plate.

North America is surrounded by the Arctic Ocean in the north, the Caribbean Sea in the south, the Atlantic Ocean in the east and the Pacific Ocean in the west. The main land mass of North America is divided into three countries – Canada in the north, which occupies the largest part of the continent; the United States of America in the middle; and Mexico in the south. North America can also be divided into four main geographical regions. They are the Great Plains that stretch from the Gulf of Mexico in the south, to the northern parts of Canada; the mountainous west, including the Rocky Mountains and the low-lying Great Basin between the Rockies and the coastal mountain range, the Sierra Nevada; the high north-eastern plateau called the Canadian Shield; and the Appalachian Mountains in the southeast.

People power

Today, the population of the continent includes three major groups of people – Native American, European-American and African-American. The earliest inhabitants of the continent were indigenous Native American tribes such as the Inuit, Hupa, Sioux and Mohawk.

Arrival of the Europeans

By the 16th century, Spanish and Portuguese colonies were established in Mexico, and in the 17th century several British and French colonies were settled in the United States and Canada. Thereafter, the spread of the European population was so swift that by the end of the 18th century there were about 3.2 million European-Americans.

▲ **Name game**
It is commonly believed that the continents of North and South America were named after Amerigo Vespucci, a famous Italian explorer of the 16th century.

The European settlers brought a large number of African slaves to America, who later became an important part of the American population, especially after they were set free following the American Civil War. The Native American populations, however, were severely depleted due to war, disease and loss of their homes. Today, the United States, Canada and Mexico also have sizable Asian immigrant populations, including people from India, Japan and China. In Canada, English and French are the two official languages. The United States does not have an official language, but English is the most commonly used language. In Mexico, Spanish is the official language.

▼ **The land of opportunity**
People from all over the world come to North America, especially the United States, to fulfil their dreams.

▲ **Prairie land**
North American prairies are most suitable for growing wheat, barley and maize. The Prairie Provinces of Canada (Manitoba, Saskatchewan and Alberta) are especially suited and are one of the world's top wheat producers.

▼ **New York, New York!**
The city of New York in the United States is the financial capital of the world.

Central America and the West Indies

Further south of Mexico are seven small countries, which form Central America. They are Belize, Costa Rica, Nicaragua, Honduras, El Salvador, Panama and Guatemala. These countries are independent, and have their own governments and currencies. However, El Salvador uses the US dollar. To the southeast of the main land mass of North America, in the Caribbean Sea, are numerous small island nations. These are collectively called the West Indies. They include Cuba, Jamaica, Barbados, the Virgin Islands, as well as many others.

Flora and fauna

The climate in the continent of North America varies greatly from north to south and east to west. This variation in weather creates a wide variety of terrain, ranging from the icy cold tundra to the temperate forests, grasslands, deserts and even warm, tropical forests. Trees that are most commonly found in this region are maple, oak, chestnut, birch, cedar and pine. The fauna in these areas is equally diverse and includes big cats such as mountain lions and jaguars. Reptiles such as rattlesnakes and geckos, and birds such as hawks, owls, turkeys and roadrunners are also a part of the North American landscape. Foxes, wolves, bobcats, polar bears, grizzly bears and black bears are also found here.

▲ **Huge and menacing**
The grizzly is second to only the polar bear in size.

Try these too:

Features of the Earth (p 22–23), The Native Americans (p 124–125), New Lands – the Age of Exploration (p 134–135)

South America

South America is the fourth largest continent in terms of land mass and ranks fifth in population. The South American continent is connected to the continent of North America and lies below it. Most parts of this continent lie south of the equator, although a small part lies above it. South America lies between the Pacific and Atlantic Oceans.

Key facts:

- The countries of the Western Hemisphere located south of the United States are together known as Latin America. Most people from these countries speak Spanish and Portuguese, which are derived from the Latin language.
- The table-like mountains on the Guiana Highlands are called *tepuis*. These mountains were formed millions of years ago. The Auyán-Tepui in Venezuela is home to the world's highest waterfall, the Angel Falls. These falls drop 979 metres (3,212 feet).
- Atacama Desert in Chile stretches from the Pacific Ocean to the Andes. This area has become dry and desert-like as it receives very little rain. It is rich in salt basins and minerals. In fact, the soil here is so rich in minerals that they can simply be dug out from the surface.
- The Andes is the longest mountain range in the world. It stretches across nearly 7, 200 kilometres (4,500 miles). The northern part of this mountain range lies close to the equator and the southern end is close to Antarctica.

South America is made up of 12 independent countries, all of which, except for French Guiana, have their own government and currency. French Guiana is a member of the European Union.

The South American landscape

The continent of South America can be geographically divided into five main regions – the Andean region, the Guiana Highlands, the Amazon Rainforest, the Brazilian Highlands and the Pampas. The Andean region runs from top to bottom along the western side of the continent. It includes the area on each side of the Andes Mountains. The Guiana Highlands along the north-eastern coast are home to some of the most impressive table (flat top) mountains. The Brazilian Highlands run along the eastern coastal areas. The Amazon Rainforest lies between the Guiana and Brazilian highlands, on either side of the mighty Amazon River. The Pampas are fertile plains that lie south of the Brazilian Highlands.

▲ **South America's green canopy**
The Andes mountain range extends continuously along the west coast of South America. This mountain range is about 7,000 kilometres (4,400 miles) long and has an average height of about 4,000 metres (13,000 feet).

▼ **A city by the sea**
A view of the Brazilian city of Rio de Janeiro from behind the famous statue of Jesus Christ, known as Christ the Redeemer located on top of the Corcovado mountain overlooking the city. Rio is known for its tourist beaches of Copacabana and Ipanema and its colourful carnival held every year.

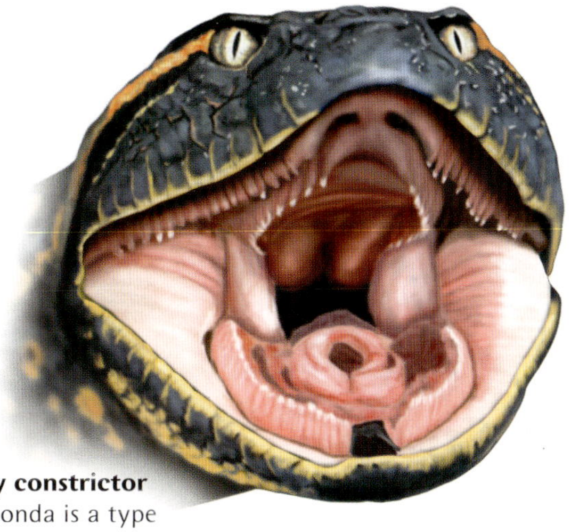

▲ **Heavy constrictor**
The anaconda is a type of boa found in the Amazonian rainforests of South America. Also known as water boa, it squeezes its prey to death and is therefore called a constrictor. The green anaconda, the largest member of its family, can grow up to 10 metres (33 feet) in length.

▶ **The green canopy**
The Amazon Rainforest spreads across as many as nine countries. About 60 per cent of this rainforest is located only in Brazil. It constitutes over half of the world's remaining rainforests.

People power

The original inhabitants of South America were native tribes. The early tribes were nomadic hunters, but later civilizations, such as those of the Chavín and Inca ruled various parts of the continent. In the 1530s, with the arrival of the Spanish conquistadors followed by the Portuguese, Europeans began to settle in South America. Africans were brought to South America as slaves.

Today, most South American countries show a strong Spanish influence, as many of them were under the Spanish until the early 1800s. The main languages spoken in South America are Spanish and Portuguese. However, other native languages, as well as English and French, are spoken in some places.

Flora and fauna

The main geographic regions of the South American continent have different climates and a varied range of plants and animals. A large part of the continent is close to the equator and therefore very hot, but the southern tip is cooler and some parts are very cold. The flora includes beech, ironwood, ginkgo, biloba and savannahs.

The Amazon

The Amazon is one of the longest rivers in the world and contains more water than any other river. This mighty river has its source in the Andes, near the Pacific Ocean. It flows across the South American continent into the Atlantic Ocean, through Brazil, Peru, Bolivia, Colombia and Ecuador. The rainforests adorning the banks of the river cover nearly 6,000,000 square kilometres (2,300,000 square miles). They make up about half of the remaining rainforests in the world. These rainforests are home to about 2,000 species of birds and mammals, several thousand varieties of plants and trees and almost 2.5 million types of insects.

Animals such as mountain lions, jaguars, llamas, spectacled bears, wolves and deer; birds including the flamingo, harpy eagles, woodpeckers and condor; and reptiles such as the huge anaconda, iguana and crocodiles are found across the continent.

◀ **Tango in harmony**
South America is a delightful mix of Native Americans, Africans and Europeans. This is evident in its food, culture, music and arts.

Try these too:

Features of the Earth (p 22–23), Seasons and Weather (p 32–33), The Incas and Aztecs (p 130–131), New Lands – the Age of Exploration (p 134–135)

Australia and Oceania

Oceania is a collection of several big and small islands in the Pacific Ocean. The largest of these is Australia. In fact, Australia is a continent by itself. Oceania also includes New Zealand, which is made up of two large islands – the North and South islands, and several other smaller ones.

Key facts:

- The hot, dry, desert-like central part of Australia is called the 'outback'. This is the only place where the Aboriginal tribes continue to live in their traditional way. However, very few people live in this area. Nearly 90 per cent of Australia's population lives along the coastline.
- The most ancient living reptile species, the tuatara, is found in New Zealand. It belonged to a group of beak-headed reptiles that first appeared over 200 million years ago. The tuatara can live up to 100 years.
- The first Europeans to settle in Australia were prisoners from Britain. In the 1780s, when Britain's prisons were full and there was no place to keep criminals and convicts, the British government sent shiploads of prisoners to Australia.

The small islands in Oceania are divided into Melanesia, Micronesia and Polynesia. Melanesia is a group of islands towards the northern and eastern parts of Australia. It includes countries like Papua New Guinea (which shares a land border with Indonesia), Fiji, Vanuatu, and the Solomon Islands. North of Melanesia is the Micronesia group of islands. There are hundreds of Micronesian islands, the most well-known of these are Palau, Kiribati, Guam, the Marshall Islands and the Federated States of Micronesia (a group of over 600 islands and islets). To the east of Australia, situated in the southern and central Pacific Ocean, are the Polynesian islands. There are more than 1,000 Polynesian islands, which include Samoa, Tuvalu, Tonga, the Cook Islands and Easter Island. Many of Oceania's islands are territories of other countries, such as the United States, the United Kingdom, France, New Zealand and Australia. Hawaii, which is a state of the United States, is part of the Oceania group of islands.

▲ An unknown continent
The early inhabitants of Australia are believed to have come from Southeast Asia about 40,000 years ago. The continent remained unknown to others until the 17th century when Dutch explorers first came here. The British arrived in the late 1700s and soon colonized the region.

▼ The blood rock
Uluru, which is also called Ayers Rock, is the largest single rock known in the world. It is 348 metres (986 feet) tall and measures 9.4 kilometres (5.8 miles) in circumference. The aboriginal people of Australia believe that this region was once covered by an ocean. This ocean threw up the blood-coloured rock to show its grief for the people who died in a battle fought on its shores.

▶ Truly Australian
The koala, along with the kangaroo, is considered a symbol of Australia. This marsupial is found along the eastern coast of the country. Its name has been derived from an Aboriginal word that means "does not drink". This cuddly animal feeds solely on the leaves of eucalyptus trees.

People power

Australia and most Oceania islands were once populated by Aboriginal people, who sometimes moved around and settled on new islands, as the Maori did when they travelled to New Zealand about 1,000–1,500 years ago. In the 19th century, Europeans began settling in Australia and in various parts of Oceania. Today, the populations of these islands are a mixture of Aboriginal people, Europeans and descendants of Asian settlers. English is spoken in most countries, but Aboriginal populations also speak their own languages.

Flora and fauna

A large part of Australia is a desert, surrounded by dry grasslands. The weather is cool and temperate in the southeastern parts, while in the north it is warm and tropical.

▲ **City down under**
A view of the Sydney Harbour, showing the Sydney Opera House and the Harbour Bridge.

Some animals and birds, which are found only in Australia, are kangaroos, platypus, emus, wombats and koalas. The flora of Oceania is similar to that found in Indonesia and the Philippines. Some trees that are commonly found here are acacia, ash, yucca, sassafras and rhododendron. There are very few native land animals on these islands. However, there are several species of birds and different types of lizards, crocodiles, snakes, insects and fish.

Try these too:

Features of the Earth (p 22–23), New Lands – the Age of Exploration (p 134–135), Colonial Empires (p 136–137)

Great Barrier Reef

The Great Barrier Reef is the largest coral reef in the world. It is situated in the Coral Sea just off the coast of Queensland, in northeast Australia. This reef, which is more than 2,000 kilometres (1,243 miles) long, consists of close to 900 small islands and about 3,000 coral formations. This natural wonder is so huge that it can even be seen from outer space.

Europe

Europe is not a geographically separate continent like most of the other continents. It is, in fact, the western part of the huge Eurasian land mass. Europe is bound by the Arctic Ocean to the north, the Atlantic to the west and the Mediterranean Sea, Black Sea and Caspian Sea to the south. In the east, it merges with Asia. There is no clear boundary between the two continents. However, the Ural Mountains, which run through the western edge of central Russia, partially separate the two continents.

▲ **Peninsular Europe**
The European continent is a collection of several peninsulas, both large and small.

Key facts:

- The Alps stretch across several European countries including Austria, Slovenia, Italy, Switzerland, Liechtenstein, France and Germany. They consist of the Western Alps and the Eastern Alps. The highest peak in the Western Alps is Mont Blanc, on the border between France and Italy. The highest peak in the Eastern Alps is Piz Bernina in Switzerland.
- The northernmost parts of Norway are located above the Arctic Circle. This particular region is also known as the 'land of the midnight Sun'. This is because every year during the summer, for several days, the Sun does not set and during the winter, for many days, the Sun does not rise.
- The European Union (EU) was formed in 1992 to bring all European countries together for their common good. There are a total of 25 member countries in this union. The euro is the common currency that can be used in the member countries.

Europe is the world's second smallest continent and its population is the third largest. It is made up of more than 40 independent countries. The European continent has several peninsulas (land covered on three sides by water) on its southern and western sides. The British Isles and Iceland, which are separate islands, are also part of Europe. The southern peninsulas are hilly and mountainous, as is the land just north of them. This area contains the Pyrenees, Alps and the Carpathian Mountains. North of these mountains are low plains, valleys and plateaus. In the northern Scandinavian Peninsula, the Scandinavian Mountains run along the western side, while the eastern side is flat and low-lying.

Due to the eastern boundary of Europe merging with Asia, the areas of some countries straddle both continents. These are Russia, Kazakhstan, Armenia, Turkey, Cyprus, Azerbaijan and Georgia. Europe can be divided into four parts – Northern, Southern, Eastern and Western Europe. The Western European countries are more advanced and developed, whereas many Eastern European countries are underdeveloped due to years of political upheavals and conflicts.

▼ **Europe's cultural capital**
Bruges, a Belgian port city is filled with medieval buildings and has a fine collection of medieval and modern art.

◂ **The Holy city**
Vatican City is the smallest independent state in the world. It is an enclave of Rome and is ruled by the Pope. The most famous landmark in the Vatican city is St Peter's Basilica.

▴ **The mighty Alps**
The Alps are divided into Western and Eastern Alps. The Western Alps are located in Italy, France and Switzerland, while the Eastern Alps run through Austria, Germany, Italy, Slovenia, Lichtenstein and Switzerland.

People power

Humans first began settling in Europe about 40,000 years ago. Early civilizations, trade, and industrial development have led to the movement and mixing of races. One native tribe that still exists is the Laplanders of Scandinavia. The continent is divided into many different countries, most of which have their own language, which means that many different languages are spoken here.

Flora and fauna

As human beings have lived in Europe for so many thousands of years, many of the forests and natural vegetation have been reduced by agriculture and grazing by cattle. However, there are still many spruce and pine forests in the north; oak, beech and birch in the central parts of Europe; and cypress and olive trees in the south. Europe's native wildlife includes animals, such as the brown bear, wolf, fox, lynx, wildcat, hedgehog and badger; reptiles, such as the adder and viper; and birds such as owls, hawks, vultures and eagles.

Countries in Europe

Northern Europe:
Norway, Sweden, Finland, Iceland, the Republic of Ireland, Denmark, the Faroe Islands, Estonia, Latvia, Lithuania and the United Kingdom
Southern Europe:
Spain, Portugal, Gibraltar, Greece, Andorra, Albania, Italy, Croatia Bosnia and Herzegovina, San Marino, Vatican City, Cyprus, Serbia and Montenegro, Malta, Slovenia, Turkey and Macedonia
Eastern Europe:
Belarus, Bulgaria, Czech Republic, Hungary, Moldova, Poland, Romania, Russia, Slovakia and Ukraine
Western Europe:
Belgium, Luxembourg, Liechtenstein, the Netherlands, France, Germany, Switzerland, Austria and Monaco

▴ **Pride of Paris**
The Eiffel Tower in Paris, France, is one of the most recognized monuments in the world.

Try these too:

Europe in the Middle Ages (p 126–127), The Renaissance (p 132–133), Ancient Architecture (p 158–159), Modern Architecture (p 160–161)

Africa

Africa is the second largest continent in the world. It lies south of Europe, joined to Asia by the Isthmus of Suez and separated from Europe by the Mediterranean Sea. To the west lies the Atlantic and to the east, the Red Sea and the Indian Ocean. The equator cuts across the main land mass.

Key facts:

- Nearly half of Africa's plant and animal species are found in the rainforests in north-west and central Africa. These rainforests are the second largest in the world. However, today nearly 90 per cent of this region has been destroyed by humans. This has in turn destroyed the habitats of several native species of animals and of the pygmy tribes.
- The 'Cradle of Humankind' is the earliest known site of human civilization on Earth. Situated close to Johannesburg, in South Africa, this site consists of several limestone caves within which prehistoric fossils have been well preserved.
- Lakes Victoria, Tanganyika, Albert, Edward and Kivu are the Great Lakes of Africa. They are located in the Great Rift Valley in East Africa. Lake Victoria is the world's second largest freshwater lake.
- The Nile is the world's longest river. It has two arms: the White Nile (the longest arm), which begins in Lake Victoria in East Africa, and the Blue Nile, which begins in Lake Tana in Ethiopia. The Nile drains into the Mediterranean Sea.

There are 54 countries on the African mainland and nearby islands. Africa has a population of more than 800 million, which is the second highest among all continents. Sudan, in the north, is Africa's largest country and the Gambia, in the west, is the smallest. However, the island republic of Seychelles is even smaller than the Gambia. The continent can be divided into seven main regions. They are the Sahara desert in the north, the Sahel, or dry areas bordering the southern side of the Sahara, the rainforests in the northwest, the Ethiopian Highlands in the northeast, mineral-rich South Africa, the Great Lakes in the east, and the savannah, or grasslands, further east of the Great Lakes.

People power

The native people of Africa can be divided into North Africans and sub-Saharan Africans. The native tribes of the north were the Berbers but, in the 7th century, the Arabs settled along the northern coast and drove the Berbers deep into the Sahara and beyond, into the Sahel.

Sub-Saharan tribes include Basarwa, or the Bushmen of the Kalahari Desert, the Masai of Kenya, the Twa pygmies and Tutsi of west and central Africa, the Amhara and Gurage of Ethiopia. In the 16th century, the Portuguese came to Africa to trade. They were followed by Dutch, British, French and German settlers. British colonists settled in large numbers in South Africa, Rhodesia and to a smaller extent in Kenya, whereas French colonists settled in Algeria and other parts of north and west Africa.

▼ **Tribal homes**
Many African tribes continue to live in small, mud houses with thatched roofs, some of which are brightly coloured.

▲ **Human race**
In the mid-20th century, anthropologists discovered bones that proved that the human race originated in the Dark Continent. From the bones, scientists were able to deduce that humans probably inhabited Africa as long as seven million years ago.

▲ **The mother city**
The oldest city in South Africa, Cape Town is also one of the most beautiful cities in the world with several peaks rising high in and around it.

Flora and fauna

Most parts of Africa have hot tropical weather. The areas along the northern coastline have Mediterranean trees and plants like cypress, pine, oak and olive. In the Sahara, the main vegetation is the date palm, while acacia and baobab are common in its cooler parts. The wildlife in these areas includes a variety of snakes, scorpions, camels, giraffes, foxes and warthogs. The west African rainforests are home to a range of animals like okapi, elephants, pygmy hippos and gorillas. South Africa is home to a wide variety of plant and animal life. The giant protea and thick-leaved small plants are the most characteristic vegetation of these parts. The most common animals here are the impala and springbok deer, white rhino, baboon and zebra. The savannah is also the home to the mighty African lions, elephants and antelope.

▲ **Standing tall**
Kilimanjaro, in Tanzania, is the highest mountain in Africa. This mountain has three peaks and is a dormant volcano. The central peak, Kibo, which is more than 5,800 metres (19,300 feet) tall, is the highest point in the continent. Although the mountain is very close to the equator, this peak is covered with snow throughout the year.

Try these too:

Features of the Earth (p 22–23), The First Mammals and Birds (p 82–83), Ancient Mesopotamia and Egypt (p 116–117)

◀ **The king of savannah**
The lion, the most majestic of all animals, is mainly found in the African savannah. Lions were once found in abundance across the Dark Continent. Today they are confined to sanctuaries and other protected areas.

◀ **Life on the desert**
Sahara, the largest desert in the world, divides the continent of Africa into North and Sub-Saharan Africa. Today, about 2.5 million people live around this desert.

Swahili Coast

The coastal areas from southern Somalia to northern Mozambique – through Kenya and Tanzania – form the Swahili Coast. This area was once very rich as people here traded in spices, gold, ivory and slaves. The most profitable trading relations were established with sea traders from Oman and India. In fact, the Sultan of Oman ruled this region during the 19th century. This relationship has greatly influenced the people of this region, a fact that is clear from their culture and traditions. The Swahili language is a mixture of the native Bantu language and Arab as well as some Indian words. The majority of the people here still follow Islam, but their food, customs and traditions are African.

Asia

Asia is the largest continent in the world and also the most populated. It forms the central and eastern part of Eurasia. The Isthmus of Suez is Asia's border with Africa. Its border with Europe is not clearly defined, but the Caspian Sea, Ural River and Ural Mountains form a natural border between these two continents.

▲ **Disappearing species**
Orangutans are endangered with a few animals found only in the rainforests of Borneo and Sumatra.

Most of Asia lies in the Northern Hemisphere, but the equator cuts across some of the islands in Southeast Asia. It is surrounded by the Arctic Ocean in the north, the Indian Ocean in the south, the Bering Sea and Pacific Ocean to the east, and the Red Sea and Mediterranean Sea to the southwest. Asia can be divided into six parts – North Asia, South Asia, Central Asia, East Asia, Southwest Asia and Southeast Asia. There are more than 50 countries in the continent, some of which are island nations in Southeast Asia. From the north to the south, Asia stretches from Siberia in the Arctic Circle to the southern tip of the Malay Peninsula. From the east to the west, it spans from Cape Dezhnev in Siberia, on the Bering Strait, to Turkey, which is partly in Europe.

▲ **Large and populous**
The continent of Asia accommodates about 60 per cent of the world's total population.

People power

Asia is a mixture of a number of cultures and religions. The six divisions of the Asian continent roughly divide not only the land, but also the people and their cultures. Even within these six divisions there are differences between the people and culture of each country and region. West Asians are of European or Arab descent; the Siberians in North Asia belong to tribes native to those regions; East Asians and Southeast Asians, like the Chinese, Japanese, Vietnamese, Koreans, Malaysians, Indonesians and Filipinos, are all different groups of Mongoloid; while the South Asian Indians and Sinhalese are descended from the ancient Aryan and Dravidian peoples of India. It is obvious that such a wide variety of people speak an equally large number of languages. They also follow many different religions. Some of the most popular Asian religions include Hinduism, Buddhism, Jainism, Zoroastrianism, Sikhism, Islam and Christianity.

◀ **Labour of love**
The Taj Mahal, in Agra, India was built by the Mughal emperor Shah Jehan, in the memory of his wife Mumtaz Mahal. It took more than 20 years to complete the mausoleum of white marble. The Taj Mahal is regarded as one of the wonders of the medieval world.

Tibetan plateau

The Tibetan Plateau, also known as the Qinghai-Tibetan Plateau, is a large area in Central Asia that rose up because of tectonic movements that took place some 55 million years ago. It was formed when the Indo-Australian plate crashed into the Eurasian plate. The plateau, which is about 5,000 metres (16,404 feet) high, is the home of the Himalayas. It covers much of Tibet and is popularly referred to as the 'roof of the world'. Seven of Asia's biggest rivers begin their journey from this plateau. They are the Yangtze, Huang Ho, Indus, Ganges, Brahmaputra, Mekong and Salween.

Flora and fauna

The climate in Asia ranges from hot and tropical in the southern parts, to icy tundra in the north. The plants and trees of the continent naturally reflect this diversity. In the cold north there are lichen, moss and flowering shrubs; grasslands are common in the northeast; desert shrubs and palms grow in Arabia; mango, banyan, neem, pine and palms grow in the south and southeast; and bamboo, cherry, plum and maple grow in the east. Asia is also home to a wide variety of animals such as the elephant, rhinoceros, ibex, hippopotamus, lion, tiger, cheetah, panda, brown bear, camel and different types of monkeys, numerous snakes, crocodiles and insects, and birds such as cranes, parrots, eagles, bulbuls and woodpeckers. Among the most popular animals are the Asiatic lion, the Bengal tiger, the one-horned rhinoceros and the Asian elephant. All of these animals are considered endangered.

◂ Ethnic mixture
Hong Kong is a global centre for finance and trade. This former British colony is now partially under the control of the Chinese government, which is responsible for Hong Kong's defence and foreign relation policies. Chinese constitute over 90 per cent of the population of Hong Kong. However, the culture of this country is a mix of East and West.

Key facts:

- Baikal Lake, in the southern part of eastern Siberia, is the world's largest freshwater lake by volume. It is also the deepest lake at 1,637 metres (5,371 feet). It is surrounded by mountains and fed by the waters of over 300 rivers and mountain streams.
- The Yangtze is the longest river in Asia. It flows from west to east, from the Tibetan Plateau into the East China Sea. It covers a distance of 6,380 kilometres (3,964 miles) and divides China into two parts – North and South China.
- The Indonesian island of Java is the most populated island in the world. The number of people living on this island is greater than the number of people on the Australian continent, which is almost 60 times bigger than Java in terms of land area.

Try these too:

Features of the Earth (p 22–23), Ancient India and China (p 118–119), Medieval Asia (p 128–129), Colonial Empires (p 136–137)

◂ A cut above the rest
The Himalayas are located between India and the Tibetan Plateau. They run through Pakistan, India, Nepal, Bhutan and China. Mount Everest, at 8,850 metres (29,035 feet), is the highest peak not only in the Himalayas but also the world.

The Poles – the Arctic and Antarctica

At the top and bottom of the Earth's imaginary axis, lie the North and South Poles. The North Pole is the northernmost point on Earth and is situated in the Arctic Ocean. The South Pole is the southernmost point and is situated in Antarctica, the southernmost continent.

▲ Discovering the South Pole
For centuries, people kept searching for the elusive 'Southern Continent'. Antarctica was finally discovered in 1911, by the Norwegian explorer Roald Amundsen.

▲▼ People of the Arctic
Inuit, or eskimos, are the native people of the Arctic region. Their native language is Inuktitut. Earlier, all Inuit lived in dome-shaped snowhouses called igloos. However, today most Inuit live in houses made of wood.

The Arctic region includes all areas that fall within the Arctic Circle. Parts of Russia, Alaska, Canada, Greenland, Norway, Sweden, Finland, Iceland and the Arctic Ocean are part of the Arctic region. All the areas within this region have cold temperatures throughout the year and the Arctic Ocean itself is mostly covered with ice. The land around the Arctic Circle is flat, with some low hills, and the land closest to the poles is ice-covered mountains. Antarctica lies within the Antarctic Circle. It is surrounded by the Southern Ocean. Antarctica is the fifth largest continent, but the least populated. In fact, Antarctica has no native inhabitants. Only scientists and researchers from all over the world stay there to carry out research and studies. Nearly the entire continent is covered with ice. It is the coldest place on Earth.

People power

The Arctic region is inhabited by native populations like the Inuit and Aleuts of North America and Greenland, and the Laplanders of Sweden, Norway and Finland. However, when the Europeans arrived, many native people were driven away from their homes and now most of them live on specially marked areas of land, called reservations.

▸ Frozen water
The ice covering the Antarctic Ocean melts in the summer to form large chunks of icebergs. Huge slabs of permanent ice, or ice shelves, also float in the Antarctic Ocean. The Ross ice shelf is the largest of these.

▲ **Equipped for the pole**
The body of the polar bear is covered with white fur. This helps the animal to blend in with the snow and ice. However, the skin underneath the fur is actually dark in colour. The fur is waterproof, helping the bear to remain dry and warm at all times. The animal simply shakes off the water from its body after a swim.

Life in the Arctic

Around the Arctic Circle some trees, plants and grasses grow. However, near the poles the weather is extremely cold. This region is called the tundra. The tundra has very little soil and not enough sunlight for trees to grow. The ground beneath the surface also remains frozen throughout the year, not allowing trees to grow roots deep into the ground. Therefore, only plants that are rootless or have short roots, such as lichens and small shrubs, can grow here. The Arctic Ocean is home to creatures such as whales, walruses, seals, plankton and numerous types of fish and birds. On land there are polar bears, foxes, lemmings, reindeer and musk-ox. Not all animals live in the Arctic throughout the year. Most mammals and birds are found here only in the summer.

Hostile environment

There are no native mammals, reptiles or amphibians in Antarctica. The wildlife of this area includes toothed whales, seals, squid, octopus and numerous fish species as well as birds, such as penguins, albatross, gulls and terns. Very few plants grow at the South Pole. There are no trees or flowering plants, only lichen, fungi and grass grow in some parts. However, the islands around the main continent have flowering plants and ferns.

Auroras

Auroras are beautiful natural displays of coloured light that occur near the polar regions. There are two types of auroras – aurora borealis, or northern lights, and aurora australis, or southern lights.
These colourful lights occur in the magnetic fields near the poles when high-energy particles from the Sun react with gases in the Earth's atmosphere.
This phenomenon has been named after Aurora, the Roman goddess of dawn. This is because the reddish glow seen in the northern night sky gives an appearance of the Sun rising from the north.

Key facts:

- In some places, the Antarctic ice sheet is 2.5 kilometres (1.6 miles) thick. Antarctica does not have alternate days and nights. Instead, it has long sunny stretches and long periods of darkness.
- Penguins are birds that have adapted to living in water. They are covered with thick feathers and their wings are paddle-like flippers. Unlike other birds that can fly, or walk and run on land, the penguin cannot fly at all and it walks very clumsily. However, it is an excellent swimmer.
- In the polar regions, when warm air above the ground mixes with cold air near the ground, a thin cloud of water vapour is formed. Because of the cold weather in these places, the water particles turn into ice and appear like millions of tiny, shiny diamond pieces. This shiny fog is called 'diamond dust'.
- Admiral Robert E. Peary, a renowned American explorer, is believed to be the first person to reach the North Pole. Peary, his companion Matthew Henson and four Native Americans accomplished this feat on 6 April, 1909.

Try these too:

Features of the Earth (p 22–23), Seasons and Weather (p 32–33), Bears (p 40–41), Marine Mammals (p 50–51), Flightless Birds (p 58–59)

Ancient Mesopotamia and Egypt

Mesopotamia and Egypt are two of the world's oldest human civilizations. The Mesopotamian civilization was located in the area between the Tigris and Euphrates rivers in Southwest Asia. This is the area of modern-day Iraq, Syria and Turkey. The Egyptian civilization grew along the banks of the River Nile, in North Africa. The Egyptian and the Mesopotamian civilizations were both river valley cultures. They developed and flourished because of the clever ways in which they used their rivers.

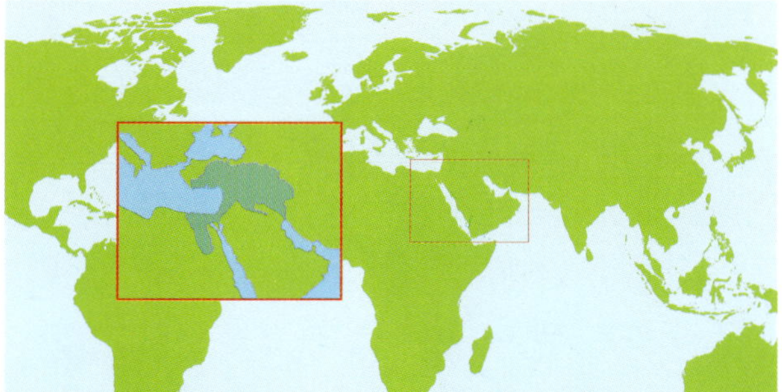

▲ Location of the ancient civilizations of Egypt and Mesopotamia.

Key facts:

- The Ancient Mesopotamians invented the first calendar. Their calender was based on the movement of the Sun and Moon. The calendar had 12 months, except every fourth year, which had 13 months.
- The Sumerians invented the wheel. They made carts and wagons to transport people and goods. They also used the wheel to make pottery.
- Ancient Egyptians believed in life after death. According to them, the soul of the dead person travelled to another world and another life. This is why they buried food, clothes and everything else that a person would need, along with the dead body.
- The gods and goddesses of the Ancient Egyptians and Mesopotamians were part-human and part-animal forms. These deities represented various natural elements like the Sun, Moon, heaven, sky and water. They also had gods of love, war, protection, childbirth, agriculture and magic.

The Mesopotamian civilization began around 5000 BC, when people began to learn how to grow crops and to live as a community. These early people, called the Sumerians, learned to use water from the Tigris and the Euphrates by making canals, dykes and tanks. They watered the hot and dry land to grow grain for food, such as wheat, chickpeas and barley. They also began rearing domestic animals such as cattle, fowl and dogs. As the civilization grew and thrived, small city-states were formed, each with its own fortress. The Sumerians traded with the Persians and the Indus Valley people. They made pottery, carved metal objects, stone sculptures and mud-brick buildings. They also began weaving cloth with linen fibre. They even invented cuneiform, an early written language.

▼ Carvings on clay
The word 'cuneiform' has been derived from the Latin word *cuneus*, meaning wedge. Ancient Mesopotamians used a reed or any sharp tool to write on clay tablets, giving this ancient script its name.

Around 2000 BC, the Sumerians were defeated by the Akkadians who made Babylon their capital and began ruling southern Mesopotamia. Hammurabi was the most powerful Babylonian king. He brought the entire area of Mesopotamia under his rule. By 1350 BC, the Assyrians became powerful in the north. King Sargon spread Assyrian rule over all of Mesopotamia, right up to Thebes in Egypt. The Mesopotamian civilization ended in 539 BC, when the Persians took control of Babylon.

▶ Farming in ancient Egypt
Ancient Egyptians mainly cultivated wheat, barley, flax, fruit and vegetables. The agricultural season lasted for about nine months. Farming was stopped from July to November during the annual flooding of the Nile.

Egyptian civilization

Farming communities began developing in the areas by the river Nile around the 11th century BC. Like the Mesopotamians, the Egyptians also built canals and waterways and made tools like the plough to help them grow grain for food. By 3000 BC, the first Egyptian kingdom was formed. The king was called a 'pharaoh' and Egyptians believed that their pharaohs were gods on Earth.

Enterprising Egyptians

The Egyptians invented a kind of paper from the stem of the papyrus plant. They also invented hieroglyphics, another early written language. Early Egyptian buildings were made of mud-bricks, but later palaces, temples and pyramids were made with huge stone blocks. The most impressive structures are their temples and pyramids that contain the tombs of Egyptian pharaohs and queens. The royalty were mummified and buried along with food, fine clothes, jewellery, furniture and even servants, ready for the afterlife.

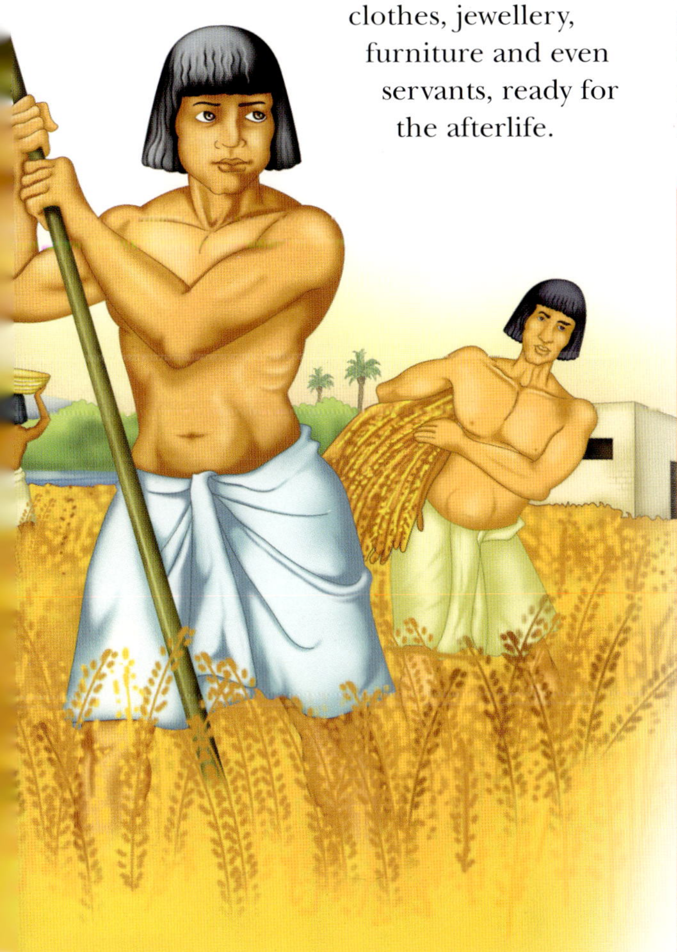

▲ **Tribute to the Sungod** The Temple at Luxor is a typical example of Egyptian architecture.

The Ancient Egyptians were very religious people. They were also equally artistic, so it was not surprising that they decorated their buildings with paintings and sculptures of their gods and kings. They also learnt to spin and weave cotton and mastered the art of glass making. The Egyptian civilization lasted for more than 3,000 years, until Alexander the Great, the king of Macedonia, invaded Egypt and defeated the Egyptians.

Try these too:

Ancient India and China (p 118–119), The Modern World (p 154–155), Ancient Architecture (p 158–159)

Ziggurats and pyramids

The ziggurats of Mesopotamia and the pyramids of Egypt are the most outstanding structures of these two civilizations. Ziggurats (see below) are huge, stepped structures that serve as a platforms for temples. Early pyramids looked similar to ziggurats, except they were hollow inside and contained tombs. The most famous pyramids in Egypt are the Great Pyramids at Giza, near Cairo.

Ancient India and China

The Indus Valley civilization in India and the Ancient Chinese civilization are the two oldest river valley cultures in the eastern part of the world. The Indus Valley civilization, also known as the Harappan civilization, developed on the banks of the Indus and Ghaggar-Hakra rivers. It was spread over present-day Pakistan, western India and parts of Afghanistan. The Chinese civilization began along the banks of the Yangtze River in central China.

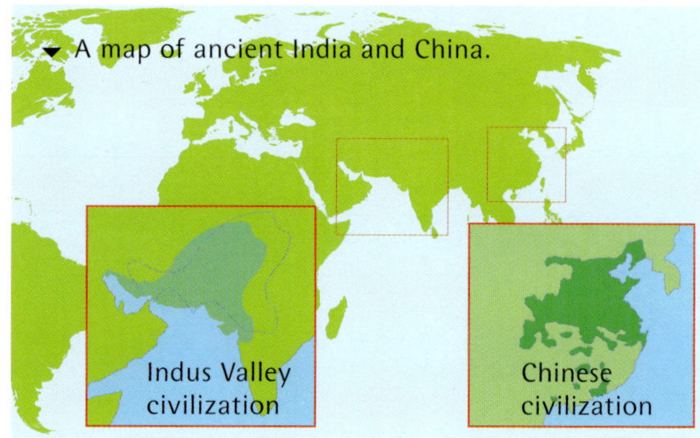

▼ A map of ancient India and China.

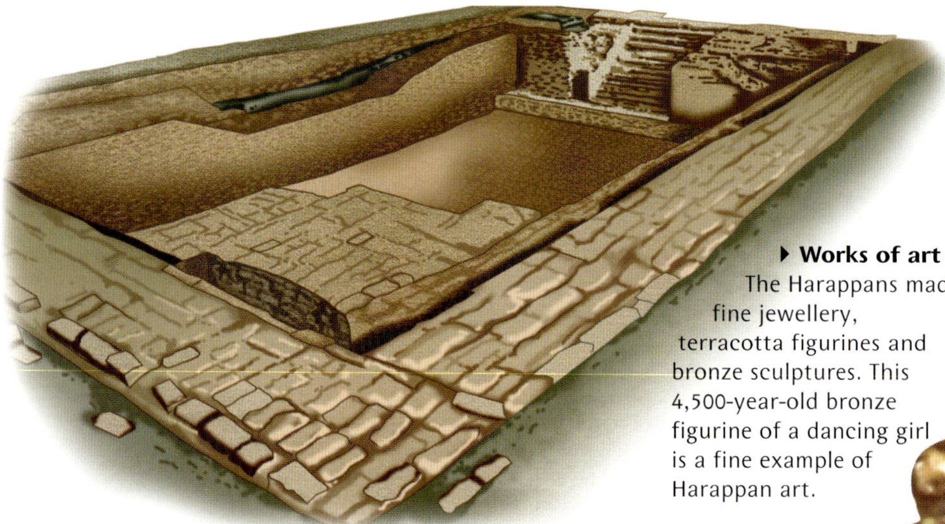

▲ **An architectural marvel**
The Great Bath at Mohenjodaro was probably the first public water tank or swimming pool. The tank was lined with closely laid plastered brick. A layer of tar was also applied on the floor and the sides of the tank to prevent it from leaking.

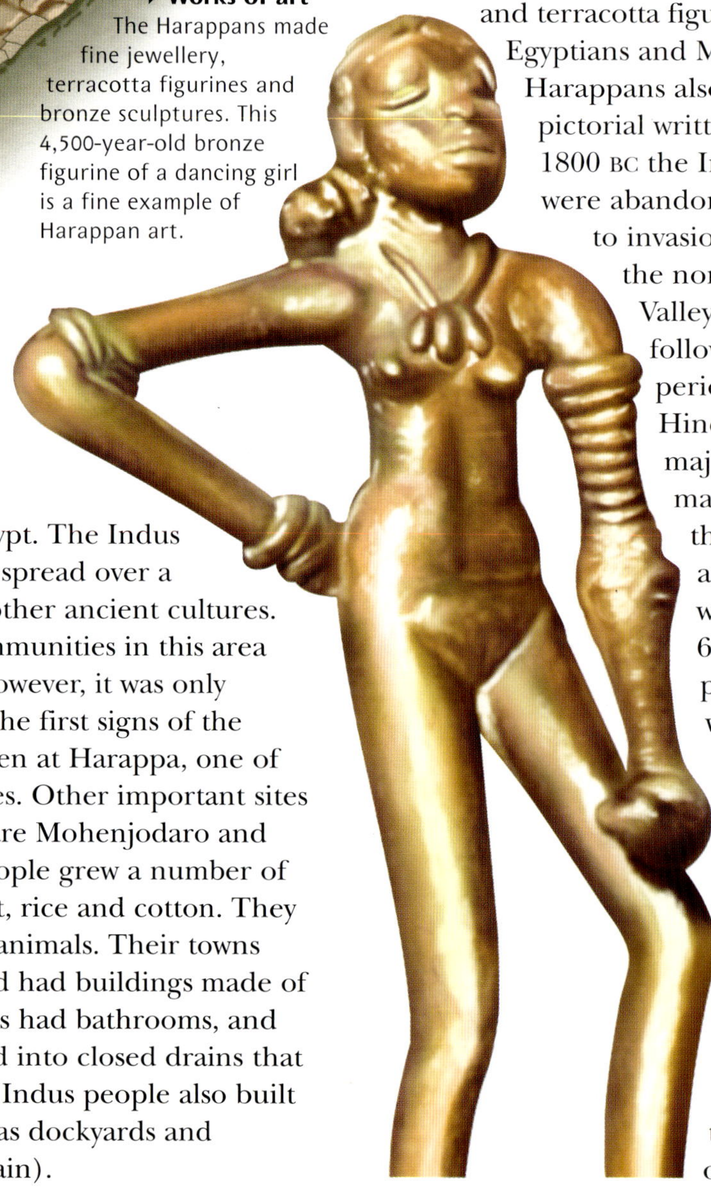

▶ **Works of art**
The Harappans made fine jewellery, terracotta figurines and bronze sculptures. This 4,500-year-old bronze figurine of a dancing girl is a fine example of Harappan art.

▼ **Metal works**
The Harappans were skilled craftsmen. They had great knowledge about metals as is evident from these household and farming tools made from copper.

The Indus Valley civilization developed at the about the same time as the civilizations of Mesopotamia and Egypt. The Indus Valley civilization was spread over a larger area than the other ancient cultures. The first farming communities in this area existed in 6500 BC. However, it was only around 4000 BC that the first signs of the Indus culture were seen at Harappa, one of the biggest Indus cities. Other important sites of the Indus culture are Mohenjodaro and Lothal. The Indus people grew a number of crops including wheat, rice and cotton. They also reared domestic animals. Their towns were well-planned and had buildings made of mud-bricks. All houses had bathrooms, and the waste water flowed into closed drains that lined the streets. The Indus people also built large structures such as dockyards and granaries (to store grain).

The Harappans built ships and were believed to have travelled to Mesopotamia and Persia. They were very artistic and made fine jewellery and terracotta figurines. Like the Egyptians and Mesopotamians, the Harappans also developed a pictorial written language. By 1800 BC the Indus Valley villages were abandoned, probably due to invasions by Aryans from the north. The Indus Valley civilization was followed by the Vedic period. At this time, Hinduism become a major religion and the main religious texts, the *Vedas*, *Brahmanas* and *Upanishads,* were written. By 600 BC, the northern part of the country was divided into 16 kingdoms and the society was divided into four castes: the *Brahmins*, or priests, the *Kshatriyas*, or warriors, the *Vaishyas*, or merchants and the *Shudras*, or labourers.

Great Wall of China

The Great Wall of China is a series of massive stone and mud fortifications that stretch across the northern border of China. The earliest walls were built in the third century BC to protect China from Mongolian and Manchurian invasions. Later, during the Qin dynasty, the wall was made bigger. Work on the wall continued until the 16th century AD, under various dynasties. A large part of the wall that we see today was built during the rule of the Ming dynasty. It is now over 6,500 kilometres (4,039 miles) long and at its highest point it is about 7.6 metres (25 feet) high.

Ancient China

Several farming villages had formed in various parts of China by 5000 BC. These villages grew in size and developed their own pottery, sculpture and architectural styles, and over the years exchanged ideas and techniques. In 2000 BC, all these scattered settlements came together under a single ruler.

Dynasties of ancient China

Ancient China was ruled by a series of dynasties, starting with the Xia dynasty. The Xia was followed by the Shang dynasty. During this period, the Chinese written language and the art of casting bronze vessels developed. During the Zhou dynasty, iron was introduced into China. The government controlled agriculture, and stored away all the surplus crops. In 221 BC, the Qin dynasty came to power. Emperor Qin Shi Huangdi unified China as a single country under his rule. He decreed that a common language (the Qin language) be used all over the kingdom. A written language with over 3,000 characters was invented and the calligraphic style of writing began developing. Coins were also introduced. After Huangdi's death, the Qin dynasty lost power and the kingdom broke up into many parts.

▼ Chinese silk
Around 3000 BC, the Chinese learnt to make silk thread from cocoons. They wove very delicate silks and painted on them.

▶ The stone of heaven
Jade represented nobility, perfection, constancy and immortality. The Chinese saw it as a link between man and god.

Key facts:

- Confucius was a great Chinese philosopher who lived in the 5th century BC. Confucianism is a religious, political and moral school of thought taught by him. His teachings have been collected in a book called *Analects of Confucius*.
- The ancient civilizations of China, India, Egypt and Mesopotamia were connected by the Silk Road. This land route stretched from China to Turkey and was used to trade in goods such as gold, silk, porcelain and jewellery.
- The written language of Harappans was made up of at least 400 symbols. However, unlike Egyptian hieroglyphics, the Indus script has still not been deciphered. This is because there are no books or carved passages in the Indus script. The only evidence of this language is on terracotta seals, which have only 4 to 5 symbols each.

Try these too:

Ancient Mesopotamia and Egypt (p 116–117), Medieval Asia (p 128–129), New Lands – the Age of Exploration (p 134–135)

Ancient Greece

The Ancient Greek civilization is considered to be the beginning of all Western civilizations. It was based not just in mainland Greece, but also on several small islands in the Aegean Sea, in Cyprus, along the Aegean coast of Turkey, in Sicily and in certain parts of Italy. Ancient Greek settlements were also located in places as far as Ukraine (in present-day Russia), Libya (in Southwest Asia), Romania and even Egypt.

▲ Location of the ancient Greek civilization.

Key facts:

- Ancient Greeks made pottery for their daily use in a variety of shapes. Some of the most common shapes were the amphora (wine jars), hydria (water jars) and krater (mixing bowls). These vessels were painted with geometric designs or human figures hunting or engaged in battle. Some depicted scenes from Greek mythology.
- In Ancient Athens only men had the right to vote or be elected to the government. Women were not sent to school. They were trained in housework and married by the time they were 13.
- Coins were introduced around 600 BC. The first coins were just lumps of gold or silver. Later, flat discs with figures of gods or goddesses, faces of kings or even messages were made.
- By 338 BC, most of Greece was under the control of the neighbouring kingdom of Macedonia. The death of Alexander the Great, king of Macedonia, in 323 BC, marked the end of ancient Greek civilization.

Long before the Ancient Greek civilization developed, other smaller, yet well-developed, cultures flourished in the Aegean islands and on the Greek mainland. The earliest of these was the Minoan civilization, which began around 3000 BC, on the island of Crete. Knossos and Phaestos were two important centres of this Bronze Age culture. About 1600 BC, the Mycenaean civilization developed on the mainland. Important Mycenaean centres were Athens and Thebes. A third, Cycladic, culture developed on the Cycladic Islands near Greece.

Aegean arts

Aegean architecture was large and impressive, and consisted of palaces and fortifications. The Minoans were artistic people who excelled at fresco painting and painting on pottery. Popular subjects were landscapes and animals. The Mycenaeans produced a number of excellent sculptural objects like plaques, statuettes, containers and masks in stone, metal and ivory. Both cultures developed their own written language and all three had elaborate burial rituals and graves filled with beautiful metal and stone objects. By about 1450 BC, the Mycenaeans destroyed the Minoan culture and by 1200 BC, they were themselves destroyed by invading Dorians.

City-states

Following the Dorian invasion were the Dark Ages, or a period of chaos. Around 800 BC, the Ancient Greek civilization began. As the civilization grew and the culture developed, colonies had to be formed in other countries to accommodate the growing population. Ancient Greece was divided into several self-governed city-states, the most important of which were Athens, Sparta, Corinth and Thebes.

By the 5th century BC, Athens became the most important, powerful and rich city-state. Democracy – a form of free and fair government elected by the citizens of a country – was first introduced in Athens.

▼ The best of Minoan
The Palace of Knossos had a rectangular courtyard with four wings, which was characteristic of Minoan architecture. The wings consisted of the royal residence, workshops, a temple, banquet halls, throne room, a theatre and storerooms.

An Athenian tribute The Parthenon is the most famous building of Ancient Greece. It stands on a citadel atop a hill in Athens. It was a temple to Athena, the Greek goddess of war and wisdom.

Art and sports

The written language of the Mycenaeans was forgotten during the Dark Ages, therefore the Greeks had to make a new language using the Phoenician alphabets. Ancient Greeks were artistic people and the arts of sculpture, pottery, architecture and painting blossomed during this period. The art and literature of this period is so exceptional that it inspires people even today. Greek poets and playwrights, including Homer and Aristophanes, have written some of the greatest literary classics.

Peloponnesian War

When Athens became powerful around the 5th century BC, the Athenians began to dominate the other city-states. The city of Sparta grew jealous and, supported by Corinth, rose against Athens in 431 BC. The Peloponnesian War lasted for 27 years. At the end of the war Athens was defeated and stripped of its powers.

In god's presence The Ancient Olympic Games were held at Olympia very four years in honour of the king of Greek gods, Zeus. The first one took place in 776 BC.

A great mind Aristotle was an ancient Greek philosopher who also made valuable contributions to politics, astronomy, medicine, geography and literature.

Try these too:

Ancient Architecture (p 158–159), Stage and Theatre (p 168–169), World of Sports (p 170–171)

Ancient Rome

The Roman civilization was the most powerful and widespread of all the ancient civilizations. At its peak, there were Roman colonies all over Western Europe, the northernmost parts of Africa and the Middle East.

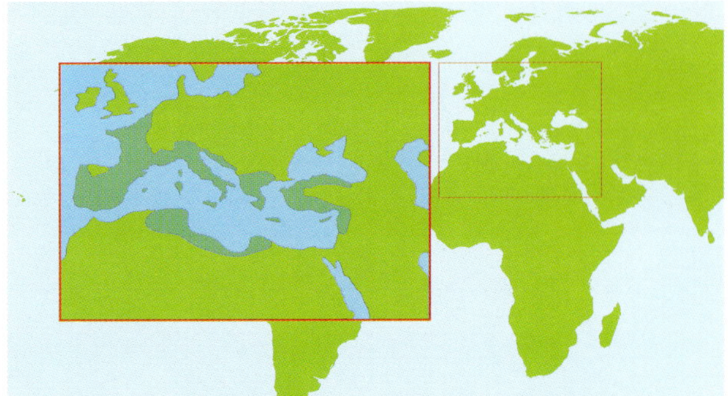

▲ Location of the Ancient Roman civilization.

▲ **Augustus Prima Porta**
This famous statue of Augustus Caesar, the first emperor of Rome is kept in the Vatican Museum.

People have lived in Rome and many parts of Italy since 3000 BC. By 1000 BC, many settlements in Italy were influenced by Greek civilization. They built stone buildings, made statues, grew crops and traded with the Greek colonies in Italy. Rome was a small collection of settlements at this time and under the control of the Etruscans who ruled most parts of Italy. By about 509 BC, the people of Rome got rid of the king and formed the Roman Republic. The Roman Republic was governed by the Senate, which comprised of heads of noble families, and the People's Assembly, which consisted of all male citizens of Rome. Around 23 BC, Octavian ended the Republic and established the Roman Empire. He took the title of Caesar Augustus and brought order and peace to the chaotic Roman realm. The Roman Empire successfully ruled Rome until AD 476, when it lost its power because of weak kings and invasions by northern barbarians.

▼ **The great Roman**
Julius Caesar symbolized the rise of Rome more than any other Roman ruler. This great military leader and politician was responsible for extending the boundaries of the Roman Empire until it became the sole superpower in the region. Although Julius Caesar was the dicatator of Rome, he never adopted the title of Emperor. However, he effectively destroyed the republic and set the foundation for a monarchy.

▶ **The legend of Rome**
According to legend, Romulus and Remus were the twin sons of Mars. They were abandoned as babies and a she-wolf nursed them. The twins were then adopted by a shepherd and in 753 BC, Romulus founded the city of Rome at the spot where the shepherd had found him and his brother. The statue of the she-wolf and the babies is the symbol of Rome even today.

Pont du Gard

The Pont du Gard is an Ancient Roman aqueduct in France. It was built in 19 BC, across the river Gardon. This three-tiered aqueduct has a road on the first level and a channel carrying water on the top level. It was part of a 50-kilometre (31-mile) long aqueduct that carried water from natural springs into the Roman town of Nîmes. This 49-metre (161-foot) tall structure, made of huge blocks of unplastered stone, has survived the ravages of time and has stood almost intact for thousands of years.

Cultural and artistic achievements

During the Roman Republic and the Empire, art, architecture and literature flourished. A lot of it was inspired by Ancient Greek culture and later also by the cultures of other areas that were brought under Roman rule. The Romans were excellent engineers. They improved roads and built several public buildings in various parts of their empire. Grand palaces, public bath houses, triumphal arches, amphitheatres and aqueducts (which carried water over long distances) were some of the common public constructions. The development of the dome and the arch during this period truly revolutionized architecture. Roman sculptures were true to life and closely resembled real people. The Romans made mural paintings, glass vessels, metal art, mosaics and pottery. They also made statues, busts and carved panels to decorate their buildings and arches, in marble, bronze, gold and silver. The period between the 1st century BC and the middle of the 1st century AD is considered to be the golden period of Latin literature. Numerous poems, essays, historical accounts and plays were written during this time.

The Ancient Roman style was a great source of inspiration for the art, architecture and literature of the Middle Ages, Renaissance period, and even of the modern world.

Ancient Romans were also keen sportsmen. They enjoyed running races, boxing, chariot racing, wrestling, swimming, hunting, ball games and board games. Stadiums, especially used for gladiatorial games, and playgrounds were common all over the Roman Empire.

◂ A place to socialize
The Romans were very particular about taking baths. Therefore, they built elaborate public bath houses in every town. Ancient Roman bath houses were not meant only for taking baths. People came to bath houses to meet friends and business associates. Apart from a pool, these bath houses also had libraries and game courts.

Try these too:

Europe (p 108–109), Europe in the Middle Ages (p 126–127), The Renaissance (p 132 –133), Ancient Architecture (p 158–159)

Key facts:

- The Ancient Romans wore long pieces of woollen cloth called togas. Togas were draped in a stylish manner, but they were not convenient or comfortable. Later, influenced by the Greeks and Egyptians, they began wearing loose linen tunics. On special occasions they wore the toga over the tunic.
- The Romans built large and magnificent public baths all over their kingdom. These baths were more like leisure centres, where there was a library, a gym and a swimming pool, as well as warm, hot and cold baths and massage rooms. The bathers were also provided with entertainment, food and drinks.
- Most Romans were poor, but those who were rich believed it was important to show off their wealth. They bought a number of slaves to work for them. Slaves did housework, carried their masters in litters when they went out, ran errands, stood guard and were at the beck and call of their masters in return for food, clothes and a place to stay.
- Latin was the widely accepted language of Ancient Rome. It was derived from Greek and served as the official and scientific language in the Western world until the 18th century. Spanish, Romanian, Portuguese, French and Italian, as well as some words in English, were derived from Latin.

The Native Americans

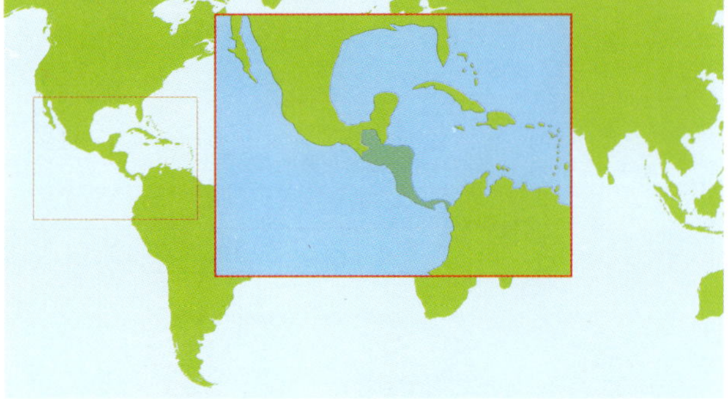

▼ Location of Ancient Native American settlements.

The very first American people lived nearly 11,500 years ago. These people are said to have come from northeastern Asia, across the Bering land bridge, which once connected America and Asia. These early people did not stay anywhere permanently – they hunted and gathered food on the move. Slowly they began settling down and living together in farming villages.

Key facts:

- Most Native American farmers and craftsmen lived in villages, in small houses. Some had just one room, while others had two or more tiny rooms. These houses were made of poles and thatch in warm areas or with 'wattle and daub', that is, clay plastered over mats made of twigs.
- Today, there are over 500 Native American tribes recognized by the United States government and many lesser-known tribes. The most well-known tribes are Cherokee, Navajo, Choctaw, Sioux, Apache, Blackfoot, Pueblo, Chippewa, Iroquois and the Inuit.

Early Mississippians settled in present-day Illinois, Wisconsin, Indiana and Kentucky around AD 900. They grew maize, made pottery and traded with people in other parts of the continent. They lived in villages ruled by a chief, who was the most powerful person. The rest of the villagers were powerless and divided into different high and low classes. These people made large mounds or platforms, which were probably religious. Other native communities included a number of small tribes who were collectively called Apache Indians, who lived in parts of Arizona and Mexico. Some groups settled down and cultivated crops, but others were fierce warrior nomads who lived in tents and hunted for food. The Inuit of Alaska and Canada form another group of Native Americans. These people were hunters and fishermen who ate whales, walruses, polar bears and musk ox. They also used the skin and bones of these animals to make boats, sledges, tools, clothes and even homes.

▲ **The mound-builders**
Mississippian mounds were usually square, rectangular or circular in shape. Temples, houses and even burial sites were built on these mounds.

▼ **Riding on ice**
Traditionally the Inuit people travelled on the komatik, a low slung sledge pulled by special sledge dogs called huskies. The person sat or lay down on this type of sledge. These sledges were made from the skin of seals or walruses. Today, however, the Inuit prefer to use snowmobiles to get from one place to another. Sledges are usually reserved for hunting and racing.

Native American clothing

The dressing style of the Native Americans depended on the climate of the place in which they lived. For instance, men in Central America wore only a cotton loincloth and women wore a dress made with a single piece of cloth, which had holes cut out for the head and hands. In some tribes women wore belts or long blouses over this dress. In the colder parts of South America, like the Andes, woollen dresses and capes were also worn, and men wore shirts, kilts and capes. The Inuit wore animal skin clothes, parkas and boots.

▲ **A remarkable victory**
The Battle of the Little Bighorn (25–26 June, 1876) was an important battle in the Indian Wars. It was a battle between the combined forces of Lakota and Northern Cheyenne tribes and the United States army. The tribal forces won the battle fought on the banks of the Little Bighorn River in eastern Montana.

Invasion of the native lands

The Native Americans lived peacefully in their new land for several centuries until the arrival of the Europeans. At first, the natives welcomed the foreigners. However, they soon turned hostile when they realized that the newcomers were there to stay. The natives were also unhappy with the Europeans as they did not respect their native culture and way of life.

This led to a series of armed conflicts between the two parties. Known as the Indian Wars, these conflicts began in the early 1600s. Some of the worst battles, however, occured after the United States had won its freedom from colonial rule. The white settlers forcibly relocated Native Americans in places far away from their homes, in an attempt to gain more territories for themselves. One of the worst incidents took place in 1838, when a huge population of Cherokee Indians were removed from their lands. About 4,000 Cherokees died during the relocation due to exhaustion and diseases.

A rich culture

The customs, traditions language and clothes of each Native American tribe is very different from the other. However, some elements are common among all tribes. The ancestors of all modern tribes were nomads who hunted large animals like bison with bows and arrows. Early native settlers were good at pottery, painting, making jewellery, carving and weaving. Most Native American tribes also share religious beliefs and ceremonies. Shamanism was a major part of their life. Shamans were priests who were believed to be able to mediate between humans and the spirit world. They were also regarded as healers and guardians of the tribes. Most religious ceremonies are accompanied by chanting, beating of drums and dancing.

▲ **Totem pole**
Native Americans believed that each tribe or individual was protected by an animal, a plant or supernatural object or being. They called this object or being 'totem'.You could not choose your totem – it chose you. The Native Americans carved the images of their totems onto poles and displayed them near their houses or on graves.

▲ **Travelling on water**
In ancient times, Native Americans used a canoe called a dugout. A dugout was built by scraping out excess wood from the middle of a log of suitable size. The two ends of the boat were then sharpened to make the boat faster.

Try these too:

The Poles – the Arctic and Antarctic (p 114–115), The Incas and Aztecs (p 130–131), New Lands – the Age of Exploration (p 134–135)

Europe in the Middle Ages

The term Middle Ages refers to the period between approximately AD 500 and AD 1400. It was the beginning of great changes in Europe. The Roman Empire had become too large and unmanageable to be ruled by one person. Also, many of the later emperors were weak and helpless against attacks from their neighbouring kingdoms. The western parts of the Empire broke away from Roman control and formed into separate countries. It was a period of endless battle, bloodshed and struggle for power.

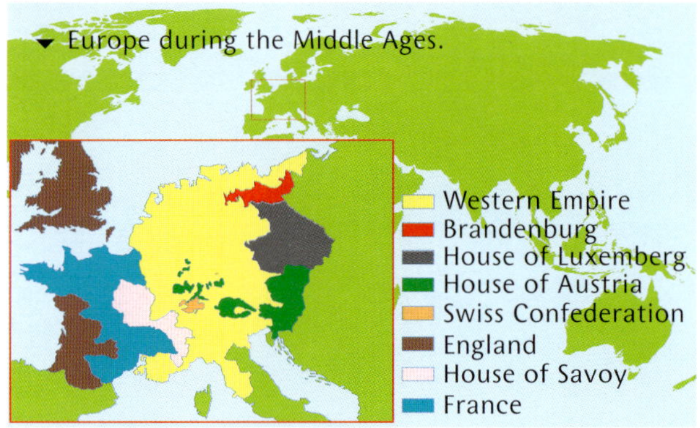

▼ Europe during the Middle Ages.

Key facts:

- Serfs paid rent in the form of livestock, such as sheep, goats, pigs and hens, or in the form of eggs, firewood or wine. The lord of the manor decided how much each peasant had to pay.
- In AD 391, the Roman Emperor, Constantine converted to Christianity and declared it to be the official religion of the Roman Empire. It was only after this that Christianity began to be accepted widely.
- Medieval craftsmen and traders were members of guilds, or associations. Each guild was responsible for setting rules, standards and prices for the products produced by their members. This ensured fairness and equality. It also assured the traders of a fixed price and safeguarded them from a bad economy.
- Around 1348, the war-torn, sickly, hungry and poverty-stricken Europe was struck by the Black Death, or plague. This terrible disease first broke out in Italy and soon spread all over Europe killing millions of people.

One of the most significant changes of this period was the spread of Christianity. A number of monasteries were built and these became centres of power and wealth. People were encouraged, sometimes forced, to convert to Christianity and Sunday mass was made compulsory.

Feudalism

By the Middle Ages, Western Europe consisted of several small kingdoms that were constantly at war with each other. Kings gifted large areas of land, called 'fiefs', to important people like barons and bishops. These barons and bishops, in return, provided the royal army with soldiers from their lands. With no single powerful ruler to protect the citizens, landlords soon became the most powerful people. They lived in manors, which usually consisted of a castle, a church, a village and fields. The peasants, or serfs, who worked in the fields were the poorest people. They had to pay rent to the lord and serve him.

The Crusades

At the end of the 11th century, Islamic Turks attacked the eastern part of the Roman Empire. The pope sent a huge army of Christians from Rome to fight against these Muslim invaders. This was the first of the many Crusades, or Holy Wars. Several more were fought between the people of these two religions over a period of 300 years. Another important war that decided the future of Europe was the Hundred Years War (1337–1453) between France and England.

◀ **The men of chivalry** The kings were served and protected by knights. These knights were young and brave warriors who were trained in warfare. Many of them fought for their kings in the Crusades. Some knights were monks, and they belonged to monasteries.

Medieval castles

The most imposing structures of the Middle Ages are castles. These large stone houses were built by barons and feudal lords to proclaim their wealth and power. These castles also doubled up as fortresses within which their owners could hide, or from where they could attack, in case of a battle. Windsor Castle and Warwick Castle are two magnificent examples.

Vikings of Scandinavia

During the Middle Ages, Europe was attacked by brave and adventurous people from the north, south and east. The Vikings of Scandinavia were the most influencial among these. They attacked Ireland, England and even Iceland. They were driven out of England by King Alfred the Great, only to return after his death. They also settled in France and eventually their kingdoms in the north joined Europe.

▼ Walls of protection
The earliest castles were made of wood and earth. As the hostilities between various European countries grew, castles began to be built of stone. They were further fortified with moats, drawbridges and portcullises.

Rule of monarchs

The first major royal dynasty to rule over large parts of Europe was that of the Merovingians. They ruled over France, Belgium, Switzerland and parts of Germany and laid the foundations for what was to become modern Europe. They were followed by the Carolingians from Austria. During their rule several schools and universities were founded, the Catholic Church became more powerful and cities and towns grew. After the Carolingians lost their power, the three important centres in Europe were Britain, France and Germany. These countries were ruled by a succession of dynasties, one sometimes taking over another.

Church art

Medieval churches were large and awe-inspiring buildings. They had arched doors and windows with stunning stained glass panels. The inner walls were decorated with paintings of scenes from the Bible or other Christian themes. The churches also had carved pillars, relief panels and statues. Many churches, monasteries and wealthy people also commissioned illuminated manuscripts. These were beautifully illustrated scrolls or books on Christian themes.

▲ A religious ruler
Charlemagne was the most popular Carolingian ruler. He was the king of Franks and Lombards, and the founder of the Holy Roman Empire. He was also a devout Catholic, and had close relations with the pope. It was the pope who crowned Charlemagne Emperor of the Holy Roman Empire.

Try these too:

The Renaissance (p 132–133), New Lands – the Age of Exploration (p 134–135), Colonial Empires (p 136–137), Ancient Architecture (p 158–159), Modern Art and Artists (p 162–163), Famous Composers (p 164–165), The Sounds of Music (p 166–167)

◀ Powerful influence
The Crusades united major European powers under the church, exposed the west to the Middle East culture and products and marked the beginning of the Renaissance period.

Medieval Asia

At the same time that Europe was being established, India, China, Japan and the Arabian countries were also going through a period of tremendous change and development. World religions like Christianity, Islam, Hinduism and Buddhism were becoming widespread. Scientific inventions, artistic development and political developments laid the foundation of the modern world.

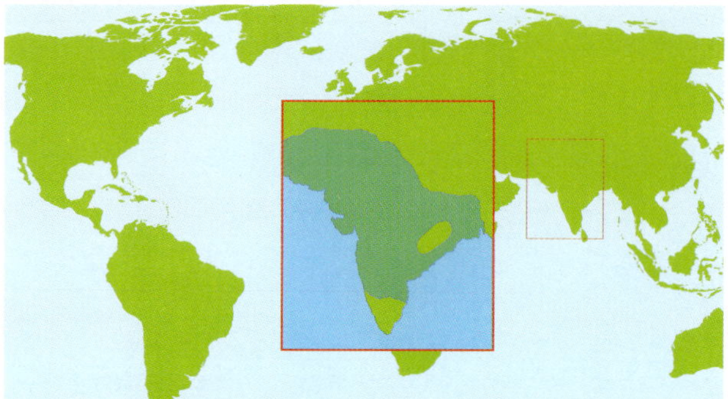

▲ Medieval Asia

Key facts:

- Around the end of the 13th century AD, the Venetian traveller Marco Polo published a book about his travels along the Silk Road, the trade route between China and the West. It was widely read by Europeans of that time and cartographers and mariners referred to it for information about Asia.
- During the Gupta period in India (AD 320–480), a surgeon called Sushruta wrote a book called the *Sushruta Samhita*. The book contains information about 300 types of surgery and 120 types of surgical instruments. Sushruta could perform a vast range of surgery. He could fit artificial limbs, and he even conducted plastic surgery.
- The people of the medieval Islamic kingdoms were mostly known as fearsome fighters. However, they were also extremely creative people who could make beautiful art objects. They produced excellent gold and silver jewellery, candle stands and containers; glass containers; ceramics; stone carvings; and even astronomical instruments.

In China, the Han dynasty brought peace and order back to the country. At the same time that Jesus was spreading the word of God in the West, Buddhism was becoming popular in China. Many people converted to this new religion. Paper was also invented in China at this time. Artists of this period were inspired to make numerous paintings of Buddhist themes.

The Golden Age

China's 'golden period' was during the rule of the T'ang dynasty, between AD 618 and 907. Landscape painting, sculpture, pottery, poetry and music, calligraphy and the manufacture of porcelain ware reached new heights. Also, the introduction of printing made it possible for books to be made in large quantities. Over the course of time, the Chinese invented several useful things including the compass, the seismograph (to measure earthquakes), the clock and gunpowder.

▸ **Towers of worship**
Pagodas are tall multi-tiered towers that were usually built in or near a Buddhist temple. Pagodas are most common in China, Japan and Korea. They combine Buddhist architectural style with that of the particular country.

Mongolian power

In the 13th century, the Mongols were the most powerful people in Asia. Led by their king Genghis Khan (1162–1227), they brought China, Tibet, Burma, Iran, Eastern Europe, and parts of Russia under their control. Between 1251 and 1259, Genghis Khan's grandson, Kublai Khan carried his grandfather's legacy forward and led a series of campaigns against China. In 1279, Kublai Khan gained control of China and became the first ruler of the Chinese Yüan dynasty.

Japan

The Japanese civilization developed later than those of its neighbours. It was only in AD 405 that Japan adopted a written language and even then they developed a writing system based on Chinese alphabets. In AD 600 Buddhism spread among the Japanese. Around this time the Yamato dynasty ruled Japan, but the real power was in the hands of the shoguns, or military generals. By the 12th century, the Yamato emperors had lost all their power. The shoguns and their powerful families, called daimyos, took over.

Ajanta

In a deep ravine in western India, there are about 30 caves. Most of these caves – in Ajanta – were used as monasteries by Buddhist monks, while the rest were prayer halls. The monasteries are called *viharas.* They have a pillared verandah, a hall and several dormitories cut into the rock. The caves used as prayer halls are called *chaitya grihas.* These are long halls cut deep into the rock. The caves are decorated with beautiful carvings and some of them have paintings, too. The caves were built in two phases. The first ones were made sometime in the second century BC, while the rest were carved between the fifth and sixth centuries AD.

India

The Mauryan Empire, established by Chandragupta Maurya, dominated northern India in the 3rd century BC. Chandragupta and his grandson Ashoka were the two great rulers of this period. At the height of Mauryan power, the kingdom covered most parts of India and Pakistan, and parts of Afghanistan.

A cultural expansion

After a brief period of instability, North India came under the control of the Gupta Empire in AD 320. Under the new rulers, art, science, architecture and literature flourished. Books were written about medicine, surgery, astronomy and mathematics.

At the same time, in South India, smaller kingdoms like the Pallavas, Cholas and Chalukyas were also expanding and producing beautiful temples, palaces, sculptures and paintings.

Rise of the Mughals

From the late 12th century, for more than 300 years, India was ruled by a series of Muslim kings from West Asia. The last Muslim kingdom of the Lodhi dynasty ended with the arrival of Babur, the founder of the Mughal dynasty. The Mughals ruled India for more than 200 years.

The Islamic World

After the fall of the Roman Empire in the Middle East, the next major event that took place in this region was the birth of Islam in the 7th century AD. The Muslims of Arabia soon took over the surrounding areas of Palestine, Egypt, Mesopotamia, Syria and Persia. From the 11th century onwards, the Middle East was ruled by various Muslim kingdoms like the Seljuk Turks, the Mameluks and the Ottoman Turks. These kingdoms terrorized Eastern Europe and blocked all land routes between Asia and Europe.

▲ Towering above all
The Qutub Minar in Delhi, the capital of India, is a great example of Mughal architecture. The minaret was built by the Muslim ruler, Qutub-ud-din-Aibak and his successors. This five-storied tower is made of red sandstone and has verses from the *Qur'an* carved on it.

◂ A marvel in stone
Mahabalipuram, a seaport town during the rule of the Pallava dynasty, is full of rock-cut temples. The beautiful Shore Temple was built in honour of the Hindu god, Shiva.

Try these too:

Asia (p 112–113), Ancient India and China (p 118–119), New Lands – the Age of Exploration (p 134 –135), The Modern World (p 154–155)

The Incas and Aztecs

The Incas and Aztecs were the two most powerful and important Native American kingdoms between AD 1400–1600. Around 1438, the South American Quechua tribe formed the Inca Empire in the Andes, with their capital at Cuzco, in Peru.

Key facts:

- The Quechua people called their kingdom Tawantinsuyu or the 'land of four quarters'. This was because the Inca kingdom was divided into four parts, each under a governor.
- The Incas often moved large groups of people from one place to another within the empire. This was because, sometimes, a large number of people were needed to farm a particular area or to mine it. Large groups of Quechua people were also moved to newly conquered areas to prevent the local tribes from revolting against the Incas.
- The people of Tenochtitlán used hollowed logs made into boats to go up and down the canals in the city. Tenochtitlán was an island in a lake that was connected to the mainland by three raised roads. Aqueducts brought drinking water into the city.
- The Aztecs used the maguey, or agave, plant for many things. The spikes on the plant were used as needles, the leaves were used to make thatched roofs, the fibre was used to make rope and the sap was used to make a drink called *pulque*.

The Incas conquered neighbouring kingdoms and tribes and made them part of the Inca Empire. At the height of Inca power, the kingdom covered parts of present-day Argentina, Chile, Peru, Bolivia and Ecuador. The Incas collected tax from all the tribes that they conquered. The tax was paid in the form of labour. Taxpayers had to work on Inca building projects, such as making mountain roads, tunnels, bridges, forts and terraces for farming. The Incas were skilled farmers. They grew corn, potatoes, chilli peppers, beans, squash, peanuts, cassava and quinoa. They built channels to bring water high up into the mountains in case the rains failed them. The Incas used hand tools such as spades, clubs, hoes, sticks and foot ploughs to dig, break and move earth. They raised guinea pigs, dogs and ducks for meat, as well as llamas and alpacas for their meat, wool and dung (which was used as fuel). They also used llamas to transport goods.

▼ The location of the empire of the Incas.

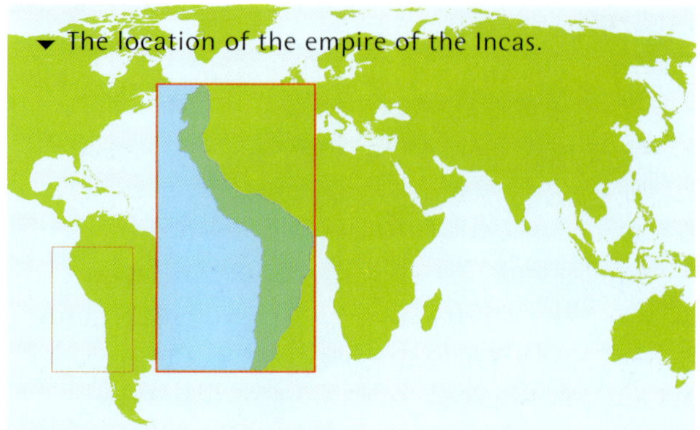

Incas worshipped nature and believed in life after death. When a king died, his body was mummified and preserved. The people would regularly offer food to it and consult it whenever they had a problem. Ordinary people were also mummified and laid to rest in tombs, along with food and water. The arrival of Spanish explorers in 1532 ended the Inca Empire. They killed Atahualpa, the Inca Emperor, and defeated the Inca armies.

▼ The Lost City
Machu Picchu is a well-preserved Inca city near Cuzco, Peru. This extraordinary city is located high on the Andes mountain, more than 2,300 metres (7,700 feet) above sea level. This city is hidden so well that it remained unknown to the outside world until 1911, when Hiram Bingham, an American historian stumbled upon the city's ruins. The city had a large palace, a huge courtyard, temples and homes for the royal staff.

Aztecs

The Aztecs were Native Americans who ruled over present-day Mexico. In fact their capital city, Tenochtitlán, was at the site of present-day Mexico City. The Aztecs ruled between 1428 and 1521, until they lost their homes and power to Spanish settlers. They were warriors who conquered many neighbouring kingdoms. Once a kingdom was conquered, its people had to pay tribute to the Aztec ruler, *Huey Tlatoani* (which meant Great Speaker). However, for a nation of warriors, they had surprisingly few weapons. Those that they had were made of stone and not metal.

An Aztec's life

The Aztecs did not have many agricultural tools either. They mostly used sticks to dig the soil and sow seeds. They had not discovered the wheel, so they had no carts. They also did not have any beasts of burden (llamas) like the Incas. However, they were good traders. They exchanged their pots, tools, baskets, cloth, jewellery and lake salt for jaguar skins, feathers, cotton and rubber from other kingdoms. The sun god (Huitzilopochtli), rain god (Tlaloc) and wind god (Quetzalcoatl) were the major Aztec gods. The Aztecs built huge temple complexes with big stepped pyramids for these gods. Human beings, especially slaves brought from conquered territories, were sacrificed regularly to please the gods.

Quipu

The Incas used brightly coloured threads called quipus to keep accounts and records of people, land, gold, animals and stored grain in their kingdom. Red threads were used to maintain army records, yellow threads for gold, and so on. The coloured threads were strung from a horizontal thread at the top and each one was knotted in a special way to record numbers and quantities. The knots at the top stood for 10,000, the ones below for 1,000 and so on and so forth until they worked their way down to one.

▲ Building bridges
The Incas built strong suspension bridges across mountains. These bridges were constructed with rope made of plaited grass woven together.

Try these too:

North America (p 102–103), South America (p 104–105), The Native Americans (p 124–125), New Lands – the Age of Exploration (p 134–135)

▲ The stone of creation
The Aztec sun stone, often mistakenly called the calender stone, is a huge carved stone dedicated to the sun god. The stone is about 3.5 metres (12 feet) in diameter and the colourful carvings are thought to depict the Aztec belief that the world went through four cycles of creation and destruction before the Aztecs came into existence.

▶ Pipe-smokers
Smoking pipes was an important part of the Aztec culture. The Aztecs smoked pipes during social gatherings and even at religious ceremonies. Pipes used by the Aztec priests during rituals were often decorated with elaborate carvings.

The Renaissance

The Renaissance period marked the end of the Middle Ages and the beginning of a more modern world. It was a period of great cultural change in Europe. Artists and writers rediscovered the classical Roman and Greek styles of art and architecture, as well as ancient books and the Greek and Latin languages.

Key facts:

- Renaissance means 'rebirth'. The name was first used by the Italian historian Giorgio Vasari, who wrote about the '*Rinascenza*' that was taking place in Italy. The word was later translated into the French 'Renaissance'.
- It was during the Renaissance period that artists regularly began signing their works. Artists began creating art to express themselves and they took pride in their work, unlike the anonymous artists of the Middle Ages.
- Cities and ports became very important during the Renaissance period. They were the centres of artistic activity and foreign trade. Banks became significant institutions as they provided money for businesses and earned huge profits.

The Renaissance period began in the 14th century AD in Italy, particularly in the city of Florence. In fact, the construction of the dome that tops the Santa Maria del Fiore Cathedral in Florence is widely regarded as the beginning of the Renaissance architecture. The start of Renaissance period itself is traced back to the Italian poet, Petrarch, who was in awe of the Ancient Roman literary works. By the 15th century, it had spread to the other parts of Europe, including France, England and Germany. The Florentines felt that the culture and style of the Middle Ages was barbaric. Therefore they looked back to the classical styles of Greece and Rome. Their art, architecture, sculpture and writing were heavily influenced by these ancient styles. Some of the greatest works of art were produced during the Italian Renaissance by artists such as Donatello, Michelangelo, Leonardo da Vinci and Raphael, and architects such as Alberti and Brunelleschi.

Pietà
Michelangelo's Pietà is one of the finest Renaissance sculptures. This marble sculpture depicts the Virgin Mary holding the body of her son Jesus, after he was crucified. The sculpture can now be found in St. Peter's Basilica in Rome. The sculpture is regarded as one of Michelangelo's greatest works.

Santa Maria del Fiore
The dome of Santa Maria del Fiore cathedral in Florence is regarded as Filippo Brunelleschi's greatest work. Its high dome was built by laying bricks in a spiral pattern on an octagonal (eight-sided) base. It was the first of its kind.

In the Middle Ages only scholars and writers read Roman and Greek classics, but the spread of education and the availability of books meant that more and more people could read by the 14th century. Renaissance people felt that it was important for everyone to constantly improve themselves and be good at a number of things, such as writing, swordsmanship and wrestling.

Elizabethan England

The Renaissance in England is also known as the Elizabethan era or the Shakespearean age. It was England's golden age of literature, architecture, science and exploration.

In England, unlike in Italy, literature gained more importance than the other arts during the Renaissance. Poets such as Edmund Spenser and John Milton, and playwrights like William Shakespeare and Christopher Marlowe wrote some of the most important English literature during this period. The architecture of this period broke away from the large, cold and dark Middle Ages style. Elizabethan buildings had high ceilings and large windows, and were decorated on the outside and the inside.

Printing press

In the early 15th century, a small-time German metalworker by the name Johann Gutenberg invented the printing press. The first book to be printed on his press was the Holy Bible. Gutenberg's invention revolutionized Western civilization. The mass production of printed books made information and knowledge much more easily available to everyone.

Reformation

By the 16th century, a number of people were unhappy with the Roman Catholic Church. They felt that the Church was becoming corrupt and misusing its power. These people broke away from the Roman Catholic Church and formed Protestant religious groups, such as the Lutherans, Calvinists and Mennonites. These groups had their own leaders and did not accept the Pope as their religious head.

In 1534, England became a Protestant country when King Henry VIII decreed that the new Church of England break away from the Roman Catholic Church.

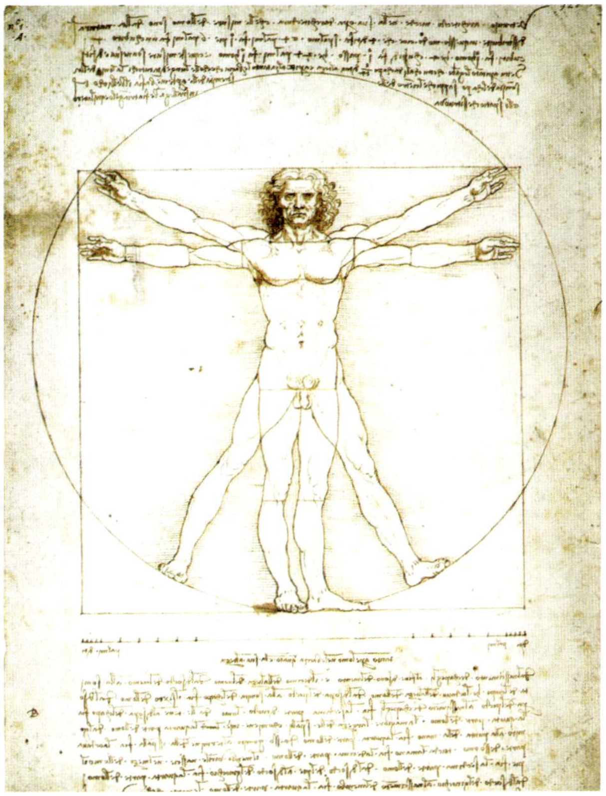

▲ **Reforming Christians**
John Calvin was one of the most important religious reformists, who established the Protestant system of Calvinism.

◂ **Renaissance man**
Leonardo da Vinci's Vitruvian Man is the most popular symbol of the Renaissance period.

Try these too:

Europe in the Middle Ages (p 126–127), Ancient Architecture (p 158–159), Modern Art and Artists (p 162–163), World Religions (p 174–175)

▾ **Michelangelo's Original Sin**
The ceiling of the Sistine Chapel in Rome was painted by Michelangelo. The ceiling contains scenes from the Book of Genesis, of which the Creation of Adam and the Original Sin are the best known.

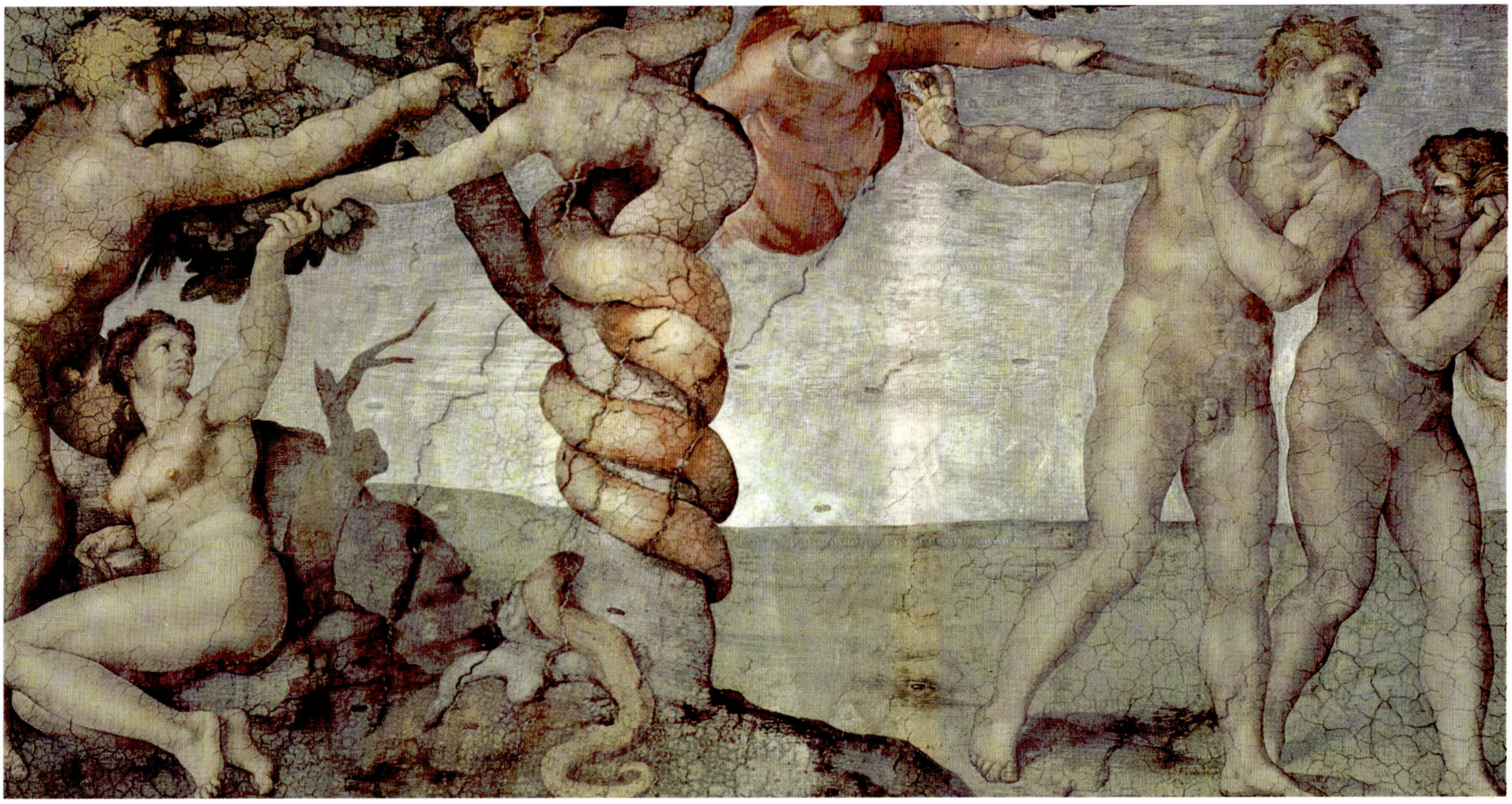

New Lands – the Age of Exploration

The period between the 15th and 17th centuries is commonly known as the Age of Exploration. During this time, European countries, such as England, Spain, Portugal, France, Germany and the Netherlands, sent out several groups of people to explore the oceans and to find out what lay beyond them. Several adventurous merchants, navigators and wealthy gentlemen led explorations for their countries or for their own personal gain.

▼ Sea routes taken by great explorers.

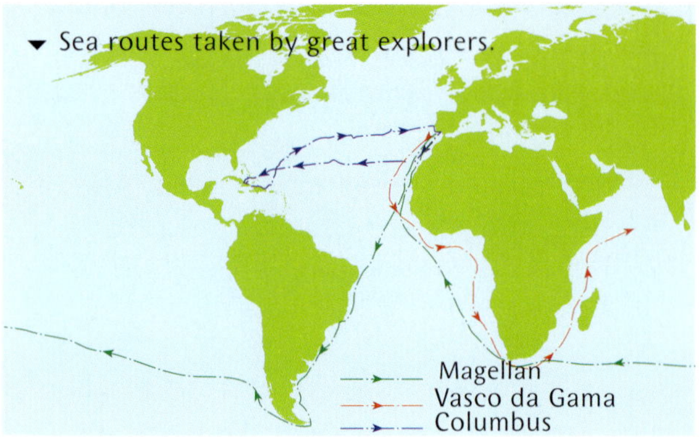

Key facts:

- People had been travelling to foreign lands since about 3000 BC. The Egyptians, Mesopotamians, Indus Valley people and Chinese travelled over land and sea to trade goods.
- Travel by land became difficult and unsafe due to the plague raging throughout Europe and because of the fierce Muslim kingdoms in the Middle East. By the 14th century shipbuilding and mapmaking had developed considerably in Europe, so travel by sea was a safer choice.
- It was the Portuguese explorer Ferdinand Magellan who gave the Pacific Ocean its name, which was derived from the Spanish word *pacifico*, meaning 'peaceful' – because he found the ocean to be very calm.

The Portuguese were the first to begin exploring sea routes. They set out for Africa under the patronage of Prince Henry the Navigator. By 1434, they had landed on the west coast of Africa. More than 50 years later, Bartolomeu Dias rounded the southern tip of the continent, the Cape of Good Hope. This meant that Europeans could sail directly to India through the Indian Ocean. In 1497 Vasco da Gama sailed along the route Dias had discovered to reach India.

Spanish explorers

The sea routes to India and China, discovered by the Portuguese, were long and extremely dangerous. This prompted the Spanish navigator Christopher Columbus to head to the west to find a quicker and much safer way to these countries across the Atlantic Ocean. After travelling for over a month, Columbus landed on an island in the Caribbean Sea, in the present-day West Indies, instead of on one of the Eastern lands. However, Columbus thought it was an island close to Asia and continued his journey to find Cuba, Haiti and the Dominican Republic. Columbus was convinced that these new lands he had discovered were the East Indies and therefore named the natives 'Indians'. Between 1493 and 1502, Columbus made three more voyages. During these trips he came upon more Caribbean islands like Jamaica, Trinidad and Tobago and Grenada. He also discovered Central America and Venezuela, in South America.

◄ **Undying faith**
Christopher Columbus died on 20 May 1506, in Valladolid, Spain. Even on his death bed, Columbus was convinced that he had discovered a new sea route to Asia.

Ferdinand Magellan was a Portuguese explorer who sailed under the banners of both Spain and Portugal. Supported by Charles I, the king of Spain, Magellan set out in 1519 to find a western route to the Spice Islands of the East. After stopping in South America for a few months in 1520, Magellan and his crew reached the Philippines in 1521. Magellan became involved in the rivalries between the natives and was killed by angry islanders. However, his crew eventually reached the Moluccas in Indonesia and one ship returned successfully to Spain in 1522. They were the first people to sail around the world.

▲ **Amerigo Vespucci**
Amerigo Vespucci was an Italian mapmaker and merchant who was he first to identify America as a new continent and not a part of the East. America was named after him.

Viking pioneers

The Vikings of Scandinavia were the earliest seafaring people to cross the Atlantic Ocean. They discovered Iceland, Greenland and Newfoundland, and sailed along the coast of Canada long before other European countries set out in search of new lands. During the period from 870–930, the Vikings settled in Iceland. In 930 the ruling chiefs established a parliament there. In 982 Eric the Red sailed from Iceland and discovered Greenland. Nearly 20 years later, his son Leif Eriksson discovered Newfoundland.

French discoveries

France was keen on exploring the west and the French mariner Jacques Cartier was the first to explore the area along the St Lawrence River in Canada. Samuel de Champlain and Sieur de La Salle followed Cartier's route a few years later. Champlain claimed Quebec for France and La Salle travelled down the Mississippi and claimed Louisiana.

English expeditions

John Cabot led the first English expedition west, to find a shorter and safer route to the spice-producing countries of the East. In 1497 Cabot landed in Newfoundland, Canada. Between 1576 and 1578, Martin Frobisher made three voyages to Canada and claimed a large part of the new land for England.

The English navigator and mapmaker James Cook undertook three historic voyages between 1768 and 1779. On the first one he charted New Zealand and the east coast of Australia. On the second he discovered several South Pacific islands and crossed the Antarctic Circle in search of Antarctica. On his last voyage he discovered Hawaii and sailed up north to Alaska. He was the first person to map the east coast of Australia.

Sir Francis Drake was one of the most well-known English explorers. He became the first Englishman to sail around the world in 1580, after travelling for about 34 months. He also raided several Spanish ships and robbed them.

▲ **Man of many talents**
As well as a fearless explorer, James Cook was an accomplished cartographer who made maps of all the places he visited.

Try these too:

Countries and People (p 102–115), Colonial Empires (p 136–137), Water Transport (p 196–197)

◀ **Sailing on**
The *Golden Hind* was a galleon that was Sir Francis Drake's flagship on his voyage around the world. Galleons were large sailing ships with many decks that were widely used in Europe between the 16th and 18th centuries. They were armed with cannons and used for both wars and explorations.

▲ **Hernando's mission**
Hernándo Cortés was a Spanish conquistador who was famous for his conquest of the Aztec empire. Hearing about the immense wealth of the Aztecs, Cortés attacked Mexico in 1519. He conquered this region and claimed it for Spain in 1521 after defeating the Aztecs in battle.

Colonial Empires

The Age of Exploration led to the Age of Imperialism in the 15th century. Europe became rich and powerful because of its conquests and colonies in other continents. In fact, many places outside Europe were European colonies at some time.

Key facts:

- The English language is one of the major contributions the British Empire has made to the world. Today, it is the second most widely spoken language in the world, used in nearly 100 countries.
- In 1776, 13 British colonies in North America signed the Declaration of Independence. These colonies joined together to form the United States of America. They were the first British colonies to become independent.
- The European colonies of Canada, Australia, New Zealand and the Union of South Africa were made dominions of the British Empire in the late-19th to early-20th centuries. This gave them the power to be completely independent.
- Today, the Falkland Islands, Gibraltar and British Antarctic Territory are overseas territories of the United Kingdom.
- The French colonial empire was the world's second largest empire after the British. During the mid-19th century France established control over parts of Asia and North, West and Central Africa.

When Europeans began discovering the countries in the East, the Caribbean and the Americas, they found that these were sources of gold, spices, silk, sugar, slaves and all kind of things that could make them rich. Portugal was the first country to establish colonies, in its neighbouring Mediterranean islands of the Azores and Madeira, around the mid-1400s. Spain, Britain, France, Germany and the Netherlands soon followed by colonizing parts of Africa, the Americas, India and Southeast Asia. Early colonies, especially in Africa, were first established as trading posts that facilitated trade in slaves, and gold, ivory and other exotic goods. Over the years, the European populations at these trading posts steadily increased and through a combination of war and peaceful treaties, the colonizers gained greater control of the colonies. Often the native populations turned to the European traders for support and protection from invading neighbours. Therefore, placed in a position of power, the European settlers took control of the administration and governance of these countries and declared them colonial territories of their respective countries. The colonial rulers collected taxes and controlled law and order, the court system, agriculture, industry and trade in the colony.

British Empire

Britain was the largest imperial power between the 16th and 19th centuries. The British Empire extended over a large part of North America, large parts of Africa and the Middle East, India, Sri Lanka, some Southeast Asian countries, several South Pacific Islands, and all of Australia and New Zealand. That is nearly one-third of all the land in the world.

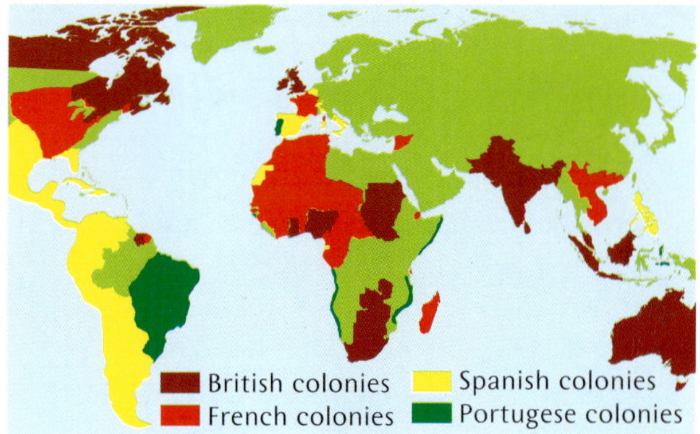

▲ **Age of empires** A map of the major powers during the Colonial age.

▼ **A colonial ruler** Queen Victoria represented the golden age of British colonialism.

Types of colonies

Britain dealt differently with each of her colonies. In Asia and Africa, companies first established trading posts, and after gaining the trust of the native kings, began governing the country. Eventually, the British monarch would declare the region an imperial territory of Britain. In some Middle Eastern countries Britain was only a protector and the country was its protectorate. This meant that the country had its own government, but was loyal to the British crown and had to obey Britain in some matters. A third type of British colony was populated only by settlers from England, and later the United Kingdom. The first among these was Newfoundland, followed by colonies in the eastern parts of North America, the Caribbean and later Australia and New Zealand.

End of the Empire

In the 20th century, the Imperial Age finally came to an end with Britain's colonies demanding independence. Britain, weakened by the two World Wars, had to eventually give in to the demands of the native populations in its colonies and grant them freedom. Most of the other Asian and African countries had gained independence by the 1960s.

Commonwealth

The Queen of England continues to be the queen of 16 former colonies, although she only holds the title and has no real powers. These 16 countries are called Commonwealth Realms. All countries that were once British colonies, including the Commonwealth Realms, are now part of the Commonwealth of Nations. There are 53 countries in this association, which co-operate and help each other in trade and development.

◂ The great statesman Cecil Rhodes played a very important role in the British colonization of Africa. He helped Britain annex many of the South African states. He also proposed the famous 'red line' – a railway network connecting all the British colonies from the north to the south of Africa. This railway line was supposed to help in the administration of the colonies as well as enable quick movement of troops through British territories. Rhodes also served as the Prime Minister of Cape Colony and founded the state of Rhodesia (modern Zambia and Zimbabwe).

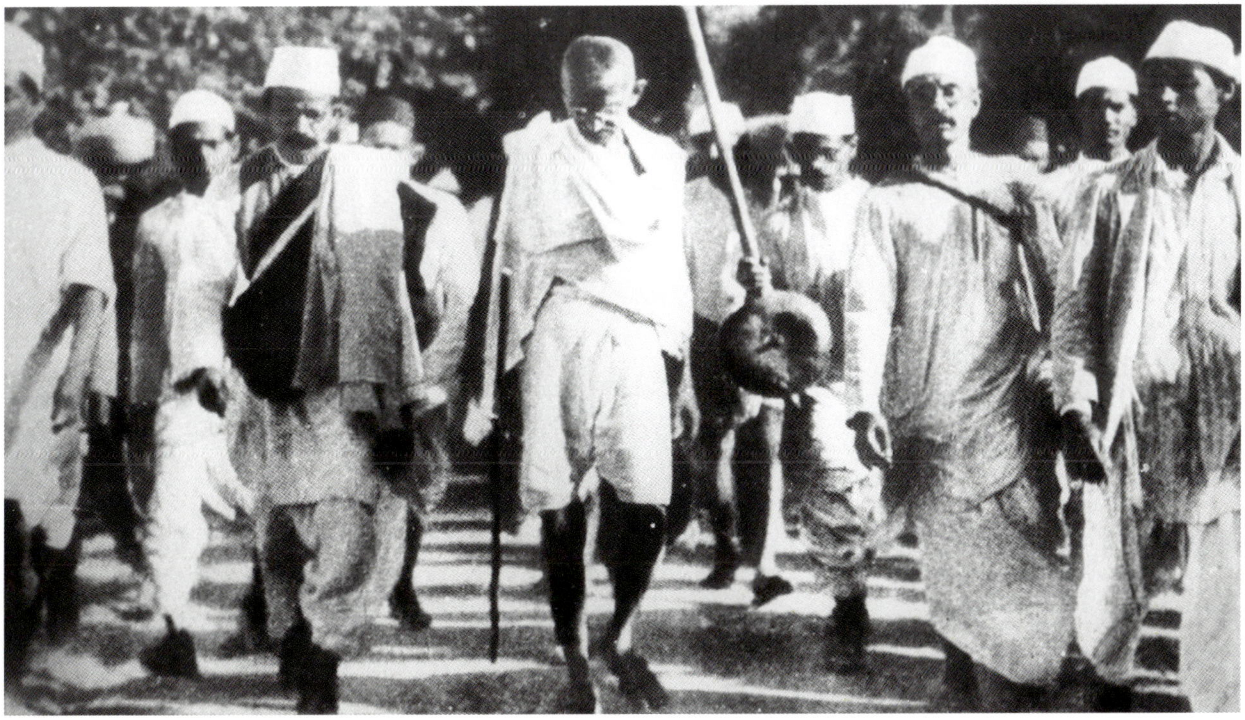

◂ Freedom at last India was the first British colony to become independent. It won its freedom on 15 August 1947, after about 40 years of struggle. Although India was led by many brave leaders throughout her struggle, Mahatma Gandhi was the most prominent of them all. It was his non-violent movement that finally drove the British out.

Try these too:

Medieval Asia (p 128 –129), New Lands – the Age of Exploration (p 134 –135), The American Revolution and Civil War (p 144–145)

The Industrial Revolution

▲ **Sowing the right way**
Jethro Tull's seed drill marked the beginning of mechanization in farming. Before that, farmers sowed by hand.

During the 18th century, Western Europe underwent great change. The main way of earning a living shifted from farming to manufacturing, and from working with one's hands to working with machines. The Industrial Revolution began in Britain and spread to the rest of Europe and to North America.

Key facts:

- One factor partly responsible for the Industrial Revolution was the excellent transportation system in Britain. Turnpike roads, navigable rivers, and canals, on which horse-drawn barges could sail, provided a good inland network, and ships sailed along the coast. These multiple transportation systems helped in swiftly transporting raw materials to factories and finished goods to cities and ports.
- The postage stamp was a significant Industrial Age invention. It led to the birth of the modern postal system. The first postage stamp was the Penny Black. It was introduced in 1840. The idea of introducing prepaid postage stamps at a very nominal cost of one penny was pioneered by Rowland Hill, a British teacher, in 1837.
- During the early part of the Industrial Revolution, Britain's gross domestic product or GDP (value of goods produced) was only £217 million (for the decade of 1800 to 1809). By 1869, British industries had raised the GDP to £633 million – an almost threefold increase within just 60 years.

Britain had good supplies of coal and iron, two of the most important materials used during the Industrial Revolution. The scientific discoveries and inventions of the 17th century paved the way for industrialization.

How it started

The earliest signs of industrialization were seen in agriculture. The invention of the seed drill, new crop rotation methods and proper breeding of animals improved farming and made it more efficient.

Changing world

Until the mid-18th century, almost everything was handmade. However, handmade products could only be made in small numbers. As the population grew, it became necessary to find ways to manufacture large quantities quickly. Machines were invented to do this.

Iron, coal and steam

An important step in the development of machines was the discovery of ways to use coal and iron. Iron could be made into hard and strong sheets, which could be used to make machines. Coal was used to produce heat and steam energy, which was used to power the machines. Steam was the most important source of energy in 18th-century England.

An early steam engine was made by Thomas Savery, an English engineer, in 1689 to pump water out of coal mines. Later, Scottish engineer James Watt designed a steam engine that could be used to run various kinds of machines.

▶ **Finding work**
The workers moved to cities to find jobs in the factories that had sprung up.

Textile industry

The textile industry in England changed almost completely because of the Industrial Revolution. Until then, wool, linen and flax yarn were spun by hand and the yarn was then used to weave cloth on handlooms. All this changed in the 18th century, with the beginning of industrialization. In 1733, John Kay invented the flying shuttle, which partly mechanized the weaving process. Then in 1770, British industrialist James Hargreaves patented the spinning jenny. This machine could spin several threads at the same time. The third invention that changed the textile industry was the water-powered spinning frame designed by Richard Arkwright. It could produce even stronger thread for yarn. However, it was only with the invention of the 'mule' by Samuel Crompton, in 1779, that good quality yarn was made. Now English textiles could be made more cheaply and quickly than anywhere else in the world.

Better quality and higher production of garments did not mean better working conditions for labourers. There was no proper health care or safety regulations for workers. Factory owners employed a large number of children as they worked hard and for less money. This situation did not change until the end of the 19th century.

'Watt' an invention!
James Watt's steam engine was largely reponsible for the advent of the Industrial Revolution.

Revolutionary invention
The spinning jenny revolutionized the textile industry. This device could spin several threads at the same time, reducing the amount of time and work required to produce yarn. With the invention of the jenny, a worker could now make eight or more spools at once.

Try these too:

Moving Ahead (p 140–141), Moving on Land (p 194–195), Water Transport (p 196–197), Air Travel (p 198–199)

Wedgwood

English pottery was yet another industry that benefited from the Industrial Revolution. Potter and designer Josiah Wedgwood set up a partly mechanized factory in Staffordshire, which produced a range of ware. The machines that mixed and ground raw materials ran on power generated by waterwheels and windmills. By 1850, the manufacture of pottery was extensively mechanized.

Moving Ahead

By about 1850, the second stage of the Industrial Revolution had begun. The most important developments of this time were the steam powered locomotive and the railways. Steam engines were also used on ships. Among the key inventions were the internal combustion engine and electricity.

▾ Setting the standard
In 1829, George Stephenson and his son, Robert, built the first modern steam locomotive, the *Rocket*. The new locomotive had many revolutionary features that were adapted into all steam locomotives built after it. A replica of the *Rocket* can be seen at the Science Museum in London.

The very first railway was a horse-drawn cart pulled along wooden rails. By the late-1700s, iron rails began to be widely used by most coal mines to transport coal. The English engineer Richard Trevithick invented the first steam locomotive, which was not very successful. In 1814, George Stephenson designed a successful steam locomotive, *Active* (which was later renamed *Locomotion*). This engine ran on rails and became the first steam locomotive ever to be used for public travel in 1825, when the Stockton and Darlington Railway employed its services. The company opened the railway to people who wanted to travel on its 40-kilometre (26-mile) route. The first successful steamship was designed by Robert Fulton, an American engineer. In 1807, Fulton inaugurated his boat, the *North River Steamboat,* with a trip down the Hudson River, from New York to Albany. Soon after, the steamboat began a regular passenger service.

▸ Picture perfect
The first practical process of photography was made public in 1839, by Frenchman Louis Daguerre. A picture was recorded on a metal plate coated with silver iodide. The plate was treated with mercury fumes and preserved by applying salt.

By the time the second phase was in full swing, Britain had lost its monopoly to the United States and Germany. The main trigger for the second phase was developments in the fields of electricity, communication and transport. In the United States, the pioneers included such great names as Thomas Alva Edison, George Westinghouse and Nikola Tesla. If steam engines dominated the first phase, it was the internal combustion engine that drove the second one. German inventors, Gottlieb Daimler and Nikolaus August Otto were the forces behind this new wave, while American businessman, Henry Ford's assembly line revolutionized factory production like never before.

Sound and light

In 1831, Michael Faraday, the famous British scientist, devised a method to generate electricity, and by 1881 American inventor Thomas Alva Edison was able to mass produce incandescent light bulbs. Meanwhile, Nikola Tesla invented electric transformers that could produce alternating current. However, it was only in 1891 that the first long-distance, high-powered transmission system was made. George Westinghouse built it for use in a gold mine in Colorado. In 1876, Alexander Graham Bell changed the way the world communicated by inventing the telephone.

It was the first time speech was converted to sound waves and sent through a wire to a receiver. By 1877, sound could also be recorded. Edison's phonograph could not only record sound, but also play it back.

Steel

Civilizations have grown and flourished because of the way in which they used metal. Starting from the Iron Age, metal has been important to man for its use in making farming tools, weapons, building equipment and for use in ornaments and currency. The invention of steel, in the 1850s and 1860s, was an important development. Steel was to become the metal of the modern world. Henry Bessemer and William Siemens were responsible for designing methods and equipment through which good quality steel could be produced in large quantities.

"Watson, I need you!" Alexander Graham Bell's first telephonic conversation was believed to have been with his assistant, Watson.

Car for the masses The Ford Model T was the first truly affordable car. It was also the first car to be mass produced on assembly lines.

Key facts:

- Thomas Alva Edison was probably one of the busiest inventors of the second Industrial Revolution. He had 1,093 design patents in his name. However, not all of his designs were original. Many of them were improvements on designs by others.
- In the late-19th century, railways were combined with electricity to make electric 'streetcars'. By the end of the century, electricity was available everywhere and streetcars became popular in many big cities of the world.

Macadam roads

Modern roads were invented by a renowned Scottish engineer named John Loudon McAdam. This enterprising inventor realized that it was important for roads to be higher than their surrounding area and that they should have smooth and hard surfaces to make them safe and easy to travel on. Therefore, McAdam made roads using a mixture of gravel and rock, with side ditches for drainage. The entire surface was compacted and fine gravel was added to bind it. This method is called macadamization.

Try these too:

Light (p 180–181), Sound (p 182–183), Electricity (p 190–191), Moving on Land (p 194–195), Water Transport (p 196–197)

The Scientific Revolution

Man has always been curious about the world around him. Knowledge about the natural world has helped scientists discover and invent things that have changed and improved our lives. Although the study of science can probably be dated to the time early man started observing the various phenomena of nature, it was in the 16th and 17th centuries that some of the greatest scientific discoveries took place.

Key facts:

- The words 'science' and 'scientist' were not in use when the Scientific Revolution began. People studying science were called natural philosophers.
- The study of the motion of bodies under the influence of forces, pioneered by Galileo, Brahe, Kepler and Newton, is called classical mechanics.
- Galileo Galilei was also an inventor as well as an astronomer. He invented a surveyor's compass and the thermometer, and vastly improved the telescope and the microscope. He also made designs for an automatic tomato picker, and a device with a candle and mirror, which could reflect light through an entire building.

In the earliest civilizations of Mesopotamia, Egypt, China and the Indus Valley, people studied the movement of the Sun and Moon. They also laid the foundations of early mathematics and medicine. In Ancient Greece, philosophers, Aristotle and Plato showed a deep interest in physics, while Ptolemy made his mark in astronomy and the movement of planets. Pythagoras studied mathematics and geometry and Hippocrates conducted research in medicine. Their work and study, and that of several other unknown scientists, formed the basis upon which modern science has developed.

Astronomy

Polish astronomer and mathematician Nicolaus Copernicus was the first to discover that the Sun was at the centre of the solar system and not the Earth, as people had believed all along. His work was further developed by scientists like Tycho Brahe and Johannes Kepler, who confirmed the theory.

Kepler's discovery
In 1604, Johannes Kepler observed a luminous stellar explosion in the sky. This proved that nothing in the Universe was indestructible. On the contrary, the Universe was constantly changing. The bright explosion of the star, called 'Kepler's supernova', was the last supernova observed in the Milky Way.

Kepler explained how planets move on elliptical paths. Italian astronomer Galileo Galilei observed sunspots on the Sun and craters and mountains on the Moon. He also discovered that Jupiter had several moons that revolved around it. These first moons, observed by him, were named the Galilean moons in his honour.

Physics

As well as astronomy, Galileo also had an interest in physics. He conducted experiments to study the movement of objects and devised a method to measure their speed. He also conducted experiments to measure the speed of light. However, it was Ole Rømer, the Danish astronomer, who first proved that the speed of light is finite. The study of motion was continued by English physicist Sir Isaac Newton. This great scientist also studied light and explained gravitational force.

A scientist par excellence
Galileo is regarded as the father of astronomy and modern physics for his contributions in these fields.

Mathematics

The French philosopher and mathematician René Descartes was the first person to demonstrate that algebra and geometry were not two completely separate branches of mathematics, but actually inseparably connected. He showed how problems in algebra could be converted and solved using geometry, and vice versa. Isaac Newton's important contributions are the binomial theorem and calculus, both important aspects of modern mathematics.

▲ The Newton effect
According to popular legend, Newton was sitting under an apple tree, when an apple fell down. He wondered why the apple had fallen down and not gone up or sideways. He soon discovered that gravity was the answer.

▲ The medical eye
The compound microscope is an indispensable instrument in modern medicine.

Biology

English scientist Robert Hooke invented a highly precise compound microscope with which he was able to study plants and animals. He coined the word 'cell', while studying the structure of plants because he thought that plant cells looked very much like monks' cells in a monastery. In 1796, Edward Jenner made an important contribution to medical science when he invented the first vaccine. The vaccine was responsible for putting an end to smallpox, which was a widespread and dreaded disease at that time.

▲ Better than cure
Jenner injected a boy with cowpox, which was not a fatal disease. He then innoculated the boy with smallpox. The boy did not fall sick and became the first to be vaccinated.

Chemistry

Several elements like magnesium, nickel, nitrogen, chlorine, tungsten, zirconium and uranium were discovered during the 18th century. French chemist Antoine Lavoisier is considered to be the father of modern chemistry. In the 1770s, he proved that oxygen, the gas responsible for life, was also responsible for burning and rusting. He also showed that oxygen combined with hydrogen produced water. Later, he published the first modern chemistry textbook with a list of substances and elements.

Baconian method

Sir Francis Bacon, the Lord Chancellor of England during the rule of James I, was a scholar and writer. In 1606, he published a book called *Novum Organum*, which explained the manner in which scientific experiments and research should be carried out. He believed that to gain a complete and correct understanding of science, it was necessary to experiment repeatedly and to carefully make observations.

Try these too:

Galaxies and Stars (p 6–7), The Sun and the Solar System (p 8–9), The Gas Giants (p 12–13), Matter (p 178–179), Light (p 180–181), Forces and Motion (p 188–189)

The American Revolution and Civil War

The American War of Independence (or the American Revolution) and the Civil War were the most important events in the early history of the United States. The Revolution led to freedom from Britain and the formation of the country, and the Civil War marked the end of slavery in the United States.

Key facts:

- The United States Constitution was adopted in March 1789. However, the situation was not very stable and for years many states resented the federal government's control over them. The election of Abraham Lincoln as President, in 1861, led to the culmination of this bitterness in the American Civil War.
- The world's first submarine was used by the Continental Navy on 6 September 1776, to sink a British ship. The attempt however, failed. The submarine, called *Turtle*, was designed by David Bushnell, an American inventor. It was made up of two shell-like parts of oak, coated with tar.
- While the Confederacy and Union were fighting the Civil War, President Lincoln issued the Emancipation Proclamation on 1 January 1863. The proclamation stated that all slaves in the Confederate States were free. A million copies of this proclamation were distributed among the slaves in the south to spread the word and start trouble in Confederacy camps.

Until about the mid-1700s most American colonists were content to be subjects of Britain. However, from 1764 onwards, Britain passed a series of acts that the American colonists found intolerable. With these acts the British government increased taxes and import duties on a wide range of commodities including sugar, indigo dye, wine, textiles, paper and tea. They also imposed taxes on all printed material such as documents, pamphlets, newspapers and even playing cards.
Britain also did not allow the United States to print their own currency notes. Angered by Britain's high handedness, the colonists decided to revolt against Britain.

Events of the revolution

The colonists formed the Continental Army, to take on the British might. They also hastily put a navy together. To begin with, the Continental Army and navy lost every battle as they did not have enough people, money or arms. However, France came to the aid of the Americans by sending them money, ammunition and even troops.

Charismatic leader George Washington's contribution in the Revolution has led to him being regarded as the father of the nation.

Britain was supported by several native tribes who hated the white colonists. A number of battles were fought and a lot of lives were lost on both sides before the British forces surrendered in defeat on 19 October 1781. In April 1782, the British Parliament voted to end the war in America and on 3 September 1783, Britain and America signed the Treaty of Paris to officially end the American Revolution.

Party at sea
The Boston Tea Party took place on the night of 16 December 1773, as an act of protest against the Tea Act. About 60 revolutionaries went aboard three British ships anchored at the Boston Harbor, and dumped their cargo of 342 boxes of tea into the sea.

Civil war

When Abraham Lincoln was elected President of the United States in 1861, he announced his intention to end slavery in the country. The southern states were not happy to hear this. The plantations in these states depended heavily on slave labour. They decided that the only way to take care of their interests was to leave the Union. South Carolina was the first state to secede from the Union. Florida, Mississippi, Georgia, Texas, Alabama, Louisiana, Tennessee, North Carolina, Virginia and Arkansas soon joined them. These 11 seceded states formed the Confederate States of America and elected Jefferson Davis as their President. This signalled the start of the Civil War. The war was fought between 23 federal states, most of which formed the northern part of the United States, and the 11 confederate southern states. The Confederacy raised an army and began the war in April 1861. They attacked Fort Sumter in North Carolina and successfully took control of it. President Lincoln responded by cutting off all supplies to the southern states. In 1863, Lincoln released the Emancipation Proclamation that set all slaves, including the ones in the southern states, free. The war was waged with several successes and failures on both sides. However, the Federal army, which was more powerful and better equipped, was eventually able to outlast its opponents. After four years of fierce fighting, the Confederates ran out of supplies and troops. Finally, on 9 April 1865, the Confederate troops gave up the fight and surrendered. The seceded states eventually rejoined the United States of America.

◀ The great General
Ulysses S. Grant is most remembered for his contribution and strategies during the American Civil War. He was solely responsible for the Union victory at Vicksburg, Mississippi, which eventually turned the tables on the Confederate States. General Grant also forced the surrender of Robert E. Lee, the most successful Confederate General at Appomattox, Virginia, effectively ending the Civil War. Later, in 1869, Grant became the President of the United States. However, he is considered to be one of the worst presidents as his administration was filled with corrupt officials.

▲ The death of a president
On 14 April 1865, after the Confederates had surrendered, President Abraham Lincoln and the First Lady celebrated by going to see a play. During the play, the President was shot dead by a Confederate supporter named John Wilkes Booth.

Declaration of Independence

The *American Declaration of Independence* was drafted by a committee specially appointed for the purpose by Congress. Thomas Jefferson, Benjamin Franklin, John Adams, Roger Sherman and Robert Livingston were the members of this committee. Jefferson wrote out the first draft of the declaration, and Adams and Franklin made some changes to it. On 28 June 1776, Jefferson's *Declaration of Independence* was presented to Congress, which then formally endorsed the Declaration on 4 July 1776 and sent copies to all the 13 colonies. The colonies signed the declaration, announcing their freedom, but Britain refused to accept her defeat until much later in 19 October 1781.

Try these too:

North America (p 102–103), South America (p 104–105), The Native Americans (p 124–125), The Incas and Aztecs (p 130–131), New Lands – the Age of Exploration (p 134 –135), Colonial Empires (p 136–137)

The French Revolution

The French Revolution was one of the most important events in the history of Europe. It took place between 1789 and 1799 and completely changed the face of French society and politics.

Expensive tastes
The extravagant spending of kings like Louis XIV on wars and palaces, such as the one in Versailles, was the reason behind the nation's heavy debts and high taxes.

Key facts:

- In 1803, Napoleon realized that it was impossible for him to defend French territories in America while he was busy fighting wars at home. In a deal called the Louisiana Purchase, Napoleon sold the Louisiana territory to the United States, at less than three cents an acre ($7 per square kilometre).
- The Napoleonic Code is the set of civil laws formulated by Napoleon in 1804. It was the first successful system to codify European civil law and is still followed in many countries.
- A major factor that influenced the French citizens to begin a revolution was the 18th century movement called the Age of Enlightenment. During this period, philosophers like Voltaire and Rousseau encouraged progress and scientific thought, and looked down upon old traditions and superstitions, promoted by the Church and the State.

By the 18th century, the population of France had grown to 25 million people, the largest in Europe at that time. Most of these people were poor, starving peasants who lived in villages. Paris was crowded, filled with merchants, traders and factory workers who felt that the king and the nobility had all the privileges while they had nothing. Taxes were high, food was scarce and the country was deep in debt. Unhappy with their situation and unwilling to tolerate it, the people of France rose up in a revolt against the monarchy.

Angry mobs

On 14 July 1789, an angry mob stormed into the Bastille prison in Paris and set some of its prisoners free in a show of rebellion against their king. This spirit of revolt soon spread throughout the country. The National Assembly was formed as the common man's government. It did away with the feudalistic landowning system and reduced the privileges of the nobility. On 26 August 1789, the Assembly published the *Declaration of the Rights of Man and of the Citizen,* which gave equal rights and freedom to all Frenchmen.

The Republic

In August 1792, Louis XVI was forced to step down from the throne. His family was imprisoned and France was declared a republic. The following year he was tried and executed by the guillotine. It was a time of widespread rioting in the country and food was still scarce. France was also at war with many of its neighbouring countries. Various factions began revolting against the National Convention, the governing body of the new Republic. The National Convention, in turn, tried to subdue the opposition. Finally, the convention was disbanded in October 1795. In the same year, the Republic was ended and the Directory, headed by five directors, took control. The Directory was replaced by the Consulate in 1799, when Napoleon Bonaparte, the French army general, overthrew it and proclaimed himself the first consul of France.

Storming of the Bastille
The revolutionaries seized the prison and killed its commander, Bernard de Launay and many of his guards. The event was significant as it was the first open rebellion against the king.

Guillotine

The guillotine was a device used for executing prisoners who were given the death sentence. It was first used on 25 April 1792 to execute a French highwayman and was the only legal method of execution in France until the death penalty was abolished in 1981. At least 20,000 people are estimated to have been executed by the guillotine during the French Revolution. The guillotine was also used to execute protestors during the Reign of Terror from 1793 to 1794.

Napoleonic era

Napoleon was one of France's most successful military generals and led the French army successfully in many battles. As a dictator and as an emperor after 1804, he brought most of Western and Central Europe under his control. He was also an excellent statesman. He made the government more centralized and efficient, improved education, taxation, banking, sanitation, and law and order.

The fall of Napoleon

It was Napoleon's ambition to conquer the whole of Europe that eventually caused his downfall. Napoleon's 1812 invasion of Russia ended in a humiliating defeat. His offensive on Germany met with an even worse fate, when he was forced to retreat in the Battle of Leipzig in 1813. The following year Britain, Russia, Prussia and Austria joined forces and captured Paris. Napoleon was arrested and exiled to the Mediterranean island of Elba. He escaped in less than 11 months, and returned to Paris in March 1815. He was then put back on the throne. However, in June he was defeated by the Duke of Wellington in the Battle of Waterloo. He was then exiled to the island of St Helena, where he died in 1821.

▼ **A stinging defeat**
In 1812, Napoleon led an army of almost 700,000 men into Russia. Lack of food, the bitter Russian winter and other logistical problems forced the French army to eventually retreat. Only 22,000 men survived the campaign.

Try these too:

Europe (p 108–109), Europe in the Middle Ages (p 126–127), Colonial Empires (p 136–137), Modern Art and Artists (p 162–163)

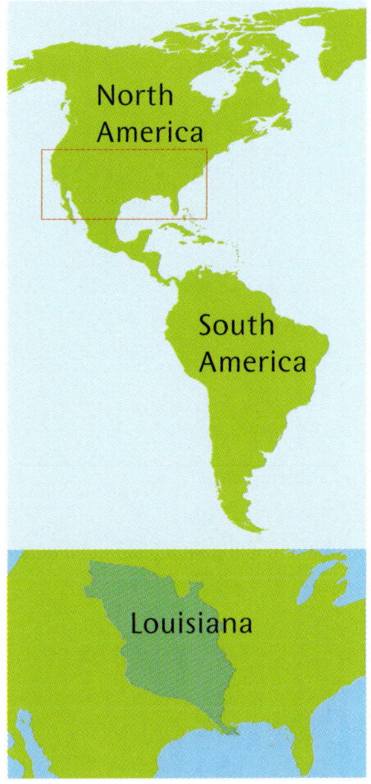

▲ **Louisiana purchased!**
In 1803, Napoleon sold the French Louisiana territory to the United States for 15 million dollars. It included the present state of Louisiana, all or parts of Missouri, Iowa, North and South Dakota, Texas, Kansas and Colorado.

The First World War and the Russian Revolution

The First World War was fought between 1914 and 1918. It was the biggest and most violent war Europe had ever experienced up until then. The First World War involved the United States as well as most of the countries in the European continent. It was also a period of great political upheaval and change. The monarchies of Germany and Austria-Hungary, and the kingdom of the Ottomans collapsed as a result of this war.

▾ Trench warfare
The heavy loss of life in the Western Front trenches is one of the most unforgettable horrors of the First World War. Thousands of soldiers were killed by firearms and poison gas, while many more died after contracting infections.

In Russia especially, the war had a profound effect. The old order ended and a Communist government came to power in 1917, following a public movement called the Russian Revolution.

The players

The First World War was also known as the Great War. It was fought between the Allied Powers and the Central Powers. The major Allied countries were Britain (and its colonies), Russia, Japan and the United States. The Central Powers included Germany, Austria-Hungary, Bulgaria and the Ottoman Empire. By the 20th century, European politics had become extremely complicated, with monarchs and leaders having treaties, agreements and secret understandings with some countries and long-standing disputes with others. This had fostered a great deal of suspicion and mistrust among various nations.

The war begins

The event that triggered the war was the assassination of Franz Ferdinand, heir to the Austria-Hungary throne, by a Serbian student. This incident made Austria-Hungary declare war on Serbia. Russia joined the war in support of Serbia, and Germany got involved in support of Austria. France and Britain, being allies of Russia, also joined the war. In 1917, the United States joined the battle by declaring war against Germany. Finally, after four years of intense fighting, peace was finally declared on 11 November 1918. The war resulted in the separation of Hungary from Austria, the formation of Czechoslovakia and Yugoslavia and the independence of Poland after more than a century of being sectioned off to Austria, Prussia and Russia. Germany was forced to give up about 10 per cent of its territories and all of its overseas colonies, reduce the size of its military and pay huge amounts in compensation to the Allies.

▾ Participants of the war
The map shows the European military alliances during the First World War. The green regions represent the allied forces, also called the Entente Powers, while the orange portion represents the Central Powers, who were so called as they were located between Russia, France and Britain. The countries marked in grey were neutral.

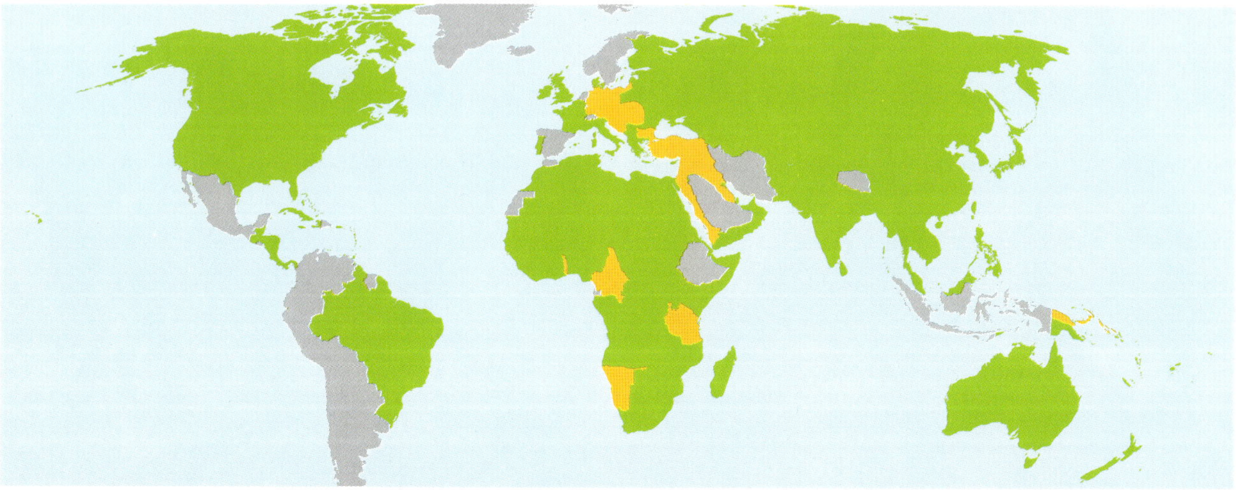

Zeppelins

Zeppelins were gigantic German airships that were used for bombing and scouting during the First World War. The first ever Zeppelin air raid on Britain took place on the night of 19 January 1915. Germany built 88 Zeppelins during the war and carried out more than 50 successful air raids on Britain.

▾ Communist Russia
As the leader of the Bolshevik Party, Vladimir Ilyich Lenin became the first Premier of the Soviet Union when the party came to power following the October Revolution.

The Russian Bolshevik Revolution

The Russian Revolution can refer to three separate events. The first revolution took place in 1905. It was marked by a series of riots protesting against the rule of Tsar Nicholas II. This revolution was not very successful, but is seen as a trigger for the revolution of 1917. The 1917 revolution was a historical movement that can be divided into two parts – the February Revolution in 1917, and the October Revolution in the same year. The Russian people had grown increasingly unhappy with the dictatorial rule of Tsar Nicholas II, the feudalistic system in the country, and the scarcity of food and extreme poverty that had resulted from the fighting in the First World War. In February 1917, the people of Petrograd, the capital city, began protesting against the Tsar. They were joined by soldiers who went on strike and refused to continue in the war. The Tsar was finally forced to give up his throne and a temporary government was formed. However, this government was weak and ineffective and, in October, the Communist Bolshevik group, led by Vladimir Lenin, took control of the Russian government. The Communists believed that all citizens had equal rights and responsibilities and that everyone should work for the benefit of the state. This model lasted for about 70 years. It was also copied in other countries including China and Cuba.

Key facts:

- Nearly nine million soldiers died on the battlefield during the Great War. Almost the same number, or more, civilians died in various countries during that time due to food shortages, being caught in the midst of land combat, being victims of air raids and due also to mass killing by enemy troops.
- The First World War saw the use of many modern combat techniques like trenches, aircraft, poison gas, tanks and machine guns.
- The event that triggered the Russian Revolution of 1905 was the Bloody Sunday massacre on 22 January 1905. A group of factory workers gathered in front of the Winter Palace in St Petersburg to present a petition to the Tsar. The Imperial Guards opened fire on the unarmed protesters, killing more than 100 people and injuring several more.

Try these too:

North America (p 102–103), Europe (p 108–109), The Second World War (p 150–151), Air Travel (p 198–199)

▸ The end of a dynasty
Nicholas II was forced to abdicate on 2 March 1917 bringing 300 years of Romanov rule to an end. The Tsar and his family were kept under house arrest in Yekatterinburg, where they were killed on 17 July 1918 by a group of Bolshevik secret police led by Yakov Yurovsky.

The Second World War

The Second World War was the largest and deadliest war in the history of the world. It was fought between 1939 and 1945 and involved almost all the nations that fought in the First World War. It was fought in Europe, Africa, Asia and the Pacific.

Key facts:

• A new and highly effective military tactic introduced by the Germans in the Second World War was the blitzkrieg. A blitzkrieg involved making a swift and intense surprise attack on enemy camps or cities.

• At least 50 million people lost their lives in the Second World War. About six million of these were killed in the Holocaust, most of whom were Jews. Several million people became homeless and nearly 70 per cent of Europe's industries were destroyed.

• When the war ended, the US Secretary of State, George Marshall drew up the Marshall Plan, according to which the US Congress contributed several billion dollars to help in the reconstruction of Europe.

• The Japanese feared that the presence of the US Navy in the Pacific would interfere with their military expansion. In an attempt to discourage US involvement in the war, Japan launched a suprise attack on the US naval base at Pearl Harbor, Hawaii. Japanese aircraft bombed the base on 7 December 1941, killing about 3,000 American soldiers.

The breakout of the Second World War is attributed to the territorial ambitions of the German dictator, Adolf Hitler, who was responsible for widespread genocide and other atrocities both before and during the war.

Why war broke out

Germany and Japan were rising powers, ambitious to increase their power and territories. Imperial Japan, led by its military generals, took over Manchuria, Korea and many parts of China. Germany, headed by Adolf Hitler, began expanding its control over neighbouring territories. Italy was ruled by the fascist leader Benito Mussolini, who entered into an agreement with Germany to co-operate in all military matters. Later, Japan also signed co-operation treaties with both of these countries. It feared the increasing power of the United States in the Pacific islands and launched an attack that eventually drew the latter into the war. In short, the atmosphere at that time was one of suspicion, fear and hatred, which ultimately led to war.

The allies

The opponents in the war were the Axis and Allied powers. The Axis nations of Germany, fascist Italy and Japan were later joined by Bulgaria, Romania, Hungary, Croatia and Slovakia. The three main Allies included Britain, Russia and the United States. They were supported by France, other European countries, the Commonwealth nations, China and a few South American countries.

▸ The stage is set
The top map shows the political division of territories between the Allied (Britain, Russia, France and United States) and the Axis powers (Germany, Italy, Japan and their allies) during the war. The bottom map depicts the drastic change that came about in the world map, following the defeat of the Axis powers.

The mighty war

The war began on 3 September 1939, after Germany invaded Poland on 1 September. There were two main theatre to the war – Western and Pacific. In the Pacific the war was mainly fought between the United states and Japan, while in the Western front the Allied forces battled the combined might of Germany, Italy and their allies. The death and destruction caused by this war surpassed anything that had ever taken place before. Horrifying new techniques like biological warfare, concentration camps and atomic bombs, as well as advanced weapons and equipment such as rockets, jet aircraft, radar and torpedoes were used. Eventually, Germany surrendered and the war in Europe officially ended on 8 May 1945. In Asia, fighting continued until Japan officially surrendered on 2 September 1945.

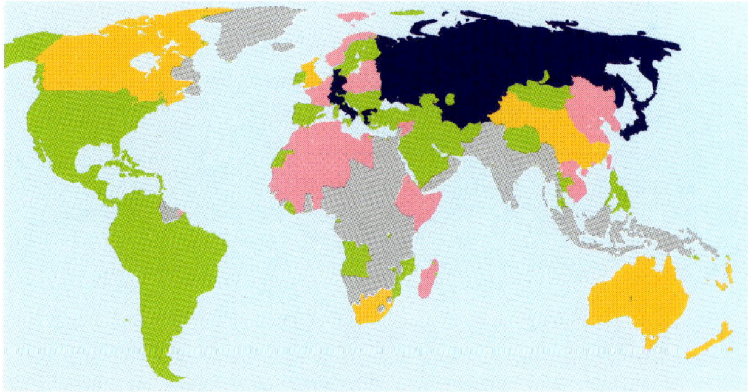

1 January 1941

Allied nations
Allied occupied territory
Axis
Axis occupied territory

1 January 1945

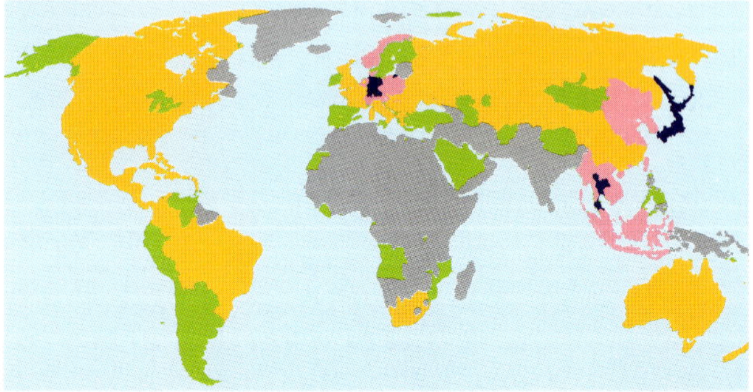

▲ **The camps of no return**
The worst atrocities during the war were committed in the Nazi concentration camps, where millions of people were, starved, tortured and mass executed.

Aftermath

The United States and the Soviet Union emerged as the two most powerful countries after the Second World War. Most countries in Western Europe formed democratic governments or continued with their pre-war governments. Countries in the east, which were allies of the Soviet Union, naturally became communist countries. Germany was divided into East and West Germany. East Germany was brought under Soviet rule, and various parts of West Germany were occupied by Britain, France and America. Japan lost all of its territories and powers and was occupied by the Allies. Korea, which was under Japanese rule until the end of the war, was divided into two parts – North and South Korea. North Korea came under the control of the communist Soviet Union, while its southern counterpart was occupied by the United States. This arrangement was politically volatile and eventually led to the Korean War.

▸ **Two of a kind**
Hitler and Benito Mussolini, the fascist Italian leader, shared radical views. Therefore, it was only natural that the two countries struck an alliance during the war. Both leaders were intolerant and merciless towards their enemies. They also resorted to violent methods to suppress any uprising within their countries.

◂ **The lethal mushroom**
The large greyish-purple mushroom cloud that loomed over Nagasaki after the atomic bombing rose about 18 kilometres (11 miles) from the point of impact. The cloud has now become a symbol of nuclear fallout.

Try these too:

North America (p 102–103), Europe (p 108–109), Asia (p 112–113), The First World War and the Russian Revolution (p 148–149), Water Transport (p 196–197), Air Travel (p 198–199)

Hiroshima and Nagasaki

The first and the only time nuclear weapons were employed in a war was in 1945, when the United States bombed the Japanese cities of Hiroshima and Nagasaki. Hiroshima was bombed on 6 August, while Nagasaki was bombed on 9 August. At least 120,000 civilians died immediately after the attack. Since then, several thousands more have died due to radiation poisoning.

The Computer Revolution

The computer was the most revolutionary invention of the 20th century. The scientific developments of the 16th and 17th centuries, along with the industrial advances of the 18th century, created the need for an efficient and safe means of storing as well as processing information. Moreover, it became necessary to solve sophisticated formulae and compute complex calculations in a quicker and easier manner than already existed.

▲ Adding up
Calculators differ from computers in that they are used for specific operations, like mathematical calculations. Modern calculators run on batteries or solar energy and are pocket-sized.

Key facts:

- There are three main categories of computers. The first includes mainframe computers, used by big companies and institutions to process a large amount of data. They are bulky and occupy entire rooms. The second includes minicomputers or workstations, accessed by multiple users. The third type is the personal computer or microcomputer used by an individual.
- A supercomputer is a particularly efficient and fast computer that is much more advanced than others of its type and time. The first one was designed by Seymour Cray in the 1960s. Today supercomputers are custom-made by large corporations.
- The computer is able to process information fed into it because of its software. A software consists of a specially encoded set of instructions called a programme. They control various parts of the computer. They also interact with human beings, process information and communicate with other software in the machine.

Computing devices like adding machines, calculators and later the computer were developed to provide solutions to these problems. The first mechanical computer was invented by Wilhelm Schickard of Germany, as early as 1623. It had wheels and cogs, like a clock, and could add and subtract six digit numbers. However, it is Charles Babbage, an English professor, who is credited with designing the first modern computer in 1833. This machine, called the Analytical Engine, was supposed to add in 3 seconds and multiply and divide in 2–3 minutes, powered by steam. Unfortunately, it was never made as Babbage died before completing work on it.

Birth of the computer

By the early 1900s, people were using adding machines, cash registers and mechanical computers operated by electricity. These early computers had to be reset manually every time a new problem had to be calculated.

During the Second World War, there were rapid improvements in the design of computing devices. The ENIAC, built for the US military during the war, was the first digital computer. It occupied about 168 square metres (1,800 square feet) of area and worked day and night solving problems. At this time, most computers were huge, almost as big as a small house. They could naturally only be used in government offices, by universities for research and by large corporations.

◀ Tough and reliable
Mainframe computers, also referred to as Big Iron, are extremely reliable, highly secure and durable. These computers can continue to work uninterrupted for several years. They can run even during repairs, making them invaluable in companies where loss of time can cause a large amount of economic setback. Reliability, Availability and Serviceability (or *RAS*) is the marketing term used to describe the qualities of mainframe computers.

Computer revolution

The widespread use of computers began only after technological developments in the 1950s and 60s when they became more accessible to the common man. Computers became interactive, they played music and games and had magnetic memories that could store information. Computer languages like FORTRAN, COBOL and BASIC were developed. The floppy disk, printer and mouse were invented, and computers were equipped for word processing.

In 1975, the Intel Corporation designed Altair 8800, the first successful personal computer. This was followed in 1977, by the Apple II, designed by Steven Jobs and Stephen Wozniak. The Apple II was the first computer with a keyboard and a colour display monitor. Jobs and Wozniak later founded the Apple Corporation. The highly successful Apple Macintosh followed in 1984. In 1982, the first portable computer was introduced by Compaq and in 1985 the first version of Microsoft Windows was launched. By this time, computers had become indispensable in commercial establishments, institutions and even homes. However, it was with the invention of the World Wide Web in 1989 that the computer truly revolutionized information processing, storage and transfer. The computer had evolved far beyond its original role as a calculating and problem solving machine. It was now capable of communication.

Contemporary devices

Computing devices took yet another huge leap forward with the invention of the cellular phone and handheld devices like the palm pilot and pocket PC. Cellular phones were originally only meant to be used as mobile telephones. However, today they are mobile computers that store and process information, allow access to the Internet, play music, and take and store photographs and video clips. Personal digital assistants (PDAs) or palm pilots and pocket PCs offer many of the same features as mobile phones, but are not able to function as a telephone. Besides being versatile, these handheld devices can be used more conveniently as they can be carried easily and used almost anywhere.

Surf on!
Internet cafes, also known as cyber cafes, offer Internet access for a particular fee. The concept and name was first proposed by Ivan Pope, a British computer professional. The first commercial Internet cafe was opened in London on 1 September 1994. A typical Internet cafe would consist of several computer stations connected to a common server, or LAN. Many people preferred Internet cafes as they were cheaper than owning a computer.

Try these too:

The Scientific Revolution (p 142–143), Magnets in Daily Life (p 186–187), Communication and Satellites (p 192–193), Air Travel (p 198–199)

Bank any time
As in most fields, computers play an important role in banking. If it were not for computers, there would not be ATMs, which help use of banking facilities like withdrawing and depositing money any time or date we choose.

Computer games

The first computer game was developed in 1952 at the University of Cambridge, by A. S. Douglas. It was a game of noughts and crosses, or tic tac toe, and was called *OXO*. The first handheld game, made in 1972, was also *Tic Tac Toe*. It had nine buttons, which would flash red or green when pushed.

The Modern World

Following the devastating Second World War, many countries spent the latter part of the 20th century recovering from their losses, both economical and political, and reorganizing. Most colonies gained independence, and monarchies gave way to dictatorships, communism or democracy.

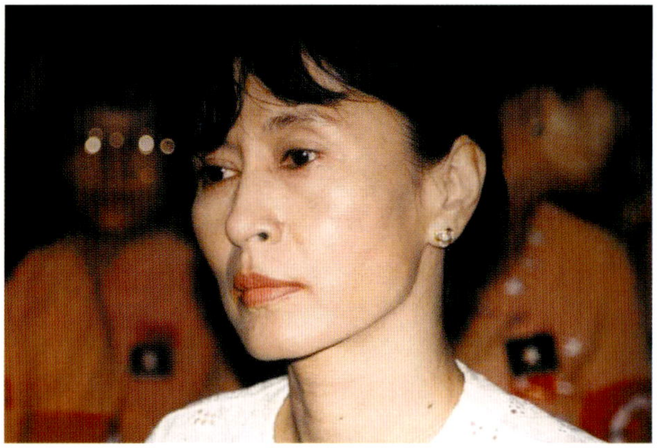

▲ A tale of grit
Aung San Suu Kyi, the Burmese activist who has been fighting for democracy in her country was placed under house arrest by the Myanmar military government in 1989. She was later released in 1995, only to be arrested again in 2003. Suu Kyi continues her struggle from within the confines of her house.

Key facts:

- The Soviet Union collapsed in 1991 as a result of the process of modernization begun by the Soviet President Mikhail Gorbachev. Ironically, this modernization broke the Soviet Union apart instead of improving it, as people demanded a complete change and break from communism.
- In 1945, the United Nations was formed with a membership of 51 countries. It is an international organization that helps to ensure peace, safety and development throughout the world.
- The Cold War between the United States and the Soviet Union was an important event that affected several countries around the world. The conflict, which began in 1947, divided the countries of the world into two groups – US supporters and Soviet supporters. It ended with the collapse of the Soviet Union in 1991.

Britain gave up most of its colonies, including India, in 1947. Queen Elizabeth II succeeded her father, King George VI in 1952. In Ireland, the Irish Free State gave up its Commonwealth membership and became a republic on 1 April 1949. Hungary and Italy also became republics. West Germany was established as the Federal Republic of Germany, and East Germany as the Democratic Republic of Germany. In 1991, Germany was reunited as one country. One of the most important events of the 20th century was the breaking up of the Soviet Union in 1991 and the formation of the Russian Federation with 15 independent republics.

The Balkans

In November 1945, the former kingdom of Yugoslavia became the Federal People's Republic of Yugoslavia ruled by the communists. The country consisted of Croatia, Macedonia, Montenegro, Bosnia-Herzegovina, Serbia and Slovenia. However, in 1991, these countries began fighting each other and by the end of the century, the Federal People's Republic of Yugoslavia was completely destroyed by the bitter racial battles of its people.

▶ The wall of separation
The Berlin Wall, symbolic of the Cold War and communism in Europe, was a 155-kilometre (96-mile) long separation barrier that divided East and West Berlin for a period of 28 years.

Asia

The second half of the 20th century was a period of war, death and destruction in many parts of Asia. When India gained independence, Pakistan was carved out of the northwestern part of the country, as well as a small part in the east. It was created as a separate Islamic country. In 1971 East Pakistan broke away and established itself as Bangladesh. In China, the civil war that had started in 1929, ended in 1949 and the People's Republic of China was established by the Communist Party under Mao-Tse Tung. In 1952, the United States withdrew its forces from Japan. Japan gained complete independence, formed a new constitution and set itself on a path of industrialization and development.

The Middle East

The state of Israel – the only Jewish state in the world – was formed in 1948. Before, as well as since its formation, Israel has been engaged in conflicts with the surrounding Arab nations of Palestine, Egypt, Syria, Lebanon, Iraq and Jordan. Two of the most important conflicts were the Arab-Israeli war of 1948 and the Suez War of 1956. In 1958, the Iranian monarchy was overthrown and military rule was established. Between 1980 and 1988, Iraq was at war with Iran. Iraq invaded Kuwait between 1990 and 1991.

Africa

In 1948, the South African government, run by descendants of European settlers, established apartheid. After years of struggle, the African National Congress finally established a native African government in 1994, with anti-apartheid hero Nelson Mandela as their first President. In Egypt, the monarchy was overthrown and the Egyptian Republic was established in 1953. In 1956 President Gamal Abdel Nasser declared that the Suez Canal was the national property of Egypt. This led to war with the United Kingdom, France and Israel, who also used the Suez route.

Americas

The United States of America rose to the position of a superpower and became a formidable contender in the race to develop powerful nuclear weapons. The Civil Rights Movement between 1955 and 1968 was a difficult period in the history of the United States. African Americans protested peacefully against the racial discrimination and inequality towards them, which led to great changes in American society. Meanwhile, most South American countries underwent a period of political chaos because of a succession of ineffective military dictatorships. Several countries in this continent suffered long periods of civil war. Cuba became a communist state in 1959 under the leadership of Fidel Castro. It is still the only communist country in the Western Hemisphere.

▾ Mission unforgettable
The Vietnam War was fought from 1965 to 1973 between the Democratic Republic of Vietnam, which ruled North Vietnam, and the Viet Cong rebels of South Vietnam. North Vietnam was supported by the United States.

Try these too:

The American Revolution and Civil War (p 144–145), The Second World War (p 150–151)

◂ Fight against apartheid
Nelson Mandela spent a large part of his life in prison. His release in 1990 marked the end of apartheid in South Africa.

▾ A rightful struggle
African Americans voiced their protests in different ways. They took to the streets demanding equal rights, and also organized bus boycotts and sit-ins at restaurants to abolish racial segregation.

Ethnic wars

The world witnessed an increase in ethnic clashes during the 20th century. An ethnic clash is fighting between two groups of people from the same area, who are racially different, speak different languages or follow different religions. These battles have often resulted in genocide, or mass killings of people belonging to a particular group. The Hindu-Muslim conflict in India and the Arab-Israeli clash in Palestine are some examples of ethnic wars.

The New Millennium

The 21st century has seen a period of relative peace in many parts of the world, but continued violence and bloodshed in others. The world has also had to face new threats and dangers like terrorism and increased global warming.

Key facts:

- East Timor, in Southeast Asia, is the youngest nation in the world. It was formerly a Portuguese colony and from 1975 it was an overseas territory of Indonesia. It gained complete independence on 20 May 2004.
- The 11 September 2001 attacks in the United States have been followed by several acts of brutal terrorism in various parts of the world. The Madrid train bombings, the attack on the Indian Parliament, the London Underground bombings and the Bali nightclub blasts are only some of the worst incidents.
- The Kyoto Protocol was brought into force in February 2005. According to this international treaty, the 156 signatory countries will actively work towards decreasing the levels of carbon dioxide and other greenhouse gases in their respective countries. Russia and the European Union have actively supported the protocol, but the United States and Australia have refused to sign it.

In the United States, the new millennium began with the election of George W. Bush as President. The United States faced its worst disaster in recent history, on 11 September 2001, when terrorists attacked the twin towers of the World Trade Center in New York and the Pentagon building in Washington. More than 2,700 people were killed in these attacks. In Mexico, Vicente Fox was elected President after the first ever free and fair polls to be held in Mexico. He is also the first opposition leader to be elected, ending the 71-year rule of the Institutional Revolutionary Party.

▲ **A tribute in light**
Two columns of light are displayed every year at the World Trade Center site to mark the anniversary of the attack.

Europe

In March 2000, the Russian Federation elected Vladimir Putin as their second President. He was also re-elected to the post in 2003. Tony Blair was elected to his second and third terms as the British Prime Minister in 2001 and 2005. He is the Labour Party's longest serving leader.

The Union

Europe first came together under the European Coal and Steel Community (ECSC) in 1951. The idea was to promote trade relations between the members and maintain peace in the region. This soon gave way to the European Economic Community in 1958.

▲ **The euro**
In 2002, the euro became the common currency of 12 member countries in the European Union.

The EEC expanded over the years and later became the European Union. By 2004, the European Union's membership had increased to 25 countries.

▸ **Katrina's fury**
The storm surge caused by Hurricane Katrina in August 2005 devastated the city of New Orleans.

Trouble continues

In the former Yugoslav Republics of Bosnia-Herzegovina and Serbia-Montenegro the violence has continued and these loosely joined federations may be further split in the near future. The former President of Serbia-Montenegro, Slobodan Milosevic, was tried by the United Nations for his role in war crimes and mass murders in Kosovo, Serbia.

They were supported in their mission by Spain, Italy, Portugal, the Czech Republic, Poland and Denmark. The long drawn-out war and US occupation of Iraq began in March 2003. In December of the same year the Iraqi dictator Saddam Hussein was arrested, and is now undergoing trial.

Try these too:

Man in Space (p 18–19), Earth's Atmosphere (p 30–31), The Modern World (p 154–155)

◂ Ineffective defence
The main battle tanks used by the coalition forces in the Iraqi invasion were much more advanced and reliable than the Iraqi T-72 tanks. Iraq's artillery and air defence also proved to be ineffective in the face of the advanced weaponry and attack aircraft of the coalition.

The Middle East

The war between Israel and Palestine continued from the previous century in spite of the peacekeeping efforts of leaders on both sides. However, in August 2005, in an attempt to improve relations between people on both sides, the Israelis began to withdraw from the Gaza Strip, which is Palestinian land occupied by the Israelis. In 2003, the United States and the United Kingdom jointly declared war against Iraq, saying Iraq had failed to prove that it had destroyed all its biological and chemical weapons and was not secretly developing nuclear weapons.

The Indian subcontinent

In 2004, Pervez Musharraf declared himself the President of Pakistan. Musharraf, formerly the Pakistani army chief, had taken control of the government in a coup at the end of the 20th century. He continues to hold peace talks with Prime Minister Manmohan Singh, who heads India's new government, which was elected to power in 2004. The United States, supported by the United Kingdom, launched an attack on Afghanistan to get rid of Osama bin Laden, the leader of the terrorist group Al-Qaeda. Bin Laden was responsible for the attacks on the World Trade Center and the Pentagon. The war in Afghanistan led to the fall of the Islamic Taliban government and the declaration of the Republic of Afghanistan with Hamid Karzai as its first leader.

▾ For the fear of flu
In 2005–2006 the world was gripped by the fear of bird flu. The H5N1 strain of the virus is also fatal to humans. This has led to a fall in the consumption of poultry, with thousands of infected birds being killed to stop the spread of infection.

▾ Killer tsunami
The killer waves that were triggered by the earthquake of December 2004 were up to 30 metres (100 feet) high and caused destruction in 12 countries.

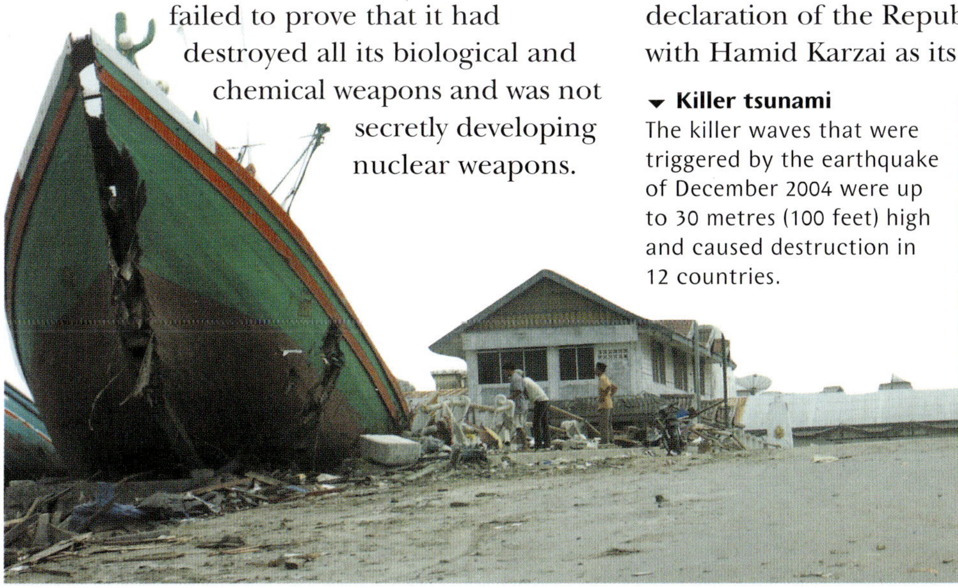

Worst disaster of the 21st century

On 26 December 2004, an earthquake measuring 9.0 on the Richter scale shook the bed of the Indian Ocean, triggering a tsunami. Indonesia was the worst affected, but Thailand, Malaysia, Sri Lanka, Bangladesh, India, the Maldives and even the East African countries of Kenya, Somalia and Tanzania felt the effects of this powerful quake. Over 280,000 people died in this disaster, more than half of them in Indonesia.

Ancient Architecture

Architecture and building technology date back to when man first began settling down and living in houses. Buildings are often considered as status symbols that declare the power and position of their owners. A great deal of ancient architecture and some of the grandest buildings ever built were religious structures, such as temples and churches. Palaces and tombs are also grand and important structures of the ancient world.

Key facts:

- Medieval homes were timber-framed. The timber was pegged together and fixed with braces to form the frame. The spaces between the pieces of timber were filled with wattle-and-daub, rubble, or brick, and plaster was applied over the filling to even it out. The upper floors of some houses were 'jettied' out, or projected out, so that more space was created.
- The Babylonians used clay to cement their bricks and the Egyptians used lime and gypsum. The Romans used a substance that was very similar to modern-day concrete. It was made by mixing volcanic ash with lime obtained from burning limestone.
- Two types of floor plans were used in medieval churches. They were the Latin cross and the Greek cross. The Latin cross plan looks like a crucifix. The altar in this plan is located at the far end. The Greek cross plan looks like a plus sign – it has four equal arms. The altar in this type is situated at the centre, where the arms intersect.

In the Neolithic period, or Stone Age, buildings were made of rough stone boulders and covered with thatched roofs. Remains of such structures have been discovered at Skara Brae in Orkney, Scotland. In warmer areas, buildings had walls made from the bark of trees and woven grass or wattle-and-daub (woven mats plastered with mud). In the advanced civilizations of Mesopotamia, Egypt, the Indus Valley and China, sun-dried mud bricks were used. Rich people used kiln-fired mud bricks as they were stronger.

The pyramids and temples of Egypt are among the most amazing surviving buildings of the ancient world. These enormous structures are made up of huge blocks of hand-cut stone, many of which are beautifully carved.

Classical style

Ancient Greek and Roman buildings were designed in what is now called the classical style. Examples of early buildings and domestic architecture have not survived in Greece because they were made using easily perishable materials like wood and mud bricks.

▲ **Monumental glory**
The Abu Simbel temple near Aswan in Egypt is guarded by massive rock-cut statues of the pharaoh, Ramses II.

Greek temples, on the other hand, were grand and beautiful structures made of limestone blocks decorated with carved marble panels and statues. Some of the grandest buildings, like the Parthenon in Athens, were built entirely from marble. Most Greek buildings were square or rectangular in shape, were surrounded by columns, and had a front and back 'porch'. The roofs of these buildings were made of wooden beams covered with terracotta, or sometimes marble, tiles.

The Romans copied the Greek style, but improved it with some of their own innovations. They developed the use of the true arch and the dome. These were extremely important developments in the history of architecture. The Greeks, as well as the Romans, liked to decorate their buildings. They made carvings on pillars and walls, and used lots of free-standing statues.

▼ **The pyramids at Giza**
The three most famous pyramids are at Giza near Cairo. The Great Pyramid, built about 2600 BC, by the Pharaoh Khufu, is 137 metres (450 feet) high.

Medieval style

By the Middle Ages, Christianity had spread to most parts of Europe. This meant that many new churches had to be built. The two main building styles of the medieval period were the Romanesque and the Gothic. Medieval churches were tall soaring structures with pointed-arch windows and doorways. Gothic churches had a special feature called 'flying buttresses'. These were additional supporting structures that were built along the outer walls of the building. Gothic churches also had beautiful stained-glass windows (made from pieces of coloured glass), which illustrated stories from the Bible. Durham Cathedral in England and the Cathedral of Pisa in Italy are Romanesque cathedrals that exist even today, while Salisbury Cathedral in England and Notre Dame de Paris, in France, are outstanding examples of Gothic religious architecture.

The other important structures built during the medieval period were castles and fortified walls. Immense stone castles were built to protect their lordly owners during this time of war and violence, and many still remain well preserved, for example, the Tower of London and Windsor Castle in England.

Renaissance

Renaissance architecture returned to the classical style of graceful columns, domes and perfectly proportioned geometric buildings. The style began in Italy and was popularized by great architects like Brunelleschi, Bramante and Michelangelo. The Santa Maria del Fiore in Florence and St Peter's Basilica in Rome are two outstanding examples of Italian Renaissance architecture. In England, the style was a mixture of the old Gothic and new European styles from France, Italy and Flanders. This was called the Elizabethan style of architecture, known for its use of round arches, pillars and domes as well as gabled turrets (small towers with sloping roofs), mullioned windows (windows with vertical divisions in wood or stone) and decorative designs like scrolls and lozenges (four-sided, elongated diamond-like shapes).

▲ **Stonehenge**
Stonehenge in Wiltshire, England, is widely considered to be the most famous prehistoric standing-stone monument in Europe. It is believed that it was built between 3000 and 1500 BC. It consists of several tall standing stones, or megaliths, set in a circle. These are surrounded by a ditch and a raised earthen circle.

Pantheon

The Pantheon in Rome was built around 27–25 BC by the Roman consul Marcus Agrippa. It was originally built as a temple to seven Roman gods who represented seven planets. In the 7th century AD the Pantheon was converted into a church. Most of the building was destroyed in a fire in AD 80, but the dome survived intact. The Pantheon is probably the oldest important building that has been continuously used since it was first constructed.

Try these too:

Ancient Mesopotamia and Egypt (p 116–117), Ancient Greece (p 120–121)

Some of the most important Renaissance buildings in England were designed by the well-known architect, Inigo Jones. The Queen's House at Greenwich and the Banqueting Hall in Whitehall, London, are two of his best known designs.

▼ **Notre Dame**
This famous gothic cathedral in Paris was completed in 1345.

Modern Architecture

Architectural styles in the 19th and 20th centuries made a clean break from the classical and ornamental styles. During this period, buildings reflected the spirit of the Industrial Age through their simple yet sensible and elegant designs. New types of building materials were responsible for some of the great changes and achievements in modern building technology.

Pathbreaker
The Reliance building is regarded as the ancestor of modern skyscrapers.

Key facts:

- In 1857, the first safety elevator for passenger service was used in a retail store in New York City. It was first demonstrated, by its inventor, Elisha Otis, in 1854. The development of the elevator made it possible for architects to let their buildings soar skywards.
- In the 1920s, a group of Dutch artists formed the De Stijl group. Works of art by this group consisted of vertical and horizontal lines, and use of primary colours – red, blue and yellow. Though the group mostly produced paintings, their style deeply influenced the Bauhaus and the International Style of architecture.
- In the 1950s, American inventor and architect Buckminster Fuller developed the geodesic dome, the only man-made structure in which strength increases in proportion to size. It is a lightweight structure that is easy and quick to construct. The surface of the dome is made up of intersecting polygons (geometric shapes with five or more sides) formed by a network of connecting rods.

The discovery of iron and steel inspired completely new building designs. In 1779 English ironmonger Abraham Darby built the first iron bridge, over the Severn River. It showed that cast iron could be used as a building material. In 1851, an English gardener named Joseph Paxton designed a gigantic glass house as the venue for the Great Exhibition in London. The gorgeous Crystal Palace used 84,000 square metres (900,000 square feet) of glass. In the late 19th century, the innovative French engineer Gustav Eiffel erected the Eiffel Tower, which is considered one of the greatest masterpieces in iron even today. The 300-metre (984-foot) tall Eiffel Tower took two years to build.

Early modernism

By the second half of the 19th century, the combination of cement and sand, to form concrete, freed buildings from the use of columns, beams and thick walls for support. This along with the invention of reinforced concrete paved the way for wider and taller buildings. A further improvement to concrete was made when cast iron was replaced with steel as reinforcement material. Steel is more flexible than iron and is fireproof.

The 16-storeyed Reliance Building in Chicago, USA, was the first to substitute solid walls with 'curtain walls' which were made largely of glass. The building was supported entirely by its inner steel framework and appeared light and airy in spite of its size.

The Iron Bridge
The world's first bridge made of iron can still be seen in Shropshire, England.

Art Nouveau

The Art Nouveau style became popular towards the end of the 19th century, in protest to the emerging plain and stark modernistic style. Art Nouveau buildings were richly decorated and patterned, and they were often built in unusual shapes and colours. Antoni Gaudí of Barcelona and Victor Horta of Brussels were two of the most famous Art Nouveau architects.

International style

The International Style of architecture developed in Europe and the United States. The buildings in this style imitated the plain, stark appearance of machines. They were geometrical and simple in design. Some of the important European architects who popularized this style were Walter Gropius, Ludwig Mies van der Rohe and Le Corbusier. Gropius and Mies van der Rohe served as directors of the Bauhaus, a famous school of Modern art and architecture, in Germany. In the 1930s these architects fled Nazi Germany and settled in the United States. Their unique architectural style has deeply influenced several modern architects. Some of the most well-known buildings of the International Style are the United Nations headquarters, the Seagram Building and the Lever House – all located in New York City.

One of the most important American architects, who designed in the International Style, was Frank Lloyd Wright. Some of his best-known buildings include the famous Guggenheim Museum in New York City, the Kauffman House in Pennsylvania, and his own home, Taliesin West in Arizona.

◂ **Sears Tower, Chicago**
Built in 1974, this was the world's tallest building at 443 metres (1,457 feet) until the opening of the Petronas Towers in Kuala Lumpur, Malaysia in 1997.

▴ **UN Headquarters, New York**
Designed by a distinguished Commute of architects, this houses the General assembly building where member nations meet and the Secretariat Building, home for the 3,500 staff of the United Nations.

Try these too:

Europe (p 108–109), The Industrial Revolution (p 138–139), Ancient Architecture (p 158–159)

▾ **Geodesic dome, Vancouver**
This stunning building was the centrepiece of Expo 1986, and it houses an Omnimax cinema screen at the Science World complex.

Modern Art and Artists

Modern art, or art that was produced between the late 19th and 20th centuries, can be divided into a number of art movements, styles and techniques. During this period art began to be produced for art's sake. Artists expressed their feelings in their works and used them to communicate with the world. Before this time, art was mainly used for religious and social purposes.

Key facts:

- Collages are artistic works created by pasting bits of paper, ribbons, buttons, photographs, newspaper clippings and other materials and objects on a flat surface. Collage was invented by Pablo Picasso in 1912, when he used a piece of oilcloth with a caning design (thin strips of bamboo cane woven to form a decorative pattern) in his artwork *Still Life with Chair Caning*. The collage technique was also used by many Surrealist painters.
- Works of art made after the 1960s are generally categorized as Contemporary Art, which is usually inspired by issues such as human rights or politics. It often combines drawing, painting and sculpture, as well as photography, film and installation art. Contemporary compositions often combine audio and video clips, live performances, and even the Internet.
- The American sculptor Alexander Calder invented the mobile in 1931. Mobiles are kinetic, or moving, sculptures. They usually consist of shapes hung from carefully balanced, movable rods.

The earliest modern art movement was Romanticism. Romantic artists expressed strong feelings in their paintings of nature and landscapes. This was a complete break from the ancient and medieval traditions of images of human figures with perfect bodies and expressionless faces. English painter J.M.W. Turner and French painter Eugène Delacroix were two of the most famous Romanticists. French artists Claude Monet, Pierre-Auguste Renoir and Edgar Degas were well-known Impressionist artists. They used short, swift brush strokes to try and capture the ever-changing look of natural light. Paul Cézanne and Vincent van Gogh were post-Impressionists, who were both deeply inspired by this style. Cézanne later invented a new style, which inspired the 20th-century Cubists, while van Gogh inspired the development of Expressionism and Fauvism.

Early 20th century

The early 20th century witnessed the birth of Expressionism in Germany, Cubism and Fauvism in France, and Futurism in Italy. These innovative styles moved even further away from the traditional idea of realistic beauty. Post-Impressionist artist Paul Gauguin and Fauvist leader Henri Matisse were inspired by brightly coloured Japanese silk-screen prints. Their work was attractively coloured and the objects and figures they painted were not intended to look realistic.

Cubism was introduced by Georges Braque and Pablo Picasso. This style used angular and fragmented forms, and inspired other 20th-century movements, for example Futurism. Expressionists like Edvard Munch and Emil Nolde, made abstract paintings that expressed horrible torment and anxiety. The Futurists Giacomo Balla and Umberto Boccioni, were more keen on showing the power and speed of technology in the modern world. The Dada movement started as a protest against what its supporters saw as outdated artistic and cultural standards of society. The violence and tragedy of the First World War led to the development of Surrealism that reflected the disenchantment of people who suffered from the war.

▸ ***The Thinker***
This famous sculpture was finished by Ausguste Rodin in 1902 . It shows a man in deep thought and contemplation. *The Thinker* was inspired by the *The Divine Comedy*, a well-known epic poem by Dante. The original sculpture is in a park in Paris, France, but 20 other casts can be seen around the world.

◂ **Setting the style**
Jackson Pollock's *Mural on Indian Red Ground* is the most famous example of his unique 'drip and slash' style of painting. With this style Pollock ushered in an era of abstract expressionism.

▴ **Conveying pain**
Painted by the famous Norwegian expressionist painter Edvard Munch in 1893, *The Scream*, gives a vivid impression of anguish and extreme mental pain. The swirling patterns and intense colours only add to the overall impact of the painting. This masterpiece was stolen from the Munch Museum in Oslo, Norway, in 2004.

Art in the United States

After the Second World War, the United States became the centre of artistic innovation and development. New styles like Abstract Expressionism, Pop Art, Op Art, Minimal Art and Photorealism were born. Some of the most famous Abstract Expressionist artists, including Jackson Pollock, William de Kooning and Mark Rothko, had unique styles. Jackson popularized action art or drip painting; de Kooning specialized in abstract and geometric human figures, and still life compositions; and Rothko expressed his emotions by filling his canvases with large areas of one or two colours.

Earth art

Earth art is made outdoors using natural materials such as soil, rocks and plants. The works are usually very large and do not normally survive for very long as they are unprotected and subject to weather conditions. One of the most famous works of land art, or earth art, is *Spiral Jetty* in Great Salt Lake, Utah. It was created in 1970 by the renowned American artist Robert Smithson.

Pop Art can be defined as art that is inspired by common everyday objects like soda cans and advertisements. It was art that was especially meant to appeal to ordinary people. Andy Warhol and Roy Lichtenstein were two well-known Pop artists.

Since the mid-20th century, new forms of art, which combine music, film, photography, and personal demonstrations, as well as electronic and digital art, have become popular. Art became interactive, inviting the viewer to participate and experience it.

◂ ***Liberty Leading the People***
This painting by Eugene Delacroix commemorates the French Revolution of 1830, which ended absolute monarchy in France. Delacroix used it as a political poster for the revolution.

Try these too:

Europe (p 108–109), Ancient Greece (p 120–121), The Renaissance (p 132–133), The French Revolution (p 146–147)

Famous Composers

Classical music generally encompasses music produced in the tradition of concert music. It is believed that the common norms of classical music developed between the mid-1500s and the early 1800s. The term itself was coined only in the early 19th century, to refer to the golden period of concert music.

▲ **Born musician**
Johann Bach belonged to a family that had produced musicians for more than 200 years.

▶ **Maestro at work**
Beethoven's achievements are all the more remarkable because he was completely deaf during the last eight years of his life. In fact, Symphony Number 9, his last complete symphony, also known as the Choral Symphony, was composed while he was completely deaf and is hailed as a masterpiece.

The Classical era is often traced from the time of Bach to that of Beethoven. Many great composers lived during this period. Some of them were Bach, Haydn, Mozart, Vivaldi, Tchaikovsky and Beethoven.

Antonio Vivaldi (1678–1741)

Antonio Vivaldi was an Italian violinist and composer of the Baroque period. He became a priest in 1703, but because of his ill health he spent most of his life as a music teacher at a girl's orphanage in Venice. He composed operas as well as concertos for instruments, the most famous of his compositions being the *Four Seasons*.

Johann Sebastian Bach (1685–1750)

Johann Sebastian Bach is one of the most famous German composers of the Baroque period. Bach began studying music and playing the organ at a very young age. His early compositions were mostly religious pieces for the organ, but later he composed several non-religious pieces that could be played on other instruments.

Georg Friedrich Handel (1685–1759)

German composer Handel began his career in music by playing the organ and harpsichord. He produced his first composition at the age of nine. He is best known for his compositions in the English oratorio style, which combine a chorus and an orchestra to narrate a religious story, without any dramatic presentation, costumes or sets. Handel also composed several concertos and Italian operas.

Wolfgang Amadeus Mozart (1756–1791)

The Austrian classical musician, Mozart, remains one of the most popular composers ever. He began composing at the age of 6 and by the age of 35, when he died, he had written 41 symphonies, as well as operas, compositions for piano, and chamber and choral music. Chamber music compositions are performed by three to four instrumentalists, each playing one part of the composition for a small private audience. Mozart spent most of his short life in Salzburg, Austria, though he travelled to France, Germany, Italy and the Czech Republic to seek commissions.

Ludwig van Beethoven (1770–1827)

Beethoven was an extremely gifted German pianist and composer during the intervening time between the Classical and Romantic periods. He composed nine symphonies, which are compositions for orchestras; piano sonatas, which are musical pieces played by one or two solo instruments; and compositions for string quartets, which combine two violins, a cello and a viola.

Richard Wagner (1813–1883)

German musician Wagner was one of the most important composers and conductors of classical music in the 19th century. He wrote several symphonic operas – among the most impressive is *The Ring of the Nibelung*, which consists of four operas that together last about 15 hours. He also wrote several books, essays and poems.

Pyotr Ilyich Tchaikovsky (1840–1893)

Tchaikovsky is best known as the composer of the popular ballets, *The Nutcracker* and *Swan Lake*, and the operas *Eugene Onegin* and *The Queen of Spades*. This prolific Russian composer and conductor also wrote several symphonies, concertos, chamber works and solo piano pieces. His music was greatly inspired by Russian folk music.

▸ Incomplete work
Mozart died on 5 December 1791, before he could complete his last composition, the Requiem. The cause of his death remains a mystery.

◂ A masterpiece
Tchaikovsky's *Swan Lake* is the most popular and widely performed ballets of all time.

William S. Gilbert (1836–1911) and Arthur S. Sullivan (1842–1900)

Gilbert (playwright/songwriter) and Sullivan (composer) were a successful team in Victorian England. They specialized in comic operas, and developed a distinct form of the English operetta. The team also performed successfully in the United States and their work has been an important influence on modern American musicals. Some of their most well-known compositions include *The Pirates of Penzance* and *The Mikado*.

Symphony orchestra

A symphony orchestra is made up of four groups of instruments – strings, brass, percussion and woodwind. The stringed instruments include violins, cellos, double basses and violas. Percussion instruments include piano, bass drum, snare drum and timpani. The brass section includes the trumpet, French horn, trombone and tuba, and the woodwind instruments include the flute, oboe, clarinet, bassoon and piccolo.

Key facts:

- Composers are people who write original music. The compositions that they write can be for various styles and genres – jazz, classical, or elaborate pieces for large orchestras. In musical styles such as pop, rock and country, composers are usually called songwriters.
- There are two types of orchestras – chamber orchestras, and symphony or philharmonic orchestras. A symphony orchestra can have between 80–100 members playing various instruments, and a chamber orchestra has about 50, or fewer, members.
- Early orchestras were led by the concertmaster (principal violinist) or the harpsichord player. They played in the orchestra and led it at the same time. However, by the early 19th century, as compositions became more and more complex and the size of orchestras increased, conductors were needed to lead them. Many well-known composers were also conductors.

Try these too:

The Renaissance (p 132–133), The Sounds of Music (p 166–167), Stage and Theatre (p 168–169), Sound (p 182–183)

The Sounds of Music

Music has been around since time immemorial. Simple chants and rhymes gradually developed into more complex and melodious compositions with the invention of a variety of instruments. New styles of music have developed over the ages, but only some have endured the test of time.

Key facts:

- Classical musicians have to be trained, unlike those in other genres. This is because classical music is based on a formal written music format, which cannot be improvised.
- The Beatles are the most successful and influential musical act of all time. The four-member rock/pop band was formed in 1959 and during their 11-year career they had over 50 hit singles. Their music continues to sell today – 25 years after they disbanded.
- Gospel music was popularized in the early 1900s, by the preachers of the 'Sanctified', or 'Holiness' Methodist churches, who encouraged church members to declare and celebrate their faith by singing, and even dancing.

Music with soul
The American soul, rock and pop singing star, Tina Turner, born in 1939, has become a legend for her highpowered perfomances.

The term 'classical music' generally includes music composed between the mid-1700s and the early 1800s. During this period, melody, harmony and complex compositions of varying pitches and tones became important. Early music of this period was generally church music and later included music for the royal court, but towards the end of the period, music was composed more for entertainment.

Gospel, rhythm and blues and jazz

The African-American community has contributed immensely to the world of music. Their church music, called gospel music, gained in popularity during the 1930s, and many gospel singers went on to become stars. Blues originated from the songs and chants of the African-American slaves who worked in the southern US plantations. This vocal and instrumental musical style has inspired other genres like pop, rhythm and blues, rock and roll, ragtime and jazz, which enjoyed great popularity in the first part of the 20th century and is still used as part of other musical compositions. Many blues musicians like Bessie Smith, Ma Rainey and Louis Armstrong also performed jazz. Contemporary jazz musicians include Norah Jones, Diana Krall and Harry Connick Jr. Rhythm and blues (R&B) is another popular genre in the United States. It developed in the 1940s from a combination of blues and jazz. Fats Domino and Jerry Lewis were popular R&B musicians. Others include Michael Jackson and Whitney Houston.

Jazz it up
Jazz is largely an instrumental style, which often makes use of wind instruments like the trumpet, saxophone and trombone.

Gramophone record

Gramophone records were the most popular and accessible devices for playing recorded music between 1910 and the 1980s. The earliest records were made of rubber or shellac, and later they were made of vinyl. The gramophone, or long-playing (LP), record is a thin black disc with spiral grooves on its surface. The needle, or stylus, of the record player, or gramophone, played on the grooves to produce sound.

◂ Music for a cause Apart from being a talented musician, Joan Baez also participated in civil rights movements.

Pop, folk and country

In the 1950s, American and British musicians became interested in traditional folk songs and started including them in their acts. This led to the revival of old songs and the birth of the popular music genre. Joan Baez, Woody Guthrie and Harry Belafonte are amongst the most successful folk musicians. Country music is a style that developed in the southern and western parts of the United States. It combines the influences of religious music, folk and blues. Jimmie Rodgers and Hank Williams, Sr., are two famous country musicians. Pop music is among the most popular and commercially successful music genres today. It includes many types of light and catchy compositions loosely inspired by a combination of R&B, rock, hip-hop and country. Eye-catching music videos, energetic live performances and the flamboyant personalities of pop performers make it a favourite among teenagers and young people.

Rock 'n' roll, rock and metal

The rock 'n' roll genre was born in the 1950s, although the style of singing existed even earlier among the African-American community. It was originally inspired by R&B, but it soon acquired a character of its own. Quick, catchy beats made it perfect for dancing. Rock 'n' roll stars like Elvis Presley and Buddy Holly mixed in blues and country with their own music to produce yet another genre – rockabilly. This was an early style of rock music. Rock music, in fact, is inspired by musical styles that evolved since the 1940s, including blues, R&B and rock 'n' roll. Folk-rock artist Bob Dylan, the 1960s act the Beatles, the hard-rock group Deep Purple and the heavy-metal band Iron Maiden all belong to the rock genre. Heavy metal, inspired from blues and rock, is a loud, aggressive style of music in which the guitar features heavily.

▴ Material Girl Madonna is regarded as the Queen of Pop.

▾ Long live the King! Known as the 'King of Rock and Roll', Elvis influenced a generation with his music, dancing, attitude and clothes.

Electronic

Electronic music is produced by electronic equipment such as synthesizers, samplers and drum machines. This style of music developed rapidly around the 1950s, and by the late 1970s electronic dance music was born. Some electronic dance music styles include trance, techno and house music.

Hip-hop/rap

This musical style developed in the 1970s in New York City. It consists of two parts – a strong and continuous beat maintained by the disc jockey (DJ), who also adds special effects by scratching and mixing sounds, and rhythmic or rhyming lyrics. By the late 1990s, popular rappers like Eminem and Jay-Z were taking hip-hop to listeners all over the world.

Try these too:

Famous Composers (p 164–165), Stage and Theatre (p 168–169), Movie Magic (p 172–173), Sound (p182–183)

Stage and Theatre

Stage and theatre arts cover a wide range of performing arts that include acting, dance, music and mime in such forms as plays, pantomime, opera and ballet.

The oldest surviving plays date way back to the times of Ancient Greece. Renowned playwrights such as Thespis, Sophocles and Euripides wrote dramas that were presented at annual festivals and competitions. These plays usually had only three actors, who wore masks and played all of the roles, including those of female characters. The Ancient Romans continued the Greek tradition of drama, with comedy being the most popular type. Medieval plays were presented in Latin and were usually religious or biblical in nature. Plays were also sometimes acted in native languages. During the Renaissance period there was a revival of Ancient Roman and Greek plays. At this time most stages were set up in the courtyards of inns. People sat around the courtyard and on the balconies above it.

In England, the 16th century was a period of great development in the dramatic arts. Famous playwrights such as Shakespeare, Christopher Marlowe and Ben Jonson wrote tragic, comic and historical plays. These plays were performed in open-air theatres, which had two- or three-storied colonnaded balconies on three sides of the stage to accommodate the audience.

▲ **The Greek master**
Euripides was one of the greatest playwrights of Ancient Greece. He is believed to have written over 90 tragic plays.

Development of stage and light

In 17th century France, Louis XIV encouraged the theatre. Great French playwrights like Molière and Racine produced outstanding comedies and tragedies about the everyday life of ordinary people. During the 18th-century English playwrights Richard Sheridan and Oliver Goldsmith also wrote these types of plays. Around this time, playwright and director David Garrick popularized the proscenium stage or 'picture frame' stage setting in England. The proscenium stage has a large arch at the front, which creates the effect of a frame through which the performance is seen. It has since been the most popular stage design.

The introduction of gas lighting in the 19th century, and later electric lighting, changed theatre art completely. Lighting effects became more and more complex. Deliberate use of poor lighting led to the development of more exaggerated acting styles. Engaging the audience by using special effects, such as revolving stages and moving scenery, soon became possible. Some of the most important dramatic works of this period were produced by such great names as George Bernard Shaw of Ireland, Henrik Ibsen of Norway and Anton Chekhov of Russia.

◀ **The Bard of Avon**
William Shakespeare is the greatest playwright of all times. He lived during the Elizabethan Era and wrote about 38 plays, a collection of sonnets and many poems. He is often regarded as Britain's national poet.

Modern theatre

Broadway in New York City was the centre of 20th-century, post-war theatre. Realistic plays of ordinary working class people were favoured in place of the exaggerated melodrama of the earlier century. Eugene O'Neill, Arthur Miller and Tennessee Williams were among the most successful playwrights of serious plays of this period. In fact, *Death of a Salesman* by Miller and *The Glass Menagerie* by Williams are considered classics. Neil Simon, on the other hand, specialized in comedies. Musical plays like *Oklahoma!* by Rodgers and Hammerstein, and *Show Boat* by the Ziegfeld Follies were also huge successes.

Author par excellence Arthur Asher Miller was a prominent American playwright, essayist and author. His best known works include *The Crucible*, *All My Sons* and *Death of a Salesman*.

The Golden Age The reign of Queen Elizabeth I is considered to be the Golden Age of English theatre and literature. Many theatres were opened during this era. The queen herself was a talented writer and encouraged young writers.

West End and Broadway

The West End in London and Broadway in New York City are among the most prestigious theatrical venues in the world. The West End is an area on the western side of the London city centre where nearly 40 theatres are located on streets including The Strand, Drury Lane and Shaftesbury Avenue. The Broadway theatre district is located in and around Times Square in New York. Currently it is home to 39 theatres.

Key facts:

- Theatre in Ancient Greece began as a festival held in the honour of Dionysus, the Greek god of wine.
- Only men were allowed to act in plays in ancient times. In fact, until the medieval period women were not allowed on stage at all. In England, women only began appearing on stage around the 17th century. Before then boys and young men played the roles of women characters.
- Physical theatre describes all theatrical forms that use gestures, expressions and body postures instead of words. Pantomime, circus, physical comedy, mime and certain forms of puppetry can all be included in physical theatre.
- Stage and theatre arts include not only the playwrights who create the material and the actors who act it out, but also the director, the costume designer, the set designer, the lighting designer, the sound designer, the stage manager, the production manager, and the dramaturg. A dramaturg is a person who hires the actors, plans the plays and edits the play. He assists the playwright and director in producing the show.

Try these too:

Ancient Greece (p 120–121), The Renaissance (p 132–133), Famous Composers (p 164–165), Movie Magic (p 172–173)

World of Sports

Sports has always been an important part of our lives. Even ancient people devised unique forms of physical exercise and recreation. Although it was mainly regarded as a fun-filled pastime in the ancient days, sporting activities were always viewed with some amount of competitiveness even then.

Key facts:

- The Paralympic Games were first held in Rome in 1960. It is an international sporting competition, held at the same time and place as the Olympic Games, for competitors with visual and mobility disabilities and those with cerebral palsy. There are both summer and winter events in the Games.
- Sports that involve great speed and dramatic stunts are called extreme sports. These dangerous sports are popular for the thrilling rush of adrenalin produced while performing them. Bungee jumping, skydiving, whitewater rafting, BMX racing and free-diving (deep-sea diving without any breathing equipment) are some popular extreme sports.
- Sports medicine is a specialized branch of medicine concerned with preventive care and treatment of injuries. Physicians, surgeons, trainers, coaches, nutritionists, psychologists and therapists work together to develop the best physical, nutritional and mental healthcare routine to improve a sportsperson's performance and increase their active sporting life.

Today there are a variety of sports, some that are played between individuals and others that involve a team of two or more. Many of the sporting events are played on land. However, water and aerial sports have also become popular over the last few years.

Team sports

Sports played between a group of more than two people are called team sports. The number of members in a team varies according to the sport. Most team sports use a ball, which is usually passed back and forth between the players. Sports like cricket, hockey and baseball use a bat or stick to hit and move the ball. The success of a team depends entirely on the team spirit.

Athletics

Track and field, or athletics, includes many events. There are different types of races, such as sprints, long distance, hurdles and marathons, as well as race walking. There are also events like long jump, high jump, and pole vault; and throwing games like javelin, shot put and discus. Unlike team sports, most athletic sports are individual events. Some, however, are relay events in which teams of four members compete against each other.

Water sports

Water sports include a wide range of individual sports such as swimming, diving and surfing; as well as team sports such as synchronized swimming, water polo, canoeing and sailing. They are popular leisure activities in most parts of the world.

▲ **Shooting baskets**
Basketball is played between two five-member teams. At each end of the court, there is a tall post with a hoop. Each team tries to take control of the ball and score points by throwing it through their opponent's hoop.

Combat sports/martial arts

Several traditional combat sports have developed over the centuries in various parts of the world. Of these, the most popular include wrestling, boxing, karate, tae kwon do, judo, sumo wrestling and fencing. Combat sports involve two individuals engaged in combat with each other in a series of 'bouts', or rounds. The winner overcomes their opponent by utilizing their skill and physical might.

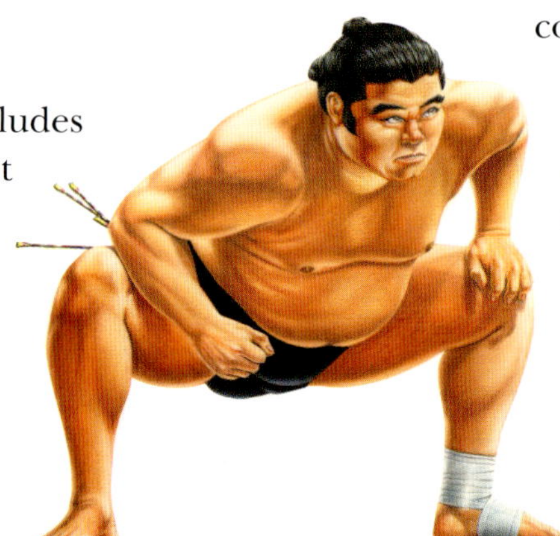

◀ **Traditional wrestling**
Sumo wrestling is a traditional and ritualistic Japanese combat sport.

▼ **All eyes on the ball**
In football 11 players try to net the ball in the opponent's goal using their feet.

Olympics

The Olympic Games is the biggest and one of the most important international sporting competitions. The earliest recorded Olympic Games was held in 776 BC in Ancient Greece, although the tradition probably dates back to even earlier times. The Ancient Olympic Games was banned in 393 AD by the Roman Emperor, Theodosius I. In 1896, French educator Baron Pierre de Coubertin revived the Olympics in an effort to promote international diplomatic relations. Since then, the Olympics have been held every four years, except in 1916, 1940 and 1944, during the two World Wars. The ancient games only had one event – a running race; other events like wrestling, pentathlon, chariot racing, boxing and even marathons were added later. The Olympic Games in Athens, in 2004, had 37 events.

Indoor sports

Indoor games, unlike outdoor games, are all-weather and anytime sporting activities. Billiards, chess and bridge are popular indoor games that require mental skills and a lot of concentration. Table tennis and gymnastics, however, require physical stamina. Today artificial turf and excellent lighting have made it possible to play even outdoor games, like tennis, hockey and basketball, indoors.

Animals and sports

Animals have long been humankind's sporting partners. The gladiators of Ancient Rome fought wild animals in closed arenas for the entertainment of spectators. Hunting, probably one of the earliest sports, calls on the skills of horses and hounds to help track and chase prey like rabbits and deer. Animals also participate in events such as horse racing, bullfighting, polo and steeplechase.

▸ **No fear**
Extreme sports like mountain climbing, skateboarding, and dirt bike racing are becoming popular despite the dangers attached to them.

◂ **Crossing hurdles**
Steeplechase started as a rural horse racing event, in which horses had to jump over fences, ditches and other obstacles. Today, artificial steeplechase tracks are made in stadiums. The term 'steeplechase' is also given to obstacle races that are part of track and field events.

Try these too:
Asia (p 112–113), Ancient Greece (p 120–121), Ancient Rome (p 122–123)

Movie Magic

The invention of the *daguerreotype* in 1839 opened up the new and fantastic world of photography. Other 19th-century inventions such as the electric bulb, celluloid film and better cameras offered exciting possibilities to innovative photographers who soon realized that it was possible to make 'moving pictures'.

Key facts:

- The first commercial film show was on 28 December 1895, in Paris, France. The Lumière brothers presented ten short films in a show that lasted 20 minutes at the *Salon Indien*, the empty basement below the Grand Café. There were 20 shows every day. The short films, or *actualities*, included a comic sequence of a gardener with a watering hose, workers leaving a factory, a horse-drawn carriage galloping towards the camera, and a train arriving at a station.
- Although the early development of film-making took place in both Europe and the United States, after the World Wars, the United States became the centre of the film-making industry. Big film studios were created, which functioned like film-making factories.
- Slapstick comedies were very popular in the silent film era. Charlie Chaplin was the most successful actor of this time. Chaplin not only acted, but also wrote, produced and directed films. *The Kid* (1921) and *The Gold Rush* (1925) were among Chaplin's most successful full-length comic films.

Early moving pictures were made by moving a series of photographs quickly to create the impression of movement. An early movie projector, called a zoopraxiscope, was invented by British photographer Eadweard Muybridge in 1879. Muybridge set up 12 cameras to record the movement of a galloping horse. These images were recorded on a rotating glass plate, which transferred them onto a screen in Muybridge's zoopraxiscope.

In the 1890s, Thomas Alva Edison and his assistant, William Dickson, invented the kinetograph and the kinetoscope. The kinetograph was a single camera that could record a succession of images onto a moving celluloid film.

▲ An error of judgment
Despite the roaring success of their short films, the Lumière brothers felt that cinema had no future.

The kinetoscope was a large coin-operated box that had a peephole at the top, through which the 'movie' could be seen. It was a popular attraction at carnivals and vaudeville shows. About the same time, in France, Louis and Auguste Lumière developed the cinematographe, a device that combined both camera and projector. It could take moving pictures and project them to several viewers. The brothers made many short films, including comic scenes and people engaged in everyday activities.

Films of this period were usually only one or two minutes long and were silent, as the art of recording soundtracks had not yet been developed. However, there was usually a live performer playing the piano or organ to accompany the film. The figures in these films appeared flat. They were shot from only one angle, as cameras were not moved around as they are now.

▸ A true legend
Greta Garbo began her career in silent movies. After attaining star status in the Silent era, Garbo went on to rule the era of the Talkies, with hits like *Anna Christie*, *Mata Hari*, *Grand Hotel* and *Ninotchka*.

The birth of the cinema

By the end of the 19th century, films began increasing in length, used different camera angles and were edited and pieced together to make a continuous story or documentary. These movies had specially composed musical scores that were performed live at each screening. Some even had a narrator and singers who lip-synched with the actors on screen. Frenchman Georges Méliès was an important film-maker of this time. His movie *Le Voyage dans la Lune* (1902) was the first fantasy film ever and it used several new techniques and special effects that had never been seen before. Dissolving one image into another, superimposing images of objects or people onto another image and hand-colouring film were just some of the techniques pioneered by Méliès. The American inventor Edwin S. Porter also made films in this new format. His best known movie *The Great Train Robbery* (1903) was nearly 10 minutes long and had 14 scenes. The movie was a big hit with audiences and proved to be a landmark achievement in the history of movie-making.

◀ Master comedian
Charlie Chaplin was a British-born actor and director who ruled the world of comic cinema during the Silent era. His work includes classics such as *The Tramp*, *The Knockout* and *Pay Day*.

◀ Blockbuster
Gladiator is one of the biggest Hollywood blockbusters in recent times. This film stars Academy Award winner Russell Crowe as Maximus Decimus Meridius in the title role, and Joaquin Phoenix as Coomodus, a blood-thirsty Roman Emperor who loved gladiatorial games. This film had spectacular visual and sound effects, and cost over 140 million US dollars to make. However, it was a huge success at the box office and grossed more than double that amount!

A new beginning

Further improvements in technique and equipment led to even longer films. Film-maker David W. Griffith pioneered the making of full-length films in the United States. He used elaborate sets and costumes, and several actors. His masterpieces *The Birth of a Nation* (1915) and *Intolerance* (1916) ran for about three hours each.

The talkies

During the 1920s 'talking films' were made in the United States for the first time. This was possible due to the invention of electronic microphones and the technique of recording soundtracks onto film, so that the images and sound ran simultaneously. The first feature-length (or full-length) talkie was *The Jazz Singer*.

▲ Drum roll
The zoetrope was the earliest device through which a moving picture could be seen. It had a hollow rotating drum, with a strip of photos or pictures. The drum had narrow slits through which the viewer could see moving pictures when the drum was rotated.

Try these too:

The Scientific Revolution (p 142–143), Stage and Theatre (p 168–169), Light (p 180–181)

The world of colour

Colour, like sound, didn't come to films until the 1920s. The Technicolor process made it possible to record colour onto film negatives. However, colour films became widespread only in the 1950s, as a means to lure television audiences back into cinemas.

World Religions

Religion has always played an important role in the lives of humans. Since time immemorial, humans have tried to explain the wonders of nature through religion. Ancient people believed in a force without any form. They believed that this force existed in the trees, animals, mountains and rivers.

Key facts:

- 'Christ' was a title given to Jesus of Nazareth. It is the Greek word for 'messiah', which means 'anointed'. According to the Old Testament, Jesus was anointed with oil. According to tradition, this ritual was applied only to prophets and kings.
- Christianity, Islam and Judaism are connected by their belief that Abraham is a holy and important figure. He is described as a patriarch (father of humankind) in the Old Testament Book of Genesis, and as a prophet in the Quran. Therefore Judaism, Christianity and Islam are also known as Abrahamic religions.
- In both Christianity and Judaism, boys and girls entering adolescence undergo special ceremonies that recognize them as young adults. Christians have a rite of confirmation, which is believed to put the young adult in direct communion with God. Jewish people conduct a ceremony at which the young girl (Bat Mitzvah) or boy (Bar Mitzvah) reads from the Torah for the first time. The ceremony is followed by a celebratory meal.

The beliefs of the ancient people led to nature worship, eventually giving birth to religion. There are many religions in the world today. Some have billions of followers, while some have only a handful of devotees.

Christianity

Christianity is one of the most widespread religions, and is followed by nearly one third of the world's population. It is a monotheistic religion, that is, Christians believe in only one god. However, they see God in three forms – the Father, the Son and the Holy Spirit, which make up the Holy Trinity of Christianity. The Christian religion is based on the teachings of Jesus of Nazareth.

Jesus was a Jew who lived in Palestine. His followers broke away from Judaism and established themselves as Christians. The Twelve Apostles, selected by Jesus from among his disciples, travelled to various parts of the world to spread the 'gospel', or the teachings of Jesus. The gospels written by the apostles and their disciples were put together as books that make up a major part of the New Testament of the Bible.

▲ **A sad reminder**
The cross is the recognized symbol of Christianity. It represents the death of Jesus Christ by crucifixion, an execution method that was popular in the Roman Empire.

Different sects

Christianity consists of three main groups – Roman Catholic, Protestant and Eastern Orthodox. Within these three groups there are a number of subgroups. Each of these subgroups have separate churches. The largest of the main groups is the Roman Catholic Church, headed by the Pope who is based in Rome. The groups differ from each other in the way that they interpret the Bible. The Church of England is a combination of both Protestant and Catholic beliefs.

◂ **The birth of a messiah**
The exact years of the birth and death of Jesus Christ are not really known. However, the Son of God is believed to have been born about 4 BC and died about AD 30. His birthday is celebrated every year on 25 December, as Christmas Day, while the day he was resurrected after being crucified is observed as Easter.

Islam

Islam was founded in the 7th century AD by the Prophet Muhammad in Arabia. Today it is the second largest religion in the world and is practised by nearly 1.3 billion people. Muhammad's teachings have been compiled to form the Quran, the holy book of the Muslim people. The word 'Islam' means 'peace' and 'obedience to God'. Islam, like Christianity, is a monotheistic religion. Muslims believe in only one God – Allah. According to the religion, 25 prophets were sent to Earth by God and Muhammad was the last of them. The earlier prophets include Adam, Moses and Jesus. There are two main sects of Islam – Sunni and Shi'a. Although there are some differences in the beliefs and customs of these sects, there are many similarities as well. The five basic beliefs of all Muslims are: faith in the finality of the prophethood of Muhammad, ritualistic prayer that has to be observed five times a day, fasting during the day for the entire month of Ramadan, sharing wealth through payment of a tax called *zakat* and the *hajj* pilgrimage to Mecca at least once during a person's lifetime.

Judaism

Judaism, the religion of the Jewish people, came into existence nearly 4,000 years ago in Palestine. It is one of the oldest religions in the world. The Jewish people believe that God created the world and continues to take care of it. They believe that God appeared on Mount Sinai and gave Moses the Ten Commandments, which have been included in their holy book, the Torah. These commandments and rules show the Jewish people the right way to live. The Torah is part of the Hebrew Bible, the Tanakh, which is the Old Testament of the Bible. Rabbis are the religious leaders and they conduct prayers at a Jewish temple, or synagogue. According to Jewish tradition, prayers should be offered three times a day. Saturday is the day of Sabbath, when no work is done and the day is spent in rest, prayer, study and feasting. There are three main Jewish sects – Orthodox, Conservative and Reform.

Bowing to God
The five ritual prayers of the Muslims is known as Salat, or Namaaz. It is one of the Five Pillars of Islam and all five prayers are compulsory. All Muslims wash themselves before offering prayers. They start the prayer by standing. This is followed by bowing and finally turning their heads to the right and left, all the while chanting prayers.

Religious celebrations

These are some important religious holidays and their significance.
Christian celebrations:
Christmas – The Birth of Christ celebrated on 25 December.
Easter – The Resurrection of Christ celebrated on 16 April.
Islamic celebrations:
Eid ul-Fitr – The end of fasting during the month of Ramadan is celebrated on the 1st day of the Islamic month of Shawwal. Shawwal is the 10th month in the lunar calendar, but the date varies every year, depending upon the appearance of the full moon.
Eid ul-Adha – To mark the end of *hajj*, the pilgrimage to Mecca, the 10th day of the month of Dhul Hijja is a day of celebration. The occasion falls exactly 70 days after the end of Ramadan.
Jewish celebrations:
Passover – The remembrance of their freedom from slavery under the Ancient Egyptians is celebrated from the 15th to the 22nd of the Hebrew month of Nisan, which falls in spring.
Rosh Hashanah – The New Year and the creation of the world is celebrated every year on the first day of the Hebrew month of Tishrei, which falls in autumn.
Yom Kippur – The holiest day in the Jewish calendar, it ends the '10 days of repentance', spent fasting and praying.

Bar Mitzvah
When a Jewish boy turns 13, he himself becomes responsible for following the Jewish religion. At this stage, the boy is said to become Bar Mitzvah.

Try these too:

Countries and People (p 102–115), Europe in the Middle Ages (p 126–127), The Renaissance (p 132–133)

Eastern Religions

Asian religions include some of the oldest relgions in the world. Most ancient relgions of the East were pagan and polytheistic, meaning the followers of these religions believed in more than one god, although they were considered different forms of the same god. Most Eastern religions are connected to each other.

▾ Creator of the world
Hinduism believes in the existence of a Supreme God who is worshipped in different forms, or as different gods, like Vishnu, Shiva, Brahma and Shakti. Brahma, the four-headed god is regarded as the creator of the world, but is not as important as the other three.

They share certain characteristics and legends – all however, are adapted to the life and times of the particular region. Hinduism, the world's oldest religion, dates back to around 1500–1300 BC. Unlike most other religions, Hinduism is not based on the teachings of a prophet. It developed from the Vedas – religious texts that were written by many learned scholars over a period of several years. The Vedas contain prayers, hymns and information about rituals. Other important Hindu texts are the Upanishads, containing information about Hindu beliefs and the teachings of ancient scholars, and the epics Mahabharata and Ramayana. Hinduism can be broadly divided into Vaishnavism, for which Vishnu is the main deity; Shaivism, for which Shiva is the main deity; and Shaktism, whose Supreme God is Shakti, or the Mother Goddess. Hindus believe that the soul is indestructible and that every person dies only to be reborn.

▸ Devoted to temples
Like Hindus, Jains believe in karma. It is said that good karma (good deeds) would help break the cycle of birth and death. For Jains, building temples is a good karma. Jain temples are usually huge complexes consisting of many temples. Most Jain temples look plain from the outside, but have magnificient interiors.

◂ A hard penance
The Buddha became enlightened while he meditated under the *Mahabodhi* tree. It is said that one day the Buddha was beset by a huge storm, but he continued to meditate. The seprent king, Muchilinda is believed to have then protected him with its hood.

Buddhism

Buddhism was founded in the 6th century BC by Siddhartha Gautama, a prince belonging to the Sakya dynasty that ruled parts of present-day Nepal. At the age of 29 Siddhartha gave up his princely life and became a monk. After six years of practising yoga and mediation, Siddhartha came to understand the human mind, the causes of all human sorrow and the path to happiness. He was thereafter called Buddha, or the 'enlightened one'. Buddhism teaches its followers to show compassion to all living creatures, to be honest and virtuous, and stresses the importance of meditation to strengthen and control the mind. The Tripitaka is the Buddhist holy book. The main Buddhist sects are Hinayana, Mahayana and Vajrayana. Buddhism is the fourth largest religion in the world.

Jainism

Jainism is a prehistoric Indian religion. According to Jain philosophy there were 24 Tirthankaras, or saints, who preached it. The last Tirthankara was Mahavira, who lived in the 6th century BC and was responsible for establishing Jainism as a religion and popularizing it. There are two main sects of Jainism – Digambara and Svetambara. All Jains are vegetarians and their religion teaches them to be compassionate to animals. Like Buddhism, Jainism also preaches non-violence and simple living.

▲ **Unique architecture**
Baha'is usually hold prayers in homes or meeting halls. However, they have seven Houses of Worship across the world, all of which have nine sides and a dome.

Sikhism

Sikhism was founded in the 15th century by Guru Nanak in Talwandi, present-day Pakistan. He was followed by nine other Gurus (teachers). The teachings of all the Gurus are contained in the *Guru Granth Sahib*, the holy book of the Sikhs, which is also considered to be the tenth Guru.

Sikhism believes in only one god, and Sikhs can be identified by the five symbols – *kara* (steel bracelet), *kirpan* (sword), *kanga* (comb), *kachha* (long shorts worn as an undergarment) and *kesh* (uncut hair).

▼ **The holiest of all**
The Golden Temple in Amritsar, Punjab, India is the most important Sikh temple. It was built between 1588 and 1601. The temple is recognized by its gold dome.

Zoroastrianism

Zoroastrianism was the state religion of Persia around the 6th century BC. It was founded by the Prophet Zarathushtra (Zoroaster). However, following the Arab invasion of Persia in 650 BC, several Zoroastrians fled Persia for India. Even today, India has the largest number of Zoroastrians. Zoroastrianism is one of the oldest religions in the world to promote the concept of one god. The holy book of the Zoroastrians is the Avesta. Fire, which is an important symbol in their religion, is the focal point in their temples.

Hindu festivals

Diwali and Dussehra are two of the most important Hindu festivals. Diwali celebrates the victory of good over evil and also marks the beginning of a new financial year. During this festival, houses are lit up with earthen lamps, new clothes are worn, firecrackers are burst, and people give gifts and sweets to family and friends. Dussehra celebrates the victory of the legendary Lord Rama in the battle against Ravana. People visit temples and say special prayers at home.

Key facts:

- Confucianism and Taoism are two traditional Chinese religions. Confucianism is based on the teachings of the 6th-5th century BC Chinese scholar Confucius. Confucius stressed the importance of each person being a responsible, dutiful and co-operative member of his family and society in order to achieve happiness and contentment. Taoism, based on the teachings of the 6th-century BC Chinese philosopher Laozi, teaches its followers to live in harmony with nature and be selfless, kind and loving. These religions have greatly influenced Chinese culture and people.
- Baha'i is a relatively new religion founded in the mid-19th century by an Iranian Muslim called Baha'u'llah. It stresses that there is only one god and that all prophets and people are part of that Supreme Being. Today, Baha'i is practised by over five million people all over the world.
- Zen is a branch of Mahayana Buddhism, founded by the Buddhist monk Bodhidharma around the 6th century AD. It is associated with the spread of martial arts like Kung Fu.

Try these too:

Asia (p 112–113), Ancient India and China (p 118–119), Medieval Asia (p 128–129), World Religions (p 174–175)

Matter

Everything around us is made of matter. All objects, living and non-living, which occupy space and have weight, are matter. Matter can be varied in shape and form. It can be hard like stone, soft like cotton, heavy like iron or light like a feather.

Key facts:

- Some fluids form crystals when they solidify. Crystals are special kinds of solids that have a regular, orderly and repeating pattern of atoms, which form a 'crystal lattice'. Some fluids solidify to form a single crystal, but most form into several interconnected 'polycrystals'.
- Ancient Greeks and Indians thought that all matter was made up of the four natural elements: earth, fire, water and air. The 6th century Indian philosopher Kanada was the first to suggest that all matter was made up of tiny particles called *Parmanu*, or atoms. However, these theories and discoveries were gradually forgotten over the centuries.
- The modern atomic theory was proposed by the renowned English physicist John Dalton, in 1803. In the latter part of the 20th century, scientists discovered the quark and the gluon. These are the smallest parts of an atom.

▸ Changing shapes
Pour coloured water into beakers of different shapes. You will see the water take up the shape of the particular beaker.

Matter can also be a liquid like water or a gas like oxygen. However, there are three basic forms of matter – solid, liquid and gas. All three states can be changed into one another, by heating or cooling. Solids have a definite shape, volume or size. Liquids have volume but they do not have a definite shape. They take on the shape of the container that holds them. Gases do not have a fixed shape or volume. They expand and fill the area or container they are put into.

What is matter made of?

Matter is made up of tiny particles called molecules, which can be further broken down into atoms. Atoms are the smallest particles that retain the chemical properties of the particular matter. The atoms of each material differ from those of other materials. Solids are made up of tightly packed atoms, which give them their shape and hardness. Liquids have atoms that are not as tightly packed as in solids, but are closer together than in gases. Gases have atoms that are spread out. Solids and liquids cannot be compressed and fitted into smaller spaces as there is not much space between their atoms. Gases, on the other hand, can be easily compressed as there is plenty of space between their atoms.

▸ Forces at play
The attractive force between liquid molecules is called cohesive force, while the one between a liquid and a solid is called adhesive force. When the cohesive force is stronger than the adhesive force, the surface of the liquid tends to curve inwards, as is the case with water drops on a waxy surface or on leaves.

▲ Solid facts
Solids have a definite shape and volume because their molecules are packed together tightly. The closer the molecules are the harder the solid. The molecules of cotton is more loosely packed than those of a stone or wood. That is why cotton is softer than the other two.

◂ **Filling up**
The molecules of a gas are spread out, as no force keeps them together. They move about in different directions at high speeds, and occupy any amount of space they can. That is why even a small amount of gas can fill an entire balloon, no matter what its shape or size.

Elements

All matter around us is made up of some basic substances called elements. Elements are substances that occur in nature. These substances cannot be made by combining other substances. The oxygen that we breathe and iron are two examples of elements. Both of these substances can be found naurally.

Compounds and mixtures

Some substances are made by combining two or more elements. Such substances are called compounds. For example, when an object made of iron is exposed to air, chemical changes take place and rust forms on its surface over a period of time. Rust is iron oxide, which is a combination of iron and oxygen. A third group of materials can be made by mixing two or more substances. These are called mixtures. Unlike compounds, mixtures are only formed through physical changes. No chemical changes occur in the substances of a mixture. For example, sugar dissolved in a glass of water is a mixture. On heating this mixture, the water evaporates and sugar remains at the bottom of the glass.

▴ **Breaking bonds**
Tearing a sheet of paper causes only a physical change, as the pieces are still that of paper. Burning a sheet of paper, however, breaks down the bonds that hold the atoms together, changing the chemical nature of paper.

Try these too:

Heat (p 184–185), Magnets in Daily Life (p 186–187), Forces and Motion (p 188–189)

Physical–chemical changes

Every time energy is added to a paricular substance or taken away from it (e.g. heating or cooling), that substance undergoes some physical changes. A physical change can be defined as one in which the state of the substance changes. However, the chemical properties of the substance remain the same. For example, water contains two parts of hydrogen and one part of oxygen when it is in its liquid state. This chemical composition remains the same even when it is a solid or vapour. This is why water can be turned into ice by cooling it and into water vapour by heating it. Both ice and water vapour can be changed back into water. If adding or taking away energy changes the substance irreversibly, then the change is chemical. For example, if paper is burnt it turns into ash and cannot be changed back into its original form.

Atomic structure

Atoms are made up of three parts. They are electrons, neutrons and protons. The neutrons and protons form the nucleus, or the centre of the atom, while the electrons travel around this nucleus. The electron has a negative electric charge and the proton has a positive electric charge. The neutron, however, has no electric charge. The number of electrons, protons and neutrons in an atom varies according to the type of atom.

Light

Light is a form of energy that helps us see. It is all around us and is produced by natural and artificial sources. Light sources also produce heat – another form of energy.

▲ **Dispersing colours**
When light enters a glass prism, it bends. Since each colour in white light has a different wavelength, they travel at different speeds. The colour with less speed is bent more than the one that travels faster, causing them to be separated. This property is called dispersion.

Key facts:

• When light falls on an object, some of it is scattered around the object, enabling us to see it. This is called 'scattering of light'. Some light is absorbed by the object and the rest is reflected. The amount of light that is absorbed depends on the nature of the object. Smooth and transparent objects like glass absorb very little, but opaque objects like wood absorb a lot and reflect very little.

• White light can be made by mixing red, green and blue light in the right proportion. These colours are called primary colours and a wide range of other colours can be produced by varying combinations of them. Unlike coloured light, coloured paints cannot be added to each other to produce white. While mixing, some colours absorb others and mixing all three together will only produce a blackish-brown colour!

• The human eye sees objects with the help of two types of cells – rods and cones. Cones can recognize colours and help form images that are bright and colourful. Rods help in seeing at night and in the dark. They cannot recognize colors, which is why everything appears black or grey at night.

The Sun is the largest natural source of light. The surface temperature of the Sun is more than 6,000° C (11,000° F) and at the centre it is nearly 13,000,000° C (23,400,032° F). All this heat makes the surface of the Sun glow brightly. This bright glow is what we see on Earth as sunlight. Other stars also produce light, but they are too far away to light up the Earth. The Moon is another heavenly body that appears to produce light, but in reality, it is just reflecting the light of the Sun.

Artificial sources of light include oil lamps, candles, incandescent bulbs and fluorescent lights. The Sun, stars, lamps, candles and bulbs are called luminous objects. Objects like trees, buildings and furniture, which do not produce light, are called non-luminous objects. These can be seen only when light falls on to them and they reflect it.

▼ **Faster than sound**
Light travels at a speed of 300,000 kilometres/second (186,411 miles/second), which is a million times faster than the speed of sound.

Colours in light

Light mostly appears to be white or yellow, but it is actually made up of numerous colours. Isaac Newton discovered that light passing through a glass prism will be broken down into violet, indigo, blue, green, yellow, orange and red (VIBGYOR). This is best demonstrated by the rainbow. The colour of the objects around us is determined by which colours of light they absorb and which ones they reflect. A red object absorbs most of the colours and reflects red. Black objects absorb most colours, to appear dark, while white ones reflect most colours, to appear white.

Seeing light

We can see ourselves in a mirror because light bounces off its surface. Polished metal, water and glass have smooth, shiny surfaces that easily reflect light. Rough surfaces scatter the reflection. Kaleidoscopes and periscopes are excellent examples of how reflecting surfaces can be used in clever ways. In a kaleidoscope, a set of two mirrors is used to create multiple reflections of coloured patterns, while in a periscope two glass prisms are used to reflect objects above through the eyepiece below.

Light travels at different speeds in different mediums. While travelling from one transparent medium to another it changes its direction slightly. This bending of light is called refraction. For example, if a pencil is placed in a partially-filled jar of water, we can see that the pencil appears to bend where it enters the water. This happens due to refraction.

Travelling light

Light can travel through empty space, even in a vacuum where there is no air. To the naked eye, light appears to travel in straight lines. Light emitted by a flashlight is an example of this. However, in reality, light travels in waves. It travels only in one direction, but in a way that is similar to ripples in a pond – with continuous crests (peaks) and troughs (valleys). Light is measured by the distance between two consecutive crests, which is its 'wavelength' and the height of the crest from the trough, which is its 'amplitude' (amount of energy). Each colour that makes up white light has a different wavelength.

Shadows

Shadows are formed when light is blocked by an object. All materials that block light even a little can form shadows. This means that even tissue paper and soap bubbles, both of which allow light to pass through them, form shadows because they are not completely transparent. However, solids, like us, form the darkest shadows. This is because we block light completely. The sharpness and the length of a shadow depend on the position of the light source and its distance from the object. A single bright beam of light coming from one direction casts a clear shadow, whereas if light is cast from several beams coming from different directions, there may not be a shadow, or it may be blurred.

◂ Reflecting colours
The kaleidoscope has a transparent compartment with bits of coloured glass or paper at one end of the cylinder and a viewing hole at the opposite end. Within the cylinder are two long mirrors that create multiple reflections of the patterns created by the coloured bits.

▴ In the candlelight
Like light bulbs, candles are artificial sources of light. They consist of a wick inside a column of solid fuel made of wax. Like all light sources candles emit heat as well as light.

◂ Skewed vision
In the picture, the line dividing the red and white surfaces seems skewed when seen through the glass of water. This is due to the refraction of light.

◂ Clear image
Reflections on still water are called specular reflections. In specular reflection, light coming from a particular direction is reflected on to a single direction, giving a clear image on the surface of the reflecting medium.

Try these too:

The Brain and Sensory Organs (p 96–97), The Scientific Revolution (p 142–143), Heat (p 184–185), Electricity (p 190–191)

Sound

Sound is a kind of energy that we can hear. Sounds are produced all around us and we hear them without actually trying to do so. This is because the human ear automatically collects sound messages and transmits them to our brain. Sound can travel through air, water and even solids, but not through a vacuum.

Musical notes
Sounds produced by musical instruments like a trumpet are usually pleasant. However, if not played well even instruments can produce unpleasant noise.

Key facts:

- Ultrasonic sound waves are used to help diagnose problems like muscular and joint injuries and pain. They are also used to scan a foetus during pregnancy and to monitor its growth.
- When an aircraft flies, it creates waves of air that push against each other and form a barrier. When the aircraft's speed exceeds the speed of sound, the barrier of air is broken, causing a loud noise called a sonic boom.

Sounds are produced by quick backwards and forwards movements, or vibrations, of an object. When an object moves, it disturbs the molecules of air around it and causes them to vibrate. This vibration travels through the air and is heard as sound. The greater the vibration, the louder the sound. As sound travels, the energy of the vibration slowly wears out and the sound fades away.

Properties of sound

Sound, like light, travels in waves. The movement of molecules in sound waves causes alternating patches of tightly bunched molecules, called compressions, and loosely spaced molecules, called rarefactions. These are shown in graphs as wave-like figures with crests and troughs, or ups and downs. Sound is measured by its wavelength, period, amplitude and frequency.

Wavelength is the distance from one crest or trough to another crest or trough, and this constitutes one cycle of the wave. The time taken for the completion of one cycle is the period of the sound.

Amplitude is the height of the wave from trough to crest, meaning the louder the sound, the bigger the amplitude. Frequency is the total number of cycles completed in a second. The greater the number of cycles, the higher the frequency and the pitch. Sound travels fastest in solids. This is because denser mediums are able to transmit vibrations faster through their tightly packed molecules. Sound cannot travel in a vacuum, because in empty space there is no medium to carry sound waves.

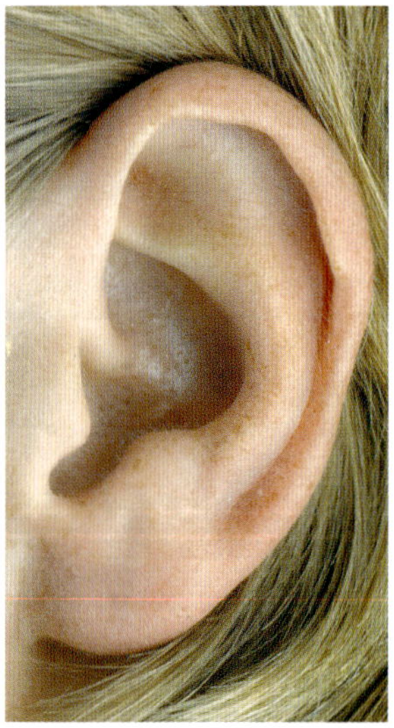

Getting an earful
The sound waves entering a human ear causes the eardrum to vibrate. These vibrations are transmitted into the inner ear, where they are converted into nerve impulses and sent to the brain.

No barriers
While sitting next to a person who is listening to music through earphones, one can sometimes faintly hear parts of the music. This is due to diffraction, by which sound waves can bend around obstacles and escape through even the tiniest openings.

Types of sound

There are two types of sounds – those that we can hear and those that we cannot. Sounds we can hear are called audible sounds. The human ear can normally hear sound that ranges between frequencies of 20 hertz and 20,000 hertz. The normal human voice is about 60 hertz. Any sound that is below 20 hertz or above 20,000 hertz is called inaudible sound, or ultrasonic sound. Some animals, like elephants and dogs, can hear ultrasonic sound. Bats can both hear and produce ultrasonic sounds.

Noise and music

Unpleasant sound is called noise. The loud sounds of machinery, aircraft taking off and heavy traffic are created by irregular sound waves that produce disagreeable sounds. Loud sounds are not only disturbing, they can also damage the eardrum and cause partial loss of hearing or deafness. Music is any pleasant sound produced by a singer or a musical instrument. It is created by regular sound waves and consists of a series of high and low frequencies, or pitches, that make up the scale. The musician controls the vibrations so that the correct pitch and amplitude are produced to make specific musical notes.

Vocal cords

Human beings produce sound through their voice box, or larynx. Within the voice box are ligaments called vocal cords. Sound is produced when air passes through a slit between the vocal cords and makes them vibrate. Many animals also produce sounds using their vocal cords. However, birds do not have vocal cords and produce sound through a bony ring called the syrinx, which is located in their windpipe.

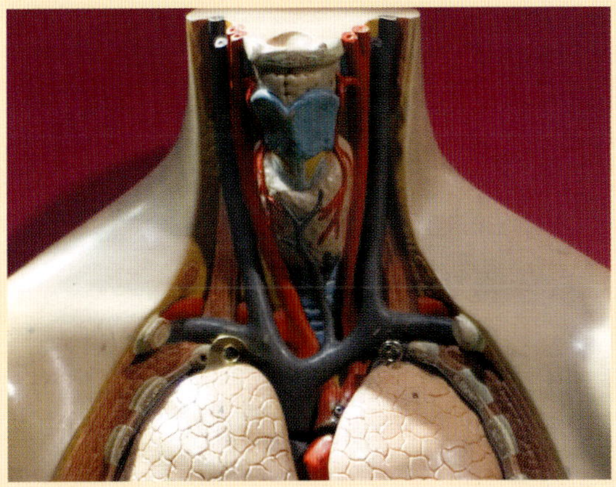

Try these too:

The Brain and Sensory Organs (p 96–97), The Scientific Revolution (p 142–143), The Sounds of Music (p 166–167)

▲ Causing ripples
Like light, sound travels in the form of waves. These waves look like ripples that are caused when a stone is thrown into a body of water.

▼ Keeping the noise out
People who work in factories and on airport runways often wear earmuffs to protect their ears from the noise.

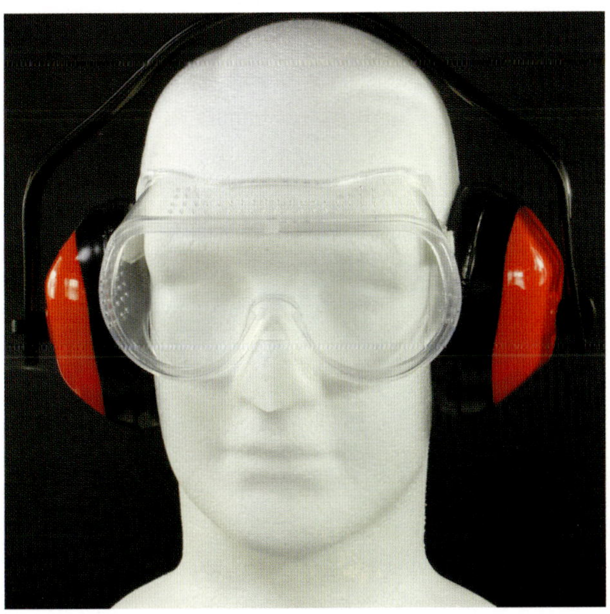

▼ Strong signals
Most male frogs have a pouch, known as the vocal sac, at the bottom of their mouths. A frog usually closes its mouth and nostrils to push air into its vocal cords to produce sound. Some of this air is sent into the vocal sac, which in turn increases the amplitude of the sound produced by the frog's vocal cords.

Heat

Heat is a form of energy. We often convert thermal (heat) energy into other types of energy to help us do work. For example, heat produced by burning coal is changed to steam power, which runs steam engines. Heat energy is constantly in motion – moving from matter with a higher temperature to matter with a lower temperature.

Key facts:

- Energy cannot be destroyed. It is merely converted from one form to another. When the energy in one object or substance reduces, it increases in another.
- Solar heat energy, or radiation, heats the land, oceans and air. The transfer of energy in the atmosphere, over land and on sea, due to differently charged atoms, results in temperature and weather or climate changes.
- The normal temperature of the human body is 37° C (98.6° F). The freezing point of water is 0° C (32° F) and its boiling point is 100° C (212° F).

◂ Energetic atoms
When metal is heated, the atoms in it gain energy and move about rapidly, pushing the neighbouring atoms away. This causes the metal to expand.

The largest source of natural heat is the Sun. Fuels like gasoline and wood produce heat. Artificial sources of light, like a candle or a bulb, also produce heat. Other sources of heat are mechanical machines, such as a saw that cuts wood or a brake that stops a car, and electrical machines, such as a television, radio or food processor. Even our body produces heat when we exercise, work or simply rub our hands together.

Properties of heat

Solids, liquids and gases expand when heated. This is because heated matter consists of molecules that are disorganized and in constant motion. A common example of this is the expansion of wooden doors and windows in hot weather. However, all substances do not expand equally. Some solids, liquids and gases expand faster and to a greater extent than others. Heat can also change the state of matter from solid to liquid or liquid to gas. Lack of heat can also result in reversing the process. The most common example of this is the change of ice into water and water into vapour and vice versa. The temperature at which any matter changes from solid into liquid is called its 'melting point' and the point at which it changes from a liquid into a gas is known as its 'boiling point'. The melting point and boiling point of each substance is different.

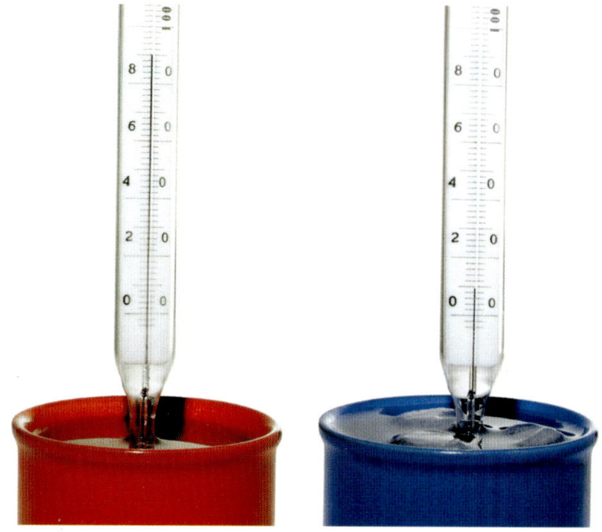

▴ Reading the mercury levels
When the bulb of a thermometer is put into a substance, the mercury in it expands and rises up the tube. The level of mercury in the tube gives the temperature of the substance it was put into.

Measuring heat

We can tell that something is hot by touching it, but to tell us how hot it is we need to use a thermometer. There are several types of thermometer, but the most commonly used types are the clinical thermometer and the laboratory thermometer. Thermometers are slim glass tubes that have a bulb containing mercury at one end.

Marking temperatures

All thermometers have temperature gradings marked on the outside. Clinical thermometers have markings from 35°–42° C (95°–107.6° F). Laboratory thermometers have markings from 0°–100° C (32°–212° F). As heat produced from different sources varies, the calorie is used as the common unit of measurement. A calorie can be defined as the unit of energy that is used to increase the temperature of one gram of water by 1° C (33.8 ° F).

Transfer of heat

There are three ways in which heat can be passed on, or transferred. They are – conduction, convection and radiation. Conduction of heat is the direct transfer of heat from a hot solid object to a cold solid object, when they come into contact with each other. The closely packed heated molecules of some solids vibrate vigorously and transfer heat to neighbouring molecules when they strike against them, thus gradually passing heat along. Metals are the best conductors, while wood and plastic are good insulators as they do not transfer heat energy. Liquids and gases transfer heat through convection. In this method, cool substances move to warm spots and warm substances move to cool spots in a circular motion. This is best illustrated by cool ocean air moving on to the land at night, while the warm land air expands and rises to move to the sea. Radiation is the method by which heat is transferred in straight lines or rays. The Sun transfers heat in this manner.

▲ ▶ **Good insulators**
Wood and plastic are very good insulators. This is because the atoms of wood and plastic are not as tightly packed as those of metals. This slows down the transfer of heat within wood and plastic. This is why houses with wooden floors or windows are able to keep out heat during summer and keep it in during winters. In the same way, plastic food containers are able to seal in or keep out heat.

◀ **Up in vapour**
The boiling point of water, when water turns into vapour is 100° C (212° F).

▼ **Moving in**
When the air over a particular region becomes warm, cooler air descends to take its place. This is best illustrated by cool ocean air moving on to the land at night, while the warm air over the land expands and rises to move over to the sea.

▲ **Cold fact**
Keep a glass of cold water on a table. After a while you will see drops of water dripping down the sides of the glass. This is due to the transfer of heat from the warmer table to the glass of cold water. As the heat is transferred, the water becomes warmer, causing the frost on the outside of the glass to melt.

Heat capacity

The rate of heat transfer in each substance is unique. While one gram of water requires 1 calorie of heat to increase its temperature by 1° C (33.8° F), the temperature of one gram of oil is raised by more than 1° by the same amount of heat. This means that the heat capacity of water and oil are not the same. The amount of heat required by each substance to increase the temperature of one kilogram of the substance by 1° C is referred to as its specific heat.

Try these too:

The Earth's Atmosphere (p 30–31), Seasons and Weather (p 32–33), The Industrial Revolution (p 138–139), Matter (p 178–179), Electricity (p 190–191)

Magnets in Daily Life

Magnets are objects that have the power to attract other metallic objects made of iron, cobalt or nickel. They also have the power to repel, or push away, other magnets. Almost all matter on Earth has magnetic power, but in most the power is very weak and not visible. Magnets occur naturally and are also man-made.

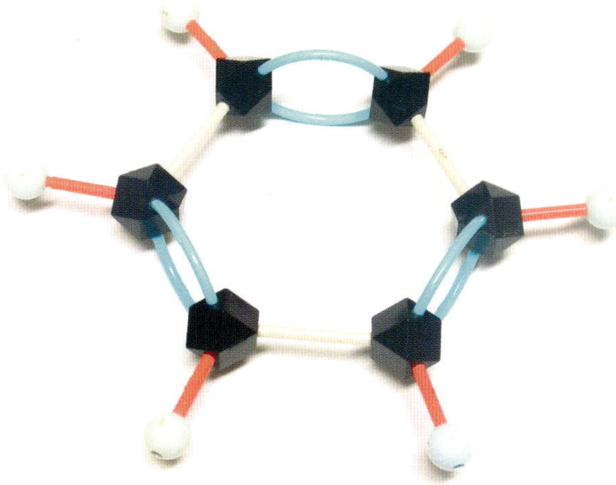

▲ **Strong attraction**
Most of the electrons in metals like iron and nickel are aligned in the same direction. That is why these metals are easily attracted to magnets.

Key facts:

- The lodestone, or magnetite, was the earliest natural magnet to be discovered. It is also the most magnetic substance on Earth. It was discovered between 800–500 BC by the Ancient Greeks and was also used in Ancient China.
- The Earth has a magnetic field surrounding it. This field protects the Earth from solar particles that break away from the Sun and come hurtling down to Earth. The Earth's magnetic field protects the planet by repelling these particles. Other heavenly bodies that have their own magnetic field are the Sun, Saturn, Jupiter, Neptune and Uranus.
- The atoms in magnetic materials themselves act like little highly charged magnets, usually facing in different directions. When these atoms line up, aligning themselves to each other's north and south poles, the material changes into a magnet.

Every magnet has a north and a south pole. Magnets are strongest at their poles and objects attracted to a magnet tend to stick to one of the poles. Magnetic north poles attract the south poles of other objects, and the magnetic south pole attracts the north pole. In other words, opposite poles attract, while like poles repel. The poles of magnetic objects always align themselves with the magnetic north and south poles of the Earth. The magnetic poles of the Earth are not the same as its geographic North and South Poles. The magnetic poles are in fact several hundred kilometres (miles) away from the geographic poles and are constantly moving. Magnets create a field of force, also known as a magnetic field, around themselves. They can affect other magnets or magnetic materials that come within this field.

Types of magnets

There are three types of magnets – permanent, temporary and electromagnets. A permanent magnet is able to retain its magnetic quality over a long period of time. However, magnetic strength varies, depending on factors like the material, size and temperature.

Temporary magnets are objects that retain their magnetic properties only for a short time. They may have been magnetized after being accidentally or intentionally put in the field of a strong magnet. These magnets usually lose their power as soon as they are taken away from the particular magnetic field. A good example is paperclips or pins that stick to magnets and, in turn, attract other clips, pins or soft iron objects.

Making an electromagnet

Electromagnets can be created by winding an electric wire around a piece of soft iron. When electric current runs through the wire, a magnetic field is created and transferred to the iron piece. The magnetic strength of such a magnet and the direction of its poles can be changed by adjusting the strength of the current passing through the wire.

▶ **Magnetic nature**
If iron filings are placed near a bar magnet, they stick to the north and south poles of the magnet. The filings, in turn, then become magnetic themselves.

Making a magnet

The easiest way to make a magnet is to place some metal in a magnetic field and vibrate it. A live electric wire, carrying a direct current (DC) can also be wrapped around the piece of metal to induce magnetism (Make sure you try this only with the help of your parents or teacher.) The third method of magnetizing a piece of metal is by stroking it with a magnet repeatedly. However, care should be taken to stroke in only one direction. Magnets lose their power if they are heated, hammered, dropped, stroked randomly or if an alternating current is passed through them.

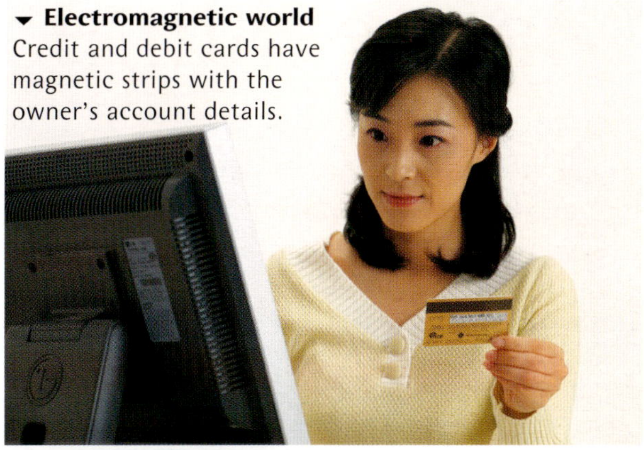

▼ **Electromagnetic world**
Credit and debit cards have magnetic strips with the owner's account details.

Where are magnets used?

Magnets are used in a number of ways in our daily life. Although we are not always aware of it, magnets are often used in electrical appliances to convert electrical energy into mechanical energy and vice versa.

Early magnets

Magnet were first used in the form of a compass. Nearly 2,000 years ago, the Ancient Chinese invented a compass, which used a small magnet that aligned with the magnetic North and South Poles of the Earth. Sailors out at sea found this compass very useful as it helped them to find out which direction they were travelling in. Compasses continue to be a major navigational tool even today.

Modern uses of magnets

Today, magnets are used in every possible area, from daily life to industries. Decorative refrigerator magnets are used to put up notes, messages and bills on the refrigerator. Audio and video cassettes are coated with magnetic material that allows music and movies to be recorded onto them. Electromagnets are used in televisions. Until the advent of plasma screens and LCDs, electromagnets were also used to help generate images on computer screens. Magnets are an important part of many of the household appliances and motor vehicles we use every day.

▲ **Moving with magnets**
Apart from bar and spherical magnets, U-shaped magnets called horseshoe magnets are also very common.

▼ **Running the house**
Magnets are used in motors that are found in appliances such as fans, dishwashers, washing machines, microwave ovens and even electric toothbrushes.

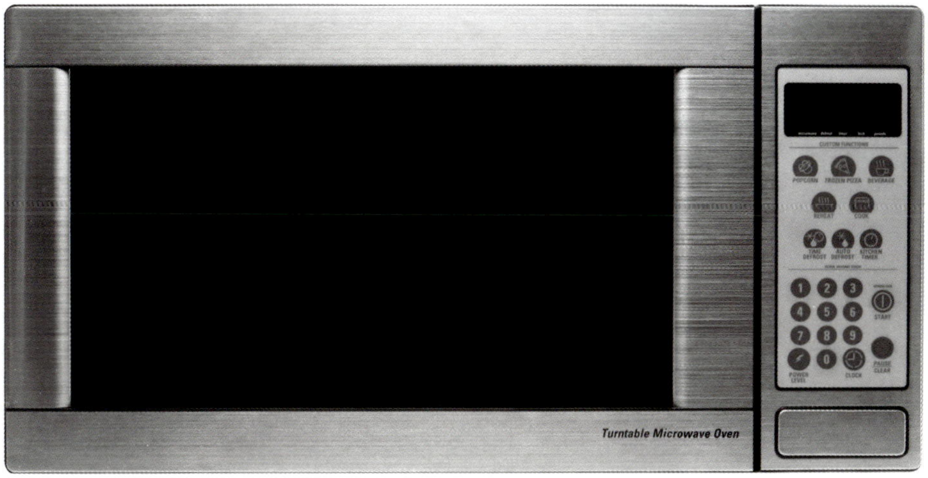

Try these too:

The Scientific Revolution (p 142–143), Computer Revolution (p 152–153), Matter (p 178–179), Electricity (p 190–191)

Forces and Motion

Force is the pull or push required to move objects. We use force all the time in our daily lives without even realizing it. Walking, lifting, running, jumping, pulling, pushing and writing are just some of the activities that require force.

Key facts:

- When two uneven surfaces rub against each other, friction is caused. Friction is a force that opposes the movement of an object by acting on it in the opposite direction. Frictional force usually produces heat.
- The mass of an object is the amount of matter in it. The greater the mass is, the heavier the object, and the heavier the object, the greater the force that needs to be applied to move it. For example, it is easy to move a ball or a puck with an ice-hockey stick, but a lot more force is required to move a rock with the same stick.
- When more than one force acts on an object, the sum of all the forces that are acting on that object is called the 'net force'. If two or more forces act together on an object in the same direction, the object can be moved faster. If the forces act in opposing directions, they cancel each other out and there is no force on the object.

Objects never move by themselves – they only move when force is applied to them. Similarly, moving objects do not slow down or come to a rest unless an opposing force is applied to stop them. This quality of constant movement or constant rest is called 'inertia'. A simple example of inertia can be seen in a ball lying on a sports field. As long as no one kicks it, the ball lies in one place without moving. When it is kicked, it begins to move and keeps moving until it hits a goalpost, net or any other obstacle.

Gravitational force

Gravity is the natural force that is exerted by all objects. This force attracts all close objects to each other. However, as the distance between two objects increases, the gravitational force decreases. Objects with larger mass are affected more by gravitational force, as they have a larger surface area. Similarly, objects with a large mass also exert more gravitational force. This is why the Earth's gravitational power is so strong. When an object is at rest it is motionless because two opposing forces are acting upon it. One is the Earth's downward gravitational pull, and the other is the upwards force exerted by the surface on which the object rests.

Heave ho!
The bigger an object, the greater its inertia. That is why you have to use a lot more force to push a heavy object compared to one that is lighter.

Light-weight!
The feeling of weightlessness on the Moon is caused by the weak gravitational force exerted by it.

It is gravitational force that attracts the Earth to the Sun and the Moon to the Earth. All planets rotate and revolve in their orbits because of gravity. We can feel this force when we try to lift any object. Those with greater mass feel heavier because of the gravitational force that pulls them down. We call this weight. The object also exerts an equal and opposite force. This upward force exerted against the gravitational force is called the apparent weight and is usually equal to the actual weight of the object.

Moving on up
Carrying objects up a flight of steps is more difficult than carrying them down. This is because you are going against the force of gravity, while climbing up.

Centrifugal and centripetal force

Centripetal and centrifugal forces are opposing forces that act on objects that are moving on circular paths. Objects set in motion normally move in a straight line, unless some other force acts upon them and changes their path. When an object, such as a ball tied to a piece of string, is swung in a circular pattern a second force acts upon the ball, attracting it to the centre of the circle. This is called centripetal force. Simultaneously, an opposing force pushes the ball outwards and away from the centre, keeping it on its path. This is the centrifugal force.

Velocity, momentum and acceleration

We measure the speed of movement of any object by its velocity, which is nothing but the distance travelled by the object in a certain period of time. It is obvious therefore that still objects do not have velocity.

When any object moves, it is said to have momentum. The amount of momentum in each object depends on how much mass makes up the object and how fast that mass is moving. We can find out the momentum of an object by multiplying its mass by its velocity.

When an object begins to move and slowly picks up speed as it travels, the object is said to accelerate. When the same object begins to gradually slow down, it is said to decelerate. In other words, acceleration and deceleration actually measure the rate of change in the speed of an object. Deceleration could be deliberate, as when you slow down a car, or also be caused by friction exerted by the surface.

▲ **Fighting friction**
Cars used in Formula One racing are specially designed for the purpose. Tyres with fewer treads help to reduce the friction between the car and the race track and achieve maximum speed. The tapered shape of the body and the airfoils, or wings at the front and the rear of the car, help to reduce air friction.

Try these too:

The Moon (p 14–15), Man in Space (p 18–19), The Scientific Revolution (p 142–143)

▶ **Forces in action**
As a bungee jumper jumps off a bridge or a cliff, the gravitational force of the Earth pulls the jumper towards it. As the jumper falls at a high speed, the air exerts a frictional force that gradually slows down the jumper, who is then pulled back by the rope.

Forces in daily life

Gravitational force: When a ball is thrown up and comes down to Earth. Cycling up a mountain is difficult, but coming down is easy.
Applied force: Pushing or kicking a ball; lifting weights
Frictional force: Car tyres rubbing against the road; striking a matchstick against the box; rollerskating on a cement road
Magnetic force: Refrigerator magnets that hold things up; a compass
Centrifugal force: Spin dryers; planets revolving around the Sun
Spring force: Pulling the trigger of a gun so that it would release a bullet; spring-loaded door hinges

Electricity

Electricity is the most commonly used form of energy. It can be easily transferred from one place to another. It can also be just as easily converted into light, heat or any other form of energy. An electric charge is created by atoms.

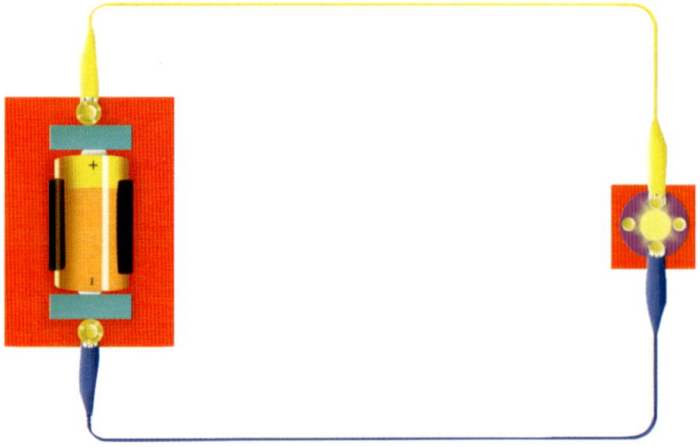

▲ As simple as that
A simple electric circuit consists of a battery or generator, which generates current. The current then passes through metal wires to a switch that controls its flow and finally into bulbs and appliances.

Key facts:

• Static electricity is created when we rub against a charged surface, like a carpet or blanket, and freely floating electrons transfer themselves on to our body. When we touch something that is positively charged, like a metal door-knob, the extra electrons on our body are attracted to the protons of the metallic object and a tiny spark of electricity is created.

• The electric bulb contains a very delicate wire called a filament. As the filament is very thin, its atoms collide more often when an electric current is passed through it. Increased atomic activity increases the heat of the wire and makes it glow. At first the light produced is reddish and as the heat increases it turns white.

• Air is usually an insulator. However, sometimes when an object is highly charged, it will pass on electric currents through air or other insulating material in the form of electric arcs. Lightning is an excellent example of this phenomenon.

The positively charged protons and the negatively charged electrons in an atom normally balance each other, making the atom neutral. However, although protons stay close to the nucleus of the atom, electrons, being loosely arranged, sometimes move to neighbouring atoms and create an imbalance in the charge of the atoms. In such cases, one atom might have more protons and becomes positively charged, while the other gains more electrons to become negatively charged. This usually happens in materials that are good conductors, like metal. A material like wood is a good insulator as its electrons do not create a charge. When the electric charge is passed on from one atom to the next in a conductor, an electric current is created.

Electric current

There are two types of electric current – direct current (DC) and alternating current (AC). Direct current always flows in one direction, whereas an alternating current keeps changing its direction. Electric current flows through electric circuits that consist of a good conductor. Copper and silver are the best conductors of electricity but as silver is very expensive, copper wires are usually used.

Voltage and resistance

The voltage, or strength, of an electric current is determined by how many electrons are sent from one end of the circuit and how many are received at the other end. In other words, there is a difference in pressure between the two ends. This is similar to the flow of water from a tank to a tap. Voltage is measured in volts. In the case of water, difference in height and increase in distance reduces pressure but, in electricity, height variations are not important. However, the distance travelled affects the quality of current. Just as water pressure decreases with friction, electric current is prevented from flowing freely because of resistance, which is caused by electrons and atoms colliding with each other. A good conductor has low resistance, while the resistance of a good insulator is high. Shorter and thicker wires have low resistance as compared to long thin wires. Resistance is measured in ohms.

▶ Lighting up homes
Electricity is generated in huge power stations. It is then carried across long distances through electric cables into our homes.

Electricity in nature

Lightning is a form of natural electricity that is most commonly found. Lightning occurs when clouds carrying a negative charge meet positively charged particles on the Earth's surface.

The human body contains a continuous flow of electric current that is created by neurons, or nerve cells, which convey electric impulses to the brain.

Some kinds of fish, such as the electric eel, can generate an electric shock to defend themselves and to hunt their prey.

Sources of electricity

The two most commonly used sources of electricity are electrolytic cells and large power generators. An electrolytic cell consists of several batteries. These batteries contain chemicals that react with each other and produce energy, which is converted into electricity. Small batteries are also used to produce power to run small machines like music systems, torches and clocks. However, batteries and electrolytic cells can only produce small quantities of electricity and we need a lot more to light our homes and offices and run household appliances like televisions, refrigerators and dishwashers.

Generating electricity

Power stations produce electricity by various methods. One method involves converting energy generated by water flowing through a dam (hydroelectricity), while in another heat produced by burning coal (thermal electricity) is used. Windmills (wind power), nuclear reactions (nuclear power) and heat from the Earth's core (geothermal electricity) are also used to generate electricity. This power is then distributed to homes, factories and offices through a grid of wires that are several thousand kilometres (miles) long.

◂ Nuclear power
In nuclear power stations, nuclear reaction is used to produce steam that is required to operate the turbines and generators.

◂ Powered by water
In hydroelectric power stations, the force of running water is used to turn the turbines, which in turn operate the generators that produce electricity. Many countries rely on hydro-electric power stations.

▸ Not so reliable
Using wind power to generate electricity is very expensive as it requires a large amount of open space. Moreover, wind is unpredictable.

Try these too:

The Scientific Revolution (p 142–143), Matter (p 178–179) Magnets in Daily Life (p 186–187), Light (p 180–181), Sound (p 182–183), Heat (p 184–185)

Communication and Satellites

Just as natural satellites like the Earth and other planets orbit around the Sun and the Moon orbits the Earth, several man-made satellites also orbit our planet. These artificial satellites are the lifelines of modern communication devices.

Key facts:

- Satellite constellations are groups of satellites that are meant to serve a common purpose. The Global Positioning System is one such constellation with six orbital planes consisting of four satellites each.
- *Sputnik 1* was the first satellite ever to be launched into outer space. It was launched on 4 October 1957, to a height of about 250 kilometres (150 miles), by the Soviet Union. The mission was to collect information about the ionosphere. Three months later the satellite burned up completely as it re-entered Earth's atmosphere.
- The Hubble Space Telescope was launched in 1990 by NASA to transmit images of outer space to astronomical stations on the Earth. The telescope sent back clear, sharp images of the Universe, which have contributed greatly to our understanding of celestial bodies and events attached to them. Images from the Hubble telescope also showed us that nearly 50 billion galaxies already exist in the Universe, while many new ones are forming.

Satellites are data centres that are equipped to collect and distribute a wide range of information. They receive signals from Earth or other heavenly bodies and send them back to Earth. Satellites help facilitate television and radio broadcasting, and assist in studies of the Earth and its atmosphere, as well as other planets and celestial phenomena. They also help in forecasting weather.

Structure of a satellite

Satellites come in different shapes and sizes. The equipment in each satellite varies according to its purpose. Most satellites have instruments for receiving and recording data, images and commands and for sending recorded information to receiving stations on Earth. All its systems are controlled by a computer. The energy required for a satellite's activities is generated through solar panels that are attached to it.

Satellite orbits

Satellites orbit Earth in a variety of orbit patterns. The three most commonly used orbits are the geostationary, the polar and the inclined orbits. Geostationary satellites appear to be stationary because they are programmed and located in such a way that they move at the same speed as Earth. Therefore, they seem to be immobile and fixed in the same place.

Polar orbit satellites are aligned with the polar regions. These satellites move along the lines of latitude, and pass over both poles in each orbit. However, since this orbit is tilted at 90° to the Equator, it passes over different latitudes in each revolution. This orbit is used by satellites that help in mapping, surveying, spying and weather forecasting.

The inclined orbit is between 0° and 90°. These satellites are only a few hundred kilometres (miles) away from Earth, and their movement is synchronized with the Sun's revolution. Satellites can also be classified depending on their height from Earth: high Earth orbit satellites are more than 35,790 kilometres (22,238.87 miles) above Earth, low Earth orbit satellites between 200 and 1,200 kilometres (124–745 miles) and medium Earth orbit satellites between 1,400 and 35,790 kilometres (870–22,239 miles).

▲ **Weather monitor**
Geostationary satellites are located above the Equator, at approximately 35,780 kilomeres (22,233 miles). They often have trouble clearly receiving and sending information to and from the poles, but are useful in making local weather forecasts.

▼ **Communicating across barriers**
A satellite dish uplinks and downlinks signals to and from communication satellites in the form of waves.

Types and functions of satellites

The three main types of satellites are communication, navigation and Earth observatory satellites. The most important of these are communication satellites. These satellites have revolutionized the world by facilitating long-distance communication through the receiving and redirecting of radio, television and telephone signals.

Early communication satellites were just metal-coated balls that could deflect signals they received back to any transmitter that was within their range. However, only very powerful transmitters could receive messages from these satellites. Today, satellites can record information and relay it to specific transmitters, and they provide a cheaper and better global communication network compared to land networks.

Communication satellites provide live television broadcasts of events happening in one part of the world to viewers all over the world, and low orbit satellites have revolutionized telephones by making mobile technology possible. People, even in the remotest parts of the world, can now communicate easily with the rest of the world. Technology has developed to such an extent that satellites can now send two or three signals simultaneously at different frequencies to different receivers. Efforts are underway to develop satellites that can even help the visually impaired to find their way.

Navigation satellites provide information for land, air and oceanic navigation. They provide signals to moving objects, which help them identify their exact location. These satellites are used for civilian and military purposes and provide three-dimensional views, and information about the speed of the vehicle, distance from target or destination and travel time.

Earth observation satellites are used for military and civilian purposes. They support reconnaissance or spying, surveying, weather forecasting, geodesic studies (mapping and observing the Earth's surface to study the changes in its crust) and monitoring of the atmosphere, oceans and land masses.

More power to the Sun

Countries such as the United States are working on a new kind of satellite known as the Solar Power Satellite, or SPS. This high Earth orbit satellite is expected to use microwave power transmission and transmit solar power to receiving antennae on the Earth. This solar power would then be used as an alternative source of energy. The satellite would have an unobstructed view of the Sun and would therefore be able to beam solar power continuously to the Earth. However, the high cost of building and maintaining such a satellite has delayed progress in this field. Efforts are now underway to find cheaper ways of building the satellite.

▲ **Signal towers**
Radio and mobile phone towers help in good reception of signals.

▼ **Finding the way**
Today, the Global Positioning System (GPS) is being used worldwide as a major navigational tool in ships, aircraft, and even cars and mine trucks.

◀ **Around the Earth**
Like satellites, space stations also orbit the Earth. The International Space Station orbits the Earth at an altitude of about 360 kilometres (220 miles). It completes one orbit around the Earth in a time period of about 92 minutes.

Try these too:

The Sun and the Solar System (p 8–9), The Rocky Planets (p 10–11), The Gas Giants (12–13), The Moon (p 14–15), Man in Space (p 18–19), The Scientific Revolution (p 142–143)

Moving on Land

Modern transport on land includes a wide range of vehicles such as bicycles, cars, buses and trains. The birth and evolution of these modes of transport can be traced back to ancient times.

Key facts:

- The earliest wheels were probably no more than slices cut off large tree trunks, which wore out easily. Gradually they were modified and made with separate pieces of wood that were joined together. The Ancient Celts further improved the wheel by using spokes and a metal rim. This made the wheel lighter and more durable.
- Early cars were all open-topped vehicles that could only seat two people. These cars did not have a steering wheel. A tiller, or a lever, adjusted the direction of the wheels. Drivers had to be well-prepared for their journey. They had to carry tools to repair their cars when they broke down. This is because petrol stations and mechanics were few and far between.
- The trains of the future will not use conventional energy sources like diesel, coal and electricity. Instead, they will use the power of magnets. Maglev, or magnetic levitation, trains are propelled by the energy from electromagnets attached to the bottom of the train.

Early humans were nomads who walked long distances in search of food. They gradually settled down and began farming. These early settlers also started to use animals to carry loads. However, they soon realized that it was necessary to invent a device that could carry greater loads and travel longer distances easily. Then, around the 5th century BC, Ancient Mesopotamians invented the wheel. At first it was just used to make pottery but later these ancient people realized that wheels could be attached to carts and used to move things and people easily.

Animal power

Early vehicles were drawn by animals. Ox and mule carts were used on farms to move goods, while horse-drawn chariots were used by people. However, most people walked as few could afford a chariot. During the Middle Ages, goods and people moved on long trains of horses, called packhorses. Often merchants and other travellers hired horses and travelled with the pack. By the 17th century, coaches and stage wagons had become popular. Royalty and rich people owned horse-drawn coaches, and wagons soon became a popular form of public transport for travelling long distances.

▲ **Pedalling on**
Today, bicycles are the choice of transport in many countries as they are environment-friendly. Special bicycles are built specially for tours and racing.

Bicycles

Bicycles were first invented in the 18th century. Early bicycles were made of wood and had to be pushed forwards by the rider's feet. Later, metal parts were used. These strange machines caught the fancy of people, but were uncomfortable and difficult to ride. By the end of the 19th century, bicycles had pedals and inflatable rubber tyres, and their designs were similar to those of modern bicycles. These changes made the bicycle easier to use and, within a few years, they were popular all over Europe and the United States. They are still the cheapest mode of transport. As bicycles became popular, the concept of motorized cycles, or motorcycles naturally gained in popularity. In 1885, the first petrol engine motorcycle was invented by Gottlieb Daimler (who also invented one of the first automobiles) and Wilhelm Maybach.

▶ **Travelling in style**
In medieval cities, hackney coaches and sedan chairs were used like local taxis.

Railways

The earliest railways were horse-drawn carriages that ran on stone tracks in Ancient Greece and Rome. In the 18th century, iron rails were introduced and horses were replaced by the steam locomotive built by English inventor Richard Trevithick. By the early 19th century, in the blossoming of the Industrial Revolution, railways became the fastest and most comfortable way to travel long distances on land. The Industrial Age also meant larger populations in cities and a greater requirement for transport around cities. This led to the replacement of horse-drawn wagons with horse-drawn trams or streetcars that ran on rails. By the 20th century, trams began running on electric power supplied from lines running overhead.

Engine power

The invention of engines that ran on steam and on fuel such as gasoline and petrol, led to the invention of cars and buses in the 19th century. The need for mass transportation in cities was also responsible for the popularization of buses. Buses were a boon to city dwellers as their routes were flexible and they could go to places that trams or trains could not. The first gasoline-powered automobiles were developed in 1886. At first, these vehicles were assembled manually. This meant that very few could be made and their cost was very high. However, in 1908, Henry Ford paved the way for the mass production of vehicles, which made them much more easily available and affordable.

Try these too:

Ancient Mesopotamia and Egypt (p 116–117), The Industrial Revolution (p 138–139), Moving Ahead (p 140–141)

◂ **Steaming ahead**
The invention of the steam engine revolutionized the railway industry.

▾ **Magnetic power**
Since there is no contact between the Maglev train and the tracks, the only friction exerted is by the air. This makes Maglev trains extremely fast.

▾ **Car track**
Cars have come a long way since they were first made. Today, superfast cars and those containing the luxuries of home are being built.

Early bicycles

The velocipede is an early ancestor of the bicycle. These Victorian scooter-like vehicles had no pedals and could not be steered. Later velocipedes had pedals, with one or two big front wheels.
The penny-farthing, or 'bone shaker', was an odd-looking cycle with one huge front wheel and one small rear wheel (hence the likening to the penny and farthing coins). These unstable cycles did not have brakes and the only way the 'wheeler' could slow down was by back-pedalling.

Water Transport

Boats were a big step in travel for early humans. Curiosity about the world around them, a sense of adventure and the search for food probably led humans to explore travelling on the water. It was the most important and, in fact, the only way to travel to foreign lands until the invention of aircraft in the 20th century.

Key facts:

- Ancient boat builders used roots or ropes to tie or stitch up wooden planks in order to make boats. With improvements in technology, they soon started using copper or iron nails, or rivets. Greek shipbuilders shaped the ends of the planks into tenon joints and interlocking mortise.
- During the Industrial Revolution horse-drawn barges were used to transport raw materials and goods along canals. The horses walked along a towpath that ran alongside the barge. In some places men pulled the barges. This system was discontinued because it was a very slow means of transportation and could not compete with the newly introduced railways.
- Submarines were used during the World Wars to make surprise attacks on enemy vessels. Early submarines were powered by electric motors and diesel engines and had to come up frequently. Today, submarines use nuclear power or liquid oxygen to propel their engines. These boats can stay underwater for several months at a time.

The earliest boats were dugouts, carved out of wooden logs. The small, early boats were probably rowed across rivers or lakes by one or two people using oars. Some boats were propelled by paddling. The commonly used paddle boats included canoes, kayaks, catamarans and gondolas. These boats are light, small and easy to manoeuvre.

Sailing vessels

Hand-paddled boats soon gave way to boats with sails attached to a central pole. These square or triangular pieces of cloth helped catch the wind and move the boat forwards faster and with less effort on the part of the oarsmen. The Ancient Egyptians and even the early Mesopotamians used paddle boats with sails. The Ancient Egyptians had a thriving shipbuilding industry and built cedar boats that were about 43 metres (140 feet) long. They also made light boats using papyrus reeds. During the Ancient Greek and Roman Empires, overseas trade, war and expanding empires led to bigger, better and sleeker vessels being designed. The Greek trireme was the swiftest warship of the 4th and 5th centuries BC. It was about 35 metres (115 feet) long and had 170 oarsmen seated in three tiers.

▲ **A boat of the past**
The coracle, made with animal skin stretched over a wooden or reed frame, was one of the earliest boats.

Greek cargo ships, on the other hand, depended more on wind power and had huge sails. Roman ships were also usually powered by sails and were very large in size, holding about 400 tonnes (394 tons) of cargo. The Vikings of Scandinavia were fierce invaders and pioneering explorers who built slim and graceful sailing vessels. They also used a small rowboat, the *faering*, for two or three people.

The medieval warship changed ship design by introducing a 'forecastle' and an 'aftcastle', at the two ends of the ship, from where soldiers launched attacks on enemies. They were shorter and stouter than earlier ships and even carried cannons. By the 16th century multi-decked ships called galleons became popular in Europe. Their sleek design made these ships even swifter.

▼ **Ships of the Vikings**
The Vikings used ships called *knarr*, to carry cargo and for exploring new lands, and longships during wars.

Flying boats

The hovercraft is a unique vehicle that can travel on water and land. It stays suspended a few centimetres (inches) above the ground or water surface with the help of an air cushion, which it creates. This ensures smooth and quick movement. The hydrofoil is a fast-moving vessel. It has ski-like projections below its hull, which help lift the boat above the water and gain great speed. Both boats are used for military purposes and also as ferries. Hovercrafts, in particular, are increasingly being used for recreational purposes.

Mechanized ships

The invention of the steam engine during the Industrial Revolution made it possible to mechanize boats and ships. Steam engines were used to power large paddle wheels and, later, propellers that helped to move both. Ships also began to have wheels for steering instead of tillers. Steam ships soon became an extremely popular mode of transport. they were widely used for inland ferries on lakes and rivers. Large ships even carried hundred of passengers across vast oceans. Steam boats were slowly replaced with diesel-powered vessels in the early 20th century.

Modern shipping

Unlike ships of the past, modern ships are not built entirely of wood. Iron made ships and submarines stronger, more waterproof and safer to travel in. Today, even materials like aluminium and fibreglass are used. Ships come in different sizes and can be used for various purposes. Military and naval battleships include aircraft carriers, frigates and submarines. Cargo ships, and ocean liners, are among the largest ships used for civilian purposes. Car ferries and tugboats are smaller ships, while yachts and motorboats are among the smallest of all modern vessels.

Try these too:

The Native Americans (p 124–125), New Lands – the Age of Exploration (p 134–135), The Industrial Revolution (p 138–139), Moving Ahead (p 140–141), The Second World War (p 150–151)

▼ **Giants of the sea**
Some of the world's largest ships are aircraft carriers. They are used to deploy and recover combat aircraft.

Air Travel

Once humans had conquered the land and the sea, their sights were naturally set on air travel. People began exploring flight with kites, artificial wings, wooden gliders and parachutes. The first experiments date as far back as the 9th century BC. However, it was the rapid changes of the Industrial Revolution that speeded up the development of aviation.

Key facts:

- The two main types of aircraft are heavier-than-air aircraft and lighter-than-air aircraft. The first category includes all types of aeroplanes, helicopters, gliders and seaplanes, while the second category includes hot air balloons and airships.
- Early gliders had wooden frames and canvas bodies, which made them light and suitable for floating on air. However, they were not safe, especially while landing. Later, aluminium was used, but the rivets and bolts that joined the aluminium sheets tended to increase the weight of the glider and slow it down. Modern gliders are made using seamless fibreglass or carbon fibre, which overcomes the problem of additional weight.
- Airships, or dirigibles, were among the earliest aircraft. They had stiff or flexible bodies filled with hydrogen or helium, which helped them float. Engine-driven airships, called Zeppelins, were used by Germany in the Second World War to attack enemy lands. Today, airships, or blimps, are used to advertise products.

Hot air balloons were the first 'aircraft'. In 1783, the Montgolfier brothers launched an unmanned hot air balloon in France, which was a large linen bag filled with hot air. The light, hot air carried the balloon over a distance of 2 kilometres (1.3 miles) for a total of 10 minutes. Later, with improved designs, hot air balloons could reach a height of nearly 2,400 metres (8,000 feet) and travel several hundred kilometres (miles).

Gliders

Gliders were the next step in the development of aeroplanes. The earliest glider design was made by Englishman George Cayley in 1804. Gliders used aerofoils, or specially designed wings that could use wind power and the rising hot air in the atmosphere to stay afloat. Modern gliders use motors to help in propulsion. They are used in aerobatic shows and for recreational flying.

The birth of the aeroplane

The invention of the internal combustion engine, in the late 19th century, was an important turning point in the development of flying machines. In 1903, Americans Wilbur and Orville Wright used the petrol engine to propel their first successful powered fixed-wing aircraft, the Wright *Flyer* biplane. This aircraft was capable of flights ranging from twelve seconds to one minute. Later the brothers went on to improve their aircraft's design and its performance.

In 1910, their Model 'B' *Flyer* set a record by flying at the speed of about 60 kilometres/hour (37 miles/hour). The design of aeroplanes swiftly advanced, especially because of the First and Second World Wars. By 1919, commercial passenger flights were operating between the United States and Canada.

▲ **Flying high**
The first manned balloon flight was made on 21 November 1783.

Early aeroplanes

The three main types of early aeroplanes were monoplanes (with a single set of wings), biplanes (with two main wings, one below the other) or tri-planes (with three wings, one below the other). Monoplanes were discontinued during the First World War, when tri-planes became the preferred design for fighter planes. Monoplanes were later revived in 1930, and have since remained the most popular design for aircraft.

▼ **Flying into history**
On 17 December 1903, Orville Wright took to air in the *Flyer*. His flight lasted all of 12 seconds. The longest test flight was made on the same day by Wilbur who flew the aircraft for almost a minute.

▲ **The giant of the skies**
The *Airbus A380* is the world's largest passenger aircraft. It can carry over 500 passengers.

Helicopters

The modern motor-driven helicopter was designed by Slovakian inventor Ján Bahyl in 1905. Helicopters carry fewer people and can only travel short distances. However, they hardly need any space to land and take off as they can do so vertically. They are propelled by rotating overhead blades and are used for military purposes as well as rescue operations, aerial photography and fire-fighting.

Jets

Jet engines took air travel to a higher level, by getting rid of propellers and relying on the power generated by the discharge of a powerful jet from the tail of the aircraft. These aircraft fly at heights of between 3,048–4,572 metres (10,000–15,000 feet). They were used extensively during the Second World War and later on became popular commercially. These aircraft can travel at speeds of about 680–900 kilometres/hour (420–580 miles/hour), and carry between 400 to 600 passengers. In the 1960s, the invention of the supersonic jet revolutionized aviation. These machines could travel faster than the speed of sound. The only supersonic jet to fly commercially was the Concorde, which could fly at a height of 17,500 metres (60,000 feet) at more than twice the speed of sound. However, the Concorde was retired from operation in 2003 due to increasing safety concerns.

▲ **Mighty choppers**
Helicopters have both military and civil uses. Military helicopters are used for transporting soldiers, weapons, and medical and food supplies.

Amphibious aircraft

Seaplanes, or flying boats, are unique machines capable of both flying in the air and floating on water. They can reach remote areas that don't have level land or landing strips. These aircraft were widely used during the Second World War for spying and rescuing stranded soldiers. By the 1950s, they had lost their importance because helicopters and aircraft carriers became increasingly popular.

Try these too:

Man in Space (p 18–19), Ancient India and China (p 118–119), The First World War (p 148–149), Communication and Satellites (p 192–193)

ARCTIC OCEAN
Greenland
(DENMARK)
ICELAND
ALASKA
(U.S.A.)
Arctic Circle
CANADA
UNITED KINGDOM
IRELAND
FRANC
NORTH
PACIFIC
OCEAN
UNITED STATES
NORTH
ATLANTIC
OCEAN
PORTUGAL
SPAIN
MOROCCO
ALGER
Western
Sahara
THE
BAHAMAS
Tropic of Cancer
HAWAIIAN
ISLANDS
(U.S.A.)
MEXICO
CUBA
DOMINICAN
REPUBLIC
HAITI
JAMAICA
BELIZE
Puerto
Rico
ST. KITTS AND NEVIS
ANTIGUA AND BARBUDA
DOMINICA
ST. LUCIA
ST. VINCENT AND
THE GRENADINES
BARBADOS
GRENADA
TRINIDAD AND
TOBAGO
GUATEMALA
HONDURAS
EL SALVADOR
NICARAGUA
COSTA
RICA
PANAMA
MAURITANIA
MALI
CAPE VERDE
SENEGAL
THE GAMBIA
GUINEA-BISSAU
GUINEA
BURKINA
FASO
SIERRA
LEONE
LIBERIA
CÔTE
D'IVOIRE
GHANA
TOGO
BENIN
VENEZUELA
GUYANA
SURINAME
French Guiana
(FRANCE)
COLOMBIA
EQUATORIAL GUINEA
SAO TOME AND PRINCIPE
Equator
Equator
GALAPAGOS
ISLANDS
(ECUADOR)
ECUADOR
PERU
BRAZIL
BOLIVIA
SOUTH
ATLANTIC
OCEAN
French Polynesia
(FRANCE)
Tropic of Capricorn
PARAGUAY
CHILE
URUGUAY
ARGENTINA
SOUTH
PACIFIC
OCEAN
Falkland Islands
(Islas Malvinas)
(U.K.)
South Georgia and the
South Sandwich Islands
(U.K.)
Antarctic Circle
SOUTHERN OCEAN

ARCTIC OCEAN
Arctic Circle
RUSSIA
FINLAND
EST.
LAT.
POLAND
BELARUS
UKRAINE
MOLDOVA
ROMANIA
HUNGARY
BULGARIA
GREECE
GEORGIA
ARMENIA
AZERBAIJAN
KAZAKHSTAN
MONGOLIA
UZBEKISTAN
KYRGYZSTAN
TURKMENISTAN
TAJIKISTAN
NORTH KOREA
SOUTH KOREA
JAPAN
NORTH PACIFIC OCEAN
TURKEY
CYPRUS
LEB.
SYRIA
IRAQ
ISRAEL
JORDAN
IRAN
AFGHANISTAN
CHINA
KUWAIT
PAKISTAN
NEPAL
BHUTAN
BANGLADESH
Taiwan
Tropic of Cancer
IBYA
EGYPT
SAUDI ARABIA
QATAR
UNITED ARAB EMIRATES
OMAN
INDIA
BURMA
LAOS
THAILAND
VIETNAM
CAMBODIA
CHAD
ERITREA
YEMEN
SUDAN
DJIBOUTI
ETHIOPIA
PHILIPPINES
FEDERATED STATES OF MICRONESIA
MARSHALL ISLANDS
CENTRAL AFRICAN REPUBLIC
SOMALIA
SRI LANKA
PALAU
MALDIVES
MALAYSIA
SINGAPORE
UGANDA
KENYA
Equator
NAURU
KIRIBATI
DEMOCRATIC REPUBLIC OF THE CONGO
RWANDA
BURUNDI
INDONESIA
PAPUA NEW GUINEA
SOLOMON ISLANDS
TANZANIA
SEYCHELLES
ANGOLA
ZAMBIA
MALAWI
INDIAN OCEAN
SAMOA
VANUATU
FIJI
MOZAMBIQUE
ZIMBABWE
AMIBIA
BOTSWANA
MADAGASCAR
MAURITIUS
Tropic of Capricorn
New Caledonia (FRANCE)
AUSTRALIA
LESOTHO
SWAZILAND
SOUTH AFRICA
SOUTH PACIFIC OCEAN
NEW ZEALAND
OCEAN
SOUTHERN OCEAN
Antarctic Circle
tica

Index

D

E

F

G

H

I

T

U

Picture Credits

Picture credits (l: left; r: right; m: middle; c: centre; t: top; b: bottom):

Robert Frederick Ltd.: 6tl, 6bl, 66ml, 9t, 16t, 16b, 17b, 20t, 20b, 21b, 24c, 26, 27, 30, 31, 32br, 33br, 32–33t, 39tl, 38–39c, 44b, 70t, 70b, 71t, 72, 80t, 81t, 86b, 88, 89tl, 89tr, 89m, 90r, 91l, 92, 93, 94bl, 94bm, 95, 96c, 97b, 98–99b, 116bc, 144b, 149r, 164t, 164b, 168l, 168r, 169t, 172t, 172b, 173b; **National Aeronautics and Space Administration (NASA):** 6br, 6tl, 8t, 9m, 10t, 10b, 11b, 11t, 12t, 12m, 12bl, 12br, 13, 14m, 14–15b, 16t, 18b, 18t, 19b, 19t, 107br, 111t, 188t, 192t, 193t; **Andreas Guskos:** 19c; **Lloyd S. Clements:** 35br; **Q2A Database:** 34–35b, 34t, 35t, 36t, 36b; **Tony Alt:** 39m; **Mark Bond:** 38t; **Lyndsey McCall:** 50tl; **Fernando Rodrigues:** 50bl; **Jan Martin Will:** 50–51bc; **Joel Bauchat Grant:** 53br; **Andy Lim:** 63t; **Tony Campbell:** 73t; **Joe Tucciarone:** 81b; **Koval:** 84r; **Mohammed Suleiman Ismail:** 84t; **Paul Cowan:** 85l; **Jason Vandehey:** 86b; **Martin Cerny:** 90tl; **Arcturus Publishing Limited:** 98m, 99m; **Leah Anne Thompson:**101m; **Bethan Collins:** 101tl; **Johnny Lye:** 101br; **Scott Rothstein:** 101tr; **United Nations Environment Programme:** 102t; **Dragan Trifunovic:** 102b; **Scott Lomenzo:** 103b; **SF Photography:** 103m; **United Nations Environment Programme:** 104t, 106t, 108t, 110t, 112t, 114t; **Vinicius Ramalho Tupinamba:** 105b; **Tan, Kim Pin:** 107t; **Dmitrii Dikikh:** 108b; **Amra Pasic:** 109tl; **Damien Dewitte:** 110–111bc; **Socrates:** 111mt; **Nicolas Raymond:** 110bl; **Keith Levit:** 111mb; **Josue Adib Cervantes Garcia:** 112m; **ARTEKI:** 112b; **Wang Sanjun:** 113b; **Olga Lis:** 115t; **Darwin Cruikshank:** 115b; **B. Speckart:** 116b; **Stuart Taylor:** 117b, 129t; **TAOLMOR:** 119b; **Wizdata, Inc.:** 121t, 187t; **Vladimir Ivanov:** 121b; **Anthony Smith:** 122bl; **Chad Bontrager:** 123b; **John L. Richbourg:** 124m; **Nast/Loc. Gov.:** 125tl; **Edward Chin:** 128b; **Heather Lewis:** 129b; **Paul Prescott:** 130b; **Franc Podgorsek:** 139r; **National Railway Museum:** 140b; **Ijan Sempoi:** 141t; **Lebrecht Music and Arts Photo Library/photolibrary:** 147b; **Anthony Smith:** 152t; **Bettmann/CORBIS:** 152b; **Andres Rodriguez:** 153b; **Eduard Cebria:** 153t; **Carsten Medom Madsen:** 154b; **Vietnam Memorial:** 155b; **Library of Congress:** 155m; **Marcus Tuerner:** 156m; **Sonja:** 156b; **A. S. Zain:** 157b; **Stephen Inglis:** 159t; **Lynn Watson:** 161m; **Les Byerley:** 162; **Vladimir Pomortzeff:** 165b; **Michelle Donahue Hillison:**170t; **Library of Congress, Prints and Photographs Division, FSA-OWI Collection:** 169b; **Erich Schlegel:** 171tl; **Allan Kilgour:** 171bl; **Paul Whitted:** 171tb; **Jim Parkin:** 171tr; **Pichugin Dmitry:** 171mt; **movieposter.com:** 173t; **photolibrary.com:** 174t; **Socrates:** 178ml; **O'Jay R. Barbee**: 178t; **canismaior:**178bl; **Stacy Anderson:** 178–179c; **Igor Leonov:** 179t; **Andrea Danti:** 179b; **Larry St. Pierre:** 181tr; **Stinjin Peeters:** 180t; **Bruce Wheadon:** 181b; **Myrthe Krook:** 181m; **Lalit Dalal:** 181tl; **EcoPrint:** 183br; **Winthrop Brookhouse:** 183tr; **Joe Gough:** 184bl; **Irina Tischenko:** 185mr; **Scott Rothstein:** 185mc; **vm:** 186t; **Ana Vasileva:** 188br; **Emil Pozar:** 189b; **Jim Parkin:** 190b; **Barry G. Hurt:** 191b; **Andrew Barker:** 192b; **Yan Vugenfirer:** 195b; **Paul B. Moore:** 196b; **David Burrows:** 197t; **Brad Whitsitt:** 198b; **Neumann:** 199b; **other illustrations Q2A property**